Jesus Christ for the Modern World

American University Studies

Series VII
Theology and Religion
Vol. 77

PETER LANG
New York • Bern • Frankfurt am Main • Paris

Douglas McCready

Jesus Christ for the Modern World

The Christology of the Catholic Tübingen School

PETER LANG
New York • Bern • Frankfurt am Main • Paris

BT
198
,M3985
1990

Library of Congress Cataloging-in-Publication Data

McCready, Douglas
    Jesus Christ for the modern world : the Christology
of the Catholic Tübingen School / by Douglas McCready.
        p. cm. — (American university studies. Series VII,
Theology and religion ; v. 77)
        Includes bibliographical references.
        1. Jesus Christ—History of doctrines—19th century.
2. Jesus Christ—History of doctrines—20th century.
3. Tübingen School (Catholic theology)   4. Catholic
Church—Doctrines—History—19th century.   5. Catholic
Church—Doctrines—History—20th century.   I. Title.
II. Series.
BT198.M3985   1991   232'.0943'473—dc20   90-33275
ISBN 0-8204-1337-2   CIP
ISSN 0740-0446

The paper in this book meets the guidelines for permanence and durability
of the Committee on Production Guidelines for Book Longevity of the
Council on Library Resources.

© Peter Lang Publishing, Inc., New York 1991

Printed in the United States of America.

ACKNOWLEDGEMENTS

No book is the product solely of its author. This one is no exception. Many people have helped me along the way. Their aid and encouragement have made this a better product. And while they deserve credit for their help, I alone am responsible for any errors or omissions.

Temple University's Religion Department encouraged me along the way and was generous with financial help. Leonard Swidler, my Doktorvater, Gerard S. Sloyan, and Gerhard E. Spiegler oversaw the initial version of this study, offering helpful suggestions and stylistic guidance. At the University of Tübingen, the staff of the Catholic Theological Faculty's library helped me make full use of their resources, and Walter Kasper and Hans Küng took time from their busy schedules for interviews. My family has patiently endured many hours while I researched, wrote, and revised this study.

The following publishers have kindly permitted me to use significant portions of their works. Full bibliographic citations may be found in the bibliography beginning on page 327:

Alba House, Staten Island, NY: Josef Neuner and Heinrich Roos, *The Teaching of the Catholic Church* (1967).

Crossroad/Continuum, New York, NY: Walter Kasper, *The God of Jesus Christ* (1984).

Doubleday & Company, New York, NY: Hans Küng, *On Being a Christian* (1976), and *Does God Exist?* (1980).

Echter Verlag, Wurzburg, W. Germany: Aloys Grillmeier and Heinrich Bacht (editors), *Das Konzil von Chalkedon* (1954).

InterVarsity Press, Leicester, UK: H. H. Rowden (editor), *Christ the Lord* (1982).

Kösel Verlag, Munich, W. Germany: J. R. Geiselmann, *Jesus der Christus* (1965).

Pantheon Books of Random House, New York, NY: Karl Adam, *The Christ of Faith* (1957).

Sheed & Ward, Ltd., London, UK: Karl Adam, *Christ Our Brother* (1931), and *The Spirit of Catholicism* (1946).

TABLE OF CONTENTS

Preface ix

Chapter I.   Introduction 1

Chapter II.   Friedrich W. J. Schelling 27

Chapter III. Johann Sebastian Drey and Johann Adam Möhler 39

Chapter IV.   Franz Anton Staudenmaier
                   and Johannes Evangelist Kuhn 73

Chapter V.   Paul Schanz 105

Chapter VI.   Karl Adam 119

Chapter VII. Josef Rupert Geiselmann 179

Chapter VIII. Walter Kasper 201

Chapter IX.   Hans Küng 261

Chapter X.   Conclusion 297

Bibliography 327

Index 343

PREFACE

Who is Jesus Christ? What did he do that makes him so important? These are questions many people are asking today; they are questions that have been central to the faith and belief of those who call themselves Christians ever since Jesus turned to his followers and asked, "What are people saying about me?"

We live in a world different in many ways from the one Jesus lived in. But the world is not as different as many have been led to believe; if anything, ours is an age of greater anxiety and tension than the was the world of Jesus and the early Church. Our world differs from earlier eras in terms of what it calls its historical consciousness and its self-conscious pluralism.

Historical consciousness designates the modern recognition that we live in a historically-conditioned world; things do change over time. The concept becomes controversial when it is extended to mean that everything is historically *determined* and history is the ultimate boundary of human experience. It is this move that transforms history into historicism. When this happens, absolutes are replaced by relativity.

The second major element of modern consciousness is pluralism of thought and practice. Pluralism can mean recognition that different beliefs and practices exist in the world and people should, for the most part, be allowed to hold to those beliefs and practices they are most comfortable with. But like historical consciousness it can be extended to relativize all beliefs and practices to say that they are equally valid and true.

Both historical consciousness and pluralism were facts of life in the nineteenth century when the Catholic Theological Faculty was established at the University of Tübingen. Those who have constituted the Catholic Tübingen School within that faculty during the past 173 years have tried to appropriate the values arising out of historical consciousness and pluralism without compromising Christian faith or practice. This has never been an easy task, but the conflict and turmoil within the Roman Catholic Church during the period has only made the job more difficult.

The Catholic Tübingers have dealt with a wide range of issues and continue to do so. Although they suffered an eclipse between the revolutions of 1848 and Vatican II, they significantly influenced the results of Vatican II, and recently the latest member of the school was named bishop of Stuttgart. Tübingers have made their most important contributions in ecclesiology and the concept of doctrinal development. But they have always been forced to look at Jesus Christ and the significance of his person and work. For several this was a major part of their work. In the twentieth century Catholic Tübingers have been instrumental in showing the importance of history and humanity for Jesus without compromising his deity and timelessness.

In the following chapters, we will look at the christological work of eight members of the Tübingen School as well as that of one man who influenced most of them (Schelling) and one man who was attracted to the School but has been in conflict with recent members on specifically christological concerns. In a concluding chapter, we will assess the strengths and weaknesses of Tübingen Christology and its potential contribution for Protestant as well as Catholic theologians.

Abington, PA   D. M.
May 14, 1990

x

CHAPTER I

INTRODUCTION

In the latter part of the twentieth century, Christology has returned to the fore as a subject for both scholarly and popular consideration. As so often in the past, Christianity has been challenged by external forces, both religious and secular, to reexamine its teaching and practice, in fact, its very reason for being. At some point, this means Christians must look anew at their doctrine of Jesus Christ because they have expressed their *raison d'être* in terms of who Jesus is and what he has done and said. This is Christology: the reflective and systematic study of the person and work of Jesus Christ.[1] The effort of a school of Catholic theologians at the University of Tübingen to explain Jesus Christ to the modern world is the subject of this study.

After several centuries of turmoil, and even open conflict, the early Church set forth some basic statements about Jesus Christ which received general, if not universal, acceptance until the last century.[2] Although these decisions were not meant to forestall further investigation into Christology, they did set limits for such study and established a foundation upon which theologians might explore other areas of Christian doctrine. In practice, however, too many have considered the early conciliar decisions to preclude further work in Christology.

The early Church fathers recognized a necessary relationship existed between the various areas of doctrine and modifications or developments in one area were likely to require changes in others. They saw questions regarding Jesus Christ as central, requiring a rethinking of the doctrine of God on the one hand and the meaning of being human on the other. Changes in Christology would have the most far-reaching impact on all theology. Equally important, changes in other areas of theology might require rethinking one's Christology.

From its earliest days, Christianity has claimed to be an historical religion. That is to say, if certain events that Christians claim to have occurred did not, the doctrines associated with them are false.[3] Thus, should Jesus never have lived, should the events of his earthly life (especially the Resurrection) never have occurred, or should the gospel writers' claims about Jesus and his work as recorded in the New Testament be demonstrably untrue, then the very validity of Christianity as a religion would be called into question. Critical studies of the past two hundred years have made this a focal issue, but the denial of one or more of these claims has challenged Christianity from the days of Jesus himself.

As the early Church sought to clarify its understanding of Jesus, it faced a constellation of interlocking issues. Among these was the desire to represent faithfully the content of biblical revelation, to define and show the way for human salvation, and to use his life as a model for how one should live. Intimately related to this desire was a particular understanding of the nature of God, of the human condition, and of the value of creation. In each area, early theologians were forced to respond to criticism from contemporary philosophies and religions as well as to the contents of the increasingly well-defined Bible. Serious conflicts arose from incompatible attempts to use these various resources. Today, similar disagreements reflect the quandary the early Church faced regarding its place in the world. But now the battles are waged in classrooms and scholarly journals with only printer's ink spilled, whereas the earlier battles sometimes spilled over into the streets and led the Roman emperors to intervene to stop the bloodshed.

As people tried to integrate the biblical evidence with their experiences, they faced a dilemma. New Testament passages describe Jesus in terms consistent with possession of both deity and humanity. The former emphasize how Jesus differed from humans and the latter how much he was one of us. To make things more difficult, the nature of the evidence seemed to require that both be true simultaneously. This was compatible with neither Jewish nor Greek thought. The Church spent some four hundred years of heated argument before it was able to arrive at language a majority would accept. The problem was made more difficult as the theologians involved tried to incorporate or respond to elements of contemporary philosophy and religion that demonstrated some affinity to the Christian doctrines. They struggled to determine what they could accept without compromising their beliefs, where they could draw valid analogies, and what they might cite as precursive thought for apologetic purposes. The key problem they faced was an apparently unbridgeable gulf between the spiritual and material realms, particularly as presented in gnostic thought and Greek philosophy.

Early attempts to develop a Christology consisted of one group's trying to hold together the two strands of biblical evidence against groups on either flank. On one side were some Jewish Christians who saw in Jesus a great, human prophet and example to others but who rejected any claim to his deity as incompatible with divine monotheism.[4] On the other were those influenced by gnostic speculation and Greek philosophy and, denying the Incarnation as incompatible with the pure spiritual nature of God, rejecting any real humanity in Jesus. He only appeared to be human, neither being born in a stable of a virgin nor dying on a cross. The basic division remains even today, although the terms of the debate have changed and the philosophies and religions interacting with Christianity are different.

Historically, theologians within the Church consensus have agreed that Jesus must be understood in terms of concurrent and complete deity and humanity. Both his essential being and his actions partake of these two properties the early Church defined as natures. Jesus remains one person, however, and the natures are neither blended nor schizophrenically divided within him. That this situation exists, classical theologians agree, but there is no consensus on how to explain it.

The process of turning this understanding of Jesus into doctrinal formulas began in A. D. 325 at Nicea, in response to a challenge to the accepted understanding of who Jesus was. It ended, for all intents, at Chalcedon in A. D. 451, where the council dealt only with the narrow issue of the constitution of Jesus' person and excluded all other christological concerns (although the council affirmed explicitly the creed resulting from Nicea and Constantinople). Thus, Chalcedon did not intend to put an end to christological thought, only to delineate the proper bounds for carrying on such thought. Amity within the Church, however, did not result. This was because some rejected the definition of Chalcedon and others pushed forward to a more precise and controversial statement about the implications of Chalcedon.[5] Modern theologians have reopened the question of the meaning of Chalcedon, and some have denied it outright.

Hermeneutical Issues

One of the problems caused by the normative status of Chalcedon is common to all hermeneutical question of how we are to relate material coming from another age and culture to our own age and culture. This is the problem of contextualization.[6] If we accept the transcultural normativity of the Christian Scriptures and, derivatively, of doctrines drawn from the Scriptures, this becomes complicated.[7] First, the transcultural element must be identified and explained in terms of its biblical context(s). Then, this understanding has to be translated into the language and thought patterns of the audience for whom the theology is being written (sometimes by a person or persons of a different culture from that of the intended audience). The result must be both clear to the audience and faithful to the source.[8] As the translator presents the new product, he or she not only must ensure the content of the message has not been altered to say something other than the original, but also that the meaning of that content is now clear to the audience where it previously was not. This process is needed in every culture in every generation. In this process, a distinction between meaning and its expression may be useful. Meaning is what the author intended the audience to understand; its expression is how it is presented for that audience and how it applies to the audience. Because expression encompasses application, it is apt to change over culture and age. If we are to distinguish meaning and expression, we must take care to ensure that an expression or application does not mask a changed meaning.

The hermeneutical issue has always been important, but with modern developments in linguistics, philosophy, history, and the social sciences (as well as a broadening of the meaning of the term hermeneutics itself), it is doubtful if serious theology can be done today without some understanding of modern hermeneutics.[9] This understanding is needed for two reasons. Where questionable christological theories have been advanced under Enlightenment or post-Enlightenment influence, theologians need to understand the presuppositions and methodologies used in reaching the disputed conclusions in order to address them adequately. New developments in hermeneutics also may provide insights that enable theologians to reach a fuller understanding of the subject than was previously possible through having a better grasp of one or both cultures involved, or providing a clearer explanation of some point of christological doctrine. Gadamer's contention that the interpreter needs to recognize and then fuse the two different horizons of the author and the interpreter exemplifies this.[10]

Too often, problems in Christology (and other areas of theology) arise when theologians fail to recognize or admit the doctrine in question was stated in a different historical, philosophical, or linguistic context than that of the theologians, and on the surface its meaning may be entirely different or even incomprehensible to a modern audience. This difference must not be ignored, but neither should it be overdrawn; it is as wrong to see a difference in substance where only a difference of expression exists as it is to deny any difference at all.

The interaction between Christian revelation and cultural context has characterized christological work throughout the history of the Church. It can be seen most clearly in the early Church and in the developments of the past 150 years. In the main, Christian theology has progressed in response to theories judged to be in some way unacceptable. Doctrinal inadequacy has always been a ground for doctrinal pronouncements, and each of the early Church councils was called to deal with a theological view seen as inadequate or false. Today, social and political concerns have come to have a greater impact on theological understanding, and frequently these have had a christological component or led to a christological conclusion.[11] The history of christological development has been recorded in detail by many historians and theologians; to repeat these accounts here would serve no useful purpose except as it relates directly to the focus of this study.

We have assumed there are both christological doctrines and theologies about Jesus Christ. In every age it is the task of theologians to translate christological doctrines into theologies. This entails both critical review of doctrine to ensure it has been properly drawn from the relevant evidence (which entails other decisions) and is as accurate and comprehensive as possible (but never more comprehensive than the sources warrant). It equally requires accurate translation of that doctrine, using the best scholarly tools and familiarity with modern culture, into the language of the culture. It is not necessary, however, for the culture to accept the theology for the translation to be valid, only that the culture understand it. Throughout history, many theologians have attempted with varying degrees of success and various receptions to develop Christologies. The range of Christologies is probably as broad today as it has been at any time in the history of the Church.

The classical christological teaching of the Church, almost uniformly since Chalcedon, has been that Jesus Christ is one person in two natures (as defined in the language of the philosophical thought of that time) and that he is the unique source of human salvation. As much as this sentence says, it leaves much unsaid. Among those who fully accept this statement of Christology there exists much disagreement over the meaning of the parts of the statement, particularly over the "how" aspect. Other theologians today reject one or both parts of the statement and offer differing formulations. The practical belief of the Church too often has not reflected its statement of formal belief. This is true for both conservatives and liberals, but in equal and opposite ways. Too often, the "average Christian" has thought of Jesus as God walking the face of the earth and downplayed or ignored his humanity. Some of modern Christology's opposing emphasis on Jesus' humanity has been in reaction to this monophysitic tendency in traditional popular Christology. Until recently, this monophysitic tendency has been strongest in Roman Catholic thought and has had a doctrinal and practical impact on Catholic theology.[12]

Christian theologians of all stripes have been attempting to do Christology in light of the shift in perspective toward a greater appreciation of the human as well as with a range of other issues. These include the growing historical consciousness of the nineteenth century; philosophical and theological progress deriving from Kant, Hegel, Schelling, and Schleiermacher (to name the most prominent influences); a growing familiarity with the people who adhere to religions other than Christianity; the development of various biblical-critical methods; and the impact of new scientific discoveries and theories.

Protestant theologians pioneered in the development of christological theories in the nineteenth and early twentieth centuries with adoptionism, kenoticism, the moral and exemplary views of liberalism, and a skeptical outlook toward much of the New Testament material as traditionally understood. In the second half of this century, Roman Catholics have been instrumental in the development of new christological thought. With the freedom Vatican II offered, these scholars have appropriated the methods and presuppositions of earlier Protestants, drawn on their particular Catholic and cultural backgrounds, and tried to come to grips with modern philosophy and social science. In doing so, they have not only restated christological doctrine; they have often reformulated it as well. Leading examples of this are Piet Schoonenberg, who has inverted the essence of Chalcedon,[13] and Hans Küng,[14] who has been attacked by some Catholics for his views regarding the person of Christ. Recently, Küng suggested the salvific work of Christ must be limited in its extent to Christians alone because other religions are salvific in their own right.[15] The strong Hegelian strand in Karl Rahner's theology has colored his Christology and led him to suggest the classical christological statements need to be understood in new and different ways.[16] Although these Catholic theologians, along with Edward Schillebeeckx and Jon Sobrino, are the best known among contemporary Catholic christologists, some other Catholic theologians want to interact with modern thought but think the theologians mentioned above have given away something essential to christological doctrine.

Many Protestants are likewise dissatisfied with the options of simply repeating the age-old creeds or abandoning them to modern reformulations of Christology within an anthropocentric and anti-supernaturalistic framework. Robert Krieg has suggested the work of the Catholic Tübingen School offers a possible solution to the dilemma,[17] but Krieg has not worked out his suggestion in detail. In this study we will attempt to do some of that work by tracing the history of the christological work of the members of that School, examining the place of the Catholic Tübingen School in the christological debates of the past century and a half, and evaluating the School in terms of both its own standards and the needs of a contemporary Christology as suggested by the various participants in the modern debate.

Origin of the Catholic Tübingen School

The Catholic Tübingen School arose out of the attempt of a small number of German Catholic theologians to come to grips with contemporary philosophy and culture at the beginning of the nineteenth century. With few exceptions, Roman Catholicism had not participated in the Enlightenment or the initial response to it. To the extent that Catholicism had recognized these developments within the European society in which it existed, it had reacted defensively. The earliest and primary exceptions to this occurred in the German states. A variety of theological programs was proposed, each with the express aim of making Christianity understandable to contemporary philosophers and people of culture. Although the primary focus was not necessarily the cultured among the despisers of religion, as Schleiermacher put it in his *Reden*, the people in the pews were not the intended audience. The theologians involved in these efforts hoped to make Christianity intellectually respectable. Their strategy was to present Christianity in terms of contemporary German philosophy (primarily that of Kant, Hegel, Fichte, Jacobi, Schelling, and Schleiermacher) and to respond to attacks on Christianity presented in terms of these philosophies. Most of their efforts were ultimately condemned by Rome, but that of the Catholic Tübingen School survived and continues to influence Roman Catholic theology in the twentieth century. O'Meara suggests Tübingen remained a legitimate, if not endorsed, view because the Tübingers were "noted for their strong attachment to Catholic orthodoxy and their devotion to the Church" as well as for being careful scientific theologians.[18]

Although the Catholic Tübingen School is certainly related to the Catholic theological faculty of the University of Tübingen, it is not coextensive with it.[19] The faculty was established in 1817 by Johann Sebastian von Drey. The University of Ellwangen had been dissolved and the king, feeling a responsibility to his new Catholic subjects, desired the continued existence of the Ellwangen theological faculty. Tübingen became unique among German universities by having both Protestant and Catholic theological faculties, a situation still relatively uncommon in German universities, which tend to have one or the other. Drey's move to Tübingen was a deliberate attempt to be in a position to interact intelligently with Protestant theologians of his time—Tübingen was renowned as a center of Protestant thought—and with those philosophers who were becoming increasingly influential in Germany. The most important of these were reflected in the viewpoints of the Protestant Tübingen faculty, where Hegel and Schelling had been students. Drey believed theology would develop more fruitfully in competition and confrontation with other confessional views by enabling mutual criticism and preventing monolithic claims.[20]

The early Catholic Tübingen School marked an attempt to move away from the Jesuit-influenced scholasticism characteristic of much Roman Catholicism of that era. The flowering of the School would be bracketed on the other end by the renewal of the earlier thinking in the form of Neo-scholasticism after the revolutions of 1848.[21] Between the two scholasticisms, two generations of Tübingers tried freely but critically to integrate new developments in history, biblical criticism, and philosophy into Catholic tradition.[22] With a paramount concern for history expressed in terms of living tradition and drawing on patristic writings, the Tübingers sought to resolve the tension between an enduring, meaningful ideal and its presence in a multi-faceted historical presence.[23] They demonstrated this primarily through their work on ecclesiology.

Catholic Tübingen Theology

Reinisch and Adam have suggested the distinctive feature of the Catholic Tübingen School was its close synthesis of speculative and historical theology, combining study of the form and derivation of dogma with a sympathetic awareness of contemporary problems and intellectual trends.[24] A different way of saying this is that the Tübingers tried to interact with modern thought and respond to contemporary concerns without compromising their faith as Catholic Christians. This means that what made the Catholic Tübingen School a school was not unity of method or conclusion, for this rarely existed, but a commonality of spirit. Many of the Tübingers have been original and independent in their work, and tensions have existed between members from the early days. Even those scholars who have questioned the very existence of the School admit to a unity within the early faculty.[25]

We maintain a similar unity of spirit exists even today—a unity over time with earlier faculty, if not always among current faculty—so we find it possible to speak of a Catholic Tübingen School in response to today's trends and problems. This is not to say the School can be traced in an unbroken chain back to Drey or that the majority of the faculty has ever been part of the School. It is simply to say that the spirit of Drey and his early colleagues has been reflected in succeeding generations of Tübingen theologians and continues to be today. Not all faculty have been members of the School, nor have all members of the School have been on the faculty. Those who were not on the faculty were students at Tübingen, however, and their study at Tübingen decisively influenced their theology.[26] In the same way, some leading members of the School were not trained at Tübingen but, attracted to the spirit and scholarship of the school, came to teach at Tübingen.[27]

Ben F. Meyer, in a recent book on Christology, has suggested that

> the Christian dilemma dates from the late seventeenth century and is objectified in the accounts of knowledge that grew up with the Enlightenment. In so far as these accounts of knowledge are themselves in turn found to be inadequate and are revised, intellectual integrity is again open to concrete redefinition.... With a *basic breakthrough* in the account of knowledge the Christian dilemma might be radically resolved, cracked open, and the way cleared for constructive projects irreducable [*sic*] to theological salvage operations.[28]

This is the situation to which the Catholic Tübingen School has sought to respond from its inception. Modern philosophies and theologies have instilled doubt about the human ability to know (epistemology) and about the accuracy and trustworthiness of the sources of Christian belief, consequently, about the logical outcomes of these beliefs. It is not only in the twentieth century that the concept "God" has been considered problematic. Schupp said relating the term "God" to history and historicity in a meaningful way is the basic problem of theology.[29]

Drey, as the founder of the Catholic Tübingen School, concentrated his theological work on this apologetic concern to make God meaningful in a society where traditional understandings and expressions had lost their meaning and value. He found his key to a systematic and theological expression of God's reality in Romanticism and German Idealism. These sources, which overlapped in their outlook, colored the thought of the nineteenth century Tübingers.[30] They have continued to influence twentieth century Tübingers. Drey himself drew heavily on the earlier Schelling, particularly in his "Vorlesungen über die Methode der akademischen Studiums."[31] Others were influenced more by Hegel. Kasper in this century has drawn on the later work of Schelling. Despite their use of

Schelling and Hegel (and Schleiermacher), Tübingers never drew uncritically from German Idealists. In fact, Staudenmaier, in the mid-nineteenth century, provided one of the most penetrating critiques of Hegel.[32]

Building on Drey's apologetic foundation, later Tübingers wrestled with issues raised by their non-Catholic contemporaries. Foremost among these was that of the *raison d'être* of the visible, institutional Church. This was not only a problem of Catholic versus Protestant, but even more one arising out of the Romantic and German Idealist consciousness. Hegel and Schleiermacher were particularly influential. The Tübingers had drawn from these same sources to construct their theologies, but never uncritically. As with Staudenmaier's critique of Hegel, they readily and sharply criticized their contemporaries at points where they were inconsistent with Catholic Christianity. Such criticism was not limited to outsiders. Tübingers have not hesitated to criticize one another when they appeared to accept too readily methods or conclusions contrary to the spirit of Catholicism.

In avoiding a theology determined by a philosophical system (Hegel) on the one hand, or one acting primarily out of human feeling on the other (Schleiermacher),[33] the Tübingers tried to steer a middle course by emphasizing freedom (both divine and human) and historicity without denying the validity of philosophy and feeling in their proper, subordinate place. In so doing, they restored the tension within Christian theology which the determinist and subjectivist poles had relaxed. Because they wanted to offer a dynamic theology better able to dialogue with their age than could the existing, static posture of the Catholic Church, they reconceptualized tradition into a living whole and revelation into an organic divine plan unfolding in history.[34] This is in sharp contrast to tradition seen as a once for all, unchanging deposit. Kasper, a century and a half after the founding of the school, has written:

> Theology today is characterized by a considerable tension between history—especially exegesis—and dogmatics. Theology must allow itself to be developed through the presentation of the historically expressed word and Christology, which are the unfolding of the immanent logic of faith.[35]

Concern for the role of tradition led the Tübingers to emphasize the Holy Spirit as the giver and empowerer of tradition in their theology. Möhler saw the Spirit as the moving force in and behind the Church when it was established and ever since. Kasper seeks to revive the Spirit Christology of the patristic period in a purified form. Pneumatology was neither new nor unique to Tübingen, but it has been a central and enduring emphasis. This emphasis has not always been biblically grounded, however. Möhler's early pneumatology owed much more to philosophy than to exegesis or systematic theology, and he backed off considerably in his later works in order to establish a more objective basis for the Church. Kasper's work is more biblically grounded, but he needs to step carefully to avoid the Adoptionism that threatens every pneumatic Christology.

The primary concern of Tübingen theologians from Drey to the present has been history. This is in no way to denigrate their other concerns; it is merely to note that they emphasized that Christ lived and died in history, the Church and its members exist in history, and the Spirit acts in history. Tradition is the Church living and developing in history, and revelation has occurred in history. History is the presupposition and medium for the realization of the other concerns expressed by the Tübingen theologians.

Seckler notes the Catholic Tübingen School was interested in three dimensions of history. The School had, first, an historical-critical interest in researching the past. When historical reality mediates truth, we need to study the forms and dynamics by which truth is mediated in order to understand better the truth being communicated. Drey believed the Bible needed to be studied critically because it was the foundation of all theology, but he was unhappy with the negative thrust of contemporary criticism.

The second dimension was the joining of speculative and historical. In this, one grasps the logic of history from the inside, inductively studying the parts in order to comprehend the whole. Drey considered this to be the task of the theologian. *Wissenschaftliche* theology enables us to recognize the accidental truths of history as the necessary truths of reason.

Third, the individual data of faith need to be evaluated and correlated. By themselves, they are "blind and dumb." Bringing many of them together only creates a greater mass of blind and dumb data. The theologian-historian needs to distinguish true from false and important from unimportant. Then he or she must fit the pieces together to create a coherent interpretation. That which does not fit into the interpretation is meaningless to the theologian. This is not, however, a subjective work by the theologian because he or she lives within history and must place him or herself under the history and tradition of the Church.[36] In so doing, the theologian is no mere chronicler of names, dates, events, and dogmas, but instead is attempting to integrate, interpret, and apply them to the contemporary Church.

The Challenge of History

For much of the history of the Church, history was understood as the record of what had happened and was open to the possibility of supernatural events and causes in history as well as natural ones. This does not necessarily mean people of earlier times were more naive, ignorant, or superstitious than moderns. They may have been, but a fundamental shift in how people perceive and relate to reality took place during the seventeenth and eighteenth centuries under the label "The Enlightenment," and this has led to a new and different understanding of historiography and a redefinition of history.

In the post-Enlightenment period, students of history passed from trying to understand history "wie es eigentlich gewesen," as did von Ranke, to approaching it relativistically, as did Troeltsch. He saw history as God marching through the world. Each religion was the response of a particular culture to God's activity. As Knitter puts it, the Absolute is manifest in all history, but no manifestation of the Absolute can itself be absolute.[37] Troeltsch, following Hegel, saw Christianity as consummating these religious developments. But not only does truth have different cultural forms, people are too trapped within their own culture to understand and appreciate different cultures. Third, based on the first two claims, he denied we can judge one religion as inferior to another. One can be more relevant to its culture's needs and more understandable, but this is a functional judgment of utility, not a judgment of truth. A religion's truth lies in its acceptance by adherents and its ability to fit into its cultural environment.[38] Knitter has shown this issue is central to any attempt to bring classical Christology into dialogue with modern culture because the particularism of the former appears incompatible with the pluralism of the latter. Whether the issue is particularism versus pluralism, mutually exclusive particularisms, or some other incompatibility, this clash has characterized the christological task for nearly 20 centuries. It is, if anything, even more difficult today than in the past.

Because an essential element of Christianity's self-witness is that Jesus Christ was an historical person and because the Church has existed in history for almost 2000 years, Christianity must take history seriously. It may not, however, allow itself to become swallowed up in historicism thereby eliminating its transhistorical and absolute claims. As Klaus Reinhardt says,

if the historical-critical explanation of the Bible and early Christianity can
show Christianity to have an historically-conditioned appearance, this would
mean the purely historical could be removed and Christianity would become
a religion of reason. The early Tübingers recognized this danger in German
Idealism and sought to ground Christianity in God who has revealed himself
in history in a particular person and at a specific time and place.[39]

For these Tübingers, historical tradition took on a new significance
because history was not merely events that could be analyzed objectively but
depended on the living Spirit of God revealed in Jesus Christ. The Spirit
bound the Church closely to the historical Jesus in understanding history.
Reason, feeling, intuition, speculation, and concrete reality took precedence
over knowledge, abstraction, rationalism, and the contemplation of delivered
truths.[40] Despite their study of romantic and idealist philosophy, the Tübingers grounded their work in Church history, notably patristic studies.[41]

The problem of historicity has remained a major concern of Tübingen theologians to this day. Walter Kasper says it defines the task of
theology because historical consciousness can generate a relativism that
threatens Christianity's very foundations.[42]

This concern for history has characterized the Catholic Tübingen
School since the days of Drey. He tried to locate Christianity within the
widest possible context consistent with Christian faith by using philosophy
of religion and history of religions. He supported in principle the historical-
critical study of Christian origins and Scripture,[43] but he considered contemporary practice less than helpful. Theological method must have an historical basis, but theology must never be dissolved into history. Drey's
concern for history was so novel that he was the first Catholic theologian to
teach a course on the history of dogma.[44]

Lessing's denial that the accidental truths of history can ever become necessary truths of reason led the Tübingers to respond by viewing history as an organic development which was the work of God. This meant
theology was based on revelation and faith, not on human intellect.[45] The
Tübingers clearly distinguished between the eternal, unchangeable divine
truth and the human understanding of it that developed in a contingent, historically changing world.[46] This allowed them to recognize an eternally
existing truth whose expression changed over the course of history. Such was
the basis for their concept of doctrinal development. It also enabled them
to defend the position that "thought must be one with Rome in faith but not
in theological expression."[47] O'Meara says that "as the struggle to comprehend history intensified, so did the interest in mysticism. What emerged was
a new emphasis upon traditional Christian themes."[48]

The early Catholic Tübingen School represented classical theology in its Catholic manifestation. It practiced a way of historical thinking and speculation foreign to the late twentieth century, so we today could not follow its precise route even if we wanted to. Early Tübingen differs from our age in three basic ways: they preceded serious historical criticism; our age thinks of history more in terms of process and development than in terms of idea, essence, and substance; and modern theology has made eschatology central, but has done so in terms of history and freedom instead of idea and nature.[49]

These differences have not kept such recent Tübingers as Kasper from turning to the work of the earlier generations for use as a living tradition within Catholic theology today. This means the epistemology and metaphysics of today's Tübingers are not those of Drey, Möhler, and Kuhn, but have developed through dialogue with contemporary philosophies. Because these differ over time, Tübingen theology, now as then, provides a genuine and orthodox alternative to scholastic Thomism in its different forms.[50]

The nature of the Catholic Tübingen School is such that our basic lesson from it will be primarily attitudinal; each member of the school faced different challenges and dealt with them in different ways. We believe, however, that all displayed a like attitude toward these different situations, and that this included respect for, use of, and fidelity to Church tradition understood as living, not static. Each Tübinger tried to be sympathetic to contemporary thought while critically examining and appropriating it.

The Christological Framework

Traditionally, Christology has been done within the framework of Chalcedon. This provided a unified and generally accepted universe for theologians to work. Today, however, the framework focuses on the two interrelated and pluralistic poles of biblical interpretation and contemporary experience. To complicate matters further, modern theologians consider both of these to be interpreted realities, not subjects of direct and objective knowledge.[51] Moreover, modern Roman Catholic Christology has shifted from dependence on neo-Thomism with its Greek philosophical roots to different versions of German philosophy, primarily German Idealism. This is the case not only for Rahner, Kasper, and von Balthasar; even political and liberation theologians draw indirectly (through Rahner) on German Idealism and directly on the left-wing Hegelians.[52]

The basic modern shift in Christology has been one of perspective—from "above" to "below" and from ontological to functional—but this perspectival shift cloaks a fundamental shift in worldview and method. A basic reason for the shift has been the increasing difficulty today in understanding traditional christological language and concepts. Christology "from below" attempts to deal with this by presenting Christology and soteriology from the perspective of anthropology.

The basic problem this approach is responding to is how to relate ontological statements about God and Christ in themselves to statements about their significance for us. How do we relate metaphysics and history?[53] This question has occupied the Catholic Tübingen School from its inception, and it is a question that goes to the heart of the Christian religion.

Christology "from above" begins from the perspective of God and treats Jesus as the Word of God who has become human in history. Christology "from below" begins with the human Jesus found in the gospels because it maintains this represents better the New Testament evidence and correlates better with today's historical way of thinking. The former Christology tends to be more ontological, the latter more functional. Theologians agree on the meaning of Christology "from above," but a survey of different writers reveals diverse conceptions of Christology "from below," not all of them mutually compatible.

Advocates of Christology "from below" see themselves as making faith in Jesus more relevant and understandable to modern thought. This is a generally valid claim, but one relating more to the concerns of traditional christologists than to the adequacy of their method. Kasper, who challenges many traditional presentations of Christology as irrelevant and incomprehensible, raises a question for christologists "from below." He asks who the subject of the method is: the man Jesus who reveals God to us, or the Second Person of the Trinity who is revealed in Jesus' humanity? Defending the doctrine of Chalcedon, Kasper asks further how these christologists propose to make that statement more understandable.[54] Louis Bouyer says the claim that a Christology "from above" evaporates Jesus' humanity is baseless. This is the Christology that developed out of the disciples' experience and which found its initial expression in the New Testament as they came to realize the full import of what Jesus had said and done. The councils merely confirmed and defended this position. The danger in such a Christology, Bouyer continues, is not that it might be consistent with its principles but that it might become inconsistent. It was inconsistency with this position that led to one-sided emphasis on Jesus' deity or humanity. The councils sought to correct this defection and to prevent future recurrences.

In contrast to Christology "from above," Christology "from below" results from people's failure to deal adequately with Jesus' uniqueness. Either they express their agreement that Jesus was unique inadequately or they no longer grasp the fact and implications of that uniqueness.[55] Kasper argues Christology "from below" is not a viable option in itself, but he adds that the two approaches are not exclusive; only the modern starting point has made them so. It is the anthropological turn of modern theology that has led to this christological turn.[56] William Loewe has written that this age has come to experience all reality as history, but Christianity has always insisted God's revelation to us is historical and factual. Thus, divine revelation has spoken and continues to speak to human needs in human terms.[57]

Context and Theology

Christians of every period have tried to present their religion to their contemporaries as a vital and meaningful faith. In doing so, they have had at some point to deal with Jesus Christ. Today, Christology has returned to the center of Christian discussion, but it has come as a problem, not as an answer. Any answer we present on this subject must be both meaningful and satisfying; that is to say, it must offer salvation in a way that responds to human needs and it must be powerful enough to make good its offer.

Christology today must be both conscious of historicity and grounded in history. This means it should recognize the contingent nature of human existence and the way history and culture affect human action, but it should remember equally the Scripture and traditions that recount and interpret the life and death of Jesus. These latter sources challenge Christians to consider that God acts in human history. A tension has come to exist between these two aspects, but we must ask if this tension is structurally necessary or is it the result of the different presuppositions we bring to our study of theology.

The Tübingen Catholics have tried in various ways and with various tools to develop and present Christologies of the sort we have said are needed. In the following pages, we will examine various proposals they have developed and evaluate them for their adequacy and for what they can teach us about doing Christology today. We will begin with Drey, the founder of the School, and cover those Tübingers who have done serious work on Christology. Our effort will necessarily focus on those more recent members, such as Kasper and Adam, who worked in modern environments—

indeed, Kasper is our contemporary—and faced problems often little different from those we face in constructing Christologies in the late 1980's.

Conclusion

In this chapter, we have looked at the issues of contextualization and translation, hermeneutics, history and historicity, and tradition. We have also looked at the histories of christological doctrine and of the Tübingen School. Each of these will play a role in later chapters, and all are part of the environment in which today's Catholic Tübingen School does its christological work.

Mondin suggests two ways to evaluate any Christology. We can look at the writer's individual texts in light of Scripture, exegesis, tradition, and conciliar decisions; or we can pick out the guiding thoughts, methodological principles, general criteria, and fundamental postulates that ground the writer's Christology and verify its solidity.[58] We do not believe it is a matter of one or the other, but that we should use both in tandem. Individual texts ought to be consistent with one's overall principles. Both ways of evaluation ought to conform to Scripture and agree with what Christians have taught for the better part of two thousand years unless good reason can be given for a change.

1. Bernard L. Ramm, *An Evangelical Christology: Ecumenic and Historical* (Nashville: Thomas Nelson, 1985), p. 15.

2. Ibid., p. 16.

3. See, for example, I Corinthians 15:14 ff., where Paul says that if the Resurrection did not happen Christianity would rest on a lie and Christians would be deluded and pitiable persons.

4. We have no extant writings from this position, but must rely on such early fathers as Hegisippus, Jerome, Eusebius, and Epiphanius for statements of that position within the context of their polemical responses.

5. In the two centuries following Chalcedon, the Church made several attempts to reach an accord between those who accepted and those who opposed the council's christological teaching. The Monophysite opposition continued to insist Christ had but one nature; a related group argued Christ could have but one will. These Monothelites feared Chalcedon led toward Nestorianism. Leontius of Byzantium suggested the concepts of anhypostasis and enhypostasis to explain the relation of person and natures in Christ. His theology, closer to Nestorius than to Cyril, drew on Aristotelian and Neo-Platonic philosophies. Although widely accepted in the Church, Leontius' views never were promulgated as dogma by any council. Thus, they have been rejected by some as an unwarranted extension of Chalcedon based on the needs of philosophical consistency, not biblical exegesis.

    At II Constantinople (A.D. 553), considering Nestorian tendencies more dangerous than Monophysite ones, the church condemned Theodore of Mopsuestia, Ibas of Edessa, and Theodoret. The first two had been associates of Nestorius and the third was an opponent of Cyril of Alexandria. Theodore was more Nestorian than Nestorius, but none of the three had been condemned at Chalcedon. the condemnation of the "Three Chapters" was intended to show Chalcedon had not been "soft on Nestorianism." Convened by the Emperor Justinian, the council aimed to clarify the teaching of Chalcedon both to exclude persons with Nestorian sympathies from the church and to refute the charge Monophysites had made against Chalcedon in hope of winning the latter back to the Church. The council specified the one *hypostasis* of the human Jesus was the Logos and the human nature was assumed into the Logos. This decision of the council remains controversial more than 1400 years after it was promulgated.

Third Constantinople (A.D. 680–681) moved to restore the balance in Christology by condemning Monothelitism (the teaching that Jesus Christ had but one will). This teaching was the logical result of the Monophysite position, extending the unity of nature to a unity of action in Christ.

6. Contextualization is a term that has been used to designate a variety of incompatible views about the relation between theology and culture. We are using contextualization here to mean the attempt to explain theology in a way understandable by one's intended audience while retaining the meaning of the original message. It is a task of *restatement*, as opposed to *reformulation*, and it must recur in each generation and cultural group. Words change meaning, new ideas and social structures develop, and different peoples look at the world in different ways. Restatement is essentially a process of translation, but it includes application in the context of the hearers; it deals not only with different languages, but also with different world views, cultures, and histories. The key point is that the message remains essentially the same while the expression changes. This is easier said than done. Reformulation, by contrast, means a new meaning is created because the original is inadequate, incomplete, or incorrect. Although the distinction is simple in theory, it is difficult to maintain in practice because it is not a contrast between two polar opposites but two regions on a scale sharing an ill-defined common border. Although difficult, translation can be done; were this not so, communication would be impossible between individuals as well as between societies. The distinction between restatement and reformulation is a theological and philosophical one based on one's understanding of God, humanity, language, and revelation.

The issue of restatement versus reformulation is extremely important in modern Christology because some argue the decisions of the early Church councils were based on Hellenistic philosophy and distorted the truth of Scripture in the process of translation; others say these statements are perfect examples of contextualization as it ought to be done because they use Greek philosophical terminology and concepts to refute attempts to force Christianity into a Hellenistic mold. This disagreement exists among Catholic theologians at Tübingen today. Later, we will use the concept of contextualization as a criterion in our evaluation of the present value of the Christology of the Catholic Tübingen School.

7. For the purpose of this study, we will define doctrine as the truth of Christian faith which remains valid throughout all time and space; theology is the continuing attempt to translate doctrine into the language of a particular age and culture. This means each doctrine can and should appear in terms of multiple valid theologies although these theologies may never be mutually contradictory (that is to say, that which is true at one time and place may not be false at another, but it need not be meaningful or complete in the latter context).

8. This is the theory of translation proposed by Eugene A. Nida and Charles R. Taber in *The Theory and Practice of Translation* (Leiden: Brill, 1974). Some modern writers on hermeneutics deny the original author can ever know fully the meaning of his or her text and claim the text's meaning is independent of the author. This would mean the interpreter must make changes in the interpretation or translation process to fill in the gaps or even say that which the author neglected to say. Heidegger, Gadamer, Ricoeur are leading advocates of this modern approach to hermeneutics, but they are by no means alone.

9. This does not mean the theologian must accept either their procedures or conclusions unless they are persuasive. On the other hand, simply because many of their presuppositions appear to be inimical to historical Christianity is not sufficient reason to automatically dismiss these scholars. Moreover, lack of familiarity with developments in modern hermeneutics and linguistics is apt to lead to incomplete and unconvincing argumentation and erroneous conclusions which will prove irrelevant to modern objections to classical theology. It will also be to miss the benefits one can derive from modern hermeneutical and linguistic theories and thus to do less scholarly and less accurate and complete work than one thinks he or she is doing.

10. Hans-Georg Gadamer, *Truth and Method* (New York: Crossroad, 1982), pp. 337 ff.; see also Anthony C. Thiselton, *The Two Horizons* (Grand Rapids: Eerdmans, 1980), pp. xix, 10 ff.

11. This should not be surprising if the different areas of theology are interconnected and interdependent.

12. This appears to be a major element in Roman Catholic Mariological doctrine and the veneration of the saints.

13. Piet Schoonenberg, *The Christ*, trans. by Della Couling (New York: Herder and Herder, 1971). See Klaas Runia, *The Present-day Christological Debate* (Downers Grove, IL: Intervarsity, 1984), pp. 50 ff., and George H. Tavard, *Images of the Christ* (Lanham, MD: University Press of America, 1982), pp. 86 f.

14. Hans Küng, *The Incarnation of God: An Introduction to Hegel's Theological Thought as a Prolegomena to a Future Christology*, trans. by John Stephenson (New York: Crossroad, 1987); *On Being a Christian*, trans. by Edward Quinn (Garden City, NY: Doubleday, 1976); *Does God Exist? An Answer for Today*, trans. by Edward Quinn (Garden City, NY: Doubleday, 1980).

15. Hans Küng, *et al.*, *Christianity and the World Religions: Paths to Dialogue with Islam, Hinduism, and Buddhism*, trans. by Peter Heinegg (Garden City, NY: Doubleday, 1986).

16. Karl Rahner, "Chalkedon: Ende oder Anfang?" III:3–49, in *Das Konzil von Chalkedon*, edited by Aloys Grillmeier, S.J., and Heinrich Bacht, S.J., three vols. (Würzburg: Echter, 1954).

17. Robert Krieg, a theologian at the University of Notre Dame, made this suggestion at the 1982 meeting of the Currents in Contemporary Christology Study Group of the American Academy of Religion.

18. Thomas F. O'Meara, *Romantic Idealism and Roman Catholicism: Schelling and the Theologians* (Notre Dame: University of Notre Dame, 1982), pp. 4, 139.

19. The concept of a Catholic Tübingen School is a matter of dispute among Catholic scholars at Tübingen today. This disagreement appears to proceed on two levels. On one, different scholars define what it means to be a school in different ways and reach opposite conclusions based on their different understandings of "school." The two camps spend little time trying to reconcile their definitional differences because their disagreement over the continuity of theology at Tübingen is even greater. Josef R. Geiselmann, Church historian at Tübingen from 1926 to 1958, firmly advocated the concept of a Catholic Tübingen School and enveloped his position in *Die Katholische Tübinger Schule* (Freiburg: Herder, 1964). Geiselmann also

wrote several other books dealing with the major writings of specific Tübingers and edited the major writings of some of these men, especially Johann Adam Möhler. Geiselmann emphasized tradition as the major concern of the Tübingers. His writings were designed to show this concern for tradition and to provide examples of tradition at work for later theologians to emulate.

A different view comes from Rudolf Reinhardt, currently professor of Church history at Tübingen. He, too, has done a great deal of study of the history of his faculty, the essence of which appears in "Die katholische-theologische Fakultät Tübingen im 19. Jahrhundert: Faktoren und Phasen ihrer Entwicklung," in *Kirche und Theologie im 19. Jahrhundert*, ed. by Georg Schwaiger (Göttingen: Vandenhoeck und Ruprecht, 1975), pp. 55-91. Reinhardt sees two alternative interpretations of the School. In one, it would be liberal, historical-critical, and at odds with the Church hierarchy; in the other, it would be a theological community with a characteristic approach to theological issues. The key trait of the latter would be the desire not merely to repeat past formulas but to interact vitally with the thinking of each era. Reinhardt rejects both interpretations as requiring selective use of the evidence, ignoring individuals and entire groups in whole or in part (pp. 63 ff.). He traces the history of the School through six phases which show discontinuities in development. Only in the first generation, says Reinhardt, did a unity in purpose and action exist. Nonetheless, he describes Möhler as the "undisputed head" of the School and the man who, through training the succeeding generation of faculty, placed his mark unalterably upon the School. This last point is one of the few places where Geiselmann and Reinhardt are in full agreement on the history of Tübingen's Catholic faculty.

What Reinhardt says about tensions and different directions among faculty is true, but we think it is relevant only if we define the School in terms of the whole of the faculty over time. Such a definition would preclude the existence of a school at Tübingen, but nothing requires the School to be defined in that way. We offer an alternate position and suggest that a school in Reinhardt's second sense did exist and, occasionally, it might be seen in terms of his first definition. Given the political and theological shifts in Europe and within the Roman Catholic Church since the founding of the faculty in 1817, a zigzag pattern is understandable if the Tübingers meant to deal seriously with changing Church and social contexts. It is unrealistic to expect all Catholic faculty members to share the same concerns and perspectives over a period of 170 years; the continued existence of a school normally derives from its ability to respond to changes over time.

Max Seckler, a Catholic fundamental theologian at Tübingen, agrees with Reinhardt that no school existed if one defines school in terms of method and unanimity of conclusions because Tübingen's projects, methods, directions of thought, and conclusions changed with each generation. In every case, Tübingen theologians have taken contemporary viewpoints most seriously. In terms of overall intellectual attitude, Tübingen does constitute a school. It demonstrated its attitude in terms of a liberality and multiplicity of approaches. This has been the basis of its achievement. See Seckler, "Johann Sebastian Drey und die Theologie," *Theologische Quartalschrift* 158 (1978):102 f.

Elmar Klinger, "Tübingen School," VI:320, in *Sacramentum Mundi*, ed. by Karl Rahner, six vols. (New York: Herder and Herder, 1970), says there have been few followers of the early Catholic Tübingen School in the strictest sense of a Kingdom-of-God theology, immediate relationship to God, and a particular notion of faith, tradition, and Scripture. He cites Paul Schanz, Karl Adam, and J. R. Geiselmann as members of the School (we would add Walter Kasper whose major work postdates the article). Klinger adds that several other Tübingers have shared the School's keen sense of the problems of history.

Our intention is not to argue the existence of the Catholic Tübingen School—others have done this already—but to trace the development of christological thought at Tübingen and to seek to learn what it has to say that can help us in our christological work at the end of the 20th century. Excellent studies of the origin and history of the Catholic Tübingen School are available. In addition to Geiselmann and Reinhardt, see Wayne L. Fehr, *The Birth of the Catholic Tübingen School: The Dogmatics of Johann Sebastian Drey*, AAR Academy Series Number 37 (Chico, CA: Scholars Press, 1981); Karl Adam, "Die katholische Tübinger Schule," *Hochland* 24 (1926–27), and reprinted in Adams' *Gesammelte Aufsätze*, pp. 389–412, ed. by Fritz Hofmann (Augsburg: Literarisches Institut, P. Haas, 1936); Thomas F. O'Meara, *Romantic Idealism and Roman Catholicism: Schelling and the Theologians* (Notre Dame: University of Notre Dame, 1982); Fritz Hofmann, "Theologie aus dem Geist der Tübinger Schule," *Theologische Quartalschrift* 146 (1966):262–284. Donald J. Dietrich, *The Goethezeit and the Metamorphosis of Catholic Theology in the Age of Idealism* (Bern: Peter Lang, 1979), places the early Tübingers in their historical, philosophical, and ecclesiological context between 1800 and 1860. Fehr presents Reinhardt's concerns well, but on pp. 3 ff. of his book he supports the idea of a Catholic Tübingen School.

20. Seckler, *passim*.

21. John Powell Clayton, "Perspectives on Protestant and Catholic Thought in the Nineteenth Century," *European Studies Review* 10 (1980):255.

22. T. M. Schoof, *A Survey of Catholic Theology, 1800-1970* (Paramus, NJ: Paulist Newman, 1970), p. 25.

23. Ibid.; Peter Riga, "The Ecclesiology of Johann Adam Möhler," *Theological Studies* 22 (1961):569.

24. Jacob Laubach, "Karl Adam," in Leonard Reinisch (ed.), *Theologians of Our Time* (Notre Dame: University of Notre Dame, 1964), p. 94.

25. Fehr, pp. 3 f.

26. F. A. Staudenmaier is an example of a Tübingen-trained theologian who did his major work elsewhere, although he was a tutor at Tübingen for a short time.

27. Karl Adam, trained in Munich, and possibly Hans Küng, trained at the Gregorian University (Rome) and the Sorbonne, are examples of this.

28. Ben F. Meyer, *The Aims of Jesus* (London: SCM, 1979), pp. 15 f.

29. Franz Schupp, S.J., "Die Geschichsauffassung am Beginn der Tübinger Schule und in der gegenwartigen Theologie," *Zeitschrift für katholische Theologie* 91 (1969):150 f.

30. Ibid.

31. Fehr, pp. 73 ff.; O'Meara, pp. 96–108.

32. Clayton, p. 251. Clayton errs in omitting Staudenmaier from the School, apparently seeing it as limited to Tübingen faculty (see Fehr, pp. 2 f.).

33. Adam, pp. 398 f.

34. Alexander Dru, *The Contribution of German Catholicism* (New York: Hawthorn, 1963), pp. 59 f.; Robert Krieg, "Karl Adam's Christology: Toward a Post-critical Method," *Heythrop Journal* 25 (1984):459.

35. Walter Kasper, *Glaube und Geschichte* (Mainz: Matthias-Grünewald, 1970), p. 20.

36. Seckler, pp. 103 ff.

37. Paul F. Knitter, *No Other Name?* (Maryknoll, NY: Orbis, 1984), p. 26.

38. Ibid., pp. 28 ff.

39. Klaus Reinhardt, *Der dogmatische Schriftsgebrauch in der katholischen und protestantischen Christologie von der Aufklärung bis zur Gegenwart* (Munich: Ferdinand Schöningh, 1970), p. 117.

40. Ibid., p. 118.

41. O'Meara, pp. 187 f.

42. Walter Kasper, *Der Absolute in der Geschichte: Philosophie und Theologie der Geschichte in der Spätphilosophie Schellings* (Mainz: Matthias-Grünewald, 1965), p. 9; William P. Loewe, "The New Catholic Tübingen Theology of Walter Kasper: Foundational Issues," *Heythrop Journal* 31 (1980):31 f.

43. Peter Stockmeier, "Die Kirchenväter in der Theologie der Tübinger Schule," pp. 131-154, in *Theologie im Wandel*, ed. by the Catholic Theological Faculty of the University of Tübingen (Munich: Erich Wewel, 1968).

44. Fehr, pp. 5 ff.

45. John Aurrecchio, S.S.P., *The Future of Theology* (Staten Island: Alba, 1970), p. 26.

46. Dietrich, p. 250.

47. O'Meara, p. 190.

48. Ibid., p. 121.

49. Walter Kasper, *Glaube und Geschichte*, p. 188.

50. O'Meara, pp. 4 f.   We have qualified O'Meara's statement about Thomism because Kasper told the author in 1983 that he was finding Thomas increasingly valuable for his theological work, but it was the original Thomas, not thomas as interpreted by later theologians.

51. Francis Schüssler Fiorenza, "Christology After Vatican II," *Ecumenist* 18 (1980):85 f.

52. Ibid., p. 82.

53. Walter Kasper, "Christologie und Anthropologie," *Theologische Quartalschrist* 162 (1982):205.

54. Walter Kasper, "Christologie von unten?" in *Grundfragen der Christologie heute*, ed. by Leo Scheffczyk (Freiburg: Herder, 1975), pp. 145 f.

55. Louis Bouyer, "Christology from Above and Christology from Below," *Word & Spirit* 5 (1983):23.

56. Kasper, "Christologie von unten?" p. 143.   We will explore Kasper's Christology at greater length in chapter VIII.

57. Loewe, p. 41.

58. Battista Mondin, "The Christological Experiment of Hans Küng," trans. by W. Stanley Fleming, *Biblical Theological Bulletin* 7 (1977):86.

CHAPTER II

FRIEDRICH W. J. SCHELLING

The era in which the Catholic Tübingen School began was greatly influenced by the Enlightenment and responses to it. Prominent figures today from the early nineteenth century include Kant, Hegel, and Schleiermacher, but the leading influence on Catholic Tübingen was a man who was equally important at the time, Friedrich Schelling. Schelling, like Hegel, had been a student at the Protestant theological faculty of Tübingen. But he disagreed with much of Hegel's Idealism, preferring instead the Romanticism that overlapped it at points.

Schelling has influenced many theologians, but the Catholic Tübingers were among the first. J. H. Thomas, ignoring Tübingen, traces Schelling's influence down to Kierkegaard, Tillich, and process theology.[1] For nearly two centuries, Christian theologians have sought to appropriate insights from Schelling's philosophy for their theology. Some have even seen him as a Christian apologist. Thomas suggests, however, that Schelling's general approach was much more pantheistic than it was Christian. He cites Schelling as saying that whereas his positive philosophy presupposes Christianity, it is not a manifestation of Christianity.[2] This does not, however, invalidate the attempts of various theologians to use elements of Schelling's system. Drey drew on Schelling's concept of organic unity and its historical unfolding to support his Christian apologetic and particularly his presentation of the Kingdom of God; Kasper draws on Schelling's concept of divine and human freedom to support elements of his theology, but neither created a theology that stands or falls on the adequacy and coherence of Schelling's total philosophy.

Schelling himself wrote about Christ primarily in his *Philosophie der Offenbarung*,[3] but he ignored the historical details of Jesus' life as he tried to fit Christ into his philosophical system.[4] Although Schelling wrote explicitly about Christology, he influenced Tübingen Christology more through elements of his philosophical system than through his theological excursions.

Schelling was the last of the great post-Enlightenment philosophers who both believed an overarching system for all philosophy was possible and tried to construct such a system. Through his influence, Roman Catholic philosophers and theologians first accepted Romanticism and Idealism. For over three decades, Schelling was a major influence on German Catholics, who saw him as anti-Enlightenment and pro-Romantic.[5]

Schelling and Christian Faith

Schelling's philosophy was not compatible at every point with Christian theology. This would have forced the Tübingers to be selective in their borrowing even if they had not insisted theology could never be dependent upon one philosophical system but must transcend them all, using any that were useful wherever they could. In Schelling's case, this included his insistence that religion could not be institutional or dogmatic, but instead must be a mystical wrestling with an immanent God whose deity existed in revelation and whose being was history.[6] Schelling represents both the fullness and the crisis of metaphysics. He inaugurated a new era in philosophy, particularly with his understanding of God. Hegel's God was "the End" of his system in which everything came to unity and completion; Schelling's God was the beginner of something new. For Schelling, God's deity needs to be understood in a new way. God is not the all-powerful but the all-suffering, who has compassion on his creatures in a way that admits no defect in him. God is not the one who "is" (*Seiende*) but the one who "becomes" (*sein werde*).[7] Tübingen appropriated Schelling's idea of the becoming of God without the problematic side effects of modern process theology's understanding of God's becoming.

Despite areas of incompatibility, Schelling's philosophy corresponded at many points to Christian theology. The problem was that it culminated in a new understanding of Christianity that was incompatible with Christian orthodoxy. Schelling's contribution was in providing a concept of history open to the future, personal, dialogical, and christocentric.

Contrary to Hegel and Strauss, Schelling said revelation must be more than humans can conceive through reason alone; were this not so, there would be no need for revelation to occur. Revelation's only value to us is in going beyond what human reason can contribute, but this beyond is not strictly informational. The God that results from this is free because pure human reason cannot contain him. Instead, the *Vorstellung* remains the essential element of Christianity and not an optional and surpassable form. Consequently, history is the arena where truth comes to realization, being not merely the appearance and *Vorstellung* form of truth (as in Hegel).[8]

Schelling saw history as the dramatic representation of the life of God, not as salvation history. As with Hegel, this meant there were strong pantheistic tones. For Schelling, there was more to history than that, and it was this more that the Catholic Tübingers were able to use. Contrary to the Enlightenment's separation of science and history, Schelling posited a system of identity where the Absolute as transcendent ground unifies all and brings together opposites that in their finite manifestations are mutually exclusive. The Enlightenment's mechanistic world became Schelling's organic one. Life in this world is not blind, biological reality, but self-conscious spirit. The world of history is a necessarily interrelated, self-conscious, and developing process.[9]

A further difficulty for Christian theologians using Schelling is his view of the relations between Christianity, free religion, and mythology. He acknowledged his philosophy is impossible apart from Christianity, but denied the two can be simply identified. Free religion (Schelling's ideal) is only mediated through Christianity; it is not a product of it. Schelling's view of the relation between Christianity and mythology is incompatible with the Christian theology of revelation seen as a unique act of God in Christ.[10] The Tübingers were, however, in full agreement with Schelling when he said, "essential in the study of theology is the binding of the speculative and historical construction of Christianity and its principal doctrines."[11] Since Drey, this has been a leading characteristic of the Catholic Tübingen School. O'Meara says Schelling's philosophy appealed to many, but finally pleased few. Nevertheless, many of these people and their movements were lastingly influenced by Schelling, perhaps more than they knew.[12]

According to Kasper, the cross was the hingepoint of Schelling's entire philosophy, not merely of his Christology. In the cross, the revaluation of all worth and the reordering of all being stand revealed. God's deity consists in his absolute freedom and in his enduring its opposite. For Schelling, this meant a positive historical becoming in God is possible.[13] Positive for Schelling meant not that God became more or better, but that he became other than he had been.

Schelling's Christ

Although Schelling made Christ a key element in his system, and although his system appeared superficially consistent with traditional theology, he was the first to acknowledge his Christology was less than fully orthodox. This is because Schelling attempted to establish a continuity between Christianity and other religions and presents a highly speculative understanding of intra-trinitarian relations based on idealist philosophy.[14] In showing a continuity within the Trinity, he also established a distinction that verges on contradiction. Consistent with his idealist scheme, Schelling said the Incarnation is the most important and essential fact of his analysis because it makes possible the resolution of contradiction within the Godhead, and thus in all of reality, a resolution which is carried out on the cross.

While dealing with the particular concerns raised by an idealist framework, Schelling managed to respond to several concerns about Christology that continue to trouble theologians in an age that by and large has rejected idealism. He rejected any Christology exclusively from "above" or "below." Whereas Christology "from above" tries to consider the temporal in terms of the eternal, the starting point now must be that of historical reality because both the innermost spirit and highest sense of Christianity is historical. The content of this history is Jesus Christ. He is neither the teacher nor founder of Christianity; he is its content. Similarly, Christology "from below" in the sense of an historical positivism provides no solution.[15] Christology in the sense of the liberal quest of the historical Jesus is nothing more than the mirror image of the failed Christology "from above." In its attempt to see Jesus' deity through his humanity, it places both in a continuum. "Above" and "below" are not genuine alternatives, said Schelling, but exist instead in a dialectical relationship encompassing faith and history.

Schelling viewed Christ as the second power of the Godhead which operates in creation and becomes the Son at the end of creation. After becoming human, this second power redeemed the world by processively returning historical factuality to the sovereignty of the Godhead. The third power of the Godhead, the Spirit, continues this redemptive work within history.[16] We see here that the primary work of the Son is within the Trinity, although Schelling professed not to neglect its historical elements, and the Spirit is the one who acts most directly in history.

Concerned for a new view of history, Schelling abandoned traditional incarnational understandings of Christology and proposed instead a kenotic model based upon Philippians 2. Schelling's kenosis was not, however, that of the later 19th century German and British theologians. The effect of this model was that he could not begin from above, but was forced to begin in history where God has appeared concretely in Christ. Schelling's model was not concerned with the question of pre-existence, but with countering pagan presentations of the Incarnation.[17]

In terms of his philosophy, Schelling required a higher unity identical both to what God necessarily is and to what humans originally were.

Given this condition, the transcendent entity can mediate between God and humans because such a mediator must be both "fully God and fully man." Jesus Christ is the leading "historical" candidate for this role. Schelling evidently attempted to tie his philosophy closely to his biblical exegesis. White asks, however, whether Schelling could introduce Christ into his system as he did without violating the fundamental principles of that system;[18] in other words, was Schelling's exegesis consistent with his philosophy?

Schelling formulated his concept of kenosis in terms of his philosophy as well as exegetically. It is the demythologization and secularization of humanity and thus its liberation. On another level, it is the negation of negation because it is the means of reconciliation with God. In his obedience, Christ rejected all dominion that is not dependent upon God. In doing so, he became one with God and at the same time one with humanity. Schelling considered Christ's humanity to be nothing more than a continuing act of kenosis.[19]

The heart of Schelling's philosophy is the question, "Why is there something instead of nothing?" His answer was that God has made humans to become fully and self-consciously one with him and this is the essence of Christian teaching presented through Jesus Christ. Furthermore, God did not forsake humanity when it forsook him, but will be reunited with it in a post-temporal future.

Schelling said we recognize there exists some potentiality that is mediated to us by creation and at the end of creation is realized as a divine person. This potentiality became real through the activity of humanity because in and of itself it can become nothing. It comes to reality through the power of humanity, but at some moment in human consciousness it reverts to being the Lord of Being. When this occurs, it is a divine person as the Lord of Being and at the same time a divine person outside of God because it exists independent of the Father. This is the whole concept of revelation: the second potentiality externalizes itself from God and thus is the Christ,[20] and Christ is the subject of revelation.

In the Old Testament, we have nothing but an anticipation and prophecy of Christ, so the Old Testament can be understood only in and through Christianity. Because Christ is the true content of the New Testament, he binds the Old and New Testaments. Schelling added that in a philosophy of revelation the only question is that of explaining the person of Christ.[21]

Christ was the light and the power of the pagans just as the Father was the power of the Jews. But because Judaism was too narrow to include them, Christ built the floor for the pagans. Thus, paganism and Judaism constitute divided economies that had been brought together in Christianity.[22]

Schelling explained that Christian missionaries had gone to India thinking they were proclaiming something the Indians had never heard before: God had become human in Christ. The Indians, however, were not surprised because what had happened once in Christ had occurred repeatedly in India. Schelling commented that the Indians had received greater understanding from their own religion than the missionaries had from theirs.[23] We see here Schelling's idea that religion is a continuum and expresses a reconciliation of the different aspects of reality. These comments show a basic contradiction within Schelling's Christology when he tried to hold to a particular effect of Christ's coming and to a general reality of which Christ's coming is but a particular case.

The Problem of the Incarnation

Schelling raised another problem for his philosophy when he said ascribing a personhood which appears in human form to something that has a prehuman, even a preworldly, existence creates a problem. Nevertheless, he seems to have claimed Christian doctrine could have arisen in history only if Jesus Christ really existed as the son of God and was sent to earth by God at a particular point in time. White quotes Schelling as saying Christ "lived like other men, he was born and he died, and his historical existence is as fully documented as that of any other historical person." Christ was the unique son of God who was born "at a determinate time," and this was "a final but fully external event, one entirely within the sphere of other phenomena."[24] Jesus' appearance as an historical person proves God has intervened decisively in the historical process, but Schelling's philosophical principles do not permit God to enter into time in such fashion because God is utterly transcendent.[25]

Schelling also held to some sort of fall. Through this fall, humanity made God from one into three.[26] Christ, said Schelling, explained his appointed task as restoring the unity of the Godhead that was destroyed by the Fall. Theologians explain the incarnation of God in Christ empirically: that is, that God has taken human nature in a particular moment of time although we cannot understand it because God is eternally outside of time. The incarnation of God is thus an incarnation from eternity. The man Christ is in his appearance only the apex and thus far the beginning of the same, which should continue thereby from him, so that all his disciples should be members of one and the same love of which he is the head. History witnesses that God first became truly objective in Christ because before Christ who has revealed the eternal in such a way?[27]

We know the Incarnation occurred, but we cannot explain it. That which has gone out of God has made himself human or has become human. The identity of the divine and human is not substantial but it is personal. This means the person of the God-man is the divine. The change that came about in the Incarnation deals only with the form of God because the divine itself does not change. The human Jesus was created through the power of God. The second divine person has united himself with this man in so intimate a way that God and human have become one person. As a result, a substantially new principle has entered the world with the Incarnation.

Schelling presented three historical ways of understanding Christ—Eutychian, Nestorian, and Chalcedonian—and rejected each. He said Christ is from neither divine nor human nature, but came instead from a unique third nature; it is only in the Incarnation that he entered into divine and human nature.[28]

The Incarnation for Schelling was the necessary prelude to the main event: Christ's death. This was no accidental happening, but a deliberate sacrifice. For Schelling this was not a sacrifice of God himself on humanity's behalf but instead a working out or unfolding of the reality of the Godhead. Schelling did go on to say Christ has identified himself with alienated humanity and as such represents us and has taken our guilt upon himself and through his punishment made us free. Christ died in our place and we were his enemies. Schelling stressed that by his death Christ has redeemed our lives from the power of the principalities that imprisoned us. Thus, Schelling's basic understanding of the atonement was the *Christus Victor* motif of his Lutheran heritage. He called Christ the savior of humanity who necessarily died in our place. His death made it possible for people to find reconciliation with God. It was impossible for humans and unnecessary for Christ (paraphrasing Athanasius), but Christ died in the place of and for the benefit of humans.[29]

Following Christ's death in history was his exaltation. The meaning of this significant event for Schelling was that

the subject which before the incarnation was neither God nor man and submitted himself to God in his substantiality and uniqueness is [now] in his uniqueness raised up to God.[30]

Schelling explained Christ by saying that in terms of his eternal humanity Christ is outside of God and in terms of his deity he is outside of humanity. The lordship to which Christ was exalted was one he did not desire for himself (Phil 2:6). Whoever would become Lord cannot be substantially God; only the one who is "in the form of God" could be recognized by God as Lord. Schelling's distinction between God and "in the form of God" was crucial because that which is "in the form of God" must be other than God (contrary to classical exegesis of the Philippians passage). The actions and passion of Christ were a true and valid part of his history for Schelling, but the crucial element was a higher one for which his human life is but "transitional and momentary." So Christ's history is the real content of Christianity, but this history is other than what we think of when we say history because much of it occurs outside our temporal realm.

The conclusion of Schelling's Christology in terms of the classical understanding was that Christ was not essentially deity in his Incarnation because deity and servanthood are incompatible conditions. This led Schelling to a kenotic reconciliation of these two apparent irreconcilables. Furthermore, the earthly Jesus could not be deity because he professed ignorance of the end (Mk 13:13) and deity cannot be ignorant. In his *Philosophie der Offenbarung*, Schelling provided his exegesis of Philippians 2:6–11, and discussed the christological import of Hebrews and John's Gospel.

Conclusion

For all his effort and declared intention, Schelling never quite arrived at a satisfactory explanation of the person of Christ. As White points out, his use of Christ violated his own philosophical standards, especially the need for particularity of Christian revelation. He did, however, provide raw material for later theologians to construct their Christologies. Kasper says Schelling's historical method and horizon of universal history are significant for formulating Christology because history has been the great problem of classical attempts, which could not explain adequately the incarnate existence—especially the death and resurrection—of God. Kasper attributes this to use of a static concept of being. Schelling considered classical Christology to be a form of Nestorianism which spoke more of a hypothetical than a real incarnation. Because this classical view held that God could not change, it followed that history could not be significant for God, and that finally it must be nothing.[31]

O'Meara says Schelling's influence on Drey began during the 1806–1821 period when Schelling was in dialogue with Roman Catholics.

Drey was part of the second generation of Catholic theologians influenced by Schelling, standing between Zimmer and Sailer on the one hand and Staudenmaier and Möhler on the other. Of all Catholics influenced by Schelling, Drey was the most important.[32] Schelling's greatest influence on Drey was his "Vorlesungen über die Methoden des akademischen Studiums." Lectures eight and nine in particular dealt with the historical construction of Christianity and the study of theology. Drey drew his concept of history from them and followed Schelling in the view that Christianity must be constructed historically in terms of the Kingdom of God. Schelling also introduced the idea of the wedding of history and freedom which has been picked up especially by later Tübingen theologians.[33] Schelling's influence upon the early Tübingers is best summed up by O'Meara:

> Drey's disciples: Staudenmaier, Kuhn, and Möhler... related to Schelling in different ways. Staudenmaier was intent upon a faithful Catholic system that would build upon Hegel and Schelling. By the 1830's, however, the younger Tübingers such as Möhler and Kuhn had moved away from Schelling; critical of both Hegel and neoscholasticism, they preferred history to system.[34]

1. J. Heywood Thomas, "J. G. Fichte and F. W. J. Schelling," I:70 f., in *Nineteenth Century Religious Thought in the West*, ed. by Ninian Smart, *et al.*, three vols. (Cambridge: The University Press, 1985).

2. Ibid., p. 70.

3. F. W. J. Schelling, *Philosophie der Offenbarung, 1941/42*, ed. by Manfred Frank (Frankfurt: Suhrkamp, 1977); see especially pages 285–312.

4. Thomas, p. 69; Alan White, *Schelling: An Introduction to the System of Freedom* (New Haven: Yale, 1983), pp. 185 f., says Schelling's use of Christ goes well beyond what his system and method permitted.

5. The best survey in English of Schelling's influence on his Roman Catholic contemporaries is Thomas F. O'Meara, *Romantic Idealism and Roman Catholicism: Schelling and the Theologians* (Notre Dame: University of Notre Dame, 1982), which deals with all German Catholic theologians of the period, not only those from Tübingen.

6. O'Meara, p. 4.

7. Walter Kasper, "Krise und Neuanfang der Christologie im Denken Schellings," *Evangelische Theologie* 33 (1973):370 f.

8. Ibid., p. 374.

9. Gerald A. McCool, *Catholic Theology in the Nineteenth Century* (New York: Seabury, 1977), p. 69.

10. Thomas, p. 68.

11. F. W. J. Schelling, "Vorlesungen über die Method des akademischen Studiums," in *Schellings Werke*, III:326, ed. by Manfred Schröter, six vols. (Munich: C. H. Beck'sche, 1958).

12. Thomas F. O'Meara, "F. W. J. Schelling: Bibliographical Essay," *Review of Metaphysics* 31 (1977):308.

13. Kasper, p. 383.

14. Schelling, *Philosophie*, especially p. 268.

15. Kasper, p. 372.

16. F. W. J. Schelling, *The Ages of the World*, trans. by Frederick de Wolfe Bolman, Jr. (New York: Columbia University, 1942), p. 203.

17. Kasper, p. 381.

18. White, p. 186.

19. Kasper, p. 382. Kasper adds that by his use of a kenosis Christology, Schelling was able to deal with the central concerns of classical Christology without being caught up in its logical problems. This should not be construed as an endorsement by Kasper of Schelling's Christology *in toto*, however.

20. Schelling, *Philosophie*, p. 260.

21. Ibid., pp. 259 f.

22. Ibid., p. 267.

23. Schelling, "Vorlesungen," pp. 320 f.

24. White, p. 185.

25. Ibid., p. 186.

26. Schelling, *Philosophie*, p. 263.

27. Schelling, "Vorlesungen," pp. 319 f.

28. Schelling, *Philosophie*, p. 296. In saying this, Schelling has adopted a position explicitly rejected by the Council of Nicea in A. D. 325.

29. Ibid., p. 303.

30. Ibid., p. 308.

31. Kasper, pp. 380 f.

32. O'Meara, *Romantic Idealism*, pp. 92 f.

33. Klaus Reinhardt, *Der dogmatische Schriftgebrauch in der katholischen und protestantischen Christologie von der Aufklärung bis zur Gegenwart* (Munich: Ferdinand Schöningh, 1970), p. 108.

34. O'Meara, *Romantic Idealism*, p. 12

CHAPTER III

JOHANN SEBASTIAN DREY

AND JOHANN ADAM MÖHLER

Johann Sebastian Drey (1777—1853) and Johann Adam Möhler
(1796—1838) were the leading figures of the first generation of the Catholic
Tübingen School. Drey founded the Catholic faculty at the University of
Tübingen and initiated the attitude toward theology that has come to be
called the Catholic Tübingen School.[1]

Johann Sebastian Drey was born into a poor Swabian family in 1777
and decided early to become a priest. He was one of the original faculty on
the university in Ellwangen. This institution had been founded in 1812 to
care for the needs of the Catholics who recently had been incorporated into
Württemberg as Napoleon had shuffled geographical boundaries to suit his
political aims. Drey taught dogmatics at Ellwangen until it was dissolved in
1817 and moved to Tübingen with some of the theological faculty and students to establish a Roman Catholic theological faculty at that well-known
Protestant school. Drey was to remain on the Tübingen faculty until his
retirement in 1846. He died seven years later.

Johann Adam Möhler was the son of a Swabian innkeeper. Born
in 1796, Möhler was a student at Ellwangen and moved to Tübingen with
Drey to complete his studies in Church history. Called to the Tübingen faculty to teach Church history and canon law, Möhler first spent a year
traveling among German universities and auditing some of the leading
figures in German theology, Protestant as well as Catholic, before he took
up his post in 1823. During his tour, Möhler was greatly influenced by
Friedrich Schleiermacher, then teaching in Berlin. A controversialist, Möhler was forced to leave Tübingen for Munich in 1835 as a result of his
heated controversy with Johann Christian Baur, the leading light of the
Protestant faculty, over their conflicting views of the true content of Christian doctrine. Never a particularly healthy person, Möhler died in Munich
in 1838. His brief academic career was marked by a tremendous output of
books and articles as well as controversy over his two major works, *Die
Einheit in der Kirche* (1825) and *Symbolik* (1832).

Möhler has been better known among Catholic theologians than has Drey. Many have called him the father of the Catholic Tübingen School because he formed theologically the next generation of teachers at Tübingen. His outlook was exported to other faculties by students who graduated from Tübingen to teach elsewhere. More recently, Catholic scholars have tried to trace a line of thought from Möhler to some of the basic concepts regarding doctrines of Church and revelation accepted by Vatican II. This fact, plus renewed theological leadership from Tübingen Catholics, has led to a new interest in the work of Drey and Möhler, especially regarding the development of doctrine.

Neither Drey nor Möhler was primarily interested in Christology because it was not a subject of controversy among Catholics in their day. Other matters causing serious disagreement among Catholic theologians in the early 1800's received more direct consideration. This is not to say neither was interested in Christology. On the contrary, Christology was presuppositional for Drey's work on doctrinal development and apologetics, and was the foundation for Möhler's later work in ecclesiology.

Several contemporary events and conditions influenced Drey's theological program. One of the most important of these was the experience of teaching on a Catholic theological faculty at a Protestant university in the midst of a Protestant area of Germany. The attempt by several Protestant and Catholic philosophers and theologians to respond to Enlightenment skepticism, the pastoral requirements in educating future priests, and the political and religious changes resulting from the recent Napoleonic Wars also affected the initial development of the Catholic Tübingen approach to theological studies. Napoleon attempted to destroy the Catholic Church wherever he went and the Enlightenment attacked all forms of organized religion, especially those claiming an authoritative teaching. These factors caused Drey to focus his efforts in the areas of apologetics and ecclesiology. Thiel says he was also the one who brought the concept of doctrinal development into Roman Catholic theology.[2]

Christology was not the focus of Drey's theology; traditional Christology had not at that time come into question within Catholicism. Drey's concepts of doctrinal development and the nature of the Church were based on Christology and presupposed a traditional understanding of Christ. Using Schelling's idealist philosophy, Drey developed a concept of the organic unfolding in history of the Kingdom of God.

JOHANN SEBASTIAN DREY

Drey was not the first Catholic who sought to incorporate the ideas of contemporary philosophy and theology into his system. He was, however, one of the few who escaped condemnation from Rome for so doing. Drey drew on various thinkers, both Protestant and Catholic, for his ideas, but he never allowed any one to dominate his thought. He used the contemporary themes of organicism, history, consciousness, and development to restate Catholic teaching in a way his contemporaries could understand.[3] But, as McCool has said, he believed Christian faith requires no philosophical foundation outside itself because Christian tradition already has its own necessary system of ideas.[4] Because he believed this, Drey could be open to contemporary philosophy and cultural values and bring them into dialogue with Catholic tradition. Such openness has continued to characterize the Catholic Tübingen School. Drey also recognized the danger of interacting with contemporary philosophy because, as he tried to link speculation with history, he had to avoid integrating them in such a way that theology was enslaved by a particular theological tradition.[5] Drey was seeking to establish a Catholic response to the challenges posed by the Enlightenment and Kant.

Drey was heavily influenced by both Schelling and Schleiermacher, but he broke with each at crucial points because he considered their teachings at these points incompatible with Christian truth. Drey drew on Schelling's philosophy of revelation with its idea of organic unity and of the unfolding of revelation in history. He introduced Schleiermacher's idea of the development of doctrine into Catholicism but modified it in the direction of Schelling to affirm that all development was consistent with and derived from the original revelatory content. Drey was able to use these resources because he viewed Christianity as consisting of an inner essence and an outer form. The form may change, but the essence must remain the same. The form of Christianity for Drey was the Church's liturgy, discipline, and worship. Its essence was God's plan to reconcile all humanity to himself in a kingdom. The Kingdom of God was the organizing concept for Drey's entire theology. Drey distinguished his theological enterprise from the main lines of German Idealism by his insistence on the separation of humanity from an omnipotent God who can nevertheless reveal his truth to humanity throughout history. This interconnection of humanity with God without the two being confused Drey expressed as the Kingdom of God in its manifold dimensions.[6]

McCool assesses Drey's work by saying that the distinctiveness of Drey's theology was due to its exploitation of Schelling's idealism. Without Schelling's metaphysics Drey's dialectical development of living tradition within the community of the Church would be deprived of its intelligible necessity and his reflective reconstruction of historical revelation would not possess the apodictic evidence which grounds its scientific certitude.[7]

Drey's theology showed the influence of a variety of contemporary philosophers and theologians, but his theology was most clearly characterized by his concern for history and historicity. Christianity was revealed objectively in the history of creation; it was not merely subjective experience. This conviction led Drey to emphasize the history and development of revelation and the implications of history for Christian revelation.[8] Drey derived this view of history with its stress on organic development from Romanticism. Integrated with Schelling's transcendental idealism, this historical understanding enabled Drey to see theology as the systematic unfolding of historical revelation in relation to human intellectual capacities.[9] This was instrumental both to his concept of the Kingdom of God and to his introduction of the concept of doctrinal development into Roman Catholic theology. In contradiction to Schelling, however, Drey saw Christianity as so intimately linked to historical persons and events that it must be considered essentially history and not a system of ideas.[10]

For Drey, revelation must be related vitally to the present with its uniqueness, problems, and needs, but it is at the same time moving toward the fulfillment of God's purpose for his creation. The goal and content of this eschatological movement is the Kingdom of God. The Kingdom is the interpretive key to the religious understanding of history. This means Drey's was an open system, because as long as history continues the inner truth of Christianity is incomplete. The whole truth, and thus the whole system, remains unfinished until the end of time. All theology stands under this eschatological caution. An extremely important consequence of this is that our systematic knowledge is not settled and can both change and develop. Drey accepted certain past developments as settled, but as doctrine continues to develop new developments force earlier ones into new relationships.[11]

For Drey the context within which theology develops was the historical Church. Theology not grounded in the Church becomes "airy and contentless speculation." Theology is a necessary task of the Church because it makes clear the relationship between God and humans and enables the Church to make definite claims. Theology expresses what the Church is; it is not the *raison d'être* of the Church: that is to change the heart of the individual and to bring him or her nearer to God.[12]

Because the Church is an historical entity, it is able to develop theologies corresponding to the needs and thought patterns of each generation. Thus, although the essence of God's revelation is eternal, pre-existing even the Church, dogmatic expressions of that revelation can vary over time and place as the historical circumstances of the divine-human dialogue vary.[13] In saying this, Drey is applying his distinction between the kernel and shell of doctrine. This distinction raises a further problem that has remained with theology to this day: how do we distinguish between the kernel and shell of doctrine? Too often, one person's shell is another's kernel. Drey's personal theology remained consistent with the major elements of traditional Catholic teaching, but there was nothing intrinsic to his system that required this. Some who have considered themselves heirs to his theological approach have used this developmental concept to question teachings widely considered part of the kernel. Drey's views at this point appear somewhat subjective because he posited the Spirit indwelling the Church as leading it through appropriate development. This implied to Drey that doctrine progresses organically. That is to say, the test for later developments is not whether they were present at the outset, but whether they are faithful to and congruent with all that has gone before.[14]

Drey did not understand Christianity as something confined to certain beliefs, events, or writings. Instead, he saw it as a social and historical reality. This reality is the Church, which grows and persists in continuity with its origin. Because the Holy Spirit regulates the Church all development of dogma has divine authority. In the same way, Drey's understanding of the role of the Spirit led him to seek harmony in his system. Whatever is out of harmony with the whole must be a misunderstanding, error, or corruption of the development of Christianity and must be rejected.[15]

Drey's introduction of the concept of doctrinal development was a conservative move meant to defend Catholic tradition against the skepticism of the Enlightenment. He also sought to place that tradition on a more solid footing than the rigid unwillingness to interact at all with contemporary thought which characterized most Catholicism of his day. In direct opposition to Enlightenment rationalism, Drey said history was directed by a constant divine influence operative in all human religious development (primitive religions as well as the Church and Christian history). Christianity culminated this religious development and was the key to understanding human history. Because the product of the divine mind occurs in history, the human mind can, in principle, understand the patterns of this history. This is because the human mind is the finite and partial manifestation of the divine mind. The task of the theologian is defined in terms of history: it is to organize human history in accordance with the divine Ideas, the principal of which is the Kingdom of God.[16]

Contemporary critics viewed history as a series of "accidents." Drey suggested history can best be understood in terms of the unfolding revelation of God through historical actions. This means it is a revelation that is living and active in and through the Church, not merely a deposit of tradition within the Church. The consummation of this unfolding revelation is Jesus

Christ. He is not to be found simply in biblical research because he partakes of the living and continuing nature of revelation and is, as a result, available only through the Church with its living tradition. Christ passes himself on through the Church that is, in a sense, the continuation of the Incarnation.[17]

For Drey, Christianity was given historically. This makes history the main arena for the theologian. But Christianity is also divinely given; thus its history has an authoritative character. Drey says this means the theologian must begin from God's side because God is the author of what the theologian seeks to understand and so he must ground any speculation in the divine revelation. In today's language, Drey opted for a theology "from above." Fehr says Drey's view of revelation led him to regard history as the outpouring of a continual, ceaseless divine influence upon human consciousness in and through the objects and events of this world.[18] This had implications for Drey's Christology and understanding of world religions. Drey viewed history in terms of divine necessity, following the views of the earlier Schelling. Later Tübingers, beginning with Staudenmaier, saw history more in terms of divine freedom, following the later Schelling, and thus as the category for interpreting all of reality. Drey recognized the need to relate God's freedom and necessity and sought to do so in terms of the Trinity. God's activity reflects his nature and thus cannot be arbitrary because no outside force exists to constrain God. Such an understanding distinguished Drey from those of his German contemporaries who saw creation as a necessary unfolding of the divine essence.[19]

Drawing on his understanding of history, Drey sought to rehabilitate the concept of revelation by placing divine revelation within the context of human development. This meant human history was the unfolding of revelation and would culminate in the Kingdom of God. Drey saw this as the only way to ground Christianity's claims.[20] He was further convinced divine revelation must be intelligible to humans because God had given it as a way of educating humanity. This education takes place through the influence of the divine Spirit on the human spirit. This influence is a unified and consistent process that leads finally to Christianity. To be accepted as true, however, the doctrines derived from revelation must be susceptible to the same rigorous scientific examination as any other branch of knowledge.[21]

Drey said the created order can know God only if God reveals himself directly or indirectly through another person who already has this idea of God. This knowledge first appeared in primitive religion and now has culminated in the incarnation of the divine Word. Because the Incarnation is the climax of divine revelation, all revelation must lead inevitably to Christ. This divine Word came to announce and teach the Kingdom of God; this concept was the focus of all Drey's teachings. The growth of the Church's consciousness of the meaning of the Kingdom results in the development of Christian doctrine over time.[22] The upshot of this is that revelation must be real and objectively given—an historical message from God—not merely experiential.

Although Scripture is foundational, it alone is not a sufficient basis for theology because Christian reality continues to unfold from those foundational events recorded in Scripture. Such external influences as philosophy and science can have a valid role in this development. In addition, Drey saw Scripture in isolation as a dead letter that must be brought to life by the Spirit. That which the Spirit contributes is called tradition by the Church. Drey wanted to integrate tradition into Catholic theology in a new way that placed greater stress on subjective experience and historical development.[23] Burtchaell says the heart of Drey's contribution was that the continued presence of the Spirit in the Church means that in some sense new revelation develops out of old as revelation continues to unfold.[24]

Drey organized his entire theological enterprise around the theme of the Kingdom of God. This was clear in his interaction with modern thought, his ideas about doctrinal development, and his understanding of revelation. It was equally true for his Christology and soteriology. As Drey himself stated it,

> The fundamental religious outlook of Christianity and thus
> the fundamental idea of Christian theology is the idea of a
> Kingdom of God as a moral world order.[25]

Drey derived this idea of the Kingdom of God from the Bible where he found it to be the heart of Jesus' preaching. He understood the concept to mean that the existence and development of the world are grounded in God's decrees. Because God and humanity share the ability to reason, humans can conceive of and understand the idea of the Kingdom. This scriptural beginning drew Drey's attention to Schelling's thesis that all creation depends upon an original ground. Drey used Schelling's *Urgrund* concept as the theological basis for his idea of the Kingdom of God which, he contended, had manifested itself visibly in the Church. This idea was both the organizing principle for all of God's relationships to the created order and the content of divine revelation.[26] The Kingdom means that neither God nor the world can be considered in isolation from the other; they exist in an intimate relationship that derives from the Father—Son relationship within the Trinity.[27]

The idea of the Kingdom affected his anthropology and understanding of sin. Because of the intimate relationship between Creator and creation, Drey said humans are radically dependent upon and oriented toward God. This is expressed in humanity's universal religious impulse, which has developed gradually, as human reason has developed under the educational influence of divine revelation.[28] The upshot of Drey's optimistic anthropology was a human nature that needs only to be educated in order to enjoy a positive relationship to God.

Drey's understanding of sin was ambiguous. He saw it as a disturbance of the divine plan which needed to be overcome by God's revelatory activity, but he also saw it as in some sense included in the divine plan as a way by which the Kingdom of God advances.[29] Sin is an accidental, not an essential, part of human existence because the latter view would make God the author of sin. Nonetheless, he continued to view sin as within the scope of God's providence, denying it was outside God's plan for creation. Fehr suggests this shows clearly the difficulty of using an Idealist model to do Christian theology.[30]

Drey also saw sin as a refusal to accept God's sovereignty over creation and thus a basis for human blameworthiness. Sin is a misreading of reality. It clouds the reason and leads to the misunderstanding of reality. Drey concluded that sin is human self-absolutizing which results in ignorance of God and his Kingdom. The Fall caused a subjective alienation from God, but it did not change the basic human relationship to God in terms of his Kingdom. As a result of the Fall, humans now have a "proclivity toward evil" intrinsic to their nature. This can be overcome only through a re-creation or rebirth of human nature.[31]

Drey's concept of sin posed several difficulties for theology, especially for Christology, because Christology must offer an adequate response to the problem created by human sin. Sin has been described traditionally as an abnormal situation within the created order caused by human rebellion against God and thus the source of human guilt before God. The Idealist philosophers of Drey's time considered sin an essential part of God's plan for creation. It cannot be both at the same time. If God made sin a necessary part of creation, it is difficult to understand how humans can be blamed for it. God may bring evil out of good, but ethics is lost if the same act is determined and praiseworthy or blameworthy at the same time. Drey also had a problem in overcoming sin. He suggested the need for a rebirth of human nature is the only answer, but he also offered education as a way out. The former suggests that human nature is fundamentally warped or evil. Radical measures are needed to restore the broken human relationship with God; the latter presupposes that human nature is basically good and directed toward God, hence it needs only to be taught what it should do and shown the way to God. These two understandings are contradictory. Historically, each has led to a particular understanding of the person and work of Jesus Christ.

Drey's interpretation of Christianity as the culmination of all religion placed it beside all other religions as one among many, even if it is the culmination of the many. Much traditional Christian theology has seen Christianity against all other religions, as true in contrast to their falsity. Drey's position recognized all religions contain elements of value and truth, but it also laid the groundwork for abandoning the traditional idea of Christian uniqueness. This new understanding has taken root in the Vatican II documents in terms of a new openness to other religions, although these documents go further, seeing Christ as bringing salvation through non-Christian religions.

Unlike some of his contemporaries, Drey rejected immanentism and retained the traditional divine origin of religion which included a creating and sustaining God. This means Drey's God is ever active in creation and always seeking out humans to be in fellowship with him.

Given his ambiguous presentation of sin, Drey presented a remarkably traditional Christology. He did so because he drew on the full range of biblical images of Christ and his work and remained firmly committed to the christological teaching of the early Church. In his *Apologetik*, Drey developed a Christology that began with Christ's pre-existence and incarnation and continued to his death, resurrection, and final return in judgment. The presentation depended heavily upon the use of proof texts, particularly from the fourth gospel.

Drey approached the person and work of Christ historically. Jesus was a real human who lived and died in a particular place and time. He said and did certain things his contemporaries could hear, see, and record for future generations. Drey's Jesus was a man, but he was more than a man. In Jesus Christ, God entered into human history in such a way that he will never exit that history. What is more, Jesus' work in history remained incomplete at his death; his mission continues and remains valid for all time. Thus, Christianity can never be a finished product; each period should be but the preparation for the dynamic movement of Christ's ideas into the next historical period. The unifying factor here is the Kingdom of God, which is being realized within history.

Drey wrote his Christology before D. F. Strauss, so he did not interact with Strauss's critical attitude toward the Bible or with the mythological approach that saw Christ more as a philosophical than an historical truth. Drey's successors at Tübingen would take up the battle with the new skeptical approach to traditional Christianity. This is not to say Drey was unaware of the work of Richard Simon. He agreed with Simon in seeing discrepancies and other problems in the Bible but said because Catholicism was not confined to the Bible for its theology, he could employ tradition to support his dogmatics. Drey's use of the gospels in his Christology must be considered pre-critical in its unquestioning prooftexting of the traditional aspects of Christology.

Drey's Christology was traditional as well in that it is ontological, not functional. He presupposed Christ's pre-existence in the *Apologetik* by his description of Christ as the One Sent and the manner in which he described Christ as the Son. He did, however, speak directly to the matter of pre-existence when he said that Christ "claimed not merely a preworldly existence with God... but an express participation in the essence, wisdom, holiness, and power of God."[32] Drey also said Jesus was conscious of an essential relationship to God. He supported his position by citing Matthew and John as recording that Jesus claimed a special and unique knowledge of God that belongs to deity alone. Christ's relationship to the Father is one of "vollkommenen ähnlichkeit, Gleichkeit, Derselbigkeit."[33] If Jesus is of the same essence as God and has been sent by God, he should show some consciousness of this. If Jesus was conscious only that he was one sent by God, he would be no different from the Old Testament prophets. What Jesus needed to set him apart was a consciousness which participates in the divine essence. Drey said this consciousness existed and was so "pure and sincere... strong and sure" that he did not fear the Incarnation. This incarnation was not a necessary event in the sense that some earlier theologians argued the Incarnation of the Son would have occurred even had the Fall not taken place. Christ was incarnated primarily to proclaim the good news of the Kingdom of God.[34]

Christ's Incarnation is the climax of revelation as it unfolds in history. The fundamental reality of Christianity is God's becoming human. This means God's final revelation occurs through an historical individual. As an eternal being the Son gives meaning to the temporal world by bringing it into intimate contact with the Godhead. To some extent, Christ brings creation into the Godhead itself.[35]   In terms of a modified idealist philosophy, the Son mediates the Father's creative work to finite reality. Thus the created reality mirrors the Son, not the Father.[36] The Son is thus the mediator between the Godhead and creation, of redemption as well as of creation. Not only does Christ represent God to humanity, he also represents humanity and all creation before God as it ought to have been from eternity. In some way, God and the world are linked intrinsically through Christ. In fact, the divine purpose for humanity is a union with God patterned in some sense after the union of the Father and the Son in the Godhead. In the same way the Spirit is the cement of the Godhead, so the Spirit is the binding force of our union with God.

The person of Jesus Christ was the key factor arising out of his appearance in history. Christ is one who is more than human; he is the Word of God, not simply the bearer of the word. God has made his salvation visible in Christ. In addition to citing the specific claims found in the New Testament, Drey cited as evidence for his deity Christ's sinlessness in the face of temptation, his ethical righteousness, and his total lack of fanaticism.[37] Furthermore, this ethical character betrays a consciousness of the divine quality of both his mission and teaching.

Christ possesses an essential identity with the Father in both his nature and activity. His works, and not only his miracles, demonstrate Christ was of the same nature as the Father. These works also authenticate his teaching, both his claims about himself and his teaching on human need and salvation.

The crucial aspect of Christology in its humanward aspect is the work of Christ. Drey saw this work as multi-faceted and extending over eternity. In contrast to those who isolate Christ's work on the cross, Drey saw Christ's work as extending backward into eternity and also into the future. Christ is the mediator between God and creation and is the immediate cause of the existence of that creation and its relationship to God.

Christ's work continued in his incarnation and life. Drey found three aspects of the work of Christ in his earthly life. First, he founded a new religion and religious community based on his teaching and on living faith in him. Second, he came for a general moral restoration and restructuring of humanity. Third, he achieved a general forgiveness of sins and salvation from corruption with an expectation of eternal bliss. Drey said these three works can be subsumed under one—uniting all humanity into one great Kingdom of God. This Kingdom was the heart of Jesus' entire teaching. He was sent by God to be the founder and Lord of this Kingdom.[38] Through the Kingdom that Christ proclaimed, humanity was not simply brought near to God; it was enabled to participate in the wisdom and love of God himself and to enjoy an eternal relationship with God.

Christ's teaching is universal. It is not only for all peoples, it is for all times. This is so not only because it is a seed within which lies the potential for unending development, but equally it bears within itself the power of the eternal God.

Christ came to save humanity. Drey saw this salvation as being accomplished through his teaching and example as much as through his work on the cross. Christ's salvific work can be seen under the headings of education, healing, and propitiation. Christ's entire life was salvific and his obedience to the Father's will is the central aspect of his life. In his work as much as in his person, Jesus was the promised Messiah. As Messiah, he was the founder of a new covenant because he had fulfilled the old.[39] In his earthly life, Christ did not complete his work. Following his return to the Father, Christ sent the Spirit to complete this work by forming the Church and transforming it into the Kingdom of God. Drey presented Christ as the archetype of what humans are meant to be; his incarnation is the full realization of this archetype in history so others can realize it in themselves.[40]

Prophecy and miracles were important elements of Drey's apologetic for Christ's deity and the divine origin of his mission. Drey presented Christ as the fulfillment of prophecy and as the consummation of all religious development in the history of the world. Through divine providence, all world history was preparatory for Christ's incarnation. Prophecy is also an affirmation of the claim the Church makes for Christ's divine person and mission. There are three aspects to this: Old Testament prophecy of the coming Christ, Christ's own prophecy concerning events to take place in his life, and Christ's prophecy of future events. Drey said the gospels record numerous instances where Jesus shows present or future knowledge that no "normal" person could possibly possess. His primary earthly prophecy concerned his death and resurrection, however. In regard to future events, the key prophecy was that concerning the destruction of Jerusalem and the dispersion of the Jewish people.[41]

Christ's miracles confirmed both his divine person and the truth of his teaching. They also legitimated his disciples' faith in him. Contrary to some contemporary critics, Drey affirmed Christ's miracles "stand firm as historical (*historische*) actions and can only fall with the entire history (*Geschichte*) of Christ himself." The miracles stand at the center of the entire history of Jesus. If they are lost to him, the entire content and understandability of Jesus will equally be lost.[42] Drey spent considerable time in the christological section of his *Apologetik* giving specific examples from the Bible showing the importance of miracles and prophecy in validating Jesus and his ministry. The section was traditional in its content and method; much of what Drey said would soon be called into question by Protestant biblical critics. They would deny the materials could be traced to Jesus but must be seen instead as creations of the early Church intended to validate their faith in terms of contemporary religious practices and apologetics.

Conclusion

In his Christology, as in the rest of his theology, Drey appeared willing to allow the Church to decide what belongs as a part of its doctrine and what does not. By the central role he accorded to the Kingdom of God, however, Drey also appeared to see this concept as the rule by which all other aspects of Christology are measured. Dietrich says Drey nowhere sacrificed traditional Catholic dogma to the new systems of thought,[43] but we must recognize he did allow his idealism and romanticism to encroach upon his theology. At points they modified his theology to the extent that it might be applied by others in a way very different from traditional Christology yet consistent with the language used by Drey. The organic relation between God and creation, the stress on Christ's work as teacher, and the continuity between Christ and all world religions are examples of teachings that could lead far afield from traditional Catholic teaching.

Fehr suggests Drey's basic problem lay in trying to subsume all of theology under the one controlling idea of the Kingdom of God.[44] When this is seen as the unfolding of God's purpose for all creation, the tension between freedom and necessity is dissolved in favor of necessity, and evil becomes part of God's plan. The centrality of the Kingdom of God also risks equating the Kingdom with history.[45] When this occurs, the transcendent can be subsumed into the immanent and the Kingdom can appear as a this-worldly reality instead of a divine inbreaking at the end of history. This last is something Drey affirmed by saying Christ will return at the end of history to judge the world.

The stress on history as essential to Christology (and all theology) was one of Drey's most significant theological legacies. Despite a strong emphasis on the deity of Christ and his mission, Drey repeatedly said Christ entered into history, acted in history, and left a Church that exists in history to carry on his teaching. Reinhardt says Drey was unable to apply his concern for history fully in developing a Christology because he never clearly understood the relation between history and doctrine. Drey never arrived at a satisfactory way of correlating tradition with Scripture to arrive at doctrine.

A further historical problem is how to relate unique historical events to a progressive unfolding of divine revelation while retaining the uniqueness of the history and the reality of providence.[46] Fehr asks whether Drey allowed for an absolute newness in the historical events of Christ's birth, life, and death. Such newness is crucial because it is the basis for human participation in the Kingdom.[47]

We can ask further whether Drey's system allowed room for the humanity of Christ in any real sense. If history is no more than the unfolding of divine revelation, then all revelation is the work of God without any human element involved. Drey's Christology made the words and deeds of the earthly Jesus crucial for human salvation, but his system appears to require that all come from the God side of the God-man. This does not make Christ docetic, but it does ignore the human reality of Christ. Drey would probably have denied this strongly in practice, but his system appears to leave him no alternative. Drey's high Christology was in the tradition of the Roman Catholic tendency toward Monophysitism, not for the traditional reasons but because the philosophy he borrowed from Schelling required it.

Drey saw Christ's work as a recreation and restoration of human nature so it can acknowledge its fundamental relationship to God. His basic concept here was restitution: making everything as it once was because Christ repeats the path trod by Adam and through his perfect obedience undoes all Adam did to destroy the divine-human relationship. This was a patristic concept dating from Irenaeus, but Drey altered the patristic picture by positing an innate human consciousness of God that was distorted by sin. Schleiermacher introduced this concept into Christian theology and suggested the way to restore humanity's God-consciousness was for Christ to be the perfect example and teacher because he was one with a perfect God-consciousness. Drey appears to have drawn on Schleiermacher at this point without accepting every element of a Christology "from below" or of salvation with no need for propitiation.

Drey appreciated the reality and seriousness of human sin, but he was ambiguous in the way he incorporated this into his theology. The result was that his presentation of Christ's work provided three motifs that were somewhat jumbled. Drey appeared to see humanity as capable of being educated before it is healed or its sin propitiated. This was a reversal of the classical understanding of Christ's work and raises the question of "why the cross?" if Christ's example and teaching could lead humanity back to God.

An anthropology is equally involved: are humans ignorant of God or are they guilty before him? Drey seems to have been unsure when we look at the parts of his doctrine. Traditional Christology is there, but Drey appears to have been uncertain how to integrate it with other sources he used for his Christology.

Drey presented the Kingdom of God as the heart of Jesus' message, but this also included Jesus as bringer and king of this Kingdom. He said Jesus' message deals very much with himself and his work because no one enters the Kingdom apart from Jesus. In saying this, Drey introduced a strong eschatological element into Christology, for in fact Jesus pointed to the future.

Drey presented a traditional, but inexact, Christology. In it he emphasized the critical place of history and tried to enter into dialogue with contemporary lines of thought. Part of Drey's difficulty was that these lines did not mesh well with the tradition Drey sought to preserve and defend. Drey was not, however, concerned primarily with Christology in his writing or teaching; it was but an element of his work in fundamental theology. It remained for later Tübingers to treat Christology as a discrete topic. Only in the present century has the subject become a central theme for Tübingen theologians.

JOHANN ADAM MÖHLER[48]

Johann Adam Möhler was the most interesting of the nineteenth century Catholic Tübingers, and the most influential. Many consider him the leader of the Catholic Tübingen School even though he was a student of the founder of the School. In addition, Möhler may have been the most complex figure to teach at Catholic Tübingen prior to Hans Küng. Möhler's theology passed through three distinct stages, which were more discontinuous than Möhler was willing to admit. Some see Möhler's development in terms of the organic model he and Drey utilized, but continuity appears often submerged under contradictions of earlier positions.

Defense of the Church

Möhler was concerned primarily with the nature of the Church and the development of its doctrine. His three stages correspond to his increased study of contemporaries and of Church history and his reaction to events within the Catholic Church. During the first stage, Möhler lectured on canon law. His theology was scholastic in a sense reminiscent of Bellarmine. This brief period was followed by a span when his theology was Spirit-centered, during which he wrote the *Einheit*. As he became more involved in the study of Church history, Möhler shifted to a Christ-centered theology and stayed with this for the rest of his short life.

As with Drey, the focus of Möhler's theological interest was not primarily christological. His primary concern was the nature of the Church. As his ecclesiology matured, he came to see Christology as increasingly important for supporting his ecclesiological position. The emphasis by the early Tübingers on the importance and nature of the Church was in reaction to the Enlightenment and post-Enlightenment denigration of the organizational idea of the Church as the seat of worship and witness. Such eminent individuals as Immanuel Kant had been content to deal with God in a purely individualistic setting and shown no interest in participation in the Church nor any comprehension of the spiritual importance of such participation.

With the Church being challenged to justify its very existence, the Tübingers took up the struggle to show not only the importance of the Church as a visible entity but also the validity of the Roman Catholic claim to be the only true Church. In his earlier writings, Möhler sought to defend the divine element in Christianity against the attacks of deism and rationalism. Later, he made anthropology central and argued against Hegel and the Idealists for the ontological separation of humanity from God.[49] Whereas Möhler's picture of the Church in the *Einheit* had caused him problems with the Catholic hierarchy, the picture in the *Symbolik* led to verbal conflict with the Lutherans, especially with the Tübingen Lutherans led by Ferdinand Christian Baur.

Möhler wrestled with the question of how to relate religion, revelation, tradition, and dogma throughout his theological career. In the *Einheit*, he emphasized the subjective element; later, in the *Symbolik*, he stressed the objectivity of sin and of salvation through the revelation in Christ.[50]

As a part of the early Catholic Tübingen School, Möhler was influenced by his mentor Drey and by Schelling, but he also drew on Hegel and Schleiermacher. Adam pointed out that, as his theology matured, Möhler drew much more on Irenaeus, Tertullian, Vincent of Lerins, and Petavius.[51] Given the major shift in his thought that occurred between the *Einheit* and the *Symbolik*, Athanasius and Anselm must also be counted among Möhler's primary sources. As Adam noted, however, Schleiermacher and Hegel not only provided Möhler with further insights into Christian thought; they also served as targets against which he developed his thought. The fundamental argument Möhler had with them concerned how Christianity related to human existence. Möhler saw both thinkers as pantheistic and evolutionary. Hegel and Schleiermacher viewed human existence in terms of continuity and fulfillment; Möhler saw it in terms of discontinuity and restoration. This would significantly influence Möhler's Christology as he drew further away from them in developing his theology.

Geiselmann said Schleiermacher risked making creation, salvation, and the Church moments in humanity's development of divinity while Hegel risked making human spiritual life the medium by which deity came to self-consciousness. Both called the uniqueness of human existence into question.[52] Hegel's most significant contribution was the dialectic which Möhler used to relate and reconcile positions previously seen as parallel. This was part of Möhler's effort to get behind dogma to its historical context.[53] Voss suggested the contemporary German influence on Möhler derived more from the common Romantic worldview shared by Hegel, Schelling, and Schleiermacher than the specifics of their philosophies. He also said the Romantic influence must not be allowed to overshadow the importance of Möhler's Catholic inheritance.[54]

Möhler rediscovered a sense of theological development and of viewing Christianity as an organic whole instead of as a collection of theses. In doing so, he rejected the rationalism of much contemporary Catholicism and reopened theology to the influence of the Spirit and the idea of history. His writings helped inspire the understanding of the Church as the mystical body of Christ that has come to the fore since Pius XII's letter on the subject in 1941.

Ecclesiology

We can understand Möhler's doctrine of the Church best in terms of the relationship between original and copy. The former is Jesus Christ, the truth incarnate; the copy is the Church. Although truth has been incarnated in Christ, its appearance cannot be merely the transitory history of a long-dead individual whom we can only remember. Instead, this embodied truth which is Jesus appears and continues to work through the Church. The Church represents Christ—he who has hypostatically united deity and humanity in one divine Person—to humanity.[55] Some have altered this teaching to present the Church as the continuation of the Incarnation itself, so the Church not only represents but also partakes of Christ essentially. To do so is to overstate the similarity between Christ and the Church and to invest the Church with more divine attributes than Möhler might wish. It can also lead to a confusion of the human and divine. Möhler sought to guard against any such confusion by balancing the idea of the Church as "the continuation of God's enfleshment in Jesus" with the idea of the Spirit indwelling the Church.

Möhler saw God as transcendent and immanent at the same time and tried to hold the two in dialectical tension. He drew on Chalcedon's "unconfused, undivided" to understand the relation of God to creation, the nature of the Church, Christology, and anthropology.[56]

In his *Einheit*, Möhler showed the influence of Schleiermacher, and the Spirit took precedence over Christ. A particular difficulty in this early writing is that Möhler did not distinguish clearly between the Spirit of God and the spirit of the community. Another point for Möhler was that dogma must reflect the inner life of the Church because this is the essence of Christianity. Thus, dogma reflects the experience of Christians, not concrete reality.

Savon said Möhler did not adequately represent the early Church fathers because he was unclear about the central position they accorded Christ in their writings.[57] He added that Möhler's explanation that his stress was on the Spirit instead of on Christ is unconvincing.[58] This christological weakness appears to have been the basis of Möhler's later discomfort with the *Einheit*, even though he steadfastly refused to repudiate any of it.

In the *Einheit*, Möhler began to show the historical perspective that characterized his later thought. Rosato sees two foci of Möhler's ecclesiology. First was the objective foundation of the Church through Christ's incarnation and glorification at specific points in time. This was balanced by the Spirit's central role in humanity's subjective appropriation of the originating events as they are present in the visible elements of the Church. Rosato says modern Catholic theologians have seen the *Einheit* as the apex of Möhler's creativity.[59] Geiselmann said that while Möhler saw Christ as the model for the Church, the Spirit was the Church's basis. This meant Christ's reconciling work was not the constructive principle of the Church, nor was the Church his institution; the non-embodied Spirit is the representative of the Godhead in Christianity.[60] Möhler's Church might be called mystical because it proceeds by unpredictable development instead of according to any particular law.

In the *Einheit*, Möhler appeared to see the Body of Christ as so caught up in the Spirit as to be itself almost divine. He drew on the hypostatic union used to describe the person of Christ and applied it to the condition of the Church. This seems to stem from his emphasis on the centrality of the Spirit as opposed to that of Christ, who partook of both deity and humanity.

In the *Einheit*, Möhler never denied any dogmas concerning Christ; he merely focused his theology on the Spirit. Because the Spirit was at the center of his ecclesiology, Möhler placed Christ outside the Church and at a distance. Although Christ was the origin of the Church, and thus its end and goal, the Spirit was the one who sustained the Church (*deren tragendes Prinzip*). It is as the originator of the Church that Christ must be external to it. The language Möhler used to relate the Spirit to the Church is that used by the Bible and traditional theology to relate Christ and the Church. For example, the mystical union occurs between the Church and the Spirit, not between the Church and Christ. Because his theology is heavily pneumatic, Möhler seems to have derogated seriously the importance of Christ and the Father. Möhler discussed Christ only in terms of his deity, ignoring all other aspects of Christ's person and work.

Möhler's Christology during the *Einheit* period was orthodox in form but not in spirit. He acknowledged the truth of all dogmas regarding the person and work of Christ, but they had little relevance for his theology as a whole. In reality, his theology depended entirely upon the activity of the Spirit. His sound understanding of Christ's person and work would stand Möhler in good stead later because it would provide the firm foundation upon which to reorient his ecclesiology.

Following the publication of the *Einheit*, Möhler became more involved in patristic studies. This proved to be a turning point in his life. He later wrote to a friend about this period, saying,

> Christ had been for me only a word, a notion.... It was while studying the Fathers that for the first time I discovered so living and new and complete a Christianity."[61]

Dietrich says that between *Einheit*, which dealt with the Spirit, consciousness, and community, and *Symbolik*, where he based objective theological truth on anthropology, there occurred a clear metamorphosis. His patristic studies led Möhler to modify his anthropology and make his theology more objective. Thus, Möhler's later work began with the historical Christ, the Word incarnate. On this basis, he reformulated his entire ecclesiology.[62] This change did not come from nowhere; it was Möhler's response to sharp criticism of his work as subjective and naturalistic by Church authorities. The criticism, joined to his patristic studies, convinced

Möhler that if he were to understand the Church in terms of its deity and humanity, he must build on Christ, not the Spirit.[63]

Möhler also saw Schleiermacher was not a sufficient foundation for his theology. He sought a firmer basis for his work than human feeling and found it in the tradition of the Church. This was a reversal of his earlier view of the Church as an abstraction of the inner life to a picture of it as an objective, historical entity which acts upon that inner life. Revelation, too, became an objective reality that serves as the basis for life and doctrine; it is not a rationalization of one's religious feelings. Religious feeling was an insufficient support for a universal religion such as Christianity is.[64]

The shift that began with his patristic studies was a return to traditional Catholicism from Möhler's period of youthful rebellion. This return was carried much further in his negative reaction to the campaign among some German Catholics to abolish clerical celibacy. He saw this campaigns an attempt on the part of liberal Catholics to make the Church more subject to the state. Möhler's great turn began with his work on Athanasius and continued with his study of Anselm of Canterbury. The latter gave him a greater appreciation for the scholasticism of the 12th and 13th centuries.

Möhler's theological shift was accompanied by a philosophical shift from Schelling and Schleiermacher toward Hegel. Möhler came to see Schelling's system as insufficiently objective to support the existence of the Church. Hegel's system ended in a concrete society, so whatever its weaknesses it was useful in giving a foundation for Möhler's theological concerns.[65] Möhler also saw a danger to historical Christianity and the historical Church in Schleiermacher's pure spirit Christianity and spiritual Church.

He concluded that an idealism that works itself out in a merely spiritual Church leads to the dissolution of historical reality into myth.[66] Möhler limited his acceptance of Hegel because he saw the same danger in his system: the historical Christ is dissolved into the Christ-idea, the Christ-consciousness of the community. The end of Hegel's Christology looked to Möhler very much like gnostic docetism.[67] Möhler's increasingly objective theology reflected his use of Hegel, but his rejection of significant elements of Hegel is seen in his sharp disagreement with Baur and the Protestant Tübingers. In contrast to the latter, he denied pure philosophical speculation can on its own principles support the absolute claims of Christ and Christianity. This finally led Möhler and the Catholic Tübingers to develop the concept of the Church as Christ living on in history.[68]

Turn to Christology

We can trace Möhler's turn toward objectivity and historicity in two major studies: *Athanasius der Grosse* (1827) and "Anselm, Erzbischof von

Canterbury" (1828).[69] In *Athanasius*, Möhler presented his first major critique of Schleiermacher's doctrine of the Trinity. It showed his increased appreciation of Christology that issued in the christocentric ecclesiology of the 1832 *Symbolik*.

In *Athanasius*, Möhler presented an Adam-Christ parallel where each represents a body of humanity. Adam represents all (because all have sinned) and Christ represents all who have been saved. This salvation results from Christ's death on the cross and his consequent resurrection which showed him to be victor over death. It was what Christ did, much more than what he taught, that constitutes the content of Christianity because Christ's teaching finds its power and justification only in his deeds. Even more basic, however, is the person who accomplished the deeds: "If Jesus is not true God, then everything is uncertain and left hanging. This is something all true Christians have believed at all times."[70] Salvation appears in terms of the restoration of humanity's original situation. This evidences a sharp disagreement with Idealism because for Möhler sin and evil are not a step in the necessary evolution of the system. They are instead a fall from the height of original creation and have their source in humanity's misuse of its freedom. Thus, they lead to human guilt and wrongdoing.

Recognizing a necessary relation between the various loci of doctrine, and certainly between anthropology and Christology, Möhler made Christology increasingly prominent in his system as a result of his changed anthropology. Further, as the human became more important in his theology as a whole, so Christ's humanity became more important for his Christology. Studying Athanasius led Möhler to view salvation in terms of deification, with new life coming from Christ, not from the Spirit.[71]

Möhler now stressed the difference in essence between Christ and humanity. The Son's sameness of substance with the Father is at the same time his distinction from humans. A oneness does exist between Christ and humanity, but Möhler qualified it to protect the certainty of salvation.[72] The heart of what Christ is is deity; humanity came later. He drew this conclusion from his qualitative distinction between God and creation and God's consequent independence of creation. Möhler used the conclusions reached at Chalcedon to deny any mixture or confusion of God and creation.[73]

Dietrich says *Athanasius* demonstrated the christological and trinitarian speculation of the early Church is incomprehensible in its historical peculiarities or its meaning for the development of ecclesiology unless belief in Christ's deity was already presupposed as dogma.[74]

Athanasius had a major impact on Möhler's appreciation of Christ and thus on his understanding of the Church. He saw the Church as built upon the incarnate Christ who is the new Man. He is the Second Adam who is both the beginning of a new human existence and the source of a divinely-created new life. This new life is the Church. Möhler's concept of the Church now centered on the Incarnation and led to a new understanding of the Eucharist as a sign of the union of God with humanity. As Christ is seen in terms of divine and human natures, so must the Church be seen. Here Möhler applied to the Church the four adverbs Chalcedon had applied to the person of Christ.

Möhler's patristic and medieval studies, particularly of Athanasius and Anselm, caused him to rethink his understanding of the Church. This led to his *Symbolik*, which could be said to constitute the final stage of his thought. His few subsequent writings were primarily defenses of the positions he staked out in *Symbolik*. *Symbolik* went through five editions before Möhler's death in 1838, each rewritten to respond to criticisms of earlier editions. Rosato says *Symbolik* constituted Möhler's final synthesis of theology in that he introduced Christology into his ecclesiology.[75] It also marked Möhler's tacit withdrawal from the controversial pneumatic theology of *Einheit*.

The organizing concept of *Symbolik* was that we can understand the Church only on the basis of Christ and the Incarnation. In a sense, the Church can be seen as the continuation of the Incarnation.[76] Möhler's reason for stressing this was his concern for the continuing importance of history. Christ did not simply appear, live, die, and disappear, so that we remember him only as a character of the past; he continues to live in and through his Church. Today Christ does invisibly that which he once did visibly on earth and will continue to do until the end of time.[77]

Möhler's new appreciation of anthropology developed in his patristic studies affected his entire understanding of theology. In particular, his acceptance of the historicity of the Fall made an historical redeemer and an historically mediating Church necessary. Substituting Christ for the Spirit as the locus of his theology enabled Möhler to achieve the objectivity his recognition of the historical context of the human predicament required. In contrast to his earlier pneumatic work, Möhler recognized the essential connection between the content of Christianity and the form in which it is mediated to us: the loss of form tends to occur at a cost to the content.

Möhler had come to see an essential relationship between the Christ of Chalcedon and the nature of the Church. He used this Christology to anchor his doctrine of the Church against the subjective intellectual movements of his day. These risked making Christianity and the Church whatever their author desired them to be. He also saw the incarnation of the Logos into history as the justification for the visible Church because

an historical, visible Christ cannot coexist with the invisible,
purely spiritual Church.... The humanity of Jesus is the
necessary and essential form of his divinity as the author of
revelation in the new Covenant. In the same way, *and even
for that very reason*, the Church with her fundamental institutions, is the essential form of the Christian Religion.[78]

To use Christology as the foundation for his study, Möhler had to
present his understanding of the person and work of Christ in some detail.
He had to justify his conclusions and show how his approach differed from
those of his Idealist contemporaries. Two points are important here. First,
Christ's coming into the world and our receiving him ended an objective dis-
union between God and humanity, reconciling the two. Second, Christ's incarnation differed qualitatively from the gracing of humanity that occurs
through the Spirit. The former constitutes a personal union whereas the
second is a "habitual" union.

Without denying his real humanity, Möhler distinguished Christ
from humanity essentially by placing him ultimately on the side of God, not
that of humanity. The Scriptures, said Möhler, continually emphasize the
person of Christ and derive all his works from his person. Because of this,
it is all the more crucial to conceive Christ as he really was because errors
concerning his person can seriously affect the faith and practice of believers.
Möhler argued Christ was one and his work comprised one whole, therefore,
the Church must equally be one. Further, by analogy, as Christ united deity
and humanity in one person, so the Church united deity and humanity in
one institution.[79]

Christ's life constituted an organic whole. Everything about it—his
work, suffering, teaching, conduct, and death on the cross—was calculated
to accomplish the redemption of humanity. The merits he obtained through
every aspect of his life were the ground upon which humanity was won back
to God. It was equally important that Christ was our prophet, priest, and
king. Had one of the three been absent, his work would be incomprehensible and inconsistent.

At some points, Möhler saw the offer of redemption as being made
based on Christ's incarnation, but at other points he emphasized the crucial
role of the cross in obtaining human salvation. Salvation consists in the
restoration of humanity's created condition. We can appreciate the magni-
tude of the change wrought by Christ only from the perspective of the Fall.
Möhler added that as the Fall was the result of a free human decision, so
the work of Christ for human salvation must be seen as his free act.

During his life, Jesus was a teacher and example. One major aspect of these was his working of miracles. In fact, said Möhler, Jesus' whole life was a miracle. His miracles had several aims. They established the credibility of Christ's words and they represented and symbolized the highest truths of God. Möhler included among these the omnipotence, wisdom, justice, and love of God; human immortality; and the worth of humanity before God. Möhler linked the growing rejection of Christ's miracles by some contemporaries with the rejection of the necessity of the visible Church because an invisible Church permits no outward manifestations, not even the incarnation of Christ.[80] In saying this, Möhler reversed his original argument from the Incarnation to the visible Church, to argue from the existing, visible Church to the necessity for the Incarnation.

Critique of Contemporary Philosophy

Möhler made a Christology built on Nicea and Chalcedon central to his later theology because he saw it as providing the only viable foundation for the theology he derived from the early Church fathers. In his patristic studies, Möhler came to see serious difficulties in the idealist thought of Schleiermacher and Schelling. This led him to draw selectively on Hegel without accepting Hegel's system, which he saw as sharing the same tendency toward pantheism as Schleiermacher and Schelling:

> *The* proper understanding lies in the mystery defined at
> Nicea and Chalcedon, the triune mystery of the unity and
> distinction of divinity and humanity in Jesus. Jesus is not
> to be found in pantheistic monophysitism. Christ's pres-
> ence in mankind is unity in distinction, as is, analogously,
> the mystery of the Spirit's work in the faithful. The con-
> substantiality of the Son with the Father is the ground of
> the separation of the Son from mankind.[81]

Each of these men had misunderstood the true relation between Creator and creation. Möhler agreed God is present in his creation, but he added that God is qualitatively different from that creation. He suggested the Chalcedonian definition of the relation between Christ's person and natures was a way to understand how God relates to creation. In particular, Möhler accused Schleiermacher of removing the complexity within the divine relationship and threatening that of the divine-human relation.[82] He said Schleiermacher paralleled the Church's relation to the Spirit to that of Christ's

Christ's humanity and deity. Yet at several points in the *Symbolik* Möhler presented the Church as the permanent expression of Christ's humanity while describing it in terms properly applied only to his deity.[83] Rosato adds that in the *Symbolik* Möhler appeared too ready to apply the deification uniquely proper to Christ's human nature to individuals and institutions within the Church. In overemphasizing Christ's presence within the Church, he risked substituting the Church for Christ.[84]

Möhler ended his life in conflict with F. C. Baur over his assertions in the *Symbolik* regarding true Christianity and in attacking D. F. Strauss' mythological approach to Christology. In his conflict with Baur, whom he saw expressing Hegel's thought in theological form, Möhler emphasized the traditional elements in Christology. In particular, he attacked Baur's denial of Jesus' necessary sinlessness.[85] Möhler's sharpest attack on Baur was his assertion that when we treat the Incarnation as a mythological argument for human dignity instead of as the act of divine providence in restoring humanity's original state, Christianity has essentially dispeared.[86]

Möhler considered Strauss' categorizing of Jesus in terms of myth both untenable and unacceptable. Möhler said myths develop over extended periods of time and within a sympathetic environment. Christ, however, lived among enemies and his words and deeds were questioned and attacked by the leaders of his society. Furthermore, the accounts of his life and teaching were compiled within a short time following his death. Thus, said Möhler, the environmental conditions were not right for a Christ-myth to develop. Möhler also understood myth to mean fantasy and said the Church could not have developed from such an insubstantial source and without an historical content. Myths are the product of limited geographical areas and are accepted only within such areas, but Christianity is a world religion. Again, said Möhler, the requisite conditions for a mythical origin are not present.[87] Möhler died soon after his criticism of Strauss, so this last part of his work remains partial and unsystematic.

CONCLUSION

Möhler's theology developed through three stages. Only the last was particularly concerned with Christ and could properly be called christo-centric. In this last period, Möhler built on the received tradition of the Church to present a traditional Christology designed to justify the very existence of the Church. This traditional approach enabled him to take the historicity of Christ's incarnation seriously in contrast to his work under Schleiermacher's influence. Fitzer says, however, that in his approach

Möhler allowed dogma to determine the conclusions of historical research. Möhler affirmed a physical and historical incarnation in contrast to what he found in Strauss. Unlike the Idealists, Möhler considered the essence of Christianity to be expressed in the scandal of the cross.

Möhler worked through a variety of theological and philosophical arguments back to the traditional Christology within which he had been raised. He did so because, however attractive these speculations might be, they were insufficient to explain and justify the existence of the Church. Further, Möhler concerned himself not merely with the Church but, in particular, with the visible Church as exemplified by Rome and nothing less than a Chalcedonian Christology could be called to testify in favor of the visibility and unity of the Church. Möhler's Christology was traditional, but it was an informed traditionalism, forged in the argumentation of the idealist-romantic era and the onset of skeptical denials of the tradition. In presenting it, Möhler sought to be biblical and consistent as well as faithful to the dogmas of the Church. The next generation of Tübingers would draw on Möhler's work, continuing the attack on Schleiermacher, Hegel, and Strauss.

Both Drey and Möhler sought to defend the traditional Christian doctrine they had grown up with, but they attempted to do so in terms of the intellectual climate within which they lived and worked. Drey's presentation of Christology was heavily philosophical, as was his entire theology. Because of this, he risked dissolving the historicity that so concerned him into the outworking of deity in time. Apart from the several dangers that we have mentioned, Drey presented a traditional, orthodox Christology. Möhler's final christological work was equally traditional. It escaped some of the dangers of Drey's because of the way Möhler applied his patristic work to his theological speculation. Möhler's work was much more historical than philosophical, but it also demonstrated familiarity with and appropriation of elements of contemporary systems he thought might be safely incorporated into his presentations. Neither Drey nor Möhler interacted significantly with the skeptical reassessment of Christology that began with Strauss' *Leben Jesu* (1835–36). This work remained for the second generation of Catholic Tübingers.

1. See note 19 of chapter one on pages 21-24 , for a treatment of the contemporary discussion concerning the existence of a Catholic Tübingen School.

2. John E. Thiel, "J. S. Drey on Doctrinal Development: The Context of Theological Encyclopedia," *Heythrop Journal* 27 (1986):302.

3. Donald J. Dietrich, *The Goethezeit and the Metamorphosis of Catholic Theology in the Age of Idealism* (Bern: Peter Lang, 1979), p. 86.

4. Gerald A. McCool, *Catholic Theology in the Nineteenth Century* (New York: Seabury, 1977), pp. 78 f.

5. Wayne L. Fehr, *The Birth of the Catholic Tübingen School: The Dogmatics of Johann Sebastian Drey*. American Academy of Religion Academy Series Number 37 (Chico, CA: Scholars Press, 1981), pp. 8 ff.

6. Dietrich, pp. 77 f.

7. McCool, p. 80.

8. Ibid.

9. Ibid., pp. 83 f.

10. Fehr, p. 135.

11. Max Seckler, "Johann Sebastian Drey und die Theologie," *Theologische Quartalschrift* 158 (1978):107.

12. Ibid., p. 108.

13. Dietrich, p. 85.

14. James T. Burtchaell, "Drey, Möhler, and the Catholic Tübingen School," in *Nineteenth Century Religious Thought in the West*, II:121, ed. by Ninian Smart, *et al.*, three vols. (Cambridge: Cambridge University, 1986). Hans Küng, who considers himself heir to the Catholic Tübingen tradition, has

applied Thomas Kuhn"s concept of paradigm shift to theology and reached sharply different conclusions about the need for continuity between current and past theological developments. See chapter nine for further discussion of Küng's Christology.

15. Seckler, p. 107.

16. Fehr, pp. 177 f.

17. This understanding of the Church, which saw it as being in some way the continuation of Christ's incarnation, was developed more completely by Möhler. The latter always sought to maintain a distinction between the essential nature of Christ and that of the Church, however. Thus, the early Tübingen position is more nuanced than it might at first appear and nowhere confuses Christ and his Church.

18. Fehr, p. 56.

19. Ibid., pp. 269, 271.

20. Fehr, pp. 23 f.

21. Ibid., pp. 118, 158 f.

22. McCool, pp. 71 f.

23. Klaus Reinhardt, *Der dogmatische Schriftgebrauch in der katholischen und protestantischen Christologie von der Aufklärung bis zur Gegenwart* (Munich: Ferdinand Schöningh, 1970), pp. 426 f.

24. Burtchaell, p. 122.

25. Johann Sebastian Drey, *Kurze Einleitung in das Studium der Theologie* (Tübingen, 1819; reprinted Frankfurt: Minerva, 1966), p. 176.

26. Dietrich, p. 130; Fehr, pp. 142 f., 148 f.

27. Fehr, pp. 200 f.

28. Ibid., pp. 210, 212 f.

29. Ibid., p. 203.

30. Ibid., pp. 221 f.

31. Ibid., pp. 219, 223 f.

32. Johann Sebastian Drey, *Das Apologetik as wissenschaftliche Nachweisung der Göttlichkeit des Christenthums in seiner Erscheinung* (Mainz, 1843; reprinted Frankfurt: Minerva, 1967), p. II:250.

33. Ibid., pp. 242 f.

34. Ibid., p. 247.

35. Dietrich, p. 82; Fehr, pp. 190 f.

36. Fehr, pp. 188 ff.

37. Drey, *Apologetik*, pp. 270 ff.

38. Ibid., pp. 279 f.

39. Ibid., pp. 293 f.

40. Fehr, pp. 230 f.

41. Drey, *Apologetik*, pp. 303 ff.

42. Ibid., pp. 337 ff.

43. Dietrich, p. 79.

44. See Fehr, especially pp. 263 ff.

45. Franz Schupp, "Die Geschichtsauffassung am Begin der Tübinger Schule und in der gegenwartigen Theologie," *Zeitschrift für katholische Theologie* 91 (1969):164.

46. Reinhardt, pp. 107 f.

47. Fehr, p. 283.

48. Little has been written on Möhler in English apart from Herve Savon, *Johann Adam Möhler: The Father of Modern Theology* (New York: Paulist, 1966). Several good articles dealing with Möhler's ecclesiology and theory of doctrinal development are available in English and his *Symbolik* and *Anselm of Canterbury* have been translated. J. R. Geiselmann prepared critical editions of Möhler's major works and supplemented these with books and articles analyzing his theology. These are listed in the bibliography on pages 328, 329, and 332.

49. J. R. Geiselmann, "Der Einfluss der Christologie des Konzils von Chalkedon auf die Theologie Joh. Ad. Möhlers," in *Das Konzil von Chalkedon*, II:393, ed. by Aloys Grillmeier and Heinrich Bacht, three vols. (Würzburg: Echter, 1954).

50. Dietrich, p. 89.

51. Karl Adam, "Die katholische Tübinger Schule," in his *Gesammelte Aufsätze*, p. 399, ed. by Fritz Hofmann (Augsburg: P. Haas, 1936).

52. Geiselmann, p. 393.

53. Thomas F. O'Meara, *Romantic Idealism and Roman Catholicism: Schelling and the Theologians* (Notre Dame: University of Notre Dame, 1982), p. 152.

54. Gustav Voss, "Johann Adam Möhler and the Development of Dogma," *Theological Studies* 4 (1943):424.

55. Geiselmann, p. 405.

56. Ibid., pp. 390 f., 392.

57. Savon, pp. 53 f.

58. Möhler, *Die Einheit in der Kirche*, p. 3, cited by Geiselmann, pp. 365 f. "Es mag befremdend erscheinen, warum ich nicht viel mehr mit Christus, dem Mittelpunkt unsers Glaubens, angefangen habe. Ich konnte allerdings zuerst erzählen dass Christus, der Sonn Gottes, vom Vater gesandt, dass er

uns Erlöser und Lehrer geworden sei und den Heiligen Geist versprochen und sein Versprochen erfüllt habe. Ich wollte aber, was billig als bekannt veranzusetzen war, nicht aufnehmen, sondern sogleich mit dem schlechthin zur Sache Gehörigen anfangen. Der Vater sendet den Sohn und deiser den Heiligen Geist: so kam Gott zu uns; umgekehrt gelangen wir zu ihm; der Heiligen Geist führt uns zum Sohn und dieser zum Vater. Damit wollte ich beginnen, was bei unserem Christwerden der Zeit nach das Erste ist."

59. Philip J. Rosato, "Between Christocentrism and Pneumatocentrism: An Interpretation of Johann Adam Möhler's Ecclesiology," *Heythrop Journal* 19 (1978):58 f.

60. Geiselmann, p. 365.

61. From a letter of Möhler's to his friend Lipp in 1843, cited in Savon, pp. 22 f.

62. Dietrich, p. 98.

63. Geiselmann, p. 380.

64. Alexander Dru, *The Contribution of German Catholicism* (New York: Hawthorn, 1963), pp. 62 f.

65. O'Meara, p. 152.

66. J. R. Geiselmann, *Lebendiger Glaube als geheiligter Überlieferung: Der Grundgedanke der Theologie Johann Adam Möhlers und der katholischen Tübinger Schule* (Mainz: Matthias-Grünewald, 1942), p. 481.

67. Ibid., p. 482.

68. Dru, p. 64.

69. *Athanasius der Grosse und die Kirche seiner Zeit besonders im Kampfe mit dem Arainismus* (Mainz, 1827); "Anselm, Erzbischof von Canterbury," *Theologische Quartalschrift* 9 (1827):435–497, 585–644; 10 (1828):62–130.

70. Paul-Werner Scheele (editor), *Johann Adam Möhler, Wegbereiter heutiger Theologie*, volume four, p. 135, ed. by Heinrich Fries and Johann Finsterholzl (Graz: Styria, 1969).

71. Geiselmann, "Einfluss," p. 398. "Jetzt setzt Möhler die Bedeutung Christi nicht mehr darin, dass er als der Logos und Sohn des Vaters uns den Geist sendet, sondern darin, dass er als der Menschgewordene unsere Versöhnung mit Gott bewirkt; nicht darin, dass er durch die Sendung des Geistes das neue Leben im Geiste ermöglicht. Sondern darin, dass er als Menschgewordener durch seinen Opfertod die Sünde innerlich und wesentlich vernichtet."

72. Ibid., p. 395, citing Möhler, *Athanasius*, I:323. Christ is "in dem Grade vor uns, die wir in ihm vergöttlicht werden, verschieden, dass nicht einmal von ihm angenommene Menschheit, mit der er sich zu einer Person verbunden, eines Wesens mit ihm geworden, in ihm entgangen ist, sondern stets werschieden bleibt."

73. Ibid., pp. 389 f., citing Möhler, *Athanasius*, I:323 f., "Der Vater war Vater, ehe er die Welt schuf; der Sohn war Sohn, ehe er Mensch wurde; und der Geist ist Geist, ehe die Kirche entstand. Gott ist in sich Vater, Sohn und Geist, und nicht erst mit der Welt, mit der Menschwerdung, mit der Kirche ist er es (Vater, Sohn und Geist) geworden. Was er nun so in sich ist, ist er ewig und unveränderlich, eben weil er es in sich ist. So ist Gott ausserweltlich."

74. Dietrich, pp. 92 f.

75. Rosato, p. 60.

76. Möhler, *Die Einheit in der Kirche*, edited by J. R. Geiselmann (Darmstadt: Wissenschaftliche Buchgesellschaft, 1957), p. 587. This is a comment by Geiselmann on Möhler's text.

77. Geiselmann, "Die Einfluss...," p. 344.

78. Möhler, *Symbolism*, trans. by James Burton Robinson from the fifth German edition (London: Gibbings, 1906), p. 417 (emphasis in original). "The ultimate reason of the visibility of the church is to be found in the *Incarnation* of the Divine Word. Has that Word descended into the hearts of men, without taking the form of a servant, and accordingly without

appearing in a corporeal shape, then only an internal, invisible Church
would have been established. But since the Word became *flesh*, it expressed
itself in an outward, perceptible, and human manner; it spoke as man to
man, and suffered, and worked after the fashion of men, in order to win
them to the Kingdom of God; so that the means selected for the attainment
of this object, fully correspond to the general method of instruction and
education determined by the nature and the wants of man.... Thus, the
church, from the point of view here taken, is the Son of God himself,
everlastingly manifesting himself among men in a human form, perpetually
renovated, and eternally young—the permanent incarnation of the same, as
in Holy Writ, even the faithful are called 'the body of Christ.' Hence, it is
evident that the Church, though composed of men, is yet not purely human.
Nay, as in Christ the divinity and the humanity are to be clearly distinguished, though both are bound in unity; so is he in undivided entireness
perpetuated in the Church" (pp. 258 f.).

79. Möhler, *Symbolik*, fifth edition (1838), p. 338. "Wie in Christo
Göttliches und Menschliches wohl zu unterschieden, aber doch auch beides
zur Einheit verbunden ist, so wird er auch in ungeteilter Ganzheit in der
Kirche fortgesetzt. Die Kirche, seine bleibende Erscheinung, is göttlich und
menschlich zugleich; sie ist die Einheit von beidem. Er ist es, der in
irdischen menschlichen Gestalten verborgen in ihr wirkt; sie hat darum eine
göttliche und menschliche Seite in ungeschiedener Weise, so dass das
Göttliche nicht von dem Menschlichen und dieses nicht von jenem getrennt
werden mag."

80. Möhler, *Symbolik*, p. 266.

81. George B. Gilmore, "J. A. Möhler on Doctrinal Development," *Heythrop
Journal* 19 (1978):394.

82. Ibid., pp. 394 ff.

83. Savon, p. 97.

84. Rosato, p. 64.

85. Joseph Fitzer, *Möhler and Baur in Controversy, 1832-38: Romantic-Idealist Assessment of the Reformation and Counter-Reformation*. American Academy of Religion Studies in Religion Number 7 (Tallahassee: American Academy of Religion, 1974), p. 75, quoting Möhler, *Neue Untersuchungen der Lehrgegensätze zwichen dem Katholischen und Protestanten* (Mainz: Florian Kupferberg, 1835), p. 139.

86. Ibid., p. 79.

87. Scheele, pp. 363 ff.

CHAPTER IV

FRANZ ANTON STAUDENMAIER

AND JOHANNES EVANGELIST KUHN

Franz Anton Staudenmaier (1800–1856) and Johannes Evangelist Kuhn (1806–1887) learned their theology in the Catholic faculty of Tübingen. Both began their teaching careers at Giessen. Kuhn then returned to Tübingen in 1837 to teach New Testament while Staudenmaier moved to Freiburg the same year to teach dogmatics. In 1839, Kuhn succeeded to the dogmatics chair at Tübingen. Although both are generally acknowledged as members of the Catholic Tübingen School, their contributions and interests differed. Staudenmaier was a systematizer of doctrinal studies and critic of contemporary thought whereas Kuhn was, like the first generation of Tübingers, a speculative and original theologian.

FRANZ ANTON STAUDENMAIER

Franz Anton Staudenmaier was one of the most brilliant figures in nineteenth century Germany Catholic theology. Born in Württemberg in 1800, he studied under Drey and Möhler at Tübingen and was ordained to the priesthood. After a year as a parish priest, he became a tutor at Tübingen. The next year, in 1830, he accepted a professorship in dogmatics at the new Catholic faculty of the University of Giessen.

Staudenmaier had broad interests and a keen mind which he used to systematize Catholic thought and present incisive criticism of contemporary philosophical and theological trends. Hunermann says Staudenmaier's life work shows both the greatness and limitations of nineteenth century Catholic theology. He tried to interact seriously with the challenges of his era, but never completed his major work, a *Dogmatik*. Nevertheless, his work should be seen as one of the first attempts of Catholic theology to engage the concerns and presuppositions of the modern world.[1] Despite Staudenmaier's familiarity with contemporary thought and his concern to interact with it, Hunermann says he must be considered a conservative, both theologically and politically.

Staudenmaier did all of his teaching and writing during the revolutionary period of the 1830's and 1840's. This colored his outlook and led him ultimately to work in the government of his state after the revolution of 1848. Staudenmaier was a prolific writer. His *Encyklopaedie der theologischen Wissenschaft* (1834) was a major achievement of its time. He also wrote four volumes of a *Dogmatik* (1844—1852) and a critique of Hegel's thought, *Darstellung und Kritik des Hegel'schen Systems* (1844). He has been credited with defending Catholic doctrine from the pantheistic influence of Hegel as well as with providing the soundest critique of Hegel to appear in the nineteenth century. In contrast to Hegel, Staudenmaier stressed God's freedom and personality.

Staudenmaier described his attempt to appropriate the work of leading German philosophers for Catholic theology by saying, "It is vain to withstand the spirit of the times.... We must recognize it, penetrate it, but not in every way adopt it."[2] O'Meara says Staudenmaier represents the Tübingen school at its best.

One of Staudenmaier's major targets was Schleiermacher, who had so influenced the first generation of Catholic Tübingen scholars. Staudenmaier considered Schleiermacher the greatest Protestant theologian since Calvin, but criticized him for developing a Christology that fell short of traditional Christian understanding of Christ as the absolute incarnate Word of God. Schleiermacher's fundamental error was in his starting point: he built his Christology, and thus his dogmatics, upon the human personality that somehow works its way up to God instead of on the spirit of Christ, a Christ who explains himself in terms of his divine origin. "The power of his God-consciousness" was not, said Staudenmaier, a sufficient basis for explaining the presence of God in Christ. Staudenmaier had a greater appreciation of the historicity of Christianity than did Schleiermacher and thus recognized a greater objectivity in Christian faith because it derived from events in history.[3] Staudenmaier did not reject the role of feeling in religion, but he refused to accord it the central position it held in Schleiermacher's theology.

Staudenmaier was equally critical of other influential contemporaries. He argued that Schelling was unable to explain how the finite derives from the infinite, so his attempt to deduce God's nature from creation must be unsuccessful. Schelling had confused finitude with sin and freedom with being—in—progress.[4] Staudenmaier's critique signaled the movement of the second generation Tübingers away from Schelling and toward other philosophical influences. He remained deeply involved with Idealism and Romanticism despite his criticisms; his framework remained idealist, but his content

became increasingly christocentric.[5] He abandoned the early Tübingen concern with metahistory and metaphysics in favor of a stress on divine freedom
and personality. His central premise was that God is a person, not an unfolding concept.[6] This shift provided a valid role for experience within
theology because persons must be experienced whereas concepts need only
be comprehended.

Staudenmaier also wrote a response to Strauss's *Leben Jesu* which
was philosophical, not exegetical, in content. He was concerned with the
idea of the life of Christ—"Jesus Christ the God-man is the Redeemer and
Savior of the world." Leaving the exegetical work to his colleague Kuhn,
Staudenmaier presented the historical and speculative arguments for traditional Christology. The Church, guided by the Spirit, must remain our only
true source for the life of Jesus. Staudenmaier attempted to demonstrate
human history is identical with divine revelation in contrast to Strauss who
had posited Christianity as no more than the mythological presentation of
an absolute philosophy.

Staudenmaier stressed that the truths of faith are historical truths
and thus factual. He based his confidence in the clarity of history on his
conviction that Christ is the center of history, thus the key to understanding
it. Hunermann suggests Staudenmaier's use of history contained a blind
spot because he did not recognize the historicity of dogma necessarily means
it is time-bound and relative.[7] This may be related to his lack of compe-
tence in historical-critical method. This lack was evident in his handling of
both Scripture and patristic sources, where he tended to harmonize texts instead of doing the hard work of wrestling with differences among them.
Basic to Staudenmaier's approach was the belief that the Church alone is
able to recognize and explain that which is Christian. This means a grammatical-historical explanation of Scripture is sufficient to draw out its truth
and significance. The task of dogmatics, then, is only to point out how the
faith of the Church remains in continuity with biblical faith. In all his work,
Staudenmaier tried to preserve Christian revelation from being dissolved
into a metaphysical system. He did not deny Scripture contained its own
metaphysic; he merely argued that this was not Idealism.[8]

Staudenmaier's Christology developed out of his fundamental anthropological concept: every person is in a unique way a revelation of God
and is responsible for allowing this to develop so God becomes transparent
through him or her self. Christ is the unique and supreme instance of
humanity. His teaching is the self-manifestation of the fullness of the
Father's presence.[9] This is the basis, but it is not the fullness of the content,
of Staudenmaier's Christology. Unfortunately, Staudenmaier never pro-

gressed far enough with his *Dogmatik* to present a formal Christology; our sources for understanding his Christology are his published articles, sections from his books, and particularly his *Encyklopaedie*, which has a major section on the person and work of Christ. In the *Encyklopaedie*, Staudenmaier devoted 70 pages to Christology and another 20 to Christ's place in revelation. Of the 70, only seven dealt directly with Christ's person; 57 discussed his work and an additional six dealt with his humiliation and exaltation. Staudenmaier organized Christ's work in terms of his offices as prophet, high priest, and king. By far the longest section dealt with his work as high priest.

The content of Staudenmaier's Christology essentially reflected the established Catholic thinking of his day with traces of German Idealism. He distinguished clearly between Creator and creation; his Christology reflected both their absolute distinction and their conjunction in the God-man Jesus Christ. Staudenmaier worked out the philosophical basis for his Christology in terms of the "Idea" he found expressed in the Old Testament wisdom literature and in the New Testament Johannine writings.

The totality of Christ's existence is the vital center of Christianity. All spiritual and moral power derives from Christ. In fact, everything stands or falls with Christ.[10] God has appeared personally in Christ; in him we have seen the Eternal One. It is impossible to explain Christ's appearance in terms of the development of the human race or the fullness of nature. Christ presents an absolute beginning because he is the author of a new spiritual creation. Jesus Christ was God enfleshed, who entered history at a specific moment in time as God's final revelation to perform the work of salvation, to redeem the human race. Jesus Christ was the God-man, the perfect connection between God and humanity.

> Christ stood in the center of the human experience of God. Christ realized the unity of God and the world. He was the primal event of life and religion.... He was not merely attached to the ultimate *Idee*, but rather was this *Idee* itself.[11]

Staudenmaier, like his mentor Drey, saw a continuity between Christianity and all other religions, with Christianity as the apex and goal of religion. Christ was the answer to the desires of all spiritual people, pagan as well as Jewish. He brought with him a new consciousness, a new age, a new reality, and a new world. Christ's entrance into history is the turning point of all history.[12] Staudenmaier argued that Christianity is the world religion because it is the truth of all religions. In Christ all the contradictions of the various religions were subsumed (*aufgehoben*) and a new oneness established. Christ appeared in the ancient world as an eternal, necessary Idea. The necessity and validity of this Idea are proven by Christ's pre-existence and his incarnation.[13]

The Person of Christ

The fundamental image of Christianity is that God was in Christ and reconciled the world to himself (II Corinthians 5:19). The Scriptures explain this in terms of a divine-human union in which the eternal Logos, who was God himself, appeared in the flesh and united himself to human existence. The evangelists present this in two ways: John in terms of the incarnation of the Logos; Matthew and Luke in terms of Jesus' supernatural virginal conception and birth.[14]

Christ appeared in the world as its savior. Staudenmaier said we can neither understand nor justify this claim unless we first know who this savior is. Thus, the person of Christ takes precedence over his work because the sufficiency of his work depends upon his person. The central concept here is that of the God-man in whom deity and humanity are hypostatically united. Staudenmaier said not only were the two natures united in Christ, but Christ himself knew this. Thus, Christ's God-consciousness was the recognition not that he was wholly dependent upon and totally agreed with God but that he was ontologically deity.

Staudenmaier said Scripture expresses Christ's divine and human natures in terms of his being Son of God and Son of Man respectively.[15] The union of these two natures is a personal union and the person is that of the Logos. Were this not so, human salvation would be impossible (Staudenmaier defined salvation in terms of restoration). Christ must be God because only God can effect a new creation; he must be human because only a human can make the satisfaction necessary to cancel the original human lapse. Further, these two acts of satisfaction and new creation must be accomplished by one person.[16] Staudenmaier's Christology faithfully reflected the Catholic tradition to this point with a clear tilt toward Apollinarianism in its emphasis on a full divine consciousness in Christ at some cost to his full humanity. The strong emphasis on Christ's deity may equally have been a reaction to Strauss and other contemporaries who called Christ's deity into question while stressing his humanity in a manner incompatible with the traditional understanding of that humanity.

Staudenmaier argued both natures of Christ were evident throughout his earthly life. He not only experienced the conditions common to human existence, he also underwent the development proper to being human. As part of the human race, Christ suffered the temptations faced by all, but he did so without sinning. In pursuing this last idea, Staudenmaier emphasized Christ's role as the Second Adam who faced the same conditions as the first but who, in not succumbing as the first did, undid the damage of the first and restored creation to its original state.

In examining the relationship between Christ's two natures, Staudenmaier said this was not an eternal relationship. It was determined by God in eternity, but it began in time. The taking up of the human nature into deity did not alter the relationship between the Son and the other persons of the Godhead. In saying this, Staudenmaier was treading the narrow line between the traditional supposition of divine immutability and the reality that after the Incarnation the Son was different from before.

The Incarnation resulted in a living and organic unity of deity and humanity. It was neither an inhabitation nor an indwelling of the divine in the human, nor was it a changing of one nature into the other nor both into a third. There existed only one "I" in Christ, the divine person, and there was no merely human person apart from his deity. The union of the two natures was not only apparent, it was "real, true, and essential."[17] Each of the options not taken by Staudenmaier had been rejected officially by the early Church but reintroduced by one or another of Staudenmaier's contemporaries.

Staudenmaier contended Christ was not simply one sent by God as were the prophets of the Old Testament. He was God's Son and very God. Were he not deity, the events of his life would make no sense. Were he not deity, the extraordinary circumstances surrounding his birth and his resurrection from the dead and ascension would be incomprehensible.[18] The content of Christ's earthly life was equally unique. No other person has ever lived who led such a holy and exemplary life as did Jesus. He was constantly aware God was with him and his entire life was an unbroken conversation with the Father. Jesus was no mere religious person; he was religion incarnate.

The Work of Christ

Christ's life serves as a special witness to the truth and divinity of Christianity. This witness is evident in his teaching, miracles, behavior, and fulfillment of ancient prophecy. Staudenmaier dealt in particular with miracles. These must be viewed in connection with his entire person and mission. Jesus did not perform miracles in order to create faith because such faith must be based on an appreciation of his entire person if it is to be true faith. Miracles can never be a definitive witness to Christ because their source can be misunderstood, as it was by Jesus' contemporaries.[19]

Through his life, Christ reconciled God and humanity and achieved true salvation for humanity. Through his work, Christ established a new communion with God, destroyed the kingdom of darkness, and founded the Kingdom of God. In contrast to Drey, Staudenmaier did not make this Kingdom the centerpiece of his theology. He did parallel Drey in seeing Christ as the subject of his own proclamation. In knowing, showing, and proclaiming God as his Father, Jesus touched on his own deity. By conceiving of Jesus' proclamation of God as self-proclamation, Staudenmaier attempted to overcome the division made by contemporary critics between Jesus the proclaimer and Christ the proclaimed.[20] If there is no difference between the messenger and the message, the critical assertion of a serious break between Christ and the teaching of the early Church is called into question at an important point. Staudenmaier's lack of exegetical work prevented his contention from becoming more than that; he did not provide serious historical-exegetical arguments for his position.

Staudenmaier denied Christ's work could be separated from his person. The work of salvation required both a human and a divine element. Equally, it must contain both objective and subjective aspects and be historical because the need for salvation exists within history. Christ is the mediator between God and humanity. As such, he not only has pointed the way to the Father; he has also led the way. Because Christ is one with God, he can bring humans into a oneness with God. This is a lesser oneness than the oneness Christ enjoys, yet it remains a oneness that participates in the divine life to the full extent humanity is able to do so.[21]

Christ's work did not end with the salvation of the world; he also established the Church to continue his work. As prophet and high priest, Christ continues to guide and direct humanity through the medium of his Church. He is able to do so because he is also king.

The Offices of Christ

Staudenmaier addressed Christ's work in terms of his three offices of prophet, priest, and king. In doing so, he showed how each office leads directly to the next so that together the three comprise the one office of savior of the world. In the Old Testament, these offices were held by different individuals. They have been brought together in Christ, however, because the savior must be able to perform all three. Furthermore, the Kingdom cannot be established until the offices have been united in one individual: "Christ proclaimed his Kingdom as prophet, he established it as high priest, and he rules it as king."[22]

Staudenmaier's exposition of Christ's three offices exemplifies his use of Scripture in his *Dogmatik*. He did not use scriptural citations in every portion, but where he did he piled up as many proof texts as he could find to support his position. The position, however, was derived from dogmatics, not from exegesis. Exegesis had no place in his *Dogmatik*, and he nowhere distinguished between various portions of the New Testament, but cited them indiscriminately. He did, however, seem to prefer Paul when it was possible to cite him.

Staudenmaier stated clearly that Christ came to save the world. In saying this, he was clearer than was his mentor Drey that Christ's primary role was to be neither teacher nor example. In fact, Christ's teaching cannot be seen apart from who he was, not least because he was the subject of his message. Staudenmaier put it succinctly: "The teaching of Christ is a teaching about Christ."[23] A key element of this teaching is the need to have faith in him. Staudenmaier said that apart from such faith neither Christ nor his message is comprehensible.

Jesus was not a teacher; he was a prophet, said Staudenmaier. Teachers pass on knowledge they have acquired from studying with other teachers and such knowledge is purely human. Christ, however, proclaimed divine truth that he knew apart from any human teacher and this points to a divine consciousness. A prophet in the Old Testament setting was a person who had been commissioned by God to appear in the name of God and proclaim the word of God. These prophets at times worked miracles through God's power. Christ appeared and proclaimed in God's name but performed miracles in his own power that flowed out of his divine nature. Ultimately, Christ was more than a prophet because he derived the truth of his teaching from his essential union with God.[24]

Not only was Christ a prophet, he was the one who effected that which he proclaimed. Staudenmaier addressed this aspect of Christ's work in terms of his office of high priest. Biblically, a priest is one who intercedes with God for other people. In the Old Testament, the high priest offered the sacrifice to atone for the sins of the nation on the Day of Atonement (*Yom Kippur*). It is necessary that Jesus be a priest because humanity cannot save itself; it needs a savior. Only God can make atonement for humanity's sins. But God is under no obligation to do so because this would mean God is somehow determined by his creation. God's work of salvation derives from his free love for his creation. This work of salvation could occur only through the suffering and death of Christ.[25]

The Old Testament high priest prefigured Christ, who is the true and eternal high priest. Whereas the Old Testament priest offered God a finite sacrifice to atone for the sins of the people, Christ offered himself as an infinite sacrifice sufficient to cover all human sin with certainty. Staudenmaier offered a long list of biblical passages to demonstrate Christ's deity and thus the sufficiency of his work for the salvation of the world.[26]

Staudenmaier interpreted the atonement not only as a work in which Christ died for humanity's sins but also one where humans were required to cooperate (*mitwirken*) in achieving this salvation. His position can be understood better in light of the contrasting positions he attacked directly. His first opponent was the Lutheran-Calvinist position which he described as mechanical and rationalistic. He equally opposed the construct whereby the loving Son offered himself as a sacrifice to appease the angry Father, thus setting the Godhead at odds with itself. He also rejected the exemplary theory of the atonement. Staudenmaier reserved his harshest criticism for two positions: the Idealist understanding of salvation as the process of divine self-unfolding, and the mythological view that was left with no more than an abstract, empty idea after it separated history from reality.[27]

The death of Christ was the heart and high point in his high priestly work, but it was by no means the totality of that work. Christ's priestly work consisted of three equally essential activities. He completely fulfilled the law in his subjective obedience to the Father; he died a redemptive death; and he interceded for and continues to intercede for humanity before God. Each activity is possible only because of that which has preceded it.[28] In these activities Christ must be seen as acting in our behalf, as our representative. Likewise, his death was the highest act of obedience. Thus, each of Christ's salvific activities subsumed and went beyond the previous acts.[29]

Staudenmaier had several additional comments regarding Christ's high priestly office that fill out the scheme of obedience, redemption, and intercession (or representation). As mediator between God and humanity, Christ was the mediator of a new covenant. As such he canceled the Jewish laws, which were unable to bring anything to fulfillment. The covenant signifies the beginning of a new time and the entry of the Kingdom of God into history.[30] In dying, Christ represented humanity in its sin, guilt, and punishment and has made humanity righteous before God. This is the objective and external aspect of salvation; a subjective aspect within the individual remains necessary. Staudenmaier thus appeared to regard the atonement as being of universal extent in its objective worth, the only limitation in practice being humanity's willingness to accept Christ's work in its behalf. Staudenmaier emphasized that in the work of atonement the Father and Son were in agreement; Christ's work reveals the inner and eternal relationship between God's love and his righteousness. These attributes exist together; neither can occur apart from the other.

Staudenmaier said little about Christ's kingship beyond its being the necessary consequence of the first two offices. Christ is king over that which he has redeemed. His realm is the Kingdom of God he proclaimed in his earthly ministry. The Tübinger's lack of emphasis on this office probably resulted from his concentration on Christ as Son of Man and Second Adam at the expense of his role as Messiah.

Humiliation and Exaltation

Staudenmaier concluded his Christology in the *Encyklopaedie* with an examination of Christ's humiliation and exaltation. He began by denying Christ's divine nature could suffer. He equally rejected the idea that Christ's human nature could suffer in isolation. Salvation could occur only if human nature were first taken up into the divine nature. When the two natures are joined, Christ's human nature could suffer blamelessly but sufficiently. It was Christ's humanity that provided satisfaction for human sin in his death and made his death the source of blessing for the human race.[31]

Christ's humiliation consisted in his becoming human. The divine nature, however, was unable to experience either humiliation or exaltation. Both changes in status were possible only because of the personal union of the two natures in Christ. The humiliation was not something forced upon Christ but was instead something he freely chose and brought about. In undergoing the humiliation of becoming human, Christ entered into the condition of those he had chosen to save. This was a necessary precondition to effecting their salvation.[32]

As the consummation of his work, Christ rose from the dead and ascended into heaven. This two-part action showed God had accepted Christ's atoning work and validated Christ's claims regarding his person and teaching. Staudenmaier pointed particularly to Christ as the judge of the world who now enjoys power and authority over creation, was victorious over death, and has achieved unity among believers.[33]

Conclusion

Because Christology was not central to Staudenmaier's theological enterprise, we must derive it primarily from comments made in his discussion of other subjects. His failure to complete the *Dogmatik* means this major work sheds no light on his later christological speculation. Staudenmaier was particularly concerned to interact with contemporary thought, but his lack of interest or ability in exegesis precluded serious interaction at the very point of Christology where his contemporaries were most involved.

Staudenmaier moved beyond Drey in a significant way through his emphasis on divine freedom. This gave the Tübingen concern to take history seriously a firm foundation that has been appropriated by Tübingen Christology in this century. In contrast to much traditional Christology, Staudenmaier was careful to protect the intimate link between Christ's person and work. In doing so, he gave clear reason for the priority of the person.

Despite his weakness in using Scripture, Staudenmaier was a firm defender of classical Christology and argued clearly and consistently for the doctrine that Christ's two natures existed in one divine person. He tried to do so without denigrating the human, and his stress on Christ's deity should be seen in connection with the denial of this deity by some of his contemporaries. Because Staudenmaier did most of his christological work while he and Kuhn were colleagues at Giessen, the imbalance of his work toward the dogmatic and away from the biblical should be considered in conjunction with Kuhn's exegetical contribution to the christological debates of that period.

JOHANNES EVANGELIST KUHN

Kuhn, like the other early Tübingers, was born in Württemberg. Slightly younger than Staudenmaier, he, too, was a student of Drey and Möhler at Tübingen. Kuhn sought to continue the theological enterprise begun by his mentors and their influence is evident throughout his work. Kuhn began his academic life teaching the New Testament first at Giessen and later at Tübingen before succeeding to Drey's dogmatics chair at Tübingen in 1839. He remained in that position until his retirement in 1882.

Kuhn was a clear thinker and adept at theological and philosophical speculation. He was also an aggressive polemicist who was at odds with the majority of his contemporaries at the time of his death. Kuhn viewed himself as an apologist for Catholicism and involved himself at every point where he felt the faith to be endangered. He created his apologetics by blending Church tradition with the results of contemporary research. Adam called him the greatest speculative mind of the Tübingen School.[34] After his death, Kuhn was virtually forgotten because his style of thinking was out of favor in the wake of the victory of Neoscholasticism in Catholic theology.

Kuhn accomplished most of his christological work during his tenure as a New Testament scholar. This work, directed primarily against D. F. Strauss, was heavily exegetical in nature. The centerpiece was his *Das Leben Jesu* (1838), of which he published only one volume of a planned multi-volume work. That this exegetical study was never completed is probably due to his appointment in dogmatics, because from that point on Kuhn concentrated on theological and philosophical speculation. He saw his life's work as investigating the connection between religion, revelation, faith, and history.

The early concern with exegesis left a mark on Kuhn's later theology. He continued to see revelation as presented in Scripture as the *norma normans fidei* and as the historically guaranteed basis for the reasonableness of Christianity.[35] Kuhn never completed his *Dogmatik*. The only systematic Christology of his later period must be drawn from his section on the Trinity, the last volume in his *Dogmatik* to be published. Kuhn continued to be fascinated by biblical and patristic theology, but was more naturally disposed toward speculation.

After flirting with the idea of abandoning theology for politics in 1848, Kuhn devoted himself to patristics for a number of years and wrote several major articles on historical theology. This marked a major shift in Kuhn's method and resulted both from his conflict with Protestant and Catholic theologians and the continued influence of Möhler. It was only the primacy of Drey's influence, says Wolfinger, that kept Kuhn from shifting his focus at this point to historical studies.[36] Geiselmann suggested Kuhn's dogmatic concept of history was influenced significantly by the doctrine of tradition emanating from Trent and from Bellarmine's anti-Protestant concept of Tradition.[37]

In addition to his Tübingen mentors, Kuhn drew from all of the major intellectual movements of his time. He studied philosophy under Schelling at Munich, but later turned toward Hegel because he found his categories more helpful for theological speculation than Schelling's abstractions. This did not diminish Kuhn's reservations about Hegel's adequacy in regard to history.[38]

Kasper says Kuhn developed toward the acceptance of Scripture as substantially complete regarding matters of faith and as enjoying a relative prominence and normativity in contrast to later tradition. Kuhn distinguished clearly between Christ's teaching and that of the apostles as the source of truth and of Church doctrine. Scripture witnesses that apostolic teaching has been preserved in the Church and serves as the basis for doctrine.[39] Reinhardt said this development resulted from Kuhn's recognition that living tradition alone could lead the Church to a subjective understanding of doctrine. Revelation must be viewed as in itself and as for us. The latter is tradition. Scripture contains the full truth of revelation, but does so in an historically-conditioned form. A fundamental incongruity exists between biblical truth and dogma which cannot be bridged by using critical tools. Only an immediate sense of the truth can provide this bridge. Kuhn tied this to a more objective revelation that permitted him to view Scripture as a valid source for establishing the faith (contra Strauss).[40]

Kuhn's work on Christology consisted of two parts. His exegetical work in response to Strauss' mythological interpretation of the gospels dealt primarily with the historicity and reliability of the gospel records. The christological portions of his *Dogmatik* were part of his speculative work on the Trinity and presented the Logos only within that context. Thus, we have a significant amount of christological material from Kuhn, but it is not such as to permit us to construct a complete Christology.

Critique of Strauss

Kuhn was foremost among the Catholic theologians involved in studies of the life of Jesus in response to Strauss' work. His *Das Leben Jesu* (1838) was a serious and scholarly attempt to respond to the problems Strauss raised.

The heart of the issue between Kuhn and Strauss was whether Christianity is basically an idea whose truth can be separated from events in the world or whether its truth remains dependent upon concrete, historical facts. In his answer to Strauss, Kuhn argued the gospels are credible as reports of the historical events they record and as reflections written to support the early Church's witness of faith. Kuhn suggested the written gospels are not simply historical records, but were written to support the apostolic kerygma and sought to defend faith with proof that Jesus is the enfleshed Messiah. Kuhn described the gospels as teleological history or alternatively as theological history.[41]

In his defense of the gospels as divine revelation, Kuhn offered the christological God-man doctrine as a parallel. Just as Christ the Savior is both human and divine, so God's revelation is human and divine. This is so because God has chosen to spread Christianity through the activity of humans. Kuhn's analogy was imperfect, because whereas he would agree Christ is the God-man without admixture or defect, he said the Scriptures can contain error. To continue the christological parallel, Kuhn's position appeared somewhat Nestorian in that he seemed to say Scripture is part divine and part human.[42]

Kuhn said the gospel writers constructed their narratives from the historical activities of Jesus, whom they considered to be the Messiah. The primary mistake on the part of both his Protestant contemporaries and post-Enlightenment critics was to ignore the living faith of the historical witnesses to Jesus and the miracles that uniquely verified his mission.

> The "wissenschaftliche" treatment of the life of Jesus limits itself principally to the early development of the human side of Jesus' Messianic consciousness, whereby the birth and childhood with their supernatural experience are not considered, and the conclusion, the resurrection which is the crown of everything, is no longer presented, as it seems to us, comprehensively, as the fulfilling from scandalous grounds.[43]

The miracles should be seen not only in terms of historical criticism but also in terms of speculative theology as verification of the apostolic kerygma.[44] The ultimate basis for the apostolic kerygma was the death and resurrection of Jesus.

The Apostolic Kerygma

The core of the apostolic kerygma as we have received it was accepted within the Church even before Paul began to write. This kerygma arose from the united voice of Jesus' disciples and their followers, and these people presented the kerygma as history. Paul, said Kuhn, had to recognize the historicity of Christianity's claim before he could become a part of the Church, and the teaching that flowed from his pen was historical in nature.[45] The teaching of Peter and Paul in Acts furnishes the foundation for an historical, evidential, and fixed actual picture of the crucified and risen Christ. This teaching is the heart of the apostolic preaching and provides a "penetrating history of Jesus of Nazareth." The striking similarity between Paul and the gospel texts offers a powerful witness to the historical truth of the accounts.[46]

The gospels were not intended to be and cannot serve as biographies of Jesus. They were concerned primarily with Jesus' *significance*. They aimed to show Jesus was the Messiah and all history had been determined by his very existence. Kuhn agreed the gospels contained material that was biographical, but he argued biography was not the primary reason the gospels were written.[47]   A scholarly, scientific biography would contain material dealing with the inner unity of the historical Jesus and the Christ of faith, but this is impossible within the parameters of modern historiography.[48]

Biblical Criticism

    Kuhn used a literary analysis of the New Testament documents in his response to Strauss. Some have called this work a precursor of modern form criticism.[49] Kuhn was the first to recognize the kerygmatic nature of the gospels. He saw them as the written deposit of a previously living tradition. Unlike modern form critics, however, Kuhn denied the post-Easter kerygma was the product of one or more anonymous communities.[50] He concluded the writers of the gospels both could and did speak the truth. Had they presented falsehood, their contemporaries would have made it known. Thus, even though they were not intended primarily as historical reports, they are historical in content and worthy of belief. Kuhn said it would be wrong to judge the gospels according to the standards of modern historical research because the gospels had another overriding purpose for their creation and modern standards of historiography did not exist when the gospels were written.[51]

    The New Testament is an historical record of a unique revelation. To understand the New Testament in this way made more sense to Kuhn than to describe it as Palestinian mythology (Strauss), or as a text to be exegeted in terms of consciousness and life (Schleiermacher). Kuhn's rejection of any mythological interpretation of the New Testament turned him away from his teacher Schelling, who saw myth as the first record of God's involvement in the world. Schelling's was a different understanding of myth from that found in Strauss' treatment of Jesus' miracles as myths, however.

    Several categories within the gospel accounts continue to be incomprehensible according to the tenets of modern critical interpretation. Primary among these are miracles and prophecy. The critical solution of either ignoring or eliminating them leads to a theology that separates the Jesus of history from the Christ of faith, as Strauss did with his Jesus myth. So said Geiselmann, who sought in the following century to apply the results of Kuhn's work to the demythologization debate with Bultmann. He put Kuhn's argument thus:

> The gospels are not sources for the life of Jesus in the
> general historical sense of the word, but witnesses from

faith to Jesus as the Christ. Whoever approaches the gospels in order to critically collect a history of the life of
Jesus from a modern historical viewpoint is traveling along
an entirely false trail because he completely misunderstands
the uniqueness of these documents. The gospels are not
"historical" [*historische*] documents, but witnesses from
faith.[52]

   Kuhn said the scientific study of the gospels has both a critical and
a theological element, but the extent to which the critical element may be
allowed to influence one's conclusions remains an open question. There are
both an internal and an external criticism. The former is a part of the
theological task, but the latter incorporates presuppositions from other
fields. Kuhn suggested these might be useful in the realm of prolegomena,
but they can never be come an integral part of the picture of the life of
Jesus.[53]
   For Kuhn, "the apostolic kerygma and our gospel were and are one
and the same: the proof of Jesus' messiahship derives from his history."[54]
The apostolic kerygma was the living proclamation of the faith in words. It
is the original and unique mediation of the faith. Thus the substance of the
kerygma is in accord with the entirety of divine revelation and says God has
spoken to us conclusively in his Son.[55] We can analyze the form and content of the kerygma from the gospels and the book of Acts. This is because
the kerygma was built upon the historical facts of Jesus' life: the memories
of his life and work, especially his passion, death, and resurrection. The
apostolic proclamation dealt not only with the story of Jesus, but went on
to present a case for the importance of having faith in him. Thus the faith
was grounded on empirical-historical facts about Jesus' life and teaching.
Granted that the apostles were creative in forming their accounts, they did
not deny Jesus' history in doing so. They did not construct legends or
myths, but instead illuminated the history they reported. They made it clear
they were reporting no common history, but were dealing instead with salvation history.[56] Part of the gospel writers' task was to show how the story
of Jesus made the various Old Testament prophecies understandable. This
was far different from using those prophecies to construct the mythical history of Jesus that Strauss had attempted.
   In his exegetical response to Strauss, Kuhn placed his greatest emphasis
on the first and fourth gospels. This appears to be because he considered
Matthew the first synoptic gospel both chronologically and canonically and

because John was a source independent of the synoptics. Because Kuhn considered each gospel to have been written from a particular theological perspective and with a particular theological purpose, he did not neglect Mark or Luke. He saw Matthew and Mark as christological, Luke as historical, and John as theological in his approach. Whereas Matthew made much use of prophecy and miracles to prove his case, John tried to show Jesus was Messiah through an historical apologetic based upon his death.[57] Luke followed a similar path when he said Jesus' resurrection summed up all that had gone before and faith in the resurrection makes faith in Jesus as the Christ and Son of God complete.[58]

The Teaching of the Fourth Gospel

John's theology, for Kuhn accepted the traditional authorship claims regarding the gospels, was the high point of New Testament theology because it presented Jesus of Nazareth as the incarnate Logos of God and the Christ. Although he did not say so explicitly, by putting it in these terms Kuhn kept the humanity and deity of Jesus together. It is important to see this, because much of his work here in *Das Leben Jesu* and in the *Dogmatik* emphasized Jesus' deity, which was the aspect of Christology under heavy attack in his day. Although the same doctrine was found in the synoptics, Acts, and Paul, John provided "greater definition and sharpness of concept and expression" than did the others.

The Logos is the divine Word through whom all that is has been called into existence. The Logos is not merely the expression of God's thought, he is the hypostatization of God's Wisdom and the Mediator of God's creative will and rule. The Logos partakes of the divine nature and is identical with God; he is God. Kuhn described the Logos as the God who appears, the manifestation of the invisible God. The Logos is also the Son of God and the Mediator of God's salvific revelation. Kuhn contrasted the revelation through the Logos with that which came through the prophets by saying that in the latter God was speaking through an alien mouth, but such was not the case when he spoke through the Logos.[59] Repeatedly, Kuhn pointed to John as proclaiming the full participation by the Logos in the divine nature.

> The relationship of Christ to God is presented as unique, one in which no other nature either in heaven or on earth participates.[60]

Pre-existence

Kuhn defended the doctrine of Christ's pre-existence against claims that it was a mythical means of affirming his divine dignity. Kuhn argued the pre-existence of Christ was taught unambiguously in Colossians and Philippians. In discussing Philippians 2:6–11, Kuhn said the Logos was the proper subject of the historical Christ and as such existed before time. The birth of Jesus, then, was not merely the birth of a human, but the incarnation of the Logos of God. The language of Colossians 1:15–20 does not lead one to think of the earthly Jesus, but of the pre-existent Word.[61] Hebrews teaches the same truth as that found in Philippians and Colossians, but it uses different language. Here, the Son participates in the divine glory and is, so to speak, God in another form. Kuhn used the German Idealist concepts of *Vorstellung* and *Ebenbild* to argue Christ is not merely the way God represents himself to humanity but is himself God.[62]

The challenge that the doctrine of Christ's pre-existence is mythological has not disappeared. If anything, it is more widespread than in Kuhn's day. Kuhn's use of the New Testament to prove his point would hardly be accepted by modern proponents of the mythological school; they have come to view the texts Kuhn used as meaning something altogether different from Kuhn's interpretation or as themselves using the language of myth.[63]

The Life of Jesus

In examining Jesus' life, Kuhn emphasized Jesus was born and raised a Jew, and this Jewishness was an integral factor in his being the Messiah. It was necessary he be a Jew, and this necessity explains his appearance in time and his rectitude in the process of development.

The birth and childhood stories explain events recounted in the apostolic kerygma. They are historical in content, though not in intent. Kuhn defended the historicity of Jesus' birth against Strauss' mythological interpretation, but he separated it from the rest of Jesus' history because it was authenticated differently. Jesus learned and developed gradually as would any other human; to think otherwise would be docetic. Yet Jesus' wisdom and learning did not come solely from human sources.[64] Kuhn said the historicity of that which the apostles proclaimed was both uncontested and presupposed in their day.

Jesus did not begin his career as a disciple of John the Baptist, as Strauss had argued. Kuhn saw the baptism by John as the beginning of

Jesus' career. This baptism was a recapitulation of the Genesis creation story where God made everything through his word alone and the Spirit hovered over the waters. At Jesus' baptism, God proclaimed the moral recreation of the world in his Son while the Spirit in the form of a dove hovered over the scene.[65]

The baptism was God's sign to Jesus that it was time for him to assume his office of Messiah. Jesus was aware of his person and destiny before the baptism, however. Kuhn said it would be impossible, both psychologically and historically, for Jesus to have become aware of his messianic destiny at the baptism or later. Jesus' temptation by Satan was equally an historical reality. Kuhn said the temptation could never have resulted in sin, only in the possibility of sin, but this possibility could never be realized. The possibility lay in the reality of human freedom, but were it realized, Christ's salvific work could never be accomplished. Jesus overcame the temptation in his human freedom, not because "he was God." The deity served only the negative function of hindering the possibility of sin as it sought to become reality. Kuhn rejected the prevalent conservative view that tended toward docetism by denying even the possibility of Jesus' sinning by removing him from the common run of humanity. Despite Kuhn's concern in this regard, his position is less than a model of clarity and does not provide a satisfactory explanation for the temptation that maintains the full integrity of Jesus' person.

Jesus' temptation was not merely the temptation of a good man, said Kuhn. It had messianic implications. That Jesus emerged from Satan's temptations unweakened and victorious demonstrated he was indeed the Messiah.

As with much christological writing before this century, Kuhn's showed limited interest in the earthly ministry of Jesus, although a complete treatment of Christology may have given this aspect more weight. Like most of his conservative contemporaries, Kuhn skipped from Jesus' birth to his death and resurrection. He said the Resurrection served to confirm Jesus as Messiah before his followers. It was this that led them to understand the concept of a suffering Messiah as presented in the Old Testament and thus explained how Jesus could be Messiah and still experience what he did. Because Kuhn, in traditional Roman Catholic fashion, viewed the Incarnation as the decisive factor in Christology, he dealt with the remainder of Jesus' life as it related to the Incarnation and its importance, but not as particularly significant in itself. It was this approach that led later theologians to charge classical Christology had tacitly denied the content of its confession by downplaying or ignoring Jesus' humanity.

Christological Titles

Kuhn also focuses on several of the christological titles. He tried
to link those of God—man and Messiah because he thought the presentation of Jesus' life can only begin from the idea of Messiah and the doctrine
of Christ must begin from the idea of the God—man.[66]

Messiah was the key title for Kuhn. Jesus was Messiah by divine
decision. His messiahship did not come by accident nor through his
grasping at divine power. On the contrary, it was a matter of Jesus' innate
personal character and was in accord with his vocation of Savior. Similarly,
Jesus' messianic consciousness could not have been the result of some sud-
den magic worked on him. Kuhn said Jesus' messianic consciousness had to
have been the result of a natural and gradual awakening of his self-
consciousness and the building up of his natural disposition under the necessary influence of such external factors as his Jewish birth, his nurture, and
his education.[67]

Being the Messiah was not simply one among many properties of
Jesus' person. It was instead the foundation upon which all other attributes
depended—it was the substance of his person. The apostolic kerygma proclaimed Jesus as Messiah in realization of the messianic promises contained
in the Old Testament and seen in the life of Jesus. This is why the gospel
writers so emphasized the theme of fulfillment in their accounts. Nonetheless, many of the Old Testament passages cited in the gospels were not
recognized by Jesus' contemporaries as messianic. This means, said Kuhn,
that the gospel writers did not simply go through their Scriptures and collect
the messianic prophecies, attributing them to Jesus. In reflecting on Jesus'
life and ministry they suddenly saw certain passages of Scripture more clearly
than they had previously and realized these, too, were messianic in intent.
Some of what they came to see and say about Jesus contrasted sharply with
contemporary Jewish messianic expectation. Contrary to Strauss, this means
the last thing the gospel writers were trying to do was to accommodate Jesus
to the accepted picture of the Messiah. Kuhn added that the writers wanted
to show events in Jesus' life were not accidental, but happened according to
God's plan which he had revealed to the prophets beforehand.[68]

Kuhn did not believe every instance of Jesus being called Son of
God during his earthly life asserted his deity. Many merely implied he was
anointed by the Spirit or equipped with divine power to perform his mission
as Messiah. Quite often the Son of God title was a synonym for Messiah or
Christ. This interpretation, said Kuhn, does not contradict higher understandings of the title, but leads to them because Jesus differed qualitatively

from other figures of Israel, including the expected Messiah. The temporal Sonship of Christ is the correlate of the eternity of the pre-existent Logos who was related to God before time. Kuhn held this position in opposition to the various early heresies that taught the relation between God and Christ began at some point in Jesus' earthly life or was only illusory.[69]

Kuhn concluded his discussion of Jesus' titles with his designation as God (*theos*). He considered this to have been used ontologically in the New Testament and said the various New Testament designations of Christ were consistent with his being God. The most prominent and controverted text in the New Testament that raises the issue is Romans 9:5. Kuhn said this verse calls Jesus God. To punctuate it to read in any other way would be arbitrary and the two possible alternatives are not grammatically strong.[70]

Although he argued strongly from the New Testament text for Christ's deity, Kuhn recognized several popular proof texts for this view were inappropriate. It appears the key for Kuhn was that the New Testament consistently portrayed Jesus using attributes and actions appropriate only to deity, and texts existed to support that conclusion.

Kuhn presented a picture of Christ pre-existent and coming "down" to earth. But he also sought to show there is a human orientation toward God and all religions exist on a continuum in which Christianity is the highest and the fulfillment of all the others. In this context, Christ is the apex of human development and the organ of divine revelation in and for the human race.

When we recognize people are sinners who have fallen away from God, we understand why they no longer reveal God, and have lost any connection with God. Applying this picture to Christ, we realize how different he is from us in his freedom from sin, his relation to God, and thus in his unique qualification to be the vehicle of divine revelation.

For Kuhn, the essence of historical revelation is that revelation has found its end and highest form in Jesus Christ and lives on in the witness of the apostles and the Church they established. That which distinguished Christ from other humans was the complete, current, and constant interworking of divine and human in him. In saying this, Kuhn appears to have seen Christ's work primarily in terms of revelation, not sacrifice. Yet, despite the serious charges Glossner made concerning Kuhn's understanding of Christ's person (an understanding that would be contrary to the dogmatic teachings of the Church if true),[71] Kuhn appears to have held that Christ's human destiny presupposed an absolute divine nature underlay it. The nature of Kuhn's writing provided no opportunity for a clear affirmation of the elements of Nicea and Chalcedon as such, but the sense that flowed through his writings was consistent with the teachings of these councils. Where he diverged, it was not from conciliar teachings, but from the popular monophysitic misapplication of them.

Early Christological Controversies

Kuhn got no further in his *Dogmatik* than the volume about the doctrine of the Trinity. Because he spent a significant portion of this large volume discussing early Church disputes over the doctrine, he was forced to deal at several points with the early christological arguments. The major thesis Kuhn repeatedly argued was that the three persons of the Trinity are identical in nature—each is God. The decisive issue, as Kuhn recognized, was the deity of Christ; the entire doctrine of the Trinity hangs on the decision as to whether or not Christ possesses divine nature.[72]

Kuhn was more modest than too many other theologians have been in dealing with the doctrine of the Trinity. He clearly acknowledged that

the divine Trinity, especially the begetting of the Son, is an inconceivable and impenetrable secret, which we ought to faithfully hold fast, even though we cannot understand it.[73]

Acknowledging no comprehensive understanding of the Trinity is possible, Kuhn did attempt to explain the doctrine to the extent he could within the limits set by revelation and speculation. He concentrated much of his argument on the relation between the Father and the Son because he recognized, as had the early fathers, that once the deity of these two divine persons was established, the doctrine of the Trinity followed more readily.

He said the Son is neither external to nor beside God the Creator. In an indivisible unity with the Father and the Spirit, the Son is himself Creator. "He is... the substantial Word and Wisdom of the Father; through him all things are thought and called into being."[74] Because the relation of Father and Son occurs within the Godhead, it is absolutely unique in kind. The relation is one of nature because the Son is called into being according to nature whereas creatures are called forth according to God's free will.

Kuhn recognized one of the principal stumbling blocks in his era was the meaning of the term "person." Although the patristic use of the term regarding the Trinity differed to some extent from its use in Christology, these two uses caused a problem simply because the term meant something significantly different from what it does now. Kuhn emphasized the fathers did not use the term in the sense of later philosophy to designate a self-conscious ego. Citing Augustine, he said the term was used in order to be able to speak about God at all, not in order to specify something in particular about God. We use the word "person," he said, in order to speak about that which is in itself inexpressible.

> [Even] if we are unable to say what the true is, we can leave no doubt as to what is contrary to the truth.[75]

Merely because the topic transcends the capacity of our finite minds, said Kuhn, does not relieve us of the obligation to express as much as our minds are able to. We must do so because the truth of the matter is so important to our religious faith that we may not permit mistaken teaching where truth is possible.

The Nicene concept of Christ is that if he is God, he must be essentially identical to the Father. There can be no half-God. The Arian concept, said Kuhn, is spiritually untenable, and because it is grounded neither in the word of God nor in the faith of the Church, it is untrue. Kuhn presented much of his positive teaching on the Trinity in the form of a response to the various heresies of the early Church. Primary among these, because of the breadth and seriousness of its impact, was Arianism.

Arianism stood in open contradiction to the essence of Christian truth and the Church's expression of that truth. The heart of this contradiction was the denial of Christ's consubstantiality with the Father. Because he is begotten (not made) of the essence of the Father (not out of nothing, as was that which was made), Christ participates fully in the divine essence.

> He is what the Father is: God. But he is not the Father. He is God not as Father, but as Son.... The Son is in every way of the Father, but he is no part of the Father.[76]

Evaluation

In his conflict with Strauss, Kuhn exemplified the Catholic Tübingen School's dialectical approach that views heresy as the antithesis that drives the Church to further development of its understanding of the faith. Strauss' theory of myth was the antithesis that helped the Tübingers reach the conclusion that the living faith of the Church is a decidedly further development out of its deposit of sacred tradition.[77]

Möhler had related the Church to Christ as virtually the continuation of the Incarnation. Kuhn rejected this view because he feared it could dissolve Christology into ecclesiology. Instead, he saw the Church as a bridge mediating saving faith to every age, serving as the stronghold of truth and providing opportunities for the individual to meet God.[78] Kuhn's position made it easier to criticize the Church's failings because these would not reflect on Christ himself, as Möhler's position would seem to have allowed (if not required).

In reflecting upon Kuhn's Christology, we should remember he never presented it as a systematic whole. We need to dig into his various writings to construct what we can of it ourselves. This means Kuhn himself might neither recognize nor accept our final product. We need, too, to recognize Kuhn was writing for an age that was only beginning to deal with the questions raised by the natural and social sciences, world religions, and the changing relation between the Church and the world.[79] Having said this, we can see both strengths and weaknesses in Kuhn's work.

Kuhn was a careful exegete who was open to reconsidering some of the Church's views on Scripture (although he was seriously dated by today's standards) and possessed a good historical background. He also had a sense for which elements were critical in the issues he faced and which were not. Although his work reflected the influence of a variety of philosophical trends, no one of these controlled his outlook. Kuhn was able to draw out that which was useful to him from thinkers with whom he disagreed fundamentally. He carried forward the consideration of the nature of living tradition that had been central to the work of the Catholic Tübingen School from its inception.

The key issue here, and one that especially concerned Kuhn in his response to Strauss, was the historicity of that tradition. Is that which the Scripture and the tradition of the Church recount about Jesus historical occurrence, or is it stories designed to convey religious truth without regard to history (myth)? Kuhn argued for the former and charged Strauss with proposing the latter. There is much truth in Kuhn's claim, but the word "myth" has always been ambiguous in its theological usage. All advocates of the use of the term assert that it designates stories as designed to convey religious truth, but not all are willing to sever the stories from historical reality. Few users of the term explain precisely where they stand on this issue. That is the first problem with using the word; the second is that the word is popularly understood to indicate religious fantasy (e.g., stories of the Greek and Roman gods and goddesses) that we might consider interesting literature but from which we never would consider deriving either historical or ethical truth. Kuhn appears to have understood myth in this second sense.

Kuhn remained faithful to Church dogma as proclaimed by the various christological councils, but he showed little hesitation to criticize inconsistency on the part of those who agreed with him in belief but not in practice. He accepted a Christology "from above," but admitted the need for what might be called a Christology "from below" as well. His picture of Christ as the end and goal of all religiosity certainly appears to be "from below." In the portions we have of Kuhn's thought, we find he, too, was guilty of emphasizing the deity of Christ to the neglect of his humanity in the same way, though not to the same degree, he warned others were doing. Although it was this deity that was under attack in Strauss' mythological interpretation, that interpretation left room for greater consideration of Jesus' earthly life than Kuhn devoted to it. He made the Incarnation the center of his Christology and thereby devoted too little consideration to the cross.

Like Staudenmaier, Kuhn left no disciples. His work presented no coherent system because he never finished any of the writing projects he began. This was not entirely his fault, however, because the Roman School that achieved dominance during the second half of the 19th century rejected his position and threatened to condemn his work. This threat led Kuhn to abstain from writing during the last two decades of his life. After several generations of neglect, however, Kuhn's memory and work were revived by J. R. Geiselmann of Tübingen, who believed Kuhn could contribute significantly to 20th century theology, primarily in the area of the use of tradition in theology.

1. Peter Hunermann, "Franz Anton Staudenmaier (1800–1856)," in *Katholische Theologen Deutschlands im 19. Jahrhundert*, II:99, ed. by Heinrich Fries and Georg Schwaiger, three vols. (Munich: Kösel, 1977). Hunermann, who teaches theology on the Catholic Tübingen faculty, has done much of the work in familiarizing modern theologians with Staudenmaier and his writings.

2. Thomas F. O'Meara, *Romantic Idealism and Roman Catholicism: Schelling and the Theologians* (Notre Dame: University of Notre Dame, 1982), p. 139.

3. Donald J. Dietrich, *The Goethezeit and the Metamorphosis of Catholic Theology in the Age of Idealism* (Bern: Peter Lang, 1979), p. 165.

4. O'Meara, p. 145.

5. Ibid., p. 146.

6. Dietrich, p. 244; O'Meara, pp. 263 f.

7. Hunermann, pp. 119 f.

8. Klaus Reinhardt, *Der dogmatische Schriftgebrauch in der katholischen und protestantischen Christologie von der Aufklärung bis zur Gegenwart* (Munich: Ferdinand Schoningh, 1970), pp. 111 f.

9. Peter Hunermann (ed.), *Franz Anton Staudenmaier, Wegbereiter heutiger Theologie*, vol. one, p. 99, ed. by Heinrich Fries and Johannes Finsterholzl (Graz: Styria, 1975).

10. Franz Anton Staudenmaier, *Encyclopaedie der theologischen Wissenschaft* (second edition), p. VI:399, six vols. (Mainz: 1840; reprinted Frankfurt: Minerva, 1968).

11. Dietrich, p. 172.

12. Staudenmaier, p. 383.

13. Ibid., pp. 385, 387 f.

14. Ibid., p. 639.

15. Ibid., pp. 636 f.

16. Ibid., p. 638.

17. Ibid., pp. 641 f.

18. Ibid., p. 402.

19. Ibid., pp. 393 ff.

20. Reinhardt, p. 114.

21. Staudenmaier, p. 643.

22. Ibid., pp. 644 f.

23. Staudenmaier, *Encyclopaedie*, p. VI:649; *Johannes Scotus Erigena und die Wissenschaft seiner Zeit* (Frankfurt, 1834), p. 215.

24. Staudenmaier, *Encyclopaedie*, pp. 646 f.

25. Ibid., pp. 657, 661 ff.

26. Ibid., pp. 664 ff.

27. Ibid., pp. 670-677.

28. Ibid., pp. 679 f.

29. Ibid., pp. 682 f.

30. Ibid., p. 691.

31. Ibid., pp. 695 f.

32. Ibid., p. 700.

33. Ibid., p. 703 f.

34. Karl Adam, "Die katholische Tübinger Schule," *Hochland* 24/2 (1926–27):393.

35. Franz Wolfinger, "Johannes Evangelist von Kuhn (1806–1887)," in *Katholische Theologen Deutschlands im 19. Jahrhundert*, II:134, ed. by Heinrich Fries and Georg Schwaiger, three vols. (Munich: Kösel, 1977).

36. Ibid., pp. 139 f.

37. Josef Rupert Geiselmann, "Der Glaube an Jesus Christus—Mythos oder Geschichte? Zur Auseinandersetzung Joh. Ev. Kuhn mit David Friedrich Strauss," *Theologische Quartalschrift* 129 (1949):436.

38. O'Meara, p. 158.

39. Walter Kasper, *Glaube und Geschichte* (Mainz: Matthias-Grünewald, 1970), p. 25.

40. Reinhardt, pp. 155 ff.

41. Johannes Evangelist Kuhn, *Das Leben Jesu* (Mainz, 1838; reprinted Frankfurt: Minerva, 1968), p. 458.

42. James T. Burtchaell, "Drey, Möhler, and the Catholic Tübingen School," in *Nineteenth Century Religious Thought in the West*, II:28 f., ed. by Ninian Smart, three vols. (Cambridge: Cambridge University, 1986).

43. M. Glossner, "Die Tübinger katholisch-theologische Schule, vom speculativen Standpunkt kritisch beleuchtet," *Jahrbuch für Philosophie und spekulative Theologie* 16 (1902):45 f.

44. Dietrich, p. 182.

45. St. Loesch, "Die katholische-theologischen Fakultäten zu Tübingen und Giessen (1830-1850)," *Theologische Quartalschrift* 108 (1927):175.

46. Ibid., p. 174.

47. Kuhn, pp. 21, 85 f., 458 f.

48. Reinhardt, p. 152.

49. Josef Rupert Geiselmann, *Die lebendige Überlieferung als Norm des christlichen Glaubens* (Freiburg: Herder, 1959) p. 45.

50. Josef Rupert Geiselmann, *Jesus der Christus. Erster Teil: Die Frage nach dem historischem Jesus* (second edition; Munich: Kösel, 1965), pp. 24 f.

51. Kuhn, pp. 85 f.

52. Geiselmann, *Die lebendige Überlieferung*, pp. 44 f.

53. Kuhn, pp. 6 f.

54. Ibid., p. 452.

55. Geiselmann, *Die lebendige Überlieferung*, p. 47.

56. Ibid., p. 46.

57. Kuhn, pp. ix-xii.

58. Ibid., pp. 454 f.

59. Johannes Evangelist Kuhn, *Katholisches Dogmatik. Zweite Band: Die christliche Lehre von der göttlichen Dreieinigkeit* (Tübingen, 1857; reprinted Frankfurt: Minerva, 1968), pp. 58 ff.

60. Ibid., p. 63.

61. Ibid., pp. 69 ff.

62. Ibid., p. 73.

63. See John Hick (ed.), *The Myth of God Incarnate* (Philadelphia: Westminster, 1977), and James D. G. Dunn, *Christology in the Making* (Philadelphia: Westminster, 1980), as examples of the modern rejection of Christ's pre-existence for mythological and exegetical reasons.

64. Kuhn, *Das Leben Jesu*, p. 441.

65. Kuhn, *Dogmatik*, p. 50.

66. Reinhardt, p. 353.

67. Kuhn, *Das Leben Jesu*, pp. 441 f.

68. Ibid., pp. 478 ff.

69. Kuhn, *Dogmatik*, pp. 66 ff.

70. Ibid., pp. 74 f. Bruce Metzger, who has done considerable work with the text of Romans 9:5, does not agree the evidence is as overwhelmingly conclusive for the reading that Christ is God as Kuhn believed. See B. M. Metzger, *A Textual Commentary on the Greek New Testament* (New York: United Bible Society, 1975), pp. 520 ff., where Metzger discusses the various alternative punctuations and the arguments for each as considered by the committee that prepared the third edition of the Greek New Testament.

71. Glossner, pp. 43 f. Here Glossner charged Kuhn held the two natures of Christ existed solely in a moral union that was based on an ideal concept and had volitional quality. The Incarnation was nothing more than a "personal appearance of God." Glossner did not say whether by the latter he meant it was of the same sort as the Old Testament theophanies or even something docetic. Glossner further charged Kuhn held the only difference between Christ and the redeemed was in grade, not in kind.

72. Kuhn, *Dogmatik*, p. 57.

73. Ibid., p. 478.

74. Ibid., p. 465.

75. Ibid., pp. 430 ff.

76. Ibid., pp. 386 f.

77. Geiselmann, *Die lebendige Überlieferung*, p. 44.

78. Dietrich, p. 178; Wolfinger, p. 153.

79. Only with Paul Schanz in the next generation will we see a Tübinger entering into serious conversation with the natural and social sciences.

CHAPTER V

PAUL SCHANZ

During the second half of the nineteenth century, the Tübingen School was eclipsed by other movements within Roman Catholic theology, especially the Neoscholasticism newly designated by Leo XIII as *the* Roman Catholic theology. Developments outside the Church, especially in the natural sciences, raised serious questions concerning the viability of traditional Christian doctrines, particularly those dealing with creation and the supernatural. In the late nineteenth century, Protestant theologians began to accept Darwinian evolution. Their biblical exegesis increasingly reflected the new critical attempts to explain Christian faith in ways consistent with the new scientific hypotheses.

It was in this environment that the third generation of Catholic Tübingers appeared. Paul Schanz (1841–1905) is the key representative of the theology of this depleted and ignored generation. Like his predecessors, Schanz was born and educated in Swabia. In addition to studying philosophy and theology at Tübingen, Schanz studied mathematics and natural science. After one year as a parish priest, Schanz returned to Tübingen as a tutor. He went on to study in Paris and Berlin before going to Rottweil to teach mathematics and science. Schanz continued to study and write on issues in mathematics and science even after he moved to Tübingen. In 1876, Schanz became professor of New Testament exegesis on the Catholic Tübingen faculty. Seven years later, he succeeded his teacher Kuhn in the chair of dogmatics and apologetics.

While teaching the New Testament, Schanz began writing commentaries on the four gospels. His style was historical-critical and philological and did not deal significantly with the theological and dogmatic content of the texts. Schanz also wrote extenively on aspects of the Church for the *Theologische Quartalschrift*, dealing particularly with the historical development of the sacraments. He wrote a significant volume on the Roman Catholic doctrine of the sacraments, but his major theological work was a three-volume Christian apologetic. The latter, soon translated into English, is the primary source for understanding his Christology.

As a third-generation Tübinger, Schanz faced a situation entirely different from that confronting his predecessors. This was the reason for his concentration on apologetics. Although Schanz was a disciple of Kuhn, the changed theological situation led him to develop his theology in a different direction from Kuhn's. The crisis in theology no longer lay in the interplay of theology and philosophy as much as in the relation between theology and the natural sciences, particularly the issues raised by naturalism. Schanz came to conclude the Christian faith and evolutionary world views were incompatible.

Heinrich Fries has said that in responding to the questions raised by natural science, Schanz remained true to the spirit of the Catholic Tübingen School. The effect of the increasing influence of science was a worldview that left no room for theology. True to the Tübingen concern to produce theology relevant to its contemporaries, Schanz constructed an apologetic that was primarily defensive. Schanz's apologetic has long since been superseded, but Fries thinks it met the needs of his time. Fries concluded Schanz never reached the height and brilliance of the earlier Tübingers, but suggested this says as much about the changed situation Schanz faced as it does about Schanz.[1]

As had his predecessors, Schanz emphasized theology could not be done apart from an understanding of both its historical and systematic elements. He continued the Tübingen concern for interdisciplinary studies by his concentration on both exegesis and theology. In keeping with the changed times, he added the natural sciences to his areas of concern. By bringing together exegesis, theology, and science, Schanz sought to specify the contribution and limits of each field. His style of theologizing was more reminiscent of Drey and Möhler's concern with the development of doctrine than of Kuhn's theological speculation.

Whereas the earlier Tübingers had grounded the Christian faith in such external criteria as miracles and prophecy, Schanz tried also to show Christianity provided an answer to humanity's current situation and state of mind. By incorporating this existential element, he sought to protect Christianity from the charge it was something external and foreign to the real needs and concerns of humanity. This led Schanz to write a number of articles dealing with contemporary apologetic concerns.[2] The full measure of his apologetics is to be found in his three volume *Apologie des Christentums*.[3] The second volume contains a long study of Christology and soteriology.

Schanz took a traditional approach to Christology, but dealt more fully with the problems raised by critical study than did his predecessors.

Schanz' apologetic showed great familiarity with the work of individual critics and with the attempts of traditionalists to respond to them. Nonetheless, Schanz followed traditional apologetic lines, basing his conclusions on Scripture and the patristic writers. He utilized his training in New Testament studies to evaluate the biblical sources, sometimes accepting the results of critics and at other times rejecting them.

The Gospels

The synoptic problem was a major issue for Schanz as he sought to explain the relationship existing among the first three gospels and then the relationship between these and the fourth. He suggested harmonization, dependence, and differing purposes for composition were the best explanations of the relationship between the gospels. Based on the witness of Papias, Schanz accepted the traditional authorship claimed for each of the gospels. He was especially concerned to defend the traditional claim that the apostle John authored the fourth gospel. He also tried to defend John against charges of being anti-Jewish by explaining the setting for his negative references to the Jews. Schanz presented the arguments for Marcan priority among the synoptics, and stated a personal preference for combining Griesbach and the Mark-hypothesis to achieve a result along the line of Augustine's. His arguments for the priority of Matthew are unconvincing today. He said the distinctive organization of the gospels came about because Jesus' teaching had been collected into various groups for homiletical and catechetical purposes, each tradition selecting certain key events out of Jesus' life. Each gospel author probably wrote out of a different tradition.[4]

Schanz agreed with critics that the gospels cannot be used as biographies of Jesus because the authors omitted too many details. The authors of the gospels recorded only those teachings and actions of Jesus that highlighted his superhuman and divine nature.[5] The gospels, said Schanz, were written for believers and presupposed a knowledge of the Christian faith. Matthew wrote to strengthen and comfort Jewish Christians, Mark sought to show gentile Christians that Jesus is the Son of God, and Luke sought to strengthen Pauline gentile Christians in their new-found faith. Matthew arranged his account of Jesus with reference to the Old Testament and showed more concern for the overall pattern than for details. Mark and Luke followed more closely the actual history of Jesus because they were not as interested in the messianic concept.

Because both internal and external evidence support the claim the gospels were written by apostles or their associates they are excellent authorities for Jesus' life, even should one not accept them as inspired writings.[6] As a result, Schanz did not hesitate to harmonize accounts where this would result in no harm to any of the accounts. He argued the authors of the gospels lacked the intellect to create, write, and preach a gospel that went so far beyond the range of contemporary Jewish thought. Had Jesus never existed or had he not spoken and acted as he did, the gospel writers would have been greater figures than the hero they created.

Using the gospels and secular historical accounts, Schanz attempted to come up with precise details regarding Jesus' life and ministry. Such details included the date of Jesus' birth, his age at the start of his ministry, the length of that ministry, and the details of his passion. Schanz explored each of these topics at length in the second volume of his apologetics. He depended primarily on the fourth gospel because it set out the major milestones in Jesus' ministry.[7] Among the synoptics, however, Luke was by far the most important and served as the stepping stone to John's account.[8]

John's focus was incarnational: the Word became flesh. The Logos Christology responded to the popular philosophy of the time, but this was not Greek philosophy. John took his lead from the wisdom books of the Hebrew Scriptures. Schanz said John introduced the Logos as something with which his readers were already familiar and which would serve to prepare the readers for the proper scope of his gospel. The fourth gospel occupies a central position among the sources for Jesus' life. It provides both the clearest statement of Jesus' deity and a three-year structure by which to organize Jesus' public career. Thus it is the only gospel that enables us to calculate the length of Jesus' public ministry. Schanz said the synoptic accounts were consistent with a multi-year ministry such as that found explicitly in John because they reported Jesus as making more than one festal journey.

The synoptic authors had a purpose similar to that intended by John in his use of a Logos Christology, but they expressed it by presenting Jesus as one who recognized his messianic calling from the start of his public ministry. Schanz said only if Jesus had understood the prophecies of the Jewish Scriptures to be about his person could he have pointed to them with such certainty to justify his words and actions. He further said it is unreasonable to read the prophecies back into Jesus' life because no figure existed in the Scriptures who could have served as a sufficient model for Jesus. Even Strauss, he said, was unable to point to any gospel narrative he could show to have been an imitation of any particular Old Testament text. Strauss was forced instead to draw pieces from various places and say that taken as a whole they provided the basis for the gospels.[9]

Mark's gospel shows Jesus to be a divine being who brought a new doctrine from heaven and confirmed his mission by performing miracles. The prohibition Mark recorded against the public announcement of Jesus' miracles was intended to prevent any misunderstanding of his messianic role. A second reason Mark included this prohibition was that he believed the miracles were neither intended to nor able to produce faith in and of themselves.[10]

The Pauline letters are so saturated with belief in Jesus' deity, said Schanz, that it is impossible to understand them apart from this perspective. Paul did not consider the Incarnation to be Jesus' initial state of existence—it was the transition period between his pre-existence in the form of God and the assumption into heaven of a glorified human nature. Paul did not derive his belief in Christ's pre-existence from popular belief or from Christ's appearance, but built his doctrine on traditions derived from John.[11] Schanz failed, however, to explain how this could be if Paul wrote nearly half a century earlier than John. Paul's belief in Christ's pre-existence served as the foundation for both his faith and his doctrine.

The Person of Christ

The New Testament uniformly portrays Jesus in all his words and deeds as a single individual and ascribes both divine and human actions to this one individual. Nowhere, however, does it attempt to explain how this can be so. Schanz said this lack of explanation can lead to christological difficulties because it is possible to understand the union of the divine and human inadequately and thereby endanger the unity of the person of Jesus. Too exact a delineation of the unity of the person can jeopardize the distinction between and integrity of the natures. According to Schanz, the hypostatic union will always make the earthly life of Jesus appear superhuman. In actuality it had but a truly human character, that of the only ideal human ever to walk the face of the earth.[12]

Schanz' presentation of the hypostatic union and its effects was an extreme example of conservative Christology, presenting a one-sided interpretation of the formula of Chalcedon. It is difficult to understand how it could have been an acceptable apologetic to anyone other than a person already committed to the position.

Like most of his Catholic contemporaries, Schanz advocated an incarnational Christology. This is to say his Christology focused almost exclusively on the Incarnation as the sufficient explanation for the entirety of Jesus' accomplishments. All else becomes virtually an addendum to the

Incarnation. The Incarnation demonstrated God's infinite love for humanity, apparently because God condescended to enter into humanity (Phil 2:6). For Tübingers from Möhler on, however, an incarnational Christology also served ecclesiologically to vindicate Catholic claims for the priority of the visible Church against what they saw as a Protestant tendency toward spiritualizing the Church.

Beginning with Möhler, the Tübingers saw the Church as the continuation of the Incarnation (Schanz was at one with this traditional Tübingen stance). The visible and physical nature of Christ's incarnation thus seemed to them to require an equally visible and physical Church to continue his work. Both the Incarnation and the cross show how much God hates sin because both were aspects of the sacrifice necessary on the part of God the Son to appease the Father's eschatological wrath and expiate human guilt.[13] In the act of becoming the God–man Jesus, as it were, carried out the whole work of human redemption. Schanz defined this redemptive work as the uniting of the divine and human and said human redemption is but a continuation of the hypostatic union achieved in the Incarnation.

What Schanz presented here was not unique to him. Most Roman Catholics, and some conservative Protestants, of his day advocated this understanding of the meaning of salvation. The modern position of Karl Rahner resembles Schanz's at this point, with its emphasis on the redemptive nature of the Incarnation. Some have criticized this position severely because it can appear to make Jesus' life, ministry, and death superfluous, all that was necessary for salvation having occurred at his birth. Understood in this way, the position raises serious ethical questions concerning the nature and character of a God who would permit the humiliating crucifixion of his Son to no real purpose. Such an understanding is contrary to the traditional Christian doctrine of God. As such, it would be rejected as not intrinsic to this view by those who, like Schanz, advocate an incarnation-centered Christology. The question remains, however, whether it is not the logical conclusion of that which advocates of this position are saying.

Schanz' christological emphasis was on the deity of Jesus. This is probably because it was Jesus' deity, not his humanity, that was under severe attack at the time. Schanz argued the New Testament was as clear about Jesus' deity as it was about his humanity. The synoptics stressed Jesus' deity from the earliest part of his ministry. John differed from the synoptics at this point because he reflected on the evidence of the synoptics in light of everything that had occurred since the cross. The key for Schanz was that John and the synoptics differed only in their emphases, not in their underlying belief. John taught Jesus' deity most clearly, but the leading Church fathers showed the synoptics also taught Jesus' deity.[14]

Prophecy and Miracles

Schanz agreed with his Tübingen predecessors that the two strongest witnesses to Jesus' deity were biblical prophecy and his miracles. A significant part of the gospels dealt with the fulfillment of prophecy. Prophecy showed Jesus to be both Son of God and Son of David; unlike Kuhn, Schanz understood Son of God to be a title of deity. Prophecy also told of a Messiah who would one day establish a new covenant, a new law, and a new kingdom. It was with this title of Messiah that Schanz was most concerned. To be the Messiah, argued Schanz, Jesus had to perform miracles. In and of themselves, these miracles showed nothing about Jesus, but in conjunction with his claim these miracles were a confirmation of his deity, they constituted a proof of his claim.

"Jesus did the works of the Father to show that he was not a mere envoy, but truly the Son of God, and God." The miracles were significant solely in that they show Jesus was the Messiah. The healings in particular were a picture of spiritual healing and served as an incentive to faith.[15] Schanz said in the fourth gospel the miracles served as a testimony that Jesus is the divine Son of God and provided a basis for faith in him. The miracles revealed Jesus' glory.[16]

In his defense of Jesus' miracles, Schanz did not entirely ignore the arguments of his opponents. He defended all the miracle accounts as true, saying the rationalist denial of the miraculous required a greater credulity than did belief in the reality of miracles.[17] He considered the alternative explanations provided by contemporary critics more difficult to believe than the gospel accounts. The effect on nature of the rationalists' explanations would have been almost as miraculous as were the biblical accounts.

Jesus' Humanity

Although he placed inordinate stress on Jesus' deity, Schanz did not ignore his humanity. Christ as a man was inferior to the Father, but this was only a temporary condition. In the eternal Trinitarian relationship, the Son could be considered subordinate (not inferior) only in the sense of being eternally generated from the Father. Schanz said Jesus was like other humans in everything except sinfulness. The Bible teaches Jesus' sinlessness both directly and indirectly. Schanz defined sinlessness as freedom—the renunciation of the world's domination and the subduing of sensuality and concupiscence. Always and everywhere, Jesus' actions were morally perfect and his knowledge without error. His human and divine knowledge and will were always in perfect accord. Schanz said because Jesus was human as well as divine, it was possible that as a man he did not know every particular the Father knows.[18]

After this concession to the human Jesus' lack of omniscience, Schanz reversed field by saying

> the Son of God made use of human nature and his connec-
> tion with earth only in so far as was necessary to fulfill his
> work of redemption, and to raise human nature to a parti-
> cipation of the divine.[19]

Such a conclusion was not only incredible to his adversaries; it is also inconsistent with the spirit of the Bible and of the early christological creeds, which emphasized Jesus' true humanity and the fullness of his human experience, as Tübingers both before and since Schanz have contended. Schanz' position was unfortunately all too representative of the Catholic defenders of orthodoxy in his day. He did point out Luke's gospel contained the fullest account of Jesus' humanity of the four, as well as carefully depicting his human spiritual activity.

Schanz accepted the position held by, among others, the early Tübingers that human nature has "an inborn striving... after the infinite and eternal, and for union with the Godhead."[20] In Jesus this union became not merely moral but was also physical. This meant it is both complete and perfect. Schanz concluded Jesus is thus perfect human and God. Because of this miraculous union, Christians since the time of Origen have called Jesus the God—man.

Jesus' human nature, however, has been "so influenced by the divine that it is entirely free of those spiritual imperfections from which no man as such is exempt."[21] Further, the Jesus who walked the earth was not merely an individual human; he was the ideal Man. As such, he was the representative and universal possession of all humanity. Because Jesus possessed a perfect human nature, he stood as a universal as well as a particular. This concept of Jesus' perfection has always been a stumbling block in the way of understanding Jesus' full humanity. Schanz was little help at this point, probably because of his focus on the Incarnation. He quoted Luke 2:40 and

52, which said Jesus grew and increased in wisdom, but refused to discuss what this meant for Jesus' person.[22]

More recent theologians have stressed that we must understand Jesus' perfection in the context of his growth and development as a human so he could learn and grow as other humans do. The key to this position is that Jesus must be seen as perfect (without error and without sin) at each level of human development, and no more be required at each step than is consistent with that step.

Schanz dealt with Jesus primarily as the Messiah. This was a result of his appreciation of biblical prophecy. He saw Isaiah, Micah, and Zechariah as portraying the Messiah in both human and divine terms. He also cited Daniel and some of the intertestamental Jewish literature to the same effect. Schanz portrayed the Messiah as being at the same time Son of David and Son of God. To him, the divine nature of the Messiah was self-evident. Without using the language, Schanz described him as prophet, priest, and king, using numerous Old Testament citations to support his conclusion. Jesus' very nature qualified him to be Messiah, but he was not installed in the office of Messiah until his baptism by John. This marked the end of his private life and the beginning of his public ministry. Schanz equated his public ministry with his work of redemption, even though he had already explained redemption in terms of the Incarnation.

Salvation

Schanz addressed this work of redemption in terms of Jesus' obedience to the Father. Essential to this was Jesus' sinlessness. Schanz responded to those critics who claimed the evidence of the gospels was insufficient to reach any conclusion regarding Jesus' sinlessness because they tell us nothing of Jesus inner life which, as Jesus himself said, is the seat of human sin. Schanz argued the gospels do indeed provide insight into Jesus' inner life, both directly through that which he said about himself and indirectly through the challenges he put before his adversaries.[23]

Despite his concern to discuss details of Jesus' filial obedience, Schanz virtually ignored Jesus' passion and death. This is the aspect theologians past and present have treated as the culmination of his obedience, there being no greater obedience than obedience unto death.

Schanz dealt briefly with the result of Jesus' death by discussing the effect of Christ's atoning work. Even here, however, he played down the place of the cross by saying only that

the God—man, by his example, his teaching and his divine
precepts really wishes to save all men and to impart his
grace to all... the grace that Christ merited for us on the
Cross.[24]

Schanz said only in the name of Jesus is salvation possible, but he did not
explain how Jesus had made salvation possible. He mentioned the cross in
several contexts but did not explain its place in Christ's work. The Incarnation appears to have had greater salvific importance for Schanz than did
Christ's death. The atonement was universal in its extent; it remains only
for individuals to accept this provision God has made for them.

Passing over the cross, Schanz proceeded to the Resurrection. This
"set a seal on Christ's entire life." Had the Resurrection not occurred,
Christ's whole life would have been meaningless. Neither his example nor
his teaching would have had a purpose. The Resurrection was the greatest
miracle of Christ's ministry. The prophets had predicted it; Jesus himself
had cited it as a witness to the unbelieving Jews. Because this event of
Jesus' life has been attacked more heavily than any other, Schanz determined
to examine the evidence for it closely. He said the proofs are both historical
and psychological. The Resurrection is taught clearly in each of the gospels
and in Paul's letters. The accounts in these sources are not entirely in
agreement—and they cannot be perfectly reconciled—but minute discrepancies cannot cancel the truth of the whole. Schanz used his earlier statement
that each gospel was written for a particular theological purpose to explain
and justify the presence of discrepancies in the accounts.[25]

The key points in Schanz' presentation of the Resurrection were the
multiple eyewitness reports, attestation the Resurrection was bodily, the
psychological predisposition of the disciples against any resurrection hope,
and the behavior of the disciples after Jesus' death which could not be explained in terms of his death alone.[26] Schanz said the basic objection of his
contemporaries to belief in the Resurrection was a predisposition against the
supernatural despite evidence contrary to this view. He concluded the
various alternatives suggested were far more incredible and lacking in evidence than were the gospel accounts.

Conclusion

Fries was generous when he said Schanz's apologetic met the needs
of his time and the changed conditions he faced were at least as significant
as Schanz' personal qualities in rendering his work less brilliant and exalted

than that of his Tübingen predecessors. Certainly the changed conditions of the last third of the century, especially the *Syllabus of Errors* (1864) and its fallout limited severely Schanz's freedom to interact with contemporary developments in the way earlier Tübingers had. This was true even of Kuhn who ceased writing during the last fifteen years of his life rather than risk a Roman censure. Schanz's apologetic, however, bears too many marks of traditional, pre-critical apologetics for us to consider this the only reason for his approach. It is possible this applies only to his christological work, because Fries, Scheffczyk, and Geiselmann, all respected modern theologians associated with the Tübingen faculty, either as students or as teachers, commented favorably on Schanz's apologetic as a whole and endorsed his place as a theologian faithful to the Catholic Tübingen School.

Schanz provided a classical Christology "from above"—certainly not in itself a bad thing—but his Christology never quite touched the ground. He worked in reaction to Christologies "from below" that never quite left the ground, and he sought to defend the deity of Christ against attempts to make him exclusively human. He often mentioned Jesus' full humanity, but almost as often he proceeded to submerge it in his deity. Schanz in many places presented a monophysitic Christology. Although he probably would have denied this warmly on hearing it so described, every time Schanz discussed the humanity of Jesus, he concluded by swallowing it up in his deity.

At many points, Schanz dealt with the results of critical exegesis and presented his own contrary conclusions. Too often these conclusions are unsatisfying even in terms of the work of his day. Having charged his opponents with selectivity in their use of evidence and refusal to allow their presuppositions to be criticized by the evidence, Schanz fell into the same error. A modern conservative, Catholic or Protestant, would be dissatisfied with Schanz' arguments even when accepting the conclusions his arguments were intended to prove.

Why Schanz concentrated on the title Messiah for Jesus in a gentile context is a mystery. Granted that it is consistent with his use of Old Testament prophecy to argue for Jesus' deity, even Schanz admitted Mark and Luke de-emphasized the title in their gospels because they wrote for gentile audiences to whom the title Messiah was not particularly meaningful. Further, this use of the messianic concept should have led him to a greater consideration of Jesus' death because Christians traditionally have understood several Old Testament passages (e.g., Psalm 22; Isaiah 53) in terms of the suffering servant who is also the Messiah. Because Schanz's Christology focused almost exclusively on the Incarnation, it failed to deal with the entirety of the biblical evidence and raised a whole new set of problems in understanding the nature of God. It ignored much of the content of Mark's gospel, which has been called a passion story with a long introduction.

In conclusion, we find in Schanz both continuity and discontinuity with the Christology of earlier Tübingers. Schanz appears to have tried to work in the spirit of early Tübingen, but his results fell far short. Granted that the times were less conducive to innovative Catholic theology, Schanz' Christology never quite came to grips with the essence of his opponents' arguments. He did better than many of his Catholic contemporaries, but it would appear he might have done better still and at the same time escaped censure by Rome. As Schanz' work differed from his mentor's, so would that of the next Tübingen christologist differ from Schanz's in consciously seeking to return to the spirit of the early Tübingers.

1. Heinrich Fries, "Paul von Schanz (1841–1905)," III:190 ff., in *Katholische Theologen Deutschlands im 19. Jahrhundert*, ed. by Heinrich Fries and Georg Schwaiger, three vols. (Munich: Kösel, 1975).

2. Ibid., p. 200. Schanz' bibliography includes books and articles on Nicholas of Cusa as mathematician and astronomer, Galileo, Christian worldviews and modern science, theology as a science, education, naturalism and spiritualism, cosmology, changing worldviews, American and French theology, authority and science, and a variety of other articles on apologetics as such, in addition to his exegetical and history of doctrine works. A complete bibliography can be found in Fries, pp. 212–213.

3. Paul Schanz, *A Christian Apology*, trans. by Michael F. Glancey and Victor J. Schobel, three vols. (New York: Fr. Pustet, 1896).

4. Schanz, II:459 ff.

5. Ibid., p. 575. Schanz was inconsistent as this point because, in other places, he said that the same gospels display Jesus' humanity.

6. Ibid., p. 486.

7. Ibid., pp. 496 ff.

8. Ibid., pp. 491 f.

9. Ibid., pp. 551, 553.

10. Ibid., pp. 563, 601.

11. Ibid., pp. 526, 529 f.

12. Ibid., pp. 577 f.

13. Ibid., p. 601. This brief comment about the cross is virtually all he has to say about Jesus' death. This is particularly interesting in that most modern Christology puts Jesus' death and resurrection in the center of his story. O'Collins has been especially critical of the disregard of this key event

sequence in Jesus' life (see Gerald O'Collins, *What Are They Saying About Jesus?* (revised edition; New York: Paulist, 1983), pp. 6 f.).

14. Ibid., pp. 517 ff.

15. Ibid., pp. 560 f.

16. Ibid., p. 564.

17. Ibid., p. 570.

18. Ibid., p. 532.

19. Ibid., p. 593.

20. Ibid., pp. 576 f.

21. Ibid.

22. Ibid., p. 579.

23. Ibid., pp. 589 f.

24. Ibid., pp. 607 f.

25. Ibid., pp. 503 f.

26. Ibid., pp. 508 ff.

CHAPTER VI

KARL ADAM

The second half of the 19th century and the early years of the 20th century had witnessed the decline and loss of influence of the Catholic Tübingen School. In 1919, however, a theologian born and raised in Bavaria, and thus not a product of Tübingen, was called to teach dogmatics on the Catholic faculty. Karl Adam (1876–1966) was to have a major impact on Roman Catholic theology during the interwar years and to return the Catholic Tübingen faculty to a position of honor and influence in modern theology. Adam originally came to Tübingen because he found the intellectual climate there more congenial to his studies than that of his first teaching position at Strassburg. He continued to teach at Tübingen until 1949, despite numerous attempts to draw him to other universities, and wrote influential books even after his retirement.

Although those who see the Catholic Tübingen School as ending with Kuhn and Staudenmaier (or possibly Schanz) have not considered Adam a member of the School, Adam himself sought consciously to be of the same spirit as his predecessors on the faculty. He has been described as one who did theology "out of the spirit of the Catholic Tübingen School."[1] Following Adam, we see a revival of the concerns of the early Tübingers and a renewed interest in their work. We can also trace a direct line from Adam through J. R. Geiselmann to Walter Kasper.

Adam was a prolific writer whose books and articles dealt in whole or in part with Christology. Because most of these books were translated into a number of languages, Adam influenced Catholic thought far beyond the bounds of Germany. His influence was such that he has been called the "forgotten forerunner of Vatican II."[2] Several of his books presented Christology and ecclesiology in terms at variance with the reigning Neoscholastic theology. This required their modification before the Church would approve their publication. Despite the continued concern of the Roman Curia, however, none of Adam's books was ever placed on the Index, nor was he ever disciplined. One reason for this was Adam's expressed opinion that theology was a community, not an individual, affair. Thus, he was willing to submit to Church authorities when required.[3]

Adam felt an affinity with the Catholic Tübingen School, especially Möhler, and was comfortable with its concern to synthesize speculative theology and historical theology with the morphology of dogmas and an openness to the currents and problems of contemporary society.[4] Hofmann has said the point where Adam's theology most clearly grew out of the old Tübingen School was in his consideration of Christ's person and work and of the mystery of revelation through him. Adam was not satisfied with merely restating the old in new words, but attempted to respond to new questions with new answers. This concern was the basis for Hofmann's statement that Adam's theology was from the *spirit* of the Catholic Tübingen School.[5] Hofmann went on to say

> Karl Adam saw Christ not only in his unity with the Father, but also in his oneness with us. We must think back to theologians like Augustine and Möhler if we want to find so intensive a consciousness of the solid bond of humans in guilt and grace as we meet in Adam.[6]

Like Möhler, Adam saw Christ and his Church as the central truth of Christianity. Adam's intense concern for the Church, evident in his best-known work, *The Spirit of Catholicism*,[7] reflected the emphasis of the Catholic Tübingen School from its earliest days. The Tübingen perspective always risked confusing Christology and ecclesiology, and Adam was not immune from this danger. Christology stood at the center of Adam's theology, but he said Jesus Christ can be known directly only through the mediation of the Church.[8]

The aspect of Adam's Christology most familiar to theologians is his renewal of Catholic interest in the humanity of Jesus. As Hofmann pointed out, however, Adam believed that unless it were anchored in his divine essence, Jesus' humanity remained unexplainable.[9] Adam was no prisoner of the proverbial ivory tower. His Christology did not merely convey theological knowledge but also fertilized the religious life of his hearers and readers because Adam's dogmatic theology and personal piety always existed in an inner unity. Adam sought in a simple and practical way to respond to people's needs and concerns in a way that could affect their daily lives. He intended theology to be practical, not otherworldly.

In describing Adam's relation to the Tübingen School, Hofmann said it was through the Tübingen tradition that Adam's Bavarian theological training reached maturity. Only in terms of the Catholic Tübingen School can one understand Adam's theology.[10]

Hofmann said for the younger generation of theologians, Adam stands with Drey, Möhler, Kuhn, and other intellectual leaders of the 19th century Tübingen School. As they had rethought the message of the Bible and the teachings of the fathers in their generations, so would Adam for the early 20th century.[11] When he assumed a chair of dogmatics at Tübingen in 1919, Adam committed himself publicly to carrying out the very heritage with which Hofmann identified him. Adam sought to continue the mission of the early Tübingers by creating for his era a theology of life that conceived the individual truths of faith in terms of their historical development and organic connection, not simply as a system of formulas and definitions. Adam wanted to respond to the claims of his time and confront the modern problems posed by phenomenology and psychology of religion with the deposit of traditional Catholicism.

The context of Adam's thought differed significantly from that of his Tübingen predecessors. Adam was a leader of the Neo-Romantic movement that followed World War I and was influenced by the life philosophy of his time. He also had a keen sense of historical development and drew heavily from Augustine. Life philosophy opposed both the Enlightenment and scientism. It was totally opposed to modern immanentist philosophy. The life that the fundamentals of Adam's theology constructed is the life of God in us as we have experienced it through the revelation we find in the Church. This philosophy, deriving from both Dilthey and Bergson, opened Adam to the non-rational element in Christ and in the Church. He saw personality as the creative carrier of life and community as an organic whole.

Drawing on psychology of religion, Adam attempted to construct a psychology of Jesus. Out of his Tübingen heritage, Adam used Möhler's Romantic theology to show the Church to be *the* way of approaching Christ and the Scriptures.[12] The philosophical and political situation existing in Weimar Germany was a strange mixture of optimism and fatalism and Adam's early work reflected this. *The Spirit of Catholicism*, written in 1924, shows clearly his optimism.

Unlike Karl Barth, whose career began about the same time, Adam never occupied himself with criticism of his culture. On the contrary, he bound himself to the prevailing culture and the new tendencies of intellectual life. Principal among these was phenomenology. Adam said only by being grounded in this method could one achieve the attitude of faith needed to grasp divine revelation. He also used this method to describe both Christ and the Church. Adam advocated a German theology answering specifically German needs in a way appropriate to Germans; he considered scholastic formulations both too difficult to understand and outdated.[13]

As significant for Adam as the trends in contemporary intellectual thought was the situation in the Roman Catholic Church of his day. Adam was trained and did most of his work in the period between the condemnation of Modernism (1907) and the first tentative attempt by Rome to come to terms with modern critical thought (1943). The papacy began to accept the methods of biblical criticism just as Adam entered retirement. The effect of this change on Adam can be seen in the new perspective to be found in his *The Christ of Faith* (1954). Pius X's condemnation of Modernism in *Lamentabili* had placed strict limits on how Catholic scholars could use the Bible as well as on the conclusion they might draw from their research. It had also required adherence to a number of dogmatic propositions regarding the person and work of Christ.[14] Most serious for Catholic scholarship, the papal condemnation of Modernism led not only to constraints on what could be said about theological topics, but equally on how it could be said.

For Adam, the heart of Christianity is Christ and the heart of Christian dogmatics is Christology. That which was implicit in Drey, Möhler, and Kuhn became explicit in Adam. Jesus Christ is the reference point for theological anthropology, soteriology, and ecclesiology. All other dogmas grow out of Christology because they describe how the mystery of Christ influences the individual and the Church. Apart from Christ, these other aspects of dogmatics would never exist. Not only is Jesus Christ the center of Christian faith, he is the ground and cause of that faith.[15] Krieg has written that

> for Adam and the Tübingen School theology does not begin
> with an understanding of the relation of God to the world
> in general or to history. Theology begins with the special,
> with the relation of God and human in Jesus Christ.[16]

As the heart of Christianity, Christ both confirms God is self-revealing and triune and acts as our path to God the Father.

Adam said the task of Christology is to understand the present reality of Christ. We receive this knowledge through tradition. Adam discovered from his work on the relation between Christology and ecclesiology that a void existed in the Christology of his age. Liberalism was not interested in Jesus as he was known by the Church but instead tried to discover a hypothetical form behind the gospels. Liberalism's polar opposite, dialectical theology, exhibited a total lack of interest in the earthly Jesus and, through its denial of the *analogia entis*, risked falling into a latent gnosticism. What was missing, he felt, was the man Jesus as he appeared in the gospel accounts. Adam further considered the Neoscholastic Catholicism of his day incomprehensible to his contemporaries and unbalanced in its presentation of the person of Jesus. The upshot of this was his dedication to the task of formulating the understanding of Jesus Christ in a new way for the Church of his day which would avoid the equal and opposite errors of Protestant liberalism and dialectical theology.[17] Because Christ is known only through the Church, Christology must direct its attention to that person whom the Church confesses as Lord. Adam further intended his research method to reflect the way the Church comes to know Christ. This meant a Christology "from below" that came to see Jesus as the Christ just as the first disciples had. Adam never saw his method as an alternative to Church tradition. He believed the Jesus of history was accessible only through the Church's belief in Christ. Further, as Kasper has argued, it is impossible to separate the Christ of faith from the Jesus of history.[18]

Christ and the Bible

To determine the primary characteristics of Christ, Adam turned to the gospels. In many ways, his biblical exegesis was pre-critical. He accepted the four gospels as accurate historical accounts of Jesus' life and ministry. He did not, however, consider them either biographies or adequate sources from which one might write a biography of Jesus. Krieg has concluded that Adam rejected critical methods in general, but accepted some of their conclusions.[19] Adam insisted on an approach that did not attempt to "go behind" the gospels because he wanted the reader to get the gospels' impression of Jesus. In this way, we can recognize Jesus' personal characteristics. One of the most important of these was Jesus' total dedication to his mission. Even more important, Jesus recognized from the outset of his ministry the unique role the Father had given him. Jesus showed this by his use of the formula, "I have come...." These statements about Jesus' supernatural origin and majesty do not stand in isolation; they always appear in proximity to other statements about Jesus' humanity with its weakness, temptation, and suffering.[20] Adam contrasted this picture of Jesus with the pictures of contemporary deities which the history of religions had attempted to use as sources for the biblical understanding of Jesus.

Adam considered the historical-critical method unsuitable for christological research. He had three reasons for this conclusion. The method begins with an attitude of skepticism toward the sources. It attempts to understand the past in terms of correlation and analogy, yet Jesus Christ is a unique individual for whom there exists no analogy or correlate. Because it presupposes a continuity within history such that nothing could have occurred in the past that does not also occur in the present, the method leaves no room for miracles or any other intervention of the supernatural into the world or its history. Adam described the "pure 'historical' Jesus" resulting from this procedure as a "simple fiction." The method makes a false distinction between the Jesus of history and the Christ of faith. As a result, it never gets to the heart of the matter.[21]

Adam was predisposed against critical methods because he believed there is scarcely any point of reference outside the gospels by which to measure Jesus. In his reading of the gospels, Adam hoped to construct a picture of Jesus' outer and inner being. With an attitude of trust toward the gospel accounts, Adam had no difficulty reconstructing the external life of Jesus. From the impression Jesus made on his disciples and contemporaries, Adam believed he could construct an accurate account of Jesus' self-consciousness and inner life. Krieg describes Adam's approach to the gospels as similar to that of reading a novel, where one would rightly expect to uncover the form of the main characters exclusively from within the story itself.[22] Adam recognized the gospels arose out of the disciples' faith experience, but denied this meant they could not be true reports and could not be understood through the faith of the Church.

Krieg says we have to understand Adam's epistemology before we can appreciate his approach to the Bible. He used a phenomenology derived from Max Scheler. If we want to get to know another person, said Adam, we must begin from a basic attitude of trust, not one of skepticism, toward our subject. Only when we display trust will others open themselves to us. He added that the question about Christ is not merely an intellectual one for us; it is one involving our whole spirituality.[23] Adam's attitude requires we first open ourselves to Christ so he can and will open himself to us. It appears to be similar to Barth's contention that to do Christian theology one must first be a Christian.

Adam considered the two biblical authors who most clearly explained the meaning of Jesus' self-revelation to be John and Paul. Paul was the first systematic theologian and John enlarged upon Paul's Christology. John went to the very heart of the Christian message, composing the most consummate picture of Christ to be found in Scripture. Later theology could add nothing, said Adam; it could only clarify, conceptualize, and systematize that which John had said more simply. Adam saw John as stressing Jesus' humanity in reaction to misunderstandings of Paul that saw him as denying Jesus' humanity in favor of his deity.[24]

In his early Christology, Adam employed no special exegesis and cited no commentaries or monographs. He used the New Testament alone as his source to develop a picture of Jesus. Reinhardt said the synoptics provided his framework for the humanity of Jesus. Adam denied the early community played any creative role in the development of the gospels' picture of Jesus. The synoptics provided Adam with the immediate impression Jesus made on his disciples while John was the source of a conceptual Christology.[25]

The heart of Adam's Christology is Jesus Christ, both God and human, who became our mediator with God through the Incarnation. In contrast to the monophysitic tendencies that characterized much of Catholic spirituality, Adam continually stressed Christ's full humanity. He said the Incarnation is the essential truth of Christianity because it grounds the truth of redemption. Adam credited Augustine as the Church father who brought out this truth most clearly. This was the approach taken by the earliest Church, he said—not to begin from the pre-incarnate Christ, but from the one who was become human. Having begun from Jesus' humanity, however, the Church went on to affirm this humanity had been taken up into divine glory. It was the "mediatory, redemptive significance of Jesus' humanity" that served as the center of Adam's theological interest.[26]

Jesus' humanity was significant because all humanity forms an organic whole whose destiny was wrapped up in that of the first man Adam. This led Adam to his Second Adam Christology. He derived this from Paul and utilized it in a kenotic direction with a humiliation-exaltation scheme. For Adam, the significance of Jesus being the Son of God was not in the raising of human nature to participation in the divine life but a descent of deity, the divine Word, to the form of a servant. Adam said the Second Person of the Trinity parted with his divine status and entered into human nature.[27]

The decisive understanding of Christ's person must come from what Jesus said about himself. His message of the Kingdom of God was eschatological, not moral. In describing himself as "the Son of Man," Jesus recognized he was more than human. Jesus' belief in his unity with God was evident from the way he saw himself as the fulfillment of Old Testament prophecy, assumed divine prerogatives, acted with divine power, and identified himself with Yahweh. Adam considered Matthew 11:25–27 to be the highest expression of Jesus' self-consciousness in the New Testament.[28]

In developing his kenotic approach, Adam did not downplay Chalcedon. He emphasized that Jesus broke through his humiliation to transcendence. Krieg suggests further that Adam used the two natures doctrine as a filter through which he interpreted the Scriptures.[29] Where he was not bound by dogma, Adam often resorted to Scotist teaching, especially in explaining Christ's human nature.[30]

The Spirit of Catholicism

Adam's first major work was his 1924 *The Spirit of Catholicism*. In this book he followed Möhler and the Catholic Tübingen School in describing the spirit of Catholicism as one that views the Church as the continuation of the Incarnation of Christ. Adam went even further back and saw himself as reflecting Augustine's ecclesiology. He described the Church as the realization on earth of the Kingdom of God. In explaining this, Adam tightly linked Christology and ecclesiology, explicitly uniting the expressed and implied concerns of his Tübingen predecessors. He said Christ is the Lord and real self of the Church and the Church is permeated with his redemptive power. The organic union of Christ and the Church is fundamental to Christian theology.

The Kingdom of God is ultimately an eschatological reality. Christ has established the Kingdom, but did so in embryonic form. The Kingdom will not reach its fullness until after his return in glory. Only then will God's rule be perfected on earth. This idea of the Kingdom also reflected earlier Tübingen thought as Adam used it to present Christianity as an unfolding organic whole that ever remains a unity even as it progresses toward an eschatological fullness.

The dogmas of Christology describe the person of the God-man and tell how the divine glory is expressed through Jesus Christ, but all other doctrines of the Church are equally stamped by Christ and express some aspect of his teaching. This is true not only of doctrine, but also of the Church's morality and worship.[31] That Christ is the head of the Church also explains its hierarchical structure. Authority in the Church derives from Christ, not the community, so its structure must of necessity be hierarchical.[32] Furthermore, Christ is the sole criterion of the Church's preaching; therefore, the Church must stick firmly with its traditional message. Thus, the Church can accept neither modernism nor the spirit of the age. The traditionalism and conservatism of the Church derive from its christocentrism. The centrality of Christ for the Church is also evident in that the controversies of the Church have been dominated traditionally by concern over the person and work of Christ.[33] Despite the antipathy Adam expressed toward the *Zeitgeist,* his consequent writings would show its influence more than this early statement would seem to warrant.

Adam followed Augustine in declaring Christ to be the source of all grace who both proclaims and effects this grace through signs he has designated. These signs are the sacraments. When Christ is permitted to be the center in this way, there is no room left for human intermediaries. In the few pages devoted to Mariology, Adam continued this emphasis. He included Mary among the creatures as one who "has no grace, no virtue, no privilege, which she does not owe to the divine Mediator." Her role for this theologian seemed to be primarily exemplary, though he also described her as "a human strand in the divine robe of our salvation."[34]

Christ came to reunite humanity with God and to do this for humanity as a whole, not as individuals. As the God-man, Christ is the source of this new humanity. Christ is the incarnate God and Savior of humanity. Adam saw the Incarnation as the basis for the Church which mediates human salvation. The Incarnation showed God has condescended to our humanity and this condescension is an enduring reality.

Adam stressed the need for a real, historical experience of Jesus on the part of the disciples. A purely supernatural experience could never claim universal validity because it could be neither tested nor controlled. Thus, against the liberal critics who denied the historicity of Jesus, Adam said the life of Jesus was historically verifiable, and against the dialectical theologians, he said it was important it be verifiable so we know what it is we claim to believe. Nevertheless, Adam rejected all attempts to prove Jesus' deity scientifically. God, he said, would not allow himself to become the object of purely human investigation.[35] Adam was saying that while Jesus was an historical personage, he was at the same time more than that. This underlay his continued emphasis on faith as a necessary ingredient in Christianity.

Adam dealt in a preliminary way with biblical criticism in *Spirit,* first by affirming the intrinsic worth of the scriptural witness, then by challenging the critical method at its source as incompatible with Christianity. This incompatibility resulted from the method's skeptical starting point and inadequacy in dealing with unique individuals and events. He agreed with Möhler that apart from the Bible we would not have the true form of Jesus' sayings. He went on, however, to say the Catholic does not derive his or her faith from the Bible because Catholic faith existed before the New Testament was written. Adam called the Bible "unerring," but also said contradictions and other difficulties exist in the gospel record.[36] The primary means

by which the experience of Jesus has been presented to humanity is tradition, not the literary records of the Bible. This tradition derived from the
apostolic kerygma and has been made alive by the Holy Spirit. Scripture is
inadequate as a complete explanation because it can deal only with that
which is past and, like all literature, is stamped by the character of its
time.[37] Adam said,

> the gospels present us with only a fragmentary record of
> Jesus, from which it is impossible to construct an exhaus-
> tive picture.... So I learn the complete Christ, not from the
> Bible, but from the uniform life of faith of the whole
> Church, a life fertilized by the teaching of the apostles.[38]

Thus, we find the living Christ only through the living Church.

The critical theology is a child of the Enlightenment and is committed to a method prescribed for it by the secular sciences. Such a
methodology is wrong because it makes Christ purely an object of knowledge
and no more than a subject of scientific investigation. Were this so,
Christianity would be but a series of ideas and notions that might be
examined, considered, and clarified insofar as they corresponded to some
"primitive Christianity."[39] To think the early community fashioned dogma
in the form of fables and myths struck Adam as absurd.

> Unlimited criticism, faulty and sterile historical or philolog-
> ical research: these things do not conduct us to the mystery
> of Christ... It cannot be that I should need, for the attain-
> ment of this infinitely important, saving reality, laborious
> historical and philological study, that I should have to
> appeal to the Higher and Lower Criticism in order to reach
> the divine mystery.[40]

Adam here has overstated the claims of historical criticism. His point,
however, was that Christ and Christianity are not the exclusive possession
of the scholar, and one's capacity to know Christ is not relative to his or her
intellect. In his pastoral concern, Adam saw the nature of Christianity as
much more in keeping with the aspirations and attitudes of the common
person, without denying the value and need of scholarly work consistent
with, not in contradiction to, the ethos of the Church.

Adam also considered the question of human salvation in *Spirit*. He
said people have a fundamental aptitude for the divine. Yet, beginning with
a sharply limited view of the extent of human salvation, he required some

connection with the Roman Catholic Church in order to receive the divine grace that gives salvation.

> Because the Church is conscious that she is the Church of humanity and that Kingdom of God to which all men whatsoever by the will of Christ fundamentally belong, she cannot admit that men can be saved by membership in other societies established by the side of and in antagonism to the primary Church of Humanity founded by Christ.[41]

Adam rooted the exclusivity of the Church in the exclusivity of Christ, the final and most perfect self-revelation of God. Thus the only road to God is through Christ, and to get to Christ one must go through the Church. Adam went on to say, however, that people can be saved despite their membership in the very non-Catholic associations he earlier condemned.

Salvation is not as sure a thing outside the Church as it is inside. Christ and his body belong indissolubly together, said Adam, and the one "who rejects the one true Church is all too easily brought... to go astray about Christ."[42] Adam stepped back again when he declared the Church's claim there is no salvation outside the Church is directed not at individual non-Catholics, but at non-Catholic Churches and communions.

> In so far as they are genuinely Catholic in their faith and worship, it can and will and must happen that there should be, even outside the visible Church, a real growth and progress in union with Christ.... Wherever the Gospel of Jesus is faithfully preached, and wherever baptism is conferred with faith in His Holy Name, there his grace can operate.[43]

Adam went on to say Catholicism teaches Christ's grace operates not only within the various Christian communions, but also in the non-Christian world.

> Wherever conscience is active, wherever men are alive to God and his Holy Will, there and at the same time the grace of Christ co-operates and lays in the soul the seed of supernatural life.[44]

Adam was saying the Catholic Church claims to be to true body of Christ and the repository of his grace while acknowledging that God's grace operates without limit. This theme would be picked up and expressed more fully at Vatican II. As Adam put it, the Church is the ordinary means of salvation, but this does not exclude extraordinary situations in which the grace of Christ visits individuals apart from the mediation of the Church and effects their salvation. Those who receive salvation in this way are incorporated into the true Church; they are saved through the Church and through the grace of Christ. Such is the case even when they are separated from the visible Church.[45]

The Spirit of Catholicism is a book about the Roman Catholic Church. Thus it is an ecclesiology, not a Christology. Yet Adam began his book by grounding the Church in Christ, for apart from Christ there would be no Church. He said a great deal about Christ in this book, but what he said was not systematic and made no pretense to be a complete Christology. That which he said, however, set forth the main themes of his later Christology and validated his place as an heir of the Catholic Tübingen School. Within ten years of the publication of *Spirit*, Adam wrote three books about Christ as well as several major articles.

Critique of Modern Christology

In 1930, Adam published a short book entitled, *Christ and the Western Mind*,[46] and a longer one, *Christ Our Brother*.[47] The first was an attempt to show that if Christ is God become human, then Christianity can in no way be dependent upon western needs or contributions. That which made Christianity what it is occurred within a Jewish context and the first apostles were Jews. The Church itself arose on Jewish soil. The Germanic mind had a strong influence upon Christianity, according to Adam, because the Germans' character led them to see Christianity as a present living force in life. This made them particularly susceptible to seeing Christianity in terms of Jesus' words: the Kingdom is "in you," with the result it laid too much emphasis on divine immanence.[48]

Adam also dealt with the skepticism regarding the deity of Christ that had begun with the Enlightenment. He charged the western denial of Christ's deity did not result from scientific inquiry or careful and comprehensive examination of sources, but derived from unbelief as a principle.

> The entire formulation of the problem of this critical
> Christology, its analysis, its argumentation, are dominated
> by this negative, *a priori* unbelief.[49]

He attacked further the demands of modern critics by challenging their basic historical presuppositions.

> Since the appearance of Christ as a direct personal entry of God into this spatial and temporal world necessarily tran- scends and annihilates all analogies and conditions of experience, the demand for analogy and correlation in the working of Christ amounts to nothing less than a tacit denial, antecedent to and prejudging all serious inves- tigation of the supernatural character of our Lord's appearance. Even before the witnesses have been heard, the claim of Jesus to divinity is rejected.[50]

Adam said the second characteristic of modern Christology is that it has permitted itself to be dominated by the spirit of the times, especially that of contemporary philosophies. As a result, he said, not only did modern Christology deny Christ's deity, it also secularized and relativized his humanity.

> The critical Christology by surrendering wholesale to this artificially blinded philosophy, borrowed from it its formu- lae and schematic constructions in order to dress up its labors of anti-Christian destruction in philosophical garb with all the attractions of modern intellectuality. In its hands not only was Christ deprived of his divinity, but even his humanity was completely secularized and con- ceived in terms of relativity.[51]

The target of Adam's acid pen was the attempt in the Germany of his day to tie Christ irrevocably to German culture and society. Within a few years, with the rise of Hitler and a resurgent German nationalism, the pressure would become even greater, as it had on the eve of World War I. Adam, however, was not Barth, and instead of supporting a Barmen-type initiative, he was initially sympathetic to the Nazis.

After Hitler's rise to power, Adam attacked the hypercritical and skeptical spirit he saw as characteristic of the modern age in his article, "Jesus Christ and the Spirit of the Age."[52] He said there existed in the philosophical realm "a strong antipathy, an outspoken resentment, toward the claims to truth and validity" made in the mysterious and miraculous elements of religion. Yet the most striking instance of the activity of the mysterious and miraculous is the person of Jesus of Nazareth. The fundamental problem for moderns encountering Jesus thus occurs at the very beginning; they have to face the preliminary question of whether knowledge of the supernatural is possible at all.

> Christ and Christianity have received the most intensive scrutiny over the centuries of any historical phenomenon, but to date no one has succeeded in demolishing even one of the bases upon which Christian preaching and teaching have depended. The efforts of radical criticism during the last two hundred years have been incapable of scientifically refuting or convicting of error a single fundamental historical assertion about Christ.[53]

The problem, said Adam, is not that Christ and his message are unable to stand before the modern intellect and conscience. The problem of today is that the effect of the Enlightenment has been to lead moderns to reject the claims of Christ even before they hear them. Modern people deny the possibility of the miraculous events in Jesus' life without even attempting a critical investigation of them.

> The question about Christ is falsely put at the outset, since what can only be maintained after full inquiry is tacitly assumed as a presupposition of the whole discussion.[54]

This presupposition is the impossibility of the miraculous.

> Today's religion is idealistic monism. Rejecting a transcendent God, people require a god tied to the world, who exists only in and through humanity, and who reveals himself only within the depths of individual personalities. When moderns apply this picture of God to Jesus, they see a man who was the first to bring to the world the message of our divine humanity. He found by experience, to an extent that no one before him had done, that we are not only like God, but equal to God and of divine descent. In this case Jesus is divine in exactly the same sense in which we are.[55]

Adam continued by saying this gentle picture of Jesus as the bringer of good news about our present condition is grossly misleading. Not only is Jesus our Savior, said Adam, he is also the messenger of divine wrath.

Adam pictured redemption as having to do with the relation between humanity and the supernatural. It occurred in a realm beyond natural experience because that is the only realm touched by original sin.[56] This presentation understated the extent of the problem of original sin by limiting its effects to the divine-human relationship. By omitting relationships among humans and with their environment, Adam left unanswered the question of how these relationships had been damaged. A further and more serious problem, particularly in light of Adam's other writings, was his apparent denigration of the role of history. If redemption did not occur in history, why should anyone care about the person or the historicity of Jesus? Strauss' mythic approach, severely attacked by Tübingers from the time of Kuhn onward, would be perfectly adequate were historicity not an essential requirement for the person and work of Christ.

Christ Our Brother

In *Christ Our Brother*, his first Christology, Adam sought to emphasize the fullness and importance of Christ's humanity. This concern for the humanity did not prevent him from understanding the deity as the ground and motive force in Christ. The latter part of his book strongly emphasized the incompleteness of Christ apart from the Church, picking up again the ecclesiological theme of his earlier *Spirit*.[57] Adam shifted between romantic, traditional, and liberal theological themes in *Brother*, but always returned to the traditional emphasis as the foundation for his Christology.

In *Christ Our Brother*, Adam sought to emphasize the reality of Christ's humanity and its implications for human practice. He did this by presenting Jesus in his life, work, preaching, and especially prayer. Adam also tried to demonstrate the mediatorial role of Christ's humanity, which he said had been sadly neglected, especially by Protestants. Adam was sharply critical of Protestantism because he saw it as undervaluing the role of Jesus' humanity in redemption. He drew this conclusion from what he considered its unacceptable exaggeration of the impotence of fallen humanity, which Luther and Calvin had described as spiritually dead. It is important to appreciate Jesus' humanity, said Adam, in order to recognize his oneness with us. It is also important if we are to value properly everything human and earthly. The humanity Adam sketched was that of a

Neo-Romantic contemporary, however, not that of a first-century Palestinian.

At the start, Adam pointed to Christ's utter devotion to his Father and his complete surrender to his Father's will. Jesus saw God's hand in everything that was and everything that happened. Adam's initial portrait of Jesus was of a man who loved nature and nature's God. He was a person who cared about people because God cared about people.

This Neo-Romantic motif was modified significantly by Adam's contention Jesus was naturally aware of his interior union with God, and he enjoyed this knowledge from his youth. "Jesus conjoins Himself and His Father in a unity in which no other creature can share."[58] This conjoining of humanity and deity appeared most clearly in Jesus' prayer life. Jesus' prayer life was the highest expression of his unity with his Father.

Adam's picture of Jesus was colored not only by the Neo-Romanticism of his era but also by the immanentism he so strenuously opposed.

> Jesus did not think of God as being utterly apart from the world, in some remote paradise, accessible only to the rapture of the disembodied spirit. He thought of God as very near to the world and as active in it.... Above all He found God in mankind. For men whether just or unjust, were children of his Father.... Jesus regards the service of our fellow men as of the very essence of religion, so that without it there is no true religion.[59]

Despite this, Adam rejected the idea that Jesus was "one of those simple enthusiasts who make a religion of the service of humanity." In and of itself, humanity did not interest Jesus.[60]

Adam's fundamental complaint against the orthodox Christology of his day was that it concentrated too much attention on Jesus' deity, and virtually ignored his humanity. This one-sided approach severed Jesus from the humanity he had come to save. Of particular concern to Adam were the concepts of Christ as the High Priest and of the Church as his Mystical Body, views he felt were insufficiently appreciated in theology.

> Eutyches, the founder of the Monophysite heresy, had no longer any place left for the priesthood of Christ in his doctrinal system.[61]

Even the non-Monophysite Churches of the East increasingly ignored Christ's role of high priest. Adam maintained this was a revolution in Christology because

> Christ no longer stands by man's side, as the representative
> and advocate of mankind, and no longer as the man, Christ
> Jesus, and the First-born of his brethren, offers the services
> of mankind to the Triune God. He has, so to speak,
> crossed over, and is now by God's side, and himself is the
> awful and unapproachable God.[62]

This removed Christ to an infinite distance from humanity, even in the Eucharist. Moreover, because he is so distant, it is easier to fear than to trust him. Jesus no longer provides any assurance of safety.

Adam argued the Christology currently in vogue in the Catholic Church was infected by this Monophysitism despite its verbal appeals to the two-nature doctrine of Chalcedon. He viewed Protestantism as even more seriously flawed at this crucial point than was Catholicism. His interpretation of this aspect of Protestant orthodoxy led Adam to develop his argument in the direction of an apologetic for the Roman Catholic Church as the one true Church of Christ because of its intimate and visible relationship to Christ, its Head.

Adam's criticism of contemporary understandings of Christology was never intended to deny Christ's full deity. Adam merely wanted to remind his readers the consubstantiality of Nicea applies equally to his humanity and to his deity. To a Church ever ready to defend Jesus' deity, Adam said Jesus also "has a purely human consciousness, a purely human will, a purely human emotional life. He is a complete man."[63] The reality of the Incarnation communicated to Jesus' humanity neither the divine nature nor its attributes. Jesus' humanity remained human even after the union.

> The Second Person of the Blessed Trinity, the Word of
> God, contributes nothing to the human nature that implies
> any enrichment of the human nature as such. What is con-
> tributed is simply the person.[64]

The Incarnation meant for Adam that God became human, not that humanity was divinized. What amazed Adam was that God came down to our level to be one of us, and did so as a little child—this was far more astounding than our being raised up to be with him.

For Adam, the Incarnation was fundamental because apart from it there would have been no redemption. It was the first manifestation and embodiment of God's salvific will. No other means of redemption God might have chosen could have revealed his will so clearly and effectively. Adam saw more than this in the Incarnation however. By its very occurrence, the Incarnation united God with humanity in a way that can never be undone.

> The vital fact is not that God dwelt bodily among us and that we can see the glory of God in the face of Jesus, but that this God is our Brother, that He is of one blood with us.[65]

Christ's deity is important because were he not true God he could not have bridged the infinite chasm separating God and his creatures, but this deity is the necessary background and empowering of his humanity. What is important *for us* is not that Jesus is God Incarnate, but that he is the New Man who returns the human race to God. In regard to Jesus himself, the deity is all-important because apart from that there could be no "for us." It is Jesus' deity that gave his redemptive work the infinite value necessary in God's sight for our salvation, and it is only Jesus' deity that enabled him to bridge the divine-human chasm.

Furthermore, the Incarnation is the supreme manifestation of God's love for his creatures. To deny Bethlehem, said Adam, is to deny the living God. In the Incarnation, Christ became not only a man, but also the Man. By virtue of the Incarnation he was able to become the head of a new human race and its representative before God.

Until all the redeemed have been incorporated into Christ, he stands incomplete. This condition will persist until the end of time because he can never be the complete Christ until all the redeemed have been incorporated into his Mystical Body. This meant for Adam the Roman Catholic Church is the "continuing life of the risen Christ; it is Christ unfolding himself in history; it is the fullness of Christ."[66] Adam drew further conclusions from this to support the validity of the Roman Catholic Church and the inadequacy of other Christian communities as vehicles of salvation.

The man Jesus who was the subject of Adam's book is essential to Christianity. The origins of the religion are inseparably bound up with his appearance in history. However imperfect the tradition about him is, it does show him to be the paradigm of pure, wise, holy, good, courageous, and perfect humanity and shows it so impressively, yet so plainly, that he must always remain the ideal man. Jesus' miracles were not random events, but reflect truly his inner nature and thus are intimately connected with his person. Jesus' miraculous character reached its climax in his resurrection. This event served as God's solemn attestation of Jesus' life.[67]

Jesus lived and thought in the language and imagery of the Old Testament. He used the Old Testament, however, not as a scholar or disciple, but as its Lord, as the one who came to fulfill it. For Jesus the Old Testament had no supreme and final authority because he himself, as God Incarnate, was that authority.[68] What Jesus had to say about God revolutionized religion. He taught God's utter supremacy and his universal fatherhood. He presented God as the deepest and ultimate meaning of life to whom service is the one thing necessary for this life. This took religion out of the realm of the exclusively natural. Although not the first to designate God as Father, Jesus was the first to use this term to bring God near to us and show his concern for us. When we understand God in this way, we must begin to respond to God from our hearts and not with mere externals. God is the Father of all, not only of the redeemed.[69] Jesus also taught the human soul has infinite value, it is called to the Kingdom of Heaven, and all humans are children of God.

Characteristically, *Christ Our Brother* was permeated with Adam's pastoral concern for the reader. "The inquiry after the personal God," he said, "is never a merely philosophical inquiry; it must also be a moral and religious act." Every other way is sacrilegious and must miss the mark. "If there be really a living God, then I can come to him only by prayerful thought, or better still, by thoughtful prayer. There is no other way to him."[70] Ultimately, Christ is our only way to God; we cannot get to God in our own power. The entire purpose of Adam's book was to show that were not Christ our brother, as a true and complete human, we never could get to God. Adam also stressed the important role of the Holy Spirit both in Jesus' earthly life and in applying to humanity the results of that life.

Adam provided the Catholicism of his day with a reminder that it needed to consider Jesus in his entirety. This was fully in keeping with the letter and spirit of Chalcedon, but not as that document had come to be misunderstood by too many conservatives, both Catholic and Protestant. In his reminder, Adam steered clear of the positions set forth by many Protestant critics who exalted Jesus' humanity at the cost of his deity. He provided good arguments for his position both from Scripture and from pastoral concern about the consequences for Christian practice of not appreciating Jesus' humanity. In recognizing the value of this book, one must not overlook the extent to which the philosophy of his time colored his perceptions and affected his Christology. *Christ Our Brother* can serve us today by reminding us of the unity of Jesus Christ and the importance of recognizing the reality of both his humanity and deity. It also warns us against allowing our theology to be so distorted by contemporary thought that Jesus becomes so much our contemporary that he neither fits into his original setting nor speaks clearly to those of other times and cultures.

To a Church that gave no more than lip service to half of the Chalcedonian definition of Christ's person which it claimed to honor, Adam said the proper understanding of the definition must be fully as expressive of Jesus' humanity as it is of his deity. This balance between and appreciation of Christ's two natures is a message that needs regular repetition to all theologians, Protestant and Catholic, because the temptation to release the tension inherent in the doctrine in one direction or the other is ever present.

Adam's strong anti-Protestant polemic makes this book less attractive to many in this post-Vatican II period than his contribution to christological study warrants. It took great courage in 1930 to write theology that diverged to any great extent from the reigning Neoscholasticism, even though what was written was correct, and even more faithful to the historic teaching of the Church. Adam was brave enough to point out the monophysitic tendency in Catholic Christology and warn of its danger. Such a Christology could only cancel the purpose of the Incarnation by distancing first God and then Christ from those they intend to save. In the past, this had led to the interpolation of mediators between Christ and humanity. The risk remained real; in fact, Protestants have often charged Roman Catholic Mariology and teaching about the intercessory role of the saints resulted directly from the distancing of Christ from his Church through one-sided emphasis on his deity. Although he addressed the first problem, Adam unfortunately nowhere answered the Protestant charge.

Jesus Christus

The major Christology of Adam's early career was *Jesus Christus*.[71] In this book, he pointed out the philosophical, historical, and theological problems regarding the figure of Jesus and faith in him were as clear for the believing theologian as for his non-believing contemporaries. The crux of the problem was the value of witnesses who were wholeheartedly committed to that to which they testified. The gospels are the primary source for our historical knowledge of Jesus and their authors were partisan. We must ask therefore whether we dare use this testimony for our historical research.

Krieg has called *Jesus Christus* a milestone in Catholic Christology because it introduced a new interpretation of the relation between Christ's two natures. This anticipated Rahner's development through Hegelian concepts of a new understanding of the mystery of the unity and distinction of natures in Christ.[72]

Reinhardt said *Jesus Christus* is clearly marked by agreement with Church dogma regarding both the historical and eternal Jesus. He suggested the theme of the book is the Christ of dogma, the One who unites in his person both divine and human natures. Adam saw no problem with the deity, but recognized Jesus' humanity was a stumbling block in the Church. Neither deity nor humanity is the key, however, but their conjunction in the one God-man Jesus Christ. Echoing the theme of his earlier Christologies, Adam emphasized it is only as our Brother, as the New Adam, that Christ can be our Savior.[73] Reinhardt seemed to miss Adam's point that the humanity of Jesus was a problem only to the extent it was not given its full worth by a Church displaying decidedly monophysitic tendencies.

Adam denied it is proper to call Jesus God; the correct way to speak of him is as the God-man. This emphasizes the incarnation of God, not the divinization of humanity. Adam suggested Jesus' humanity is the way, means, and sacrament of salvation. This led, said Kasper much later, to what was for Adam's time an astonishingly biblically-oriented Christology. At the same time, Adam challenged the demythologization programme being developed by Bultmann because he feared it would remove the vital, concrete elements of faith and replace them with an ungrounded, uncontrollable mysticism.[74]

The humanity Adam described for Jesus continued to be marked by strong Neo-Romantic elements, as can be seen in his description of Jesus as thrilling, austere, and heroic. He identified Jesus as the Son of God and as the Second Adam, but interpreted these titles in a Neo-Romantic sense. Adam's Jesus was a stately figure who attracted others to himself by his physical appearance. He contrasted Jesus with the founders of other world religions as one who enjoyed good health all his life. How else, asked Adam, could one explain Jesus regularly engaging in preaching, healing, and prayer all day and all night. Jesus was also extremely intelligent and morally good. This was evident from the impression he made on both his disciples and his enemies in his ability to argue from Scripture despite his lack of a formal education. Adam's Second Adam was an heroic figure, even something of a Nietzschean Superman.[75]

Adam introduced *Jesus Christus* by citing Dostoievskoy's claim that the deity of Jesus is the question facing modern European civilization. He agreed with Dostoievskoy this was so, but added it was incomplete "because the mystery of Christ does not consist in him being God, but in him being the God-man.... That is the heart of the early Christian proclamation."[76]

In contrast to his skeptical contemporaries, Adam affirmed Jesus' full deity, and, in contrast to Catholic practice of his time, he affirmed Jesus' full humanity. But he went on to say these two, the humanity and the deity, must be joined in the one person or there was nothing to become excited about. In his Catholic context, the humanity was the problem because for centuries the Church had been virtually monophysite in practice, creeds and councils notwithstanding. Adam raised anew the importance of Jesus' full humanity.

> Thus we determine that Christ is a complete, whole human; that for all his essential union with deity he had not only a human body, but also a human soul, a pure human consciousness, a pure human will, and a pure human emotional life; that in a complete and true sense he is one of us. It is just as important that he be human as that he be God.[77]

In becoming human, Christ became our Brother. He became not only a human like us, but the Human, the new Human, the Second Adam. This is the heart of the paradox of Christian faith: the Son of God is a true human. To dissolve the tension inherent in this paradox is to destroy Christianity.

> If one falsely or exclusively emphasizes the human or divine nature in the mystery of Christ, the mystery of salvation is distorted and thus all of Christian faith is disfigured.... He did not save us through a mysterious, inconceivable sacrificial act, but through his mediatorial service to God and humanity.[78]

Historical Christianity battled fiercely to defend the consubstantiality of the Son with the Father against Arius and it fought equally hard to defend his consubstantiality with us against the Monophysites. These battles were important. If Jesus were only human, Christianity would be an immense fraud and talk of salvation no more than a word game. Were Jesus only human, he could give us only that which is human, in all its conditionality and questionability, but he could not address our deepest need, that regarding our sinfulness and death. These would remain with us.[79] Christ's humanity is necessary, but it is not sufficient if he is to be our Savior. By standing on the side both of God and of humanity he is qualified to be the Mediator through whom we can come to the Father.[80]

For Adam, the proper subject of Christology is not the eternal Word in his divine form, nor the second Person of the triune God, but the Son of God in his human form, the exalted Son of Man, who sits at the right hand of the Father, whom God has made Lord and Christ.[81] Adam appears to have been advocating a Christology "from below" here, but one connected firmly to a high view of Christ's person based on the creeds and councils.

In order to approach Christology "from below," Adam demanded we affirm the historical reality of Jesus of Nazareth. He said today we must either accept the historical existence of the Jesus who performed miracles or deny the Christ of the gospels ever existed. It is no longer possible to accept the historical existence of Jesus and deny the supernatural character of his appearance and activity.[82] "The critical denial of the divine Christ must at the same time be a critical denial of the historical Jesus."[83] Adam attributed the growing acceptance of the possibility Christianity originated as the explanation of certain powerful ideas instead of being the work of one creative individual to the increasing influence of Hegelian philosophy on historical research. In rejecting the view derived from Hegel through Strauss that Christ was a mythological figure, Adam surveyed the early extra-biblical accounts to show they were historical accounts and not inconsistent with the gospel records. Many of the reports were written too soon after Jesus' death to qualify as myth.

Adam sharply criticized the modern worldview. Since Kant, he said, it has become skeptical, matter-of-fact, blasé, and wise before its time. It is so concerned with weighing and measuring the visible world that it has no time for the invisible. Modern Europeans are scandalized by the thought of the miraculous. They reject the supernatural not because evidence for its existence is unavailable but because they are blind and prejudiced. "Western eyes have become old and can no longer see all of reality."[84]

In response to such an outlook, Adam presented his understanding of the witness of the gospels. He agreed these were not biographies, but that the writers sought simply and objectively to organize the accounts of Peter and the other disciples as well as the recollections of Jesus' mother circulating in the community. These accounts had existed orally and were passed down in certain characteristic forms to the writers. The different thrusts of the gospels occurred because, although they were agreed in essentials, each of the sources proclaimed Jesus differently. Adam thus allowed no room for the personality and concerns of individual gospel authors to show through; all the differences already existed in the tradition each author received.[85] These gospel accounts were historically precise, however, and their precision lies in nothing else than the inner tie of the writers to Jesus and his word. They were faithful to Jesus and scrupulously respected his

words as they found them in circulation, neither adding to them nor appropriating them for other purposes.[86] The attempt of New Testament scholars to drive a wedge between the Aramaic of Jesus and the Greek of the
gospels was a fruitless exercise, according to Adam, because Jesus certainly
must have spoken Greek. The scholars act as if Palestine were an Aramaic
island in the Greek-speaking east, but Palestine was actually bilingual. If it
were not, how could Jesus have communicated with a Canaanite woman (Mt
15:22 ff.) and gentile proselytes (Jn 12:20 ff.)?[87]

Adam concluded the gospels present us with the unvarnished apostolic witness. There were no intermediaries between Jesus and the gospel
writers. The gospels contain first-hand, eyewitness testimony. Crucial for
Adam was the fourth gospel. Adam concluded it came from the traditional
source, John the beloved disciple, but Adam's language was such as to allow
either he was the source instead of the immediate writer or he was the one
who dictated to a scribe. He had to be one of Jesus' inner circle, close
enough to Jesus to be able to describe his inner life, not merely one of the
general group of Jesus' followers. On the basis of both internal and external
evidence, Adam concluded John was the source.

John wrote to fill in the gaps left by the synoptics and provided a
wealth of facts we know about Jesus' life and ministry only because of his
gospel. The key teachings are Jesus' divine pre-existence, his being ontologically divine and human, and his self-consciousness as Son of God. In the
fourth gospel we find psychological aspects of Jesus that were omitted in the
synoptics.

Adam devoted a considerable portion of *Jesus Christus* to these
inner aspects of Jesus' life. This was a result of his romantic understanding
in which Jesus' self-consciousness became a central theme. Adam did not
go as far as earlier romantics in downplaying Jesus' life out of concern for
his self-consciousness. The core of Jesus' being was in the divine Word,
even though he was a full and complete human. From the beginning, he
knew who he was and why he had come. This is clear from his expression,
"I have come..." He was a man of decisive will and purposeful actions, a
born leader who concentrated on his goal and took personal initiative. With
this aspect of his presentation, Adam out lined a neo-Romantic superman,
a "thoroughly heroic figure, the incarnate hero." He determined Jesus had
been born in the autumn of 7 B. C., and died on April 7, 30 A. D. He
began his three-year ministry at 34. Jesus was a winsome and attractive man,
Isaiah 53 notwithstanding. He was active among the poor, sick, and sinners.
The gospels picture him as a powerful, hardy, and healthy man who rarely
needed to eat and required little sleep. Jesus freely entered into the need

need of others and took their need unto himself because he alone was able to overcome it. This ability was the psychological root of his salvific work.

Adam introduced an element into Jesus' salvific work not commonly found in the theology of his day. He dealt with Jesus as the Liberator from earthly woes.

> It would be a vain endeavor to overlook the proletarian
> sound of the beatitudes and to violently reinterpret them in
> an ethical sense.[88]

Adam said Luke was foremost in presenting the Beatitudes in this social context that included liberation from earthly need, but he denied it would be legitimate to transform Jesus into a modern social reformer. Adam saw Jesus instead as offering a wholistic salvation. Jesus' love for others was all-inclusive and showed not the slightest hint of class struggle.

The heart of Jesus' being was in his prayer life. Adam pointed out the centrality and power of Jesus' prayer life for his ministry. Before Jesus acted, he prayed. When he faced a crisis, he prayed. Jesus' prayers also exhibit the unique relationship he enjoyed with the Father. He always prayed to "my Father," but he told his disciples to pray to "your Father." Never did he tell them to pray to "our Father" and include himself in the "our." When Jesus prayed, he stepped completely out of the realm of humanity and placed himself exclusively within the circle of his Father.[89] Adam's expression of this idea appears to have been somewhat at variance with his heavy stress on Jesus' true and full humanity and certainly presented Jesus as at least an extraordinary man.

Jesus' preaching showed his confidence that he exercised power and judgment. In fact, his words indicated his very presence constituted divine judgment. Adam said Jesus preached that which he was: the embodied will of God. His opening words dealt with the coming of the Kingdom of God, not directly with himself. Out of this proclamation grew Jesus' self-confession. He was of the line of the prophets, and brought that line to an end. He recognized himself as the fulfillment and completion of the prophetic office.

Adam described the Kingdom of God as an action exclusively of God. Humans play no part in bringing it into being. Their repentance and righteousness are only preparations for God's action. "Jesus understood the Kingdom of God as unbroken, eternal community of life with the Father and with himself."[90] In a sense, the Kingdom arrived with Jesus, but fundamentally it is eschatological; its coming lies in the future. Adam understood

Jesus as expecting the coming of the Kingdom in the near future because it was already approaching. He was unaware of the precise moment of its coming, but it was unlikely Jesus expected all the events of Matthew 24 to occur within one physical generation because he was speaking in terms of an eschatological generation.

The Kingdom of the Father was at the same time the Kingdom of the Son. It was Jesus' presence among the Jews that enabled him to say the Kingdom was already in their midst. This Kingdom is no static entity. It is a becoming and it is always coming. There was a tension in Jesus' concept of the Kingdom between the present and the future: the Kingdom has appeared, but it remains future. Jesus' language was eschatological, placing the future into the present. The eschatological claims he made about himself force us to see him in a new light. The gentle Galilean is the coming Judge of the world and the Lord of the coming Kingdom. Jesus recognized himself in both situations and thus designated himself as the Son of Man. This self-designation leads us to the depth of his self-consciousness. It shows that he distinguished his messianic understanding from that of his contemporaries.

The Son of Man title was unique to Jesus and found its origin and place with him.[91] The Church, however, preferred other titles to describe him. For Jesus, Son of Man was an indirect and veiled messianic claim that had a deliberate air of mystery designed to entice others to begin thinking about what Jesus had said. The root of Jesus' usage was Daniel 7:13, and this was developed further from the intertestamental literature. Jesus' understanding of the title was not limited to that of Daniel. He gave it both a deeper meaning and a new content. He invested it with a salvific as well as an eschatological content. He is both Judge of the world and the Bringer of blessedness. The eschatological task presupposes the messianic. As Son of Man, Jesus did what only God could do.[92] The basic change Jesus introduced was in joining Isaiah's suffering servant with Daniel's exalted Son of Man. He said the Son of Man must suffer and die as well as be exalted. Jesus' use of the Son of Man title was not as a dogmatic statement but as a riddle.

Jesus' message began with the theme of the Kingdom of God. With Jesus' coming, eternity had entered into time. Salvation was approaching. The "agreeable year of the Lord" (Luke 4:19) was now approaching. This content distinguished Jesus from his predecessors. He identified himself with this new thing that was happening.

Not only Jesus' words but equally his actions reveal his self-consciousness. Jesus was unique among the founders of major religions because he is the content of the faith; in the other cases, it is the leader's teaching, not his person, that is central. Jesus readily assumed authority beyond and above that of the Mosaic law, forgave sins, and healed. His claim to such authority flowed out of his consciousness of an essential oneness with God. "It was rooted in an 'I' that was God.... For his consciousness, Yahweh and his own 'I' are one and the same."[93] Jesus does not merely stand on God's side, he himself is God. His work, his teaching and action, were the work of a man who knew himself to be essentially one with God.[94]

Adam concluded his assessment of Jesus' self-consciousness and his claims about himself by raising the question of why we should believe what Jesus said, especially in light of where his claims led him. This served as the bridge to Adam's consideration of Jesus' resurrection. Because he wanted to show the validity of Christ and Christianity, Adam discussed the Resurrection before going on to the crucifixion.

Jesus' Death and Resurrection

Adam presented the Resurrection primarily from Paul's writing. Paul believed the bodily resurrection of Jesus was a demonstrable historical fact. He did not simply identify the Jesus who hung on the cross with the Christ who appeared to him and the other apostles because there was a difference as well as a continuity. Paul's account included no empty grave, but it did presuppose one.[95] The synoptic account of the empty grave was primarily apologetic. Adam worked to harmonize the major points of the various resurrection accounts, but was not particularly concerned about minor differences. He rejected any proposal that modern psychology and parapsychology might account for the Easter appearances, but affirmed instead that they had an objective metaphysical basis. The versions of such critics as Renan struck Adam as requiring more faith than did the original accounts.[96]

For Paul, Jesus' death, burial, and resurrection constituted a whole. For Adam, this indicated that the Resurrection was bodily. The body was not "flesh" in Paul's sense—the location and instrument of sin—but it was an organic form. Essentially, Jesus' resurrection body was the same body as that placed in the grave, but its form of existence was different. Paul set forth the essential oneness of the earthly and heavenly bodies in Philippians 3:21.

A further reason for requiring a bodily resurrection was that, unlike the Greeks, the Jews did not separate body and spirit. For them, the spirit was always revealed through the body. Jesus' spirit without Jesus' body would have been utterly abnormal to the Jewish disciples. There was a point of discontinuity, however, because the Jews of Jesus' day held only to a general resurrection of the dead at the end of the world. Jesus' individual resurrection did not fit their pattern; there existed no expectation from which to construct Jesus' resurrection had it not occurred in reality.[97]

The empty grave was the sole objective, externally verifiable, clearly demonstrable, and controllable element in the disciples' experience of the Resurrection. Any theory of Jesus' resurrection that deals only with a subjective experience in Galilee without at the same time considering the empty grave betrays itself as "the sterile product of an ahistorical and anti-historical Enlightenmentism."[98] Claims the disciples stole the body or were unable to find the correct grave are implausible. Adam called such explanations "simple fiction."[99] Adam did not deny the apostles had a dogmatic and apologetic interest in Jesus' resurrection; he did deny such interest must negate their historical concern. He saw no possibility, psychologically, that they could have conceived of a resurrection had it not forced its reality into their lives.

From the Resurrection, Adam passed on to the event it presupposed: Jesus' crucifixion. He had two major concerns in this: the relationship between the two natures in Christ's suffering and death, and the effect of Christ's passion.

The crucifixion concerns the death of a man who is God. This was Adam's statement of what Calvary was about. Adam said it is common knowledge that God cannot die; thus God did not die and the eternal Word did not die. The one who died was a human who was joined essentially with the eternal Word, "a man who is God."[100]

The cross is the mystery of God's self-sacrifice for humanity. The deepest expression of Jesus' consciousness of his mission was his statement that he would give his life as a ransom for many (Mk 10:45). This self-sacrifice was at the heart of his salvific work; healing, miracles, and preaching were merely external expression of this.[101]

> Christ appeared in order to free fallen humanity from their costly bondage resulting from Adam's sin and to incorporate them into a new unity and community with himself.[102]

The basis for this salvific possibility was the Incarnation. As a human, Christ was able to make satisfaction to God for our guilt, and because he is God he could overcome and erase this guilt completely. It was only in and through his human nature, however, that Christ experienced suffering and death.[103] The human nature was the instrument for achieving our salvation; the man Jesus carried out the act of obedient suffering freely. In doing so, he accomplished in the cloak of humanity the satisfaction humanity owed to its Creator.

The result of Christ's work is that we have become members of Christ. His Holy Spirit has joined us to Christ, and in and through Christ the Spirit has joined us with all those who have received the same Spirit in baptism. In other books, Adam filled out this picture as that of the Church, but here he was content with the general description of the effect of Christ's work without explanating in detail how it relates to the Church.

Fifty years after its publication, *Jesus Christus* will strike many as time- and culture-bound. Adam's philosophical framework has been rejected by a world that has seen several major wars and untold destruction since Adam wrote; biblical scholars would challenge many of his exegetical claims; and theologians would be distinctly uncomfortable with his dogmatic and methodological presuppositions. Nonetheless, Adam addressed issues that continue to challenge people interested in Jesus Christ. He has presented Jesus as a human being with the features and personality of a human being. In doing so, Adam brought Jesus near to us without reducing him to less than the sources say he is. This was no mean achievement, given the theological context in which he worked.

Jesus Christus was the summation and high point of Adam's early christological work, but he did not stop with this. As he continued, Adam refined and expanded his early presentation and entered into discussion with some of his contemporaries who were pursuing courses sharply divergent from his own. Adam also continued to make pastoral application of his Christology and to tie it to other topics in theology, especially ecclesiology.

The result of this continuing work appeared in *The Christ of Faith* (1954),[104] which, like *Jesus Christus*, was the product of Adam's classroom lectures.

The Christ of Faith

In *The Christ of Faith*, Adam traced the history of the development of christological doctrine from the early Church to the present and pointed out significant contributions to the defense of this doctrine. He attacked those forms of criticism and theological study that denied or played down the traditional Catholic dogma of Jesus as the God-man. He emphasized the Western fathers' defense of the duality of natures by emphasizing the unity of Christ's person, Leontius of Byzantium's contribution of anhypostasis and enhypostasis to christological terminology, and Boethius' clear concept of personhood.

Adam further suggested Christology consists of the study of the images of Christ that have emerged in the course of the tradition. He proposed three types of image: the images reflected in Scripture, the dogmatic images of Church doctrine, and the living images that grow out of the Church's life and thought.

Reinhardt suggested that in this volume Adam showed several significant changes in the biblical foundation of his Christology. There emerged in it a greater interest in Jesus' self-consciousness. Adam made this self-consciousness the ultimate source for Christian faith as he increasingly opposed the positions of Bultmann and Bousset.[105] Adam dealt with Jesus' self-consciousness in terms of his roles as Messiah, Son of Man, and Son of God. The high point appears in Matthew 11:25–27. Adam used the Old Testament and early Jewish sources much more than he had previously. He continued to concentrate on John and Paul because he saw their Christologies as expressing Jesus' self-consciousness in a way that the synoptics did not. Adam continued to interpret Scripture in terms of Church doctrine and the primary effect of modern biblical theology on Adam was to strengthen his appreciation of salvation history as the way to understand Jesus.

Adam began *The Christ of Faith* by stating Christ is the heart of Christianity and Christology lies at the heart of Catholic dogma. Christ is central because he confirms God is self-revealing and triune, provides the way to the Father, and gives *all* other doctrines meaning, relevance, and form.[106] Our belief in Jesus comes from the Church, not from philosophy or biblical criticism. If we seek Christ apart from the Church, using our own insight and criticism, we can never find him.

> In the Church's consciousness of faith, in her ordinances
> and sacraments, she is the living revelation of the spirit of
> Jesus, and of the powers of resurrection he issues forth.
> She is his body.[107]

Apart from the Church, even the New Testament is only a "stirring literary composition."[108] Without the testimony of the Church, the biblical evidence for Jesus would be insufficient.

> This overwhelming fact, that Christianity never was any-
> thing but the tidings of Christ, that Christ was and is the

object of contemplation and thought across many hundreds of years, assures us that the image of Christ cherished by the congregation of the faithful can never be distorted, that it is the true original image of Christ, and that therefore we must go to the living Church, and not to the critics outside the faith, if we are searching for the true Christ.[109]

Adam mounted a sharp attack on what he considered the negative criticism so evident among his Protestant contemporaries. If we rely too heavily on and esteem too highly the results of biblical criticism, we may find ourselves believing that faith depends upon these results. Protestant theology is more susceptible to this danger because in Catholicism "the living proclamation of the Church... is the true basis of Christianity," and all biblical considerations are secondary.[110]

Adam contended the Church could communicate the image of Christ to us even if the Bible had never existed. As a result, critical exegesis of Scripture never touches the substance of Christian faith. Adam's position has been overtaken by Vatican II's renewed appreciation for the Bible and its centrality in theology.

Despite his valid objections to the excesses of biblical criticism, Adam's counterproposal appears more an evasion of the challenge of the critics than a response. His severing of Scripture and tradition in order to defend dogma resembles in appearance, although not intent, Bultmann's bifurcation of faith and history in order to retain a faith that he no longer considered supportable in terms of modern historiography. Adam recognized this danger. He also differed from Bultmann significantly in the doctrines he defended, being far more in agreement with traditional Christianity. Despite his protestations to the contrary, said Adam, Bultmann's doctrine had abandoned Christ's teaching and turned revelation into philosophy of religion.

Adam charged biblical criticism treats Christianity like a corpse to be dissected and examined piece by piece, and not as the living movement it is.

The textual critic assumes that Christianity and Christology are something finished and inflexible, lying before us complete down to the last impulse and the last article, complete in the Bible and in Christian literature, in every Christian movement and institution from the early Fathers down to the present.... According to this theory, the sole source of

our faith, and its exclusive standard, would simply be the
historical evidence for it.[111]

As a Catholic Tübinger, Adam refused to understand Christianity and its
tradition in this static sense. In response, he pointed to the living quality of
Christian tradition as found only in the Catholic Church. The only valid way
to approach Christianity is through the objective spirit of the living Church,
not through the subjective spirit of the individual scholar. Further,
Christianity transcends the limits of history.

> The historical appearance of Christ and Christianity is not
> to be understood in all its aspects merely with the means of
> historiography. There will always be something left over
> that cannot be understood.[112]

Adam agreed belief in Christ includes a rational conclusion drawn from verifiable premises using philosophy and historical method, but it also contains
a supernatural element that these tools are unable to deal with adequately.
It is the supernatural element that is decisive. Ultimately, God, not history
or philosophy, makes us receptive to Christ.[113]

Adam said the Church opposes its consciousness of faith to critical
scholarship, and more than this, opposes the spirit of that scholarship with
its consciousness of the spirit of the Lord who animates its faith. To
respond to "this hypercritical scholarship" only with scholarship of its own
would mean the Church was sacrificing its very essence; to scholarship must
be joined the power of faith. It is from this that the Church has derived its
Christology, not from "dead texts willfully rearranged." As a result, the
Church has had to establish boundaries for its christologists. Such boundaries are needed only insofar as non-Catholic theologians have threatened
to disrupt Catholic Christology. Adam said the Church's guidelines for the
Catholic Christology of his day were intended only to protect the Church's
faith from the basic errors of D. F. Strauss and his spiritual heirs.

Adam regarded the miracles of Jesus as strong evidence for the
validity of Christianity. The biblical critics who followed Strauss erred in
presupposing the supernatural, and thus the miraculous, was non-existent no
matter what evidence might be offered in its defense.

> If the law of analogy and correlation is to be the guiding
> star of historical investigation, all it will recognize are

> things analogous, things similar, things causally related to
> previous events. So miracles cannot exist in this scheme of
> things. But the great characteristic of Christianity is that
> it is a history of miracles. Thus Troeltsch's two principles
> betray an unproved and unprovable presupposition that
> cuts off from the start all understanding of Christianity.[114]

This did not mean Adam saw miracles as proofs for Christianity or for
Christ. Miracles enable us to consider Christ, but they do not force us to
believe. They are always means, never ends.

Adam presented his methodology as dogmatic. This meant he did
not draw his evidence about Christ from secular sources but from the
Church's living faith. At times he combined this approach with what he
called the apologetic method. This drew solely on natural means of per-
ception, disregarding the supernatural character of the sources of Christian
faith. His apologetic method dealt with documents and the tradition in the
same way as do secular historians. Such an approach stands on the same
ground as negative criticism because this is the only way an honest and
fruitful dispute is possible.[115]

Before looking at the gospel sources for Christology, Adam set forth
his dogmatic presuppositions. Foundational for Adam was Nicea's doctrine
of the consubstantiality of the Son with the Father. Only theology built on
this foundation can be called Christian. Liberal Protestantism has neglected
Nicea as its starting point.

Chalcedon is important because it renewed the Church's appreciation for Christ's full humanity. It kept Christology within the proper
bounds, but it did not provide a positive solution to the question of how
the two natures of Christ are joined. The council provided a defense, not
a constructive solution.

> Christ is unique. He is no less than the Logos itself. His
> human nature is taken up into the Logos, but it is not en-
> tirely subsumed by it. Even after the Incarnation, Christ
> remains fully and wholly man. By stressing this last truth
> in particular, the Council of Chalcedon made the old prob-
> lem still more urgent: How can Christ be fully and wholly
> human, if this humanity does not exist of itself, but only in
> the Logos? ... This issue was clarified by the theologian
> Leontius of Constantinople and the philosopher Boethius.

In a more precise conceptual analysis they distinguished between person and nature and demonstrated that existence as person could be detached from nature.[116]

The dispute with Monophysitism confirmed that human nature need not be diminished solely because it had been united with the divine. It remains in all its peculiarity, even including acts of the will. The laws of physiology and psychology are not incompatible with human development and have a place in the Church's image of Christ.

Modern non-Catholic theology has attacked the deity of Christ on the basis of its rationalistic presuppositions. It believed Incarnation is *a priori* impossible because it does not agree with common human experience and destroys the chain of cause and effect. Thus, the theme of Christ's deity stands outside the domain of historiography. These rationalists view the matter as one solely of subjective belief.

The only genuine object of scholarly probing was to *explain* historically how the belief in Christ's divinity came to be held among men.[117]

Whereas these theologians drive a wedge between the historical Jesus and the Christ of faith, making them into very different persons, the Church in *Pascendi* rejected such a distinction. The Church further rejected the claim that only the Jesus of history can be demonstrated through historiography, whereas the Christ of faith must be viewed as the product of religious experience. The Church affirms the centrality of faith, but contends Jesus knew himself to be the Son of God and testified to this during his lifetime. Furthermore, this can be shown using historical methods.[118]

New Testament Christology

Adam considered it necessary, despite his earlier comments on the role and value of Scripture, to look to the canonical gospels for their image of Christ because it is basic: this is the image of the Christ of faith. In examining the gospels, Adam looked for the image of Christ held by believers before the gospels were written. From there, because some critics distrusted even the apostolic witness, Adam sought to get back to Jesus himself as the one sure ground in the face of all criticism. He concluded the evidence from all of these strata is consistent because it comes from one Spirit.

Adam understood the Christology of the gospels in a traditional sense. He accepted a high Christology and asserted the gospel writers intended the title Son of God in a strictly metaphysical sense.

> To sum up, we may affirm that the Gospels are agreed in their testimony that Jesus felt himself to be the fulfillment and the true content of the Old Testament, the bringer of the highest, most consummate revelation. This consciousness of his calling was rooted in his metaphysical consciousness of being the Son of God, in his clear knowledge and declaration that he and he alone was the well-beloved Son of the heavenly Father, identical with Jahve.[119]

The apostolic proclamation began with the divine Jesus. The earliest proclamation concerned not the everlasting Son of God, but the God become human. The God-man was approached in terms of his humanity, however, a humanity that has been assumed into the divine glory. The early Christian proclamation emphasized Jesus' humanity, his appearance in history, and his vindication by death and resurrection, presupposing his deity. The early apostles were more concerned with the Messiah than with God.[120] The shift to concern for Jesus' deity occurred with the onset of the Hellenistic mission. The Christian understanding of Jesus' person differed from the Hellenistic concept of divinization because the latter always occurred in the context of gnosticism and docetism. Such a picture is ahistorical, whereas Christianity held firmly to its historical content. These contrasting understandings of divinization led to conflicting understandings of salvation. The same language appears in each, but the terms have entirely different meanings.[121]   Continuing the thrust of his earlier *Jesus Christus* in *The Christ of Faith*, Adam pointed out that the declarations of Jesus' majesty were only part of the early story. Equally clear statements of his lowliness and meekness stand beside them. Jesus knew himself to be the Son of the Father, but never did he consider himself merely a god strolling across the earth after the manner of pagan myths.

In the gospels we find a picture of a Jesus who struggled, a Jesus immanent to, not sovereign above and apart from the world. This very human Jesus' desires were rooted firmly in the will of God so that all outward temptation lost its force the moment it came up against this will within in Jesus' consciousness. Jesus' moral wishes and power were perfect, but perfect only as a person's will on earth can be perfect. This is far different

from the moral perfection God possesses. Similarly, the earthly Jesus' consciousness never included the omniscience of the Father. Jesus' being was
limited in will, knowledge, and power; this is clear from the circumstances
in which the gospels describe Jesus as living his human life. It was a life of
poverty, lowliness, and homelessness.

Adam saw in the gospels a "naive and simple" historiography that
labored

> to put down without any omissions the recollections of the
> Apostles' teachings current in the community, even when
> it has to take repetitions, inconsistencies, and even contra-
> dictions in its stride.[122]

Adam contrasted this with the approach of the later apocryphal gospels.

In Paul's Christology Adam found undeniable development. This
was not a progression from one new position to another, but instead an
increasingly profound comprehension and clarification of that which he had
said earlier. This development was forced on him by his disputes with the
Jews and by the anthroposophic views of various gnostic mystery religions
of redemption.

Adam summed up the biblical witness as follows. The earliest
Christian community in Jerusalem, even Jesus' disciples during his lifetime,
had made Jesus the object of religious veneration. They recognized him as
Lord, and they performed signs and wonders in his name. This is the only
way we can account for the total absence of distinction between the belief
in Jesus found in the earliest Palestinian communities and that found in the
Hellenistic communities.[123]

The early Church certainly was aware of the importance of doctrine
and theology. It had no room for the vagaries of the anti-Christian pagan
legends. This clear concept of doctrine left room neither for a gradual unfolding of Christology nor for any alteration in the presentation of the figure
of Christ. The Hellenistic and Christian saviors are separated by "an unbridgeable abyss."

In drawing from this to develop his dogmatic understanding, Adam
used Scripture in an essentially naive manner. His citations and references
show no evidence of critical reflection or conclusions. Adam approached
Jesus in terms of his self-consciousness and claims in the same way he had
earlier in *Jesus Christus*. He had no doubt that Jesus understood himself
from the outset as the promised Messiah and King, but recognized Jesus
gave these terms an entirely different interpretation than did Jesus' contem-

poraries. Such was the reason for Wrede's "Messianic secret." Jesus refused to be understood in terms of the Jewish forms he rejected as wrong. The temptation accounts of Matthew and Luke present Jesus' messianic understanding most clearly.

Jesus' self-designation as Son of Man shows clearly his self-aware-ness. Adam said the gospels never confuse "Son of Man" and "man," but they do alternate between "Son of Man" and "I." Jesus derived Son of Man from Daniel 7:13, and the title pointed to his pre-existence. Although he never stated it in so many words, Jesus assumed his own pre-existence. This was the background to his frequent assertion that he had "come." Jesus' use of the Son of Man title went beyond that which can be explained by Daniel, however. This title was Jesus' indirect and transitional way of explaining who he was.[124]

In Matthew 26:64, Jesus made an undeniable claim to deity. Peter's confession at Caesarea Phillipi also must be understood in metaphysical terms in the full sense of the Matthew passage because of Jesus' response. In John 14:10, Jesus contrasted his relationship with the Father to that enjoyed by other devout persons. He claimed to have a unique and exclusive communion with the Father. This communion was no sometime thing. Simply because he expressed it rarely and only among his intimates is no reason to believe he experienced it only sporadically. It was the motive force of his entire life. Only in light of this special relationship does Jesus' life become clear. To understand Jesus' unique relationship with the Father is to understand the mystery of Jesus.

Because he enjoys this unique relationship, only the Son can reveal the Father to us. This was Jesus' mission and the essence of his message. Christianity claims the Son is the only way to the Father. Adam said this means "Jesus is God the Savior" and "no critical scruples can destroy this."[125]

> At no point in his life is the merest trace of a moral lack, or moral immaturity, or even need for moral development perceptible in him.... From whatever angle we consider his image, Jesus is always as we in our best moments would wish to be.... Either this man is just a literary figment of the imagination... or he is no mere man.... He is God be-come man.... The divinity cannot be removed from his life and being.... To look for mere man behind his miraculous image would be contrary to all historical analogies, and against any understanding psychology.[126]

Jesus' life and ministry reflect his deity, but his disciples came to see and accept this only gradually and not without resistance because of their traditional Jewish up bringing. It was the Resurrection that finally broke through their resistance and transformed both their spiritual outlook and religious understanding.

Adam drew heavily on Paul's Christology because he considered Paul to have "most faithfully presumed and shared the entire spirit of Jesus' doctrine and its dominant ideas."[127]   One of the concepts Paul picked up from Jesus was the Kingdom of God. The dispute the New Testament reported between Paul and the other early disciples dealt only with practical matters, never with doctrine, especially not with Christology. That which Paul taught about Jesus' person and salvific death had already become part of the established fund of Christian proclamation. Both Paul and the early disciples equated Christ with God; Paul's message presupposed this.[128] Paul also presupposed Christ's pre-existence, so he never attempted to prove it. Such pre-existence he derived from his belief in Jesus' deity. Adam listed various passages where Paul stated his belief in Christ's pre-existence.[129] Christ's full humanity was equally central to Paul's message as his deity. This was evident in his Adam-Christ parallel. It also shows in Philippians 2, where Paul set out the relationship between the man Jesus and the Son of God.

Kenosis was Paul's unique contribution to the understanding of the Incarnation. For Paul, *kenosis* did not mean Jesus' self-emptying of his deity, but "of his divine splendor, of those characteristics that are proper to God, and by which he proclaims himself as God."[130] Christ suspended the fullness of his divine qualities—the relative attributes—and used instead purely human attributes and qualities. Thus, the Incarnation was not the transformation of deity into humanity, but the suspension of the divine glory so only the humanity is visible. Adam's expression of his kenotic understanding was ambiguous. At some points he spoke of Christ emptying himself of divine characteristics, but at other times he described this as suspending their use. Given Adam's acceptance of metaphysical language, the variation is important because it affects our understanding of who Jesus is. For Adam, who Jesus is bears on what he can do. Thus, Adam's ambiguity at this point should later affect his soteriology.

Adam considered the doctrine that Christ is one person in two natures to have come from Paul. Further, Paul made it clear Christ's deity did not subsume his humanity. Instead, his human nature retained all its qualities, those associated with willing as well as those associated with doing. Christ's pre-existence was the principle that united and sustained his being and doing as well as forming his divine-human person. Paul's doctrine of kenosis enabled him to move from expressing Christ's divine person to affirming his redemptive suffering and death. Paul's theology was centered in Christ, not in Jesus, because it sought to understand the mystery of Christ in terms of his heavenly origin, that is from the side of God. According to Adam, "Paul had eyes only for the divine Christ."[131]

In John, Adam saw a warm and tender recollection of Jesus. This was for Adam a welcome supplement to Paul's systematic Christology. Adam argued both in terms of modern linguistic study and patristic evidence that John was the author of or source for the gospel bearing his name. He agreed John differed significantly from the synoptics, but he said this was because John supplemented them at essential points. John was both historically accurate and helpful in providing details lacking in the synoptics.[132]

In contrast to Paul, John was concerned primarily with Jesus' humanity. He did not see humanity as something strange and foreign to Jesus' deity. Humanity was not a condition of humiliation but a transparency and revealing of the deity. Jesus' humanity was the medium through which his divine glory could shine. Like Paul, John affirmed Jesus' deity and pre-existence, but he laid much greater stress on his full humanity than did Paul. John saw Jesus' deity and humanity as co-existing in the closest possible proximity without mixing. Thus, the incarnate Jesus was fully conscious of his unity with the Father. In becoming incarnate, the Logos partook of humanity in all of its weakness and imperfection.

John's picture of Jesus is the most consummate given us in revelation. "Later theology had nothing to add to it. All it did was clarify, conceptualize, and systematize into an ordered Christology what John had described with simple directness."[133]

Adam drew on these two canonical sources to explain what happened when the Word became human. Incarnation was the assumption of human nature into the divine person, not into the divine nature. This means Christ's humanity did not differ from ours. The way in which it was united with deity is a mystery—we cannot comprehend it. The hypostatic union is an article of faith, not of reason. Thus it is beyond, but not contrary to, faith.[134] The Church has not settled on any particular understanding of the union of the two natures, so theologians remain free to speculate. The two items involved here are the same two involved in the doctrine of the Trinity—person and nature. Nature makes a thing what it is; person is a closed entity with an independent and rational autonomy. Of the two basic Catholic understandings, Adam preferred the Scotist, which held that in Christ both created and uncreated existence were present, and went on to describe existence as an attribute of the nature, not of the person. We can see and experience only the human in Christ; the Logos remains transcendent and available only to faith.[135] Aquinas, in contrast, saw Christ's humanity as so penetrated by the Logos that the only reality of the humanity was that of the Logos. Given Adam's concern for Catholic Monophysitism, his preference for Scotus over Thomas is understandable. Adam was also sympathetic to the Scotist position that the Incarnation would have occurred even had there been no fall. This is because the Incarnation had an end in itself apart from its soteriological value.

Even though Christ's humanity remained like ours, his unity with the Godhead was such that his human self-conscious and self were assumed into the divine consciousness so completely that they are aware of the divine-human union in every respect. All of Jesus' feeling, thought, and volition occur only in the closest connection with his deity. The intimacy of the union rendered Christ incapable of sinning, even though he had a fully human will. Again, Adam followed Scotus in suggesting Christ was theoretically able to sin because sin is a capacity of true humanity but was preserved from sin through the action of divine providence. Adam's preference at this point appears to have been because Scotus emphasized more strongly the fullness of Christ's humanity than did Thomas. Thomas, said Adam, presented a Christ whose moral will was constituted differently from other humans. Jesus was metaphysically incapable of sinning, but could not know this. That is what made his temptations real.

> His incapability of sin secured immutably only the *goal* of his way, which was the fulfillment of the divine will. That he went his way as he did was for his human freedom to decide.[136]

Christ had to be free from sin—original, personal, and even the inclination to sin—if he were to effect our salvation. Christ had to be related to humanity to be our Savior, but he could not be related to human sin. Adam said every objection to the doctrine of Christ's sinlessness was a misunderstanding of the meaning of Scripture, of real humanity, or of sin.[137]

The hypostatic union came into being the instant Christ's human nature was conceived. Jesus' humanity never existed independent of the Logos. Both Scripture and the fathers affirm the union came into existence at the moment of the virginal conception. Now that it exists, the union can never be broken. Jesus was aware of this union from his childhood and thus knew himself to be God's Son. He also knew he was the Savior of the world. Jesus' humanity was so penetrated by his deity that he was aware of the presence of the triune God in his life. This knowledge could not have come through human sources; it could have come only super naturally from God. Jesus needed to know about the Incarnation, so we must conclude God gave him this knowledge as soon as his human consciousness was able to receive it. Nevertheless, Jesus' vision of God could only be as full as the fullest that humanity was capable of and thus infinitely less than God's self-comprehension.

> We can speak of a relative omniscience on the part of our Lord's human soul. It is omniscient because in principle it comprehends everything that God knows. And it is a relative omniscience because it is given only potentially, only according to its capabilities, and put into action only successively, from one case to the next, according to the decision of Jesus' free will.... It does not necessarily follow from that direct vision of God of Jesus' soul that it will have knowledge of all reality.[138]

Adam was concerned to reconcile Jesus' statement that he did not know the day of judgment with the Church's claim Jesus knows everything in the Logos. He concluded Jesus had all knowledge objectively and in principle, but he possessed it only potentially. His knowledge depended in each case upon the grace of God. Thus Jesus could not use it arbitrarily but it remained in Jesus' subconscious and could be called into his consciousness only at the proper time. Jesus could not reflect upon the day of judgment because the time was not yet right. Adam said he drew this solution from the Scotist assumption that Jesus possessed only the capacity for, not the reality of, omniscience within human limits.[139]

Adam dealt with the issue of the day of judgment in another way, too. He said Jesus' message had strong eschatological elements, but the Kingdom of God was not solely a future expectation. Its foundations were laid in the present. Jesus was not interested in when the parousia would come; he wanted to emphasize the certainty of its coming. Never did he say it would come soon after his death. In the prophetic perspective he presented, his coming and the events that followed, especially the fall of Jerusalem, meant the train of events leading toward the day of judgment had begun.[140]

It was the Logos alone that held the natures together. Because the Logos was the ground of Jesus' humanity, his human nature was more perfect than that of other humans because it was not damaged by the effects of sin as all other humans have been.

The totality and nature of the union have practical implications for the believer. Because the person in whom the natures subsist is deity, Christ as a whole is to be worshipped. Moreover, the human Jesus and even the parts of his body are to be worshipped because neither his humanity nor its parts can be divided from his divine person. In each case, however, it is God, not humanity, who is the object of our worship.

The hypostatic union did not result in an apotheosis or deification of Christ's humanity. It did lead to a divinization in which all of Christ's actions were so closely united that each of Jesus' human actions had the Logos as its subject and could be ascribed to the Logos.

Adam said the decisive thing about the Incarnation was that God has come down to humanity. The Incarnation united humanity objectively and fully with God. Christ's humanity mediates the reunion between God and humanity. Adam said Augustine was the Church father who stated this most clearly.

> Christ is the mediator not because he is God but because
> he is *God become man*.... Christ fulfills his office *in forma
> servi*.[141]

The Incarnation cannot be separated from Calvary. By entering into human nature, Christ took to himself all the possibilities that come with being human. The potential for Calvary existed in Bethlehem. This leads to the doctrine of redemption. Adam said provision for redemption presupposes the need for redemption. This is the purpose of the doctrine of original sin. "Because Adam was in his person *totus homo*, all mankind fell through his act." This means all humanity bears a burden of guilt which it has inherited from that first human. Because that guilt reaches to the roots of our human essence, only God can free us from it.[142]

Adam saw redemption as existing within the context of sin and error. Human thought, will, and body stand in need of redemption because each participates in human sin. God determined to redeem fallen humanity through the same process by which it fell under the power of sin. This meant the redeemer would have to "wear the sacrificial garment of humanity," yet remain divine. It also meant that in representing redeemed humanity Christ must be united to the totality of redeemed humanity in the same way the first human was united to the totality of humanity.[143] What Christ accomplished in this representation and recapitulation was the reunion of God and humanity in their original relationship. It is not that he prepared the way for others to follow, but that he accomplished all that was needed.

> It is not as though we were redeemed only by our imita-
> tion of Jesus' life in his meaning and spirit, and should
> follow his example.... It is not as though Christ had merely
> built the bridge across the abyss separating us from God,
> and had now given us the opportunity of crossing this
> bridge of our own accord.... Christ does not simply build
> this bridge; he is himself the bridge.... The substance of
> what we have to do to wipe out our sins has been achieved
> by Christ, yea, he is himself this achievement.... We in our
> religious life are only the extension, the unfolding, of what
> occurred once in Nazareth, an historically unfolding incar-
> nation of the God-man.[144]

Adam explained Jesus' salvific work in terms of his passion, which he described as a "suffering of atonement." This was something he took upon himself voluntarily yet necessarily if he was to be our Savior. Jesus' repeated citations of the Jewish Scriptures confirm this.

Jesus also appeared as the bringer of the new Kingdom. Only where Jesus is do we find the Kingdom and forgiveness of sins. He claimed that in him the new Kingdom had appeared, and it was this claim that gave meaning and power to his promises and commandments. Jesus' sacrificial death on the cross bore fresh witness to his claims. Grace and sacrifice are not contradictory concepts for Adam; instead, grace has become possible only because Jesus died as a sacrifice to ransom humanity from sin.[145] In saying this, Adam omitted any doctrine of election and stressed the objectivity and universality of Christ's saving work.

Sacrifice and death were not the end of Jesus' story. The Resurrection was the "crown and consummation" of Jesus' ministry. From this point on, we see him as the risen Lord, King, and Priest of the new covenant. He is also the Judge of the world, and in this final role he will lead the redeemed into the presence of the Father.

The Easter events were a matter of real history. For that reason, eyewitnesses were needed to vouch for the authenticity of the Easter events.

But the events were not merely historical, they were also salvific. To the extent they partook of salvation history, they can be understood only through the activity of the Spirit who makes that history possible. In saying this, Adam was attacking Bultmann's criteria for historicity as inappropriate to the nature of the event. Because it was a religious event, it went beyond the visible world of experience and cannot be understood completely in terms of this world. That does not mean it was unhistorical, but that it was superhistorical. The Resurrection was not merely a question for scholars. Adam said the Resurrection addresses the entirety of a person, not only the intellect. Fundamentally, it addresses the conscience and thus requires primarily a response of faith and the will.[146]

The basis for the apostolic belief in the Resurrection was both Jesus' appearances and the empty tomb. The latter guaranteed the corporeality of the former. This means the Resurrection includes both the survival and the transformation of the body.

Adam sharply attacked what he called the "destructive theological criticism" of Jesus' passion. He said Jesus was fully aware from the outset of his ministry that he could die a violent death. At Caesarea Philippi this possibility became a certainty for him. Adam explicitly denied Paul was the first to interpret Jesus' death along the lines of an Old Testament atoning sacrifice. Adam cited Luke as showing Jesus to be the source of this interpretation.[147] Adam also said "negative biblical criticism" denied the Resurrection because it determined *a priori* that because "dead men do not rise," Jesus could not have risen. Against this "established dogma of unbelief,"[148] Adam presented the biblical witness for the reality of Jesus' resurrection and related it to the practice of the early believers, which was understandable only in light of a bodily resurrection.

In looking at Adam's Christology as it developed over nearly four decades, we see both continuity and change. Adam continued to hold to the basic dogmatic themes that helped form his earliest Christology, but the earlier Neo-Romantic themes were less evident in his final Christology. Krieg says the various elements of Adam's historical context (and we might say contexts) flowed together in his Christology. These would reform what he had to say according to the changing environment and audience he faced. We should add that this shift was intentional on his part; it was part of what he understood the Tübingen School's purpose to be. Thus Adam's Jesus was primarily a Jesus as seen through the eyes of inter-war German Catholicism. That limits its value for us today. The work also bears the imprint of an inheritance from Drey, Möhler, and Kuhn, and shows evidence of a desire to avoid the biblical hermeneutics identified with Modernism.

Conclusion

In many ways, Adam's approach to Christology was pre-critical. It was also consciously dogmatic. In *Jesus Christus*, Adam said he was interested only in the "dogmatic Christ." In *The Christ of Faith*, he said his research was directed by the dogmatic method. Adam described this method as meaning our statements about Jesus are created out of the living faith of the Church which has found its true deposit in the inspired Scriptures and in the extrabiblical tradition. Krieg describes Adam's Christology as standing in every way in contrast to modern Christologies. The value he sees in this is that Adam's work can cause us to distance ourselves critically *vis-à-vis* our current practice of theology within the general framework of anthropology or history.[149]

Krieg also observes it would be wrong to consign *Jesus Christus* and *The Christ of Faith* to the museum. "The central place of Christology in Adam's thought and aspects of his theological method refer directly to contemporary theological questions."[150] First, Adam reminds us that Christology investigates the identity of an individual human being whom we can know immediately only through his followers. Thus Christology must take place within the realm of tradition using a method that synthesizes Church doctrine, Scripture, and contemporary concerns. Adam also calls on us to go beyond the critical method toward a biblical hermeneutic that draws on the images of Jesus we find in the gospels.

Adam's Christology has both strengths and weaknesses. His strong emphasis on Jesus' humanity challenged the latent Monophysitism that had ruled the Catholic Church for centuries. But Adam allowed contemporary currents to take precedence over Scripture and dogma. In this way, he compromised his interpretation of Chalcedon and the gospels. Krieg charges Adam's treatment of Jesus reflected the life philosophy of his day more than it did Chalcedon. He suggests an inadequate biblical hermeneutic may have been at the root of Adam's problem.[151]

Adam attempted to ground his Christology in human experience as well as in logic and theory. We can see this in his word pictures of Jesus. Two of Adam's students, Fritz Hofmann and Heinrich Fries, have written that Adam's images of Jesus changed their lives and led them to a deeper understanding of the Church's Christology. For Krieg, this aspect of Adam's hermeneutic presents a challenge to our age. We cannot use his pre-critical approach to the gospels, but modern critical methods have made it almost impossible to derive any picture of Jesus. Reinhardt, however, saw Adam's images of Christ as scarcely distinguishable from the liberal lives of Jesus

that were appearing during Adam's early theological training.[152] In saying
this, Reinhardt appears to have picked up on weaknesses that Krieg mentioned without recognizing the value of Adam's work in creating a full-orbed
Christology such as is necessary for a living faith.

Kasper has pointed out Adam's Neo-Romanticism led him to under-
estimate the reality of evil and thus the theological significance of the cross.
Kasper also asks whether Adam has fully appreciated the element of suffering in human history. This, says Kasper, has led him to de-emphasize the
importance of the Paschal mystery. It was not that Adam missed or ignored
the essentials, but his attitude toward nature and human ability was too
positive given the reality of the cross. Further, Adam's *Lebensphilosophie*
related only to the brief inter-war period between 19th century idealism and
20th century materialism.[153] The point of contact today, says Kasper, is
not life but freedom or liberation.[154]   Kasper's criticism of Adam is much
harsher than Krieg's. Because of its Neo-Romanticism and pre-critical
reading of Scripture, Adam's Christology is superficial and passé. Kasper
calls it a "painful reminder of the fundamentalism of the Church before
Divine Afflante Spiritu."[155]

Adam emphasized the Incarnation at the expense of the cross and
Resurrection. This contrasted sharply not only with modern critical scholarship but also with the New Testament. We would suggest both Adam and
the modern critics have erred in adopting a one-sided approach to Christ.
The New Testament documents present both the Incarnation and the death
and Resurrection as important. The image of two foci appears more accurate than that of one center.

In reaffirming the importance of Christ's humanity for Church
doctrine, Adam never failed to take his deity into account. This was an
important balance at a time when too much theology was affirming one or
the other. Although he did not carry through with his christological
program to develop a complete and coherent picture of enduring value,
Adam made a significant contribution by reintroducing Jesus' humanity to
the faith of the Church and yet affirming Jesus' deity.

> If Jesus were only a man and no more, he could only give
> us our humanity back, humanity with all of its conditional-
> ness and doubtfulness. And our deepest misery, the misery
> of our sin and death, would remain always with us. No,
> Jesuanity is an empty, soulless Christianity, a faith from
> which the heart has been torn, even if it has been pro-
> claimed by the theologians.[156]

Adam laid great stress on the mediatorial and redemptive significance of Jesus' humanity. This humanity was also the starting point for his reflections on the Church. The second controlling idea of Adam's theology was the Church as the body of Christ, the revelation and manifestation of Christ's saving power. To protect this humanity, Adam viewed the hypostatic union in static terms so the humanity would not be absorbed into the deity. He united the natures in the Logos ontologically in terms of a hegemony of the Logos and psychologically in terms of Christ's human consciousness possessing an immediate vision of God. For Adam, Christ has a divine person and a divine-human personality.[157]

Adam was particularly concerned with Jesus' self-consciousness. Jesus' entire attitude suggested he was aware of himself as Messiah. Jesus described himself as Son of Man because this enabled him to provide the content he desired for his self-presentation. The high point of Jesus' self-consciousness, however, was the title Son of God. Jesus used both of these concepts.[158]

Like his Tübingen predecessors, Adam closely related Christ and the Church. The relation was a sacramental unity in which God has appeared in the human. It is a unity where the members are joined to their head, Christ, in a visible, holy community. The Church is essential to Christianity. For Adam, the Church is nothing else than Christ living on and growing in space and time.

> The Church, which exists in its new, realized human community... is at the heart of Karl Adam's theology. But it is not the final and most profound word; the Church is what it is only through Christ. Jesus Christ—his divine-human person, his saving work, and his perpetual mediation—constitutes the proper center of his theology.[159]

Adam has much to offer the Church in the late 20th century. He had the gift of presenting the central truths of Christianity—God, Christ, Church, grace—to the people of his day in a way that answered their questions and became a truth for their lives that they could understand in their time. Hofmann has said a theology that lacks the courage to be time-bound in this way can be of assistance to no time, but runs the risk of being lost in abstract conceptualization. Thus Adam's Christology is a model for theologians who serve their own age.[160] Kasper echoes this, and adds that because he was concerned to create a theology for his time Adam is more important for his students than for his books. The latter are time-bound, but the former have learned to speak to their own time (and can teach their students to do so). Adam's students were a powerful force in the renewal of the Church that began at Vatican II.

Kasper also says the spirit of Adam's theology is the spirit of the Catholic Tübingen School. It was characterized by the unity of scientific study, attachment to the Church, and openness to the times. Kasper clarifies this by adding that scientific study is not the same as dead analysis, attachment to the Church is not the same as prescribed limits, and openness to the times does not mean chasing the latest fad.[161]

Krieg sees two ways Adam can contribute to today's Christology. First, his writings developed an approach that united Church doctrine, Scripture, and the life experience of the Church today. Second, in *Jesus Christus*, Adam required a biblical picture of Jesus that disclosed his individuality and presented a basis for his christological claims. Krieg says Adam challenges modern Christology not only to say who Jesus is but also to *show* who he is. He challenges us to explore ways to introduce a powerful picture of Jesus into our Christology.[162] When we can present such a picture—one faithful to the Scripture, to Church doctrine, and understandable in terms of our culture—we will have a vibrant Christ who can change our world as he once changed the world of his contemporaries.

1. Fritz Hofmann, "Theologie auf dem Geist der Tübinger Schule," *Theologische Quartalschrift* 146 (1966):283. Hofmann was a student of Adam at Tübingen.

2. Robert Krieg, "Zur Aktualität der Christologie Karl Adams," *Theologische Quartalschrift* 166 (1986):92.

3. "The Church community is the sole mediator of the Spirit, not the 'I,' but the 'we' is the bearer of the Spirit." Cited by Walter Kasper, "Karl Adam," *Theologische Quartalschrift* 156 (1976):254.

4. Jacob Laubach, "Karl Adam," in *Theologians of Our Time*, p. 94, ed. by Leonard Reinisch (Notre Dame: University of Notre Dame, 1964).

5. Hofmann, p. 283.

6. Ibid., p. 282.

7. Karl Adam, *The Spirit of Catholicism* (revised edition), trans. by Justin McCann (New York: Macmillan, 1946).

8. Krieg, pp. 96 f.

9. Hofmann, p. 282.

10. Ibid., p. 264.

11. Roger Aubert, "Karl Adam," in *Tendenzen der Theologie im 20. Jahrhundert*, p. 162, ed. by Hans Jürgen Schultz (Stuttgart: Kreuz, 1966); Kasper, pp. 252 f.

12. Klaus Reinhardt, *Der dogmatische Schriftgebrauch in der katholischen and protestantischen Christologie von der Aufklärung bis zur Gegenwart* (Munich: Ferdinand Schöningh, 1970), p. 325.

13. Kasper, p. 254.

14. The papal decree *Lamentabili* expressly condemned the following christological statements:

> ——the divinity of Jesus Christ is not proved from the Gospels, but is a dogma derived by the Christian conscience from the notion of the Messiah;
>
> ——while exercising his ministry, Jesus did not so speak as to teach that he was the Messiah, nor was the purpose of his miracles to prove that he was;
>
> ——It is permissible to admit that the Christ shown by history is much inferior to the Christ who is the object of faith;
>
> ——in all Gospel texts the expression "Son of God" means no more than "Messiah" and in no way signifies that Christ is the true natural Son of God;
>
> ——the doctrine concerning Christ taught by Paul and John and the Councils of Nicea, Ephesus, and Chalcedon is not that which Jesus taught but (only) what the Christian conscience has conceived about Jesus;
>
> ——the natural sense of the Gospel texts cannot be reconciled with what our theologians teach about the awareness and infallible knowledge of Jesus;
>
> ——it is obvious to anyone who is not led by pre-conceived opinions that either Jesus taught in error the proximate advent of the Messiah or the greater part of his teaching as contained in the synoptic Gospels lacks authenticity;
>
> ——a critic cannot claim unlimited knowledge for Christ without supposing what is historically inconceivable and repugnant to the moral sense, that Christ as man had knowledge of God and nevertheless in so many things did not wish to communicate the knowledge to his disciples and to posterity;
>
> ——Christ was not always aware of his own messianic dignity;
>
> ——the Resurrection of the Savior is not a true fact in the order of history but only a fact in the supernatural order and is neither proved nor provable, but something that the Christian conscience gradually developed from other facts;
>
> ——belief in the resurrection of Christ was not at the beginning in the actual fact of resurrection but in the immortal life of Christ with God;
>
> ——the doctrine of the expiatory death of Christ is not from the Gospels but from Paul.

This selection from *Lamentabili* is found in *The teaching of the Catholic Church*, ed. by Josef Neuner and Heinrich Roos (Staten Island: Alba House, 1967), pp. 172 f. Further condemnations of various aspects of biblical studies included in *Lamentabili* were equally detrimental to Catholic scholars' willingness and ability to engage in serious theological study.

15. Laubach, p. 99.

16. Krieg, p. 96.

17. Ibid., pp. 94 f.

18. Kasper, p. 256.

19. Robert Krieg, "Karl Adam's Christology: Toward a Post-Critical Method," *Heythrop Journal* 25 (1984):466.

20. Laubach, p. 100.

21. Krieg, "Aktualität," p. 102.

22. Ibid., pp. 102 f. Adam's belief he could recover Jesus' self-consciousness from his reading of the gospels is a clear example of the difference between his approach to the text and that of the hermeneutics of suspicion that governs much of modern criticism. Royce Gordon Gruenler has provided a defense of this phenomenological approach to the text in his book, *New Approaches to Jesus and the Gospels* (Grand Rapids: Baker, 1982). Gruenler suggests a phenomenological approach to the text permits him to develop the high Christology of the patristic Church using only the text accepted as authentic by such New Testament scholars as Norman Perrin. Adam used the entirety of the gospels as his source for Christology.

23. Ibid., p. 101.

24. Ibid., pp. 103 f. Such a position stands in stark contrast to the general critical attitude that John was the source of the traditional high Christologies that tended to lose sight of Jesus' humanity altogether.

25. Reinhardt, p. 334. From the conclusions Adam presented, it is clear he approached the Bible with a set of presuppositions sharply at variance with those of either the liberals or the dialectical theologians. In his willingness to accept some of the results of critical scholarship, Adam was equally distant from the prevailing Neoscholasticism that characterized the Catholic scholarship of his day. Because of the significant role he allotted to tradition and because of the powerful effect of contemporary influences, Adam's theology was not as exclusively biblical as it might appear from these sentences.

26. Laubach, pp. 97, 100, 105 f.

27. Krieg, "Aktualität," p. 99. Alec Vidler also pointed to this feature of Adam's Christology:

> The tendency of his own Christology, if we may judge rather from what he leaves unsaid than from what he says, seems to be toward a position that is equivalent to, though formally distinct from, a kenotic theory of the Incarnation (Alec R. Vidler, *The Modernist Movement in the Roman Church* (Cambridge: The University Press, 1934) pp. 229 f.).

Vidler here at this relatively early point in Adam's academic career used the method of interpreting Adam as much by what he left unsaid as by what he said. This is how post-Vatican II Catholic theologians have suggested Adam be understood. Writing in this way, Adam would have been able to publish his theology without running afoul of the anti-Modernist strictures by neglecting to discuss subjects where his position might be construed as reflecting the condemned Modernism.

28. Reinhardt, pp. 333 f.

29. Krieg, "Aktualität," p. 99.

30. Laubach, p. 105.

31. Adam, *The Spirit of Catholicism*, pp. 15 f.

32. Ibid., pp. 20 f.

33. Ibid., p. 23.

34. Ibid., pp. 113, 116–120. Adam's concern with Mary as ensuring a human involvement in the process of salvation appears out of place in a theologian noted for his emphasis on Jesus' humanity.

35. Ibid., p. 51

36. Ibid., p. 50.

37. Ibid., pp. 56 f.

38. Ibid., pp. 57 f.

39. Ibid., p. 61.

40. Ibid., pp. 63 f.

41. Ibid., pp. 169 f.

42. Ibid., p. 173.

43. Ibid., pp. 174 f.

44. Ibid., pp. 177 f.

45. Ibid., p. 180.

46. Karl Adam, *Christ and the Western Mind*, trans. by Edward Bullough (New York: Macmillan, 1930).

47. Karl Adam, *Christ Our Brother*, trans. by Dom Justin McCann (New York: Macmillan, 1931).

48. Adam, *Christ and the Western Mind*, p. 24.

49. Ibid., pp. 34 f.

50. Ibid.

51. Ibid., p. 36.

52. Karl Adam, "Jesus Christ and the Spirit of the Age," in *Germany's New Religion*, pp. 117–168, ed. by Wilhelm Hauser, *et al.*, trans. by T. S. K. Scott-Craig and R. E. Davies (New York: Abingdon, 1937). Hauer was the translators' example of the new German religion, a paganism with a strong affinity to the ruling Nazism, and Adam was the Catholic advocate of the traditional Christian faith; Karl Heim was the Protestant representative.

53. Adam, "Jesus Christ and the Spirit of the Age," pp. 124 f.

54. Ibid., pp. 125 f.

55. Ibid., pp. 129 f.

56. Ibid., pp. 162 f.

57. The first edition of *Christ Our Brother* included only the first three chapters of the 1930 version plus a chapter incorporated into *The Spirit of Catholicism*. That first edition appeared in 1926, two years after *Spirit*.

58. Adam, *Christ Our Brother*, pp. 21 f.

59. Ibid., p. 25.

60. Ibid., pp. 25 f.

61. Ibid., p. 49.

62. Ibid., pp. 49, 51.

63. Ibid., pp. 59 f.

64. Ibid.

65. Ibid., pp. 62 f.

66. Ibid., p. 196.

67. Ibid., pp. 192 f.

68. Ibid., p. 78.

69. Ibid., pp. 85, 90 ff., 104.

70. Ibid., p. 185.

71. Karl Adam, *Jesus Christus* (third edition; Augsburg: Haas und Grabherr, 1934). The influence of this book on German Catholic theology becomes clear when we realize the first edition of the book appeared in 1933, and at least three further editions appeared before 1940. *Jesus Christus* appeared in English translation in 1934 as *The Son of God* (London: Sheed and Ward), but the translation gives no indication that it bears any relation to Jesus Christus.

72. Krieg, "Aktualität," p. 100.

73. Reinhardt, pp. 331 f.

74. Kasper, pp. 254 ff.

75. Krieg, "Aktualität," pp. 98 f.

76. Adam, *Jesus Christus*, p. 10.

77. Ibid., pp. 10 f.

78. Ibid., pp. 14 f.

79. Ibid., p. 16.

80. Ibid., p. 19.

81. Ibid., pp. 20 f.

82. Ibid., pp. 25 f. Adam indicated this was particularly true since A. Schweitzer's critique of the *Leben Jesu Forschung*.

83. Ibid., p. 60.

84. Ibid., pp. 26 f., 29.

85. Ibid., pp. 73 ff.

86. Ibid., p. 79.

87. Ibid., p. 80.

88. Ibid., 135.

89. Ibid., pp. 146 ff.

90. Ibid., p. 173.

91. For a report on the status of Son of Man studies, see William O. Walker, Jr., "The Son of Man: Some Recent Developments," *Catholic Biblical Quarterly* 45 (1983): 584–607.

92. Adam, *Jesus Christus*, pp. 184 ff. For example, Jesus forgave sins, a divine prerogative in the Old Testament.

93. Ibid., pp. 199 f.

94. Ibid., p. 203.

95. Ibid., p. 233.

96. Ibid., pp. 226 ff.

97. Ibid., pp. 244, 249.

98. Ibid., pp. 245 f.

99. Ibid., pp. 246, 250.

100. Ibid., p. 274.

101. Ibid., p. 286.

102. Ibid., p. 296.

103. Ibid., pp. 302 f.

104. Karl Adam, *The Christ of Faith*, trans. by Joyce Crick (New York: New American Library, 1962).

105. Reinhardt, p. 336. Many of the changes Reinhardt mentioned as first appearing in *The Christ of Faith* were already present in *Jesus Christus* over 20 years earlier.

106. Adam, *The Christ of Faith*, pp. 17 f. (emphasis added).

107. Ibid., pp. 19 f.

108. Ibid.

109. Ibid., p. 22.

110. Ibid., pp. 23 f.

111. Ibid., p. 24.

112. Ibid., p. 27.

113. Ibid., p. 29.

114. Ibid., p. 27.

115. Ibid., p. 70.

116. Ibid., p. 57.

117. Ibid., p. 63.

118. Ibid., p. 69.

119. Ibid., p. 81.

120. Ibid., pp. 89 ff.

121. Ibid., pp. 92, 109 ff. Martin Hengel's recent work calls into question Adam's sharp distinction between Palestinian Jews and Hellenistic gentiles, but Adam's position reflected faithfully the biblical-critical conclusions of his

contemporaries. Hengel teaches New Testament on the Protestant Tübingen faculty.

122. Ibid., p. 103.

123. Ibid., pp. 100 f.

124. Ibid., pp. 133 f., 136 f., 139.

125. Ibid., p. 158.

126. Ibid., pp. 165 f.

127. Ibid., p. 182.

128. Ibid., pp. 185 f.

129. Ibid., pp. 190 f. The passages Adam cited were Rom 1:4; I Cor 8:6; II Cor 8:9; Gal 4:4; Phil 2:8; Col 1:15 ff.

130. Ibid., p. 193.

131. Ibid., p. 200.

132. Ibid., pp. 196 f., 205.

133. Ibid., p. 206.

134. Ibid., pp. 216 f.

135. Ibid., pp. 226 f., 229 f.

136. Ibid., p. 253 (emphasis in original).

137. Ibid., pp. 277 f.

138. Ibid., pp. 306 f.

139. Ibid., pp. 307-313.

140. Ibid., pp. 313–321.

141. Ibid., pp. 339 f.

142. Ibid., pp. 335 f.

143. Ibid., p. 337.

144. Ibid., p. 341.

145. Ibid., p. 357.

146. Ibid., pp. 396 f.

147. Ibid., pp. 342 f.

148. Ibid., p. 389.

149. Krieg, "Aktualität," p. 98.

150. Ibid., p. 107.

151. Ibid., pp. 100f.

152. Reinhardt, p. 336.

153. Krieg, "Karl Adam's Christology," p. 470.

154. Kasper, "Karl Adam," p. 257.

155. Krieg, "Aktualität," p. 106.

156. Kasper, "Karl Adam," p. 256.

157. Reinhardt, p. 332.

158. Laubach, pp. 101 f.

159. Hofmann, pp. 281.

160. Ibid., pp. 282 f.

161. Kasper, "Karl Adam," pp. 257 f.

162. Krieg, "Aktualität," pp. 92 f.

CHAPTER VII

JOSEF RUPERT GEISELMANN

The Catholic Tübingen School has had a strong tradition of historical concern. Its emphasis on tradition has required Tübingen theologians to be familiar with the history of the Church and of doctrine in order to recognize the context of and connections between doctrines so they can better present them to their own age. Most Tübingers have incorporated this historical interest into their dogmatics but several have made Church history their overriding concern, doing their theology within the context of their reflection on the history of the Church. Möhler is the best known of this group, but a hundred years later, Josef Rupert Geiselmann (1890—1970) undertook a major project both to define the nature of the Tübingen School and to appropriate its lessons for his contemporaries.

Geiselmann was born in Neu Ulm in 1890, and studied for the priesthood at Tübingen. These studies took place immediately after the condemnation of Modernism with the repercussions that condemnation had for Catholic theological education. Geiselmann was a student at Tübingen after its earlier glory had faded into obscurity and several years before the arrival of Karl Adam. After completing his theological studies, Geiselmann served in a parish for four years (1915—1919), and then returned to Tübingen as an instructor. In 1930, he was promoted to professor. Four years later, he became professor of scholastic philosophy and dogmatic theology. In 1949, Geiselmann succeeded to Adam's chair of dogmatics. He retired in 1958.

During his nearly 40 years at Tübingen, Geiselmann devoted himself to researching and revitalizing the theology of the Catholic Tübingen School. He prepared critical editions of the works of earlier Tübingers, particularly Möhler, as well as detailed explanations, critiques, and applications of his predecessors' work in a number of books and articles. Geiselmann also wrote a history of the Catholic Tübingen School.[1]

Historian of the Tübingen School

When Geiselmann began his research, no consensus existed regarding the nature of the Catholic Tübingen School. Both Schanz and Funk had

written articles on the subject during the decades before Geiselmann began
to teach at Tübingen, but Funk had denied any school existed in the proper
sense of the term.[2]

Geiselmann showed the Tübingen theology existed in a vital relationship with the spiritual developments of the Enlightenment, Romanticism, and German Idealism. It must be understood both as a synthesis of
these movements and as their opponent. The determining characteristic of
the Catholic Tübingen School was "the fundamental principle of the historicity of revelation." The theologians of Tübingen did not understand
historicity to mean a multiplicity of discrete, punctiliar occurrences in human
life. Instead, they saw it as the connection of the whole of that which is
mediated to humans through living tradition, a tradition to which they are
responsible and which they must appropriate according to their situation.[3]

As Geiselmann saw it, the 19th century Catholic Tübingen School
was "die glückliche Mittelstrasse" of the Roman Catholic theology of its day.
His research was directed at confirming this opinion. Tübingen theology was
no cautious tactical use of a middle way, said Geiselmann, but instead was
a vital mediating process where recognition of the substantial reality of the
truth contained in the Christian revelation led to its being reformed into a
new historical shape through accepting and rejecting historical elements.
Scheffczyk said Geiselmann's contribution was to recognize historical Tübingen thought was determined by the law of the dialectic with its doctrine of
thesis and antithesis.[4] Using this dialectic, Geiselmann was able to explain
not only the inner turbulence and pluriformity of Tübingen theology but also
to uncover the unity encompassing these differences. Geiselmann not only
used this approach in his own work, but also passed it on to his students, so
that at the end of his career he could say, "Die Schule ist nicht tot."

> Thus he was entirely in the spirit of the great Tübingers
> who manifested a thoroughly dialectical relationship over
> against the power of the spirit of the age, who assigned to
> theology the double task of being open to the claims of the
> time and yet not surrendering the self-identity and original-
> ity of that which is Christian.[5]

In his attempt to renew theology on the basis of historical thought,
Geiselmann gave the christological question a particular importance. Scheffczyk said Geiselmann's principal work on Christology, *Jesus der Christus*,
showed a mastery of the results of exegesis rarely seen in a theologian.
From these results, Geiselmann concluded the salvation history fulfilled in

Jesus Christ showed the original apostolic kerygma to consist of witness (*martyrion*) and tradition (*tradition*). In this way, he hoped to overcome the division between the Jesus of history and the Christ of faith.

Biblical Hermeneutics

Drawing heavily on the earlier work of J. E. Kuhn, Geiselmann suggested the original apostolic kerygma was based on the historical facts of Jesus' life, but its primary purpose was not to be an historical report of the events. The gospels were concerned with faith in Jesus, not with the history of Jesus, but they certainly were grounded in the empirical-historical facts about Jesus. Thus, we do not face pure history in the gospels but salvation history. In presenting Jesus' history as salvation history, the apostles were creatively forming history, but they were not denying or misusing history.[6]

Each age has its own questions about Jesus. These questions relate directly to the situation in which that age finds itself and suggest a picture of Jesus corresponding to that situation. Geiselmann sought to sketch such a picture of the historical Jesus, who is also the proclaimed Christ, suitable to his age.[7]

> Catholic systematic theology seeks to answer the question about the historical Jesus through natural historical judgment. Thus, the scriptures will be considered an historical source, although they must be critically examined.... No one denies that the gospels are kerygmatic witnesses from faith and are not historically neutral.[8]

To say the gospels are kerygmatic witnesses, and thus not historically neutral, is not to deny they can serve as reliable sources for the life of Jesus; it is only to say we cannot deal adequately with them unless we first recognize their perspective and take it into account. At other points in his work, Geiselmann offered the same warning about recognizing the values implicit in our approach to the text. Geiselmann was correct in recognizing the gospels are not value-neutral—no text is—but in affirming that we still can use them profitably.

The only way to achieve the proper understanding of the Jesus Christ of the New Testament is first to clarify the relationship of God to the world. God is immanent in the world and God is transcendent over the world. In the life and work of Jesus, God intervened in history. When we recognize this, the scandal of the course of Jesus' life and work we find in the post-Easter reports of the synoptics is canceled (*aufgehoben*).[9]

The unity of the historical Jesus with the Christ of faith constitutes the "scandal and folly" of Christianity. The apostolic witness confesses Jesus as the Christ and intends an objective unity of the Christ of faith with the Jesus of history. The double name "Jesus Christ" witnesses to the mystery of this person. Geiselmann said we must distinguish the two names but we may not divide them. Otherwise we can never hope to understand the uniqueness of this historical individual. Jesus is the name of a man who is a part of history and who made history. Christ is an honorific we give to that historical personage and behind which lies his God-given task and his work. This title also shows Jesus does not belong solely to the history of the world. To divide the Christ of faith from the Jesus of history leads inevitably to the Christ myth.[10]

Geiselmann did not satisfy himself with simply attacking the demythologization of the gospels that viewed Jesus as merely a human; he also criticized the opposing opinion that saw Jesus as God but could not conceive of him as a human. Geiselmann said one can see the prevalence of this view simply by presenting the Jesus of the synoptics to a contemporary Catholic audience and measuring the reaction. A latent Monophysitism lies hidden behind much traditional Christian orthodoxy, said Geiselmann.

The theology of the Enlightenment took the opposite course. It surrendered the Christ of heaven for a Jesus who had both feet on the ground. That age read into Jesus its own understanding of what it means to be human, defined in terms of rationalism, moralism, and individualism. The result was a preacher of morality and teacher of virtue who mirrored the spirit of the Enlightenment. George Tyrrell put the problem well when he described one liberal Protestant theologian as looking down the well of time, seeing the reflection of a liberal Protestant at the bottom, and calling it Jesus.[11] Among the questers for the life of the historical Jesus, idealists saw him as the human ideal, aesthetes as the genial artist of speech, and socialists as the friend of the poor and a social reformer.[12]

The theologies of the Enlightenment, liberalism, and dialectical theology are rooted in anthropocentrism, charged Geiselmann. The historical Jesus was theocentric. He certainly cared about people's salvation and happiness, but more than this he cared about God, his lordship, and his Kingdom. Jesus' concept of history centered on God, not on humanity.[13]

Geiselmann derived this picture of Jesus from his reading of the gospels. They alone are the proper source for the historical Jesus, but they must be seen in the light of faith. The gospels are not fictional creations of the life of Jesus; they present a careful selection of eyewitness reports that intend to show Jesus is the promised Messiah.

From the Kuhn-Strauss controversy of the previous century, Geiselmann drew several conclusions for future examination of the gospels as sources for the life of Jesus. The gospels are witnesses from faith that Jesus is the Christ and their historical accounts have been selected to achieve this purpose. This does not mean the gospels are unreliable, merely that they are selective in the history they contain.

The gospels are the written deposit of the original apostolic kerygma. Thus, they derive directly from that kerygma, even though a period of time passed between the original proclamation and its commitment to writing. Despite this passage of time, it is still possible to say something about the original apostolic faith from reading the gospels and Acts. The proclamation of Jesus was not intended merely to inform people about who Jesus was, but to awaken within them faith in this Jesus as the Christ. The apostolic kerygma contains the substance of the entire revelation God has communicated to us in Christ.

Tradition and Scripture

Geiselmann agreed with critics of Scripture that Church tradition does not reproduce the events of Jesus' life (or other reported events, for that matter) with modern historiographic detail, but said it does so in terms of their significance for readers and hearers of the gospel. This explains why the gospels are faithful to the *ipsissima vox* without being overly scrupulous about the *ipsissima verba*. The Spirit working in the Church was the source of this interpretive freedom.[14]

It is this Church kerygma, which faithfully passes on the gospel of Jesus, that keeps the gospel of Jesus alive for today. It is the gospel of Jesus, however, that grounds the kerygma and keeps it from becoming a mere idea or myth. If we valued only the gospel of Jesus, we would know only the man and would end up as Ebionites, yet if we attend only to the kerygma, we must become docetists.

> The historical Jesus and the kerygmatic Christ are not two things independent of each other, instead they stand together with an inner connection.[15]

The priority here goes to the historical Jesus and his gospel because that is the foundation upon which the kerygmatic Christ stands or falls. The kerygma exists to serve the gospel. The proper way to understand history (that is, history as the New Testament presents it) can be described as *Heilsgeschichte*, where the transcendent God enters into the history of humans for their salvation. Such a divine *Heilsgeschichte* is a prerequisite for the deity of Jesus. Otherwise, he would be merely one more of the heroes of world history or of myth.

The Resurrection provided the bridge between Jesus the proclaimer and Jesus the proclaimed, between the gospel and the kerygma. It was not a story made up by the community. Only the experience of Easter made it possible for the disciples to recognize God had entered into world history in the person of Jesus and had lifted him up from under the power of sin and death and made him Lord of the world. Easter was the inbreaking of God's new world which Jesus had proclaimed as the Kingdom of God. Strauss and Bultmann were unable to appreciate this reality because they worked in terms of a particular concept of history that predetermined their conclusions and prevented them from seeing the whole of Jesus. They concentrated so completely on the *Historie* that they missed the *Geschichte*.[16]

Jesus left no written record of his own, and the accounts that have come down to us were written well after Easter. This means the entire history of Jesus as we have it has passed through the filter of Easter. That is what is meant by the kerygma; it is an interpreted history of Jesus. Thus we have a problem. Everything we have about Jesus comes from the gospels, but they were written by believers after Easter. How can we use such materials as sources for the historical Jesus with any confidence?

Modern Biblical Criticism

Geiselmann presented the methods and conclusions of form and redaction critics regarding this issue. Although he agreed with the former about the kerygmatic nature of the gospels, he rejected the skepticism that denied them any historical worth on this account. He also had serious reservations about the skeptical conclusions of the redaction critics. Even though the gospels are not historical records of Jesus' life in the modern sense, they do have value for the historical understanding of Jesus. Therefore, we need not fear history as do some of those skeptics who want to retain the message of Jesus but reject all historical justification for doing so. Although the gospels may have been written after Easter, that does not mean there is no continuity with the pre-Easter situation.

> We always stumble across words in the gospel that unequiv-
> ocally point to the pre-Easter situation. And the kerygma
> of the early Church points back behind itself to the pre-
> Easter events. Its kerygma refers to an historical occur-
> rence, to events in history: to God's revelation in Jesus.[17]

Geiselmann was not content merely to assert this point; he mustered citations from several eminent New Testament scholars to support his claim that
the gospels are reliable records of the message, deeds, and history of Jesus
of Nazareth. He went on to add that whatever the input of the post-Easter
community, it in no way covered over the immediacy of the earthly Jesus.

> The proclamation of Jesus is not so painted over by the
> post-Easter kerygma of Jesus' apostles that it is impossible
> to crystallize Jesus' original words out from them.... The
> gospels offer much more authentic tradition than those on
> the critical side until a short time ago were willing to
> admit, especially that which concerns the passion and
> Easter tradition.[18]

The latest theological tradition clearly shows Christianity did not begin with
the post-Easter tradition of the disciples.

> The origin of Christianity is to be sought not in the Easter
> experience of the disciples and their proclamation, nor in
> the simple idea "Christ," but in an historical event, the
> appearance of Jesus of Nazareth and his message. The re-
> ports about Jesus in the gospels certainly are not pure his-
> torical reports; they stand much more in the service of the
> early Church's witness of faith, but they do not enable one
> to write a "life of Jesus."[19]

The kerygma always proclaims its source lies in Jesus' own proclamation. The early Church confirmed this by accompanying the kerygma with
the teachings which we also find contained in the gospels.

Geiselmann said J. Jeremias has given us confidence we can follow
the path of the Jesus of history without becoming engaged in a hopeless
undertaking because modern scholars have better tools and more data to do
so than did their predecessors. We have a better understanding of the con-

ditions in which Jesus lived and of his religious background. A critical factor in our better understanding of Jesus and his message is our greater knowledge and appreciation of the role of apocalyptic in his society.[20] Lohse properly characterized the gospels as the written commitments of the community tradition which are not only reports about Jesus but are equally confessions of him as the Son of God.[21]

The New Testament contains both proclamation about Jesus and proclamation by Jesus. Christ is at the same time both the bearer and the subject of the proclamation.

The question about the historical Jesus was raised first by the theology of the Enlightenment. It did so because of its opposition to the dogmatic Christ of 17th century Protestant orthodoxy. The Enlightenment question asked how Jesus actually lived in first century Palestine. The posing of this question came at the same time as the questioning of the value of the Bible and its claim to divine inspiration. Following Schweitzer, however, interest in the historical Jesus began to fade because of doubts about the value of the quest. Bultmann had no particular interest in the historical Jesus because, as he said, we cannot "get behind the kerygma" to reconstruct an "historical Jesus" with his "messianic consciousness," his "introspection," or his heroism. This would have been "Christ according to the flesh." For Bultmann it was not the historical Jesus but the proclaimed Christ who is Lord.[22] Bultmann's Jesus Christ exists only in the kerygma. This kerygma presents the *Dass* of Jesus' historicity but ignores the what and how of his proclamation.

Geiselmann said Bultmann's existential interpretation of the kerygma was not only a demythologization, but was also a dehistoricization. This was, as far as Geiselmann was concerned, a return to gnosis. "Does not docetism lurk behind this kerygmatic Christ, detached from the historical Jesus?" asked Geiselmann.[23] He suggested Bultmann replaced the message of the Galilean Jesus with the proclamation of the apostle Paul. A consistent and thorough demythologization must result in the dissolving of the unity of Jesus' historical person and leave Christ merely as a paradigm for the intentions of each individual.

When the early Christians identified the humiliated Jesus with the exalted Lord, they testified it was impossible to exclude the presentation of his history from their faith. They were unwilling to replace history with myth, making the man Jesus into a heavenly figure. They also considered the one whom the community acknowledged as Lord after Easter to be the same person as the earthly Jesus who was crucified on Good Friday. Easter made no sense apart from the earthly Jesus.

> We cannot break up the identity of the exalted with the
> earthly Lord without risking turning the Easter faith in
> Christ the Lord into a myth and replacing the historical
> Jesus with the exalted Lord.[24]

The demythologization program gives us a choice, said Geiselmann. We can
have the earthly Jesus or we can have the exalted Christ, but we cannot have
both together. Yet it was both together that the early Church proclaimed
as historical reality.

Claims of the critics to the contrary not withstanding, the question
about the earthly Jesus remains open. Geiselmann said it would be a mistake to believe otherwise because fragments exist in the synoptics that the
historian must accept as authentic if he or she wishes to remain an historian.
Moreover, the early Christians united the kerygma of the exalted Lord with
their proclamation of the earthly Jesus. The problem today is that the picture of the earthly Jesus has been almost obscured by that of the exalted
Lord. The early Church, however, held firmly to the identity of the one with
the other.

> The question about the historical Jesus is not a question
> about the simple facts of his earthly life but concerns the
> bond and tension between the proclamation of the earthly
> Jesus and that of the post-Easter community.[25]

It is a matter of the continuity of the gospel before and after Easter, of the
continuity of Jesus' proclamation with the proclamation of Jesus as the
Christ.

Geiselmann saw no problem with accepting some of the form critical conclusions regarding the ordering and setting of the various pericopes.
He rejected, however, any suggestion that the early communities invented
pericopes. He cited Luke 1:1–4 and Hebrews 2:3 as making claims for the
veracity of the biblical accounts of Jesus' life. Geiselmann also quoted Cullmann and Wikenhauser as saying, "The witness of faith of the synoptic tradition has the history [of Jesus] as its subject."[26] As Geiselmann reconstruct-
ed it, the tradition originated in individual pericopes used for preaching and
catechetical instruction. The gospel writers later organized and edited these
pericopes according to their own theological purposes.

In recognizing the theological intent of the gospel writers, the form
critics too often denied their historical concern, as if the two were incompat-

ible. Thus, the exclusively form-critical interpretation of the gospels risks transforming the historical events of Jesus' life into myth.

> We must ask, however, whether the form-critical investiga-
> tion which makes the historical facts of Jesus' crucifixion
> into a principally theological statement and thus covers the
> historical proceedings of the crucifixion with total darkness
> is justified in this instance. The early Church certainly was
> not aware of the modern way of asking historical questions.
> It was concerned with the proclamation of its Lord whom
> it saw in the light of Easter.[27]

A further opinion of many form critics that is equally problematical is the belief the people of antiquity were historically naive. Geiselmann did not pursue this matter as he might have, but the gospel reports of a widespread skepticism regarding Jesus' person and work do not appear to support the existence of such naiveté. British and American scholars have examined the historiography of the gospel writers (especially Luke) and of their age, and concluded that, although they were not moderns, they certainly were not naive.[28]

Contribution to Christology

Although much of Geiselmann's christologically-related work was an evaluation of contemporary approaches, he also offered his own conclusions. The impetus for his critiques derived from his research into the work of earlier Tübingers. He thought he recognized a family relationship between the conclusions of Strauss as discussed by Kuhn and the arguments of Bultmann. Thus Geiselmann drew on his reading of Kuhn to challenge Bultmann's methods and conclusions. As Kuhn had with his *Das Leben Jesu*, so Geiselmann concluded his *Jesus der Christus* with an examination of the perspective and aim of each gospel and a survey of the titles attributed to Jesus.[29]

Matthew was the "Jewish gospel." It portrayed Jesus as Israel's expected Messiah and was structured to prove the history of Jesus fulfilled the Old Testament's expectation. An additional theme was Israel's salvation and rejection. The Church has become the new community of salvation and its bounds encompass all the peoples of the world, gentiles as well as Jews. Matthew also dealt with the relationship between law and gospel. The gospel did not cancel the law; the law remains and has been fulfilled in the gospel. Jesus internalized the keeping of the law. No longer is mere ritual sufficient; the key is the attitude of one's heart. Geiselmann also said Matthew pictured Jesus as the new Moses, the giver of a new law.

Mark wrote before the destruction of the temple because he did not distinguish between the destruction of Jerusalem and the destruction of the world (Mark 13:24). He wanted to prove Jesus is the Christ and the Son of God. Because he was most concerned with what Jesus did, Mark included few teachings or dialogues. The "messianic secret" was not created by the community after the fact to make Jesus Messiah as the result of its Easter experience, even though he neither used the title nor saw himself as such. Jesus avoided the title because he did not want his messianic role misunderstood in the political-military sense of contemporary Jewish messianic expectation.

Luke was the historian among the gospel writers. Geiselmann suggested he wrote between 70 and 80 A. D. Luke addressed Christians in a universal context, not only those within the limits of Palestine. He presented Jesus as the Savior of the poor, sick, weak, sinners, and those held in contempt by society (especially women). Luke presented a more developed Christology than had Mark. He omitted some things that might have caused readers to think less of Jesus, such as his questions that might lead some to view him as ignorant. He also toned down Mark's passion account. Luke was unique among the gospel writers in placing a theology of the Holy Spirit beside his Christology.

John wrote no later than A. D. 100. Geiselmann based this conclusion on the dating of the Rylands fragment. John wrote in a Jewish context, not a Hellenistic one. His oppositions of light-darkness, truth-lie, and life-death are Jewish and parallel the teachings of Qumran. John recorded miracles and sayings not found in the synoptics. Whereas the synoptic Jesus spoke of God's Kingdom and lordship, John's Jesus spoke of himself as God's revelation to humanity and of his unique relation to the Father. Distinctions between John and the synoptics exist, but they are not contradictions.

John presented the person of Jesus more clearly than did the synoptics. They saw Christ as the Bringer of salvation and Son of God. Geiselmann said John was the writer who presented Jesus as a man with real flesh and blood and thus who did not raise the divine dignity to the same extent as did the synoptics.[30] Geiselmann did not consider John 1:14 a metaphysical statement. He understood it in a *Heilsgeschichte* sense to mean the Logos had given up his exalted status with God and taken upon himself the humiliation of an earthly, human existence. Geiselmann saw the two natures doctrine as a legitimate explanation of John 1:1–18, but he seems to have thought this explanation did not reach to the heart of the passage. Here he differed significantly from Kuhn, who understood John 1:14 ontologically.

Geiselmann criticized the Bultmann school for denying any of the messianic claims and titles in the New Testament can be traced to Jesus but derived instead from the early Church. He argued some of the titles, especially Son of Man, came from Jesus. This can be shown, said Geiselmann, using a criterion of reliability, and he proceeded to apply this to various of the messianic titles.

Geiselmann considered Messiah to be the central concept of dogmatic Christology.[31] The New Testament does not view Jesus' messianic role as beginning with his exaltation. The synoptics brought Jesus' messianic claims to clear expression in various ways. One of the clearest of these was Jesus' reported response to John the Baptist's question whether he was the Messiah (Mt 11 and Lk 7). Jesus' entry into Jerusalem a week before his death confirmed the Jewish messianic expectation, yet modified that expectation so as to reject the idea of a militant Messiah.

Jesus always showed great reticence regarding the title of Messiah. This was primarily because his contemporaries saw the office in strongly political terms. Jesus rejected such political implications, and only acknowledged the title openly at his trial and before Pilate. These were two times when he was directly confronted about being the Messiah and both occurred after his public ministry had ended.

> Jesus himself never expressly raised the messianic claim nor designated himself as Messiah during his public work. And yet over the story of Jesus there lies a messianic splendor, a messianic election, a messianic holiness. The messianic character of his person expresses itself in his proclamation, his actions and in the immediacy of his historical appearance.[32]

Consistent with the primary emphasis of his contemporaries in New Testament studies on the Son of Man title, Geiselmann considered this title at great length. It was this title that Jesus used to show his unique relationship to the Father, the relationship he expressed with the words "my Father." Jesus is God's unique Son: "the man Jesus as Son had no equal, he stood with his intentionality above the angels and would be surpassed by the

Father." Jesus expressed the claim of this messianic title through his actions of bringing forth the Kingdom of God and forgiving sinners.

By using the title in intimate connection with his coming suffering, Jesus showed his disciples where the heart of his messianic task lay. In the original form of this self-designation, Jesus linked the majestic form of the Son of Man as coming Judge of the world with the humiliation of his suffering and sacrifice as seen especially in the suffering servant of Isaiah 53.

> The Son of Man must go through his earthly life as the servant of God. Thus the messianic secret of the synoptics hangs together: because Jesus is the unconfessed and unrecognized servant of God, his messianic secret must not for the time being be openly expressed.[33]

In saying this Geiselmann linked the Son of Man title to that of Messiah, explaining why the Jewish expectation was not met and showing the Messiah must be more than a human, though not less.

Geiselmann recognized some patristic writers saw the Son of Man title as indicating Jesus' humanity in contrast to the Son of God title as designating his deity. He also recognized that Jesus occasionally used the title in place of "I" as a self-designation. He did not deal seriously with the New Testament scholarship that saw the alternation between Son of Man and "I" as the result of redactional work on the oral tradition. This oversight may have resulted from his lack of sympathy with that type of criticism.

Geiselmann's conclusion would not change if these points were granted. It is scarcely possible, he said, that every instance of the title was inserted by the Church after Easter. It was not a common messianic designation in Jesus' day or in the New Testament; it is found almost exclusively on Jesus' lips. If we reject the title as a self-designation of Jesus, we must reinterpret the passages in terms of the proclamation or the early history of the Church. Jesus used Son of Man language in the same way he did messianic language—indirectly and in the third person. His use was a claim to sovereignty even though he also used the title in connection with his humiliation.[34] It was this that confounded both friend and foe: Jesus paradoxically joined in his person two concepts that had been seen as mutually exclusive, saying the one who was most highly exalted must also be most severely humiliated.

Humanity of Jesus

As did his senior colleague Karl Adam, Geiselmann considered proper appreciation of Jesus' humanity essential. The first thing to remember, he said, is Jesus was a Jew. But as a Jew, he grew up in the semi-pagan, despised region of Galilee. His message was couched in eschatological terms and drew on the ideas of the Essenes and other Jewish apocalyptics. It is impossible to understand Jesus' message unless we understand the world of late Judaism and especially that of the Essenes. Geiselmann did not mean to suggest Jesus mirrored all these streams of thought but the presuppositions and ways of thinking of Jesus' day came from these sources. These were the forces that helped mold the young Jesus as he grew to adulthood and prepared to begin his ministry.

The full and unlimited humanity of Jesus has been a part of Christian teaching since the fourth century, at the latest. Geiselmann said in the Incarnation Jesus became not Man, but a man. He was an individual with a specific history, not generic humanity. His body grew physically and his mind developed intellectually. As he grew to adulthood, there was nothing about him that made him appear different or unusual to the people living in Nazareth. Jesus' humanity appears repeatedly and in a variety of ways in the gospels.

A primary focus within the general theme of Jesus' humanity during the past decades has been Jesus' human knowledge. It presents a problem because the Church teaches Jesus is both God and human. God's intellectual capacity, however, is infinite whereas human capacities are finite. Geiselmann said the Son's knowledge is equal to that of the Father, but the knowledge of the man Jesus was limited. The Bible clearly reported a limit to Jesus' human knowledge when he admitted ignorance of the time of the parousia (Mk 13:32), and Jesus likewise clearly admitted the finitude of his human knowledge in Matthew 24:36.

> Jesus is a full and complete human. The human nature certainly exists in an hypostatic union with the deity of the Logos, but the two are not mixed. With his human nature, Jesus had the knowledge of a human corresponding to his nature, one that is finite and remains finite.[35]

> It is certain that the man Jesus did not become omniscient through the hypostatic union. If such were to be claimed, it would lead to monophysitism.... On the other hand, the

claim that Jesus was equipped with only a limited human
knowledge must end in Nestorianism.[36]

In attempting to deal with this difficult subject, Geiselmann drew on the
work of Karl Rahner. Knowledge, according to Rahner, is not a univocal
term. There are many, essentially distinct "knowledges" that can exist in a
human and information does not simply pass from one "knowledge" to
another. Thus, it is possible to say one can know something in one way and
at the same time in another way not know it. Rahner added that when one
is radically united with God, he or she knows in the depths all that is yet is
unable to express that knowledge in any dimension of human existence.
Jesus was united with God in this way.[37]

The practical source of the problem of Jesus' human knowledge is
the gospel records of his ignorance of specific facts. Primary among these
is the timing of the parousia. Geiselmann argued that, despite the belief
of some Church fathers and of many modern New Testament scholars, Jesus
did not expect an immediate *eschaton*. Geiselmann understood Jesus to be
talking about an eschatological generation in Luke 21:32, not about a biological generation.[38]

Jesus' discussion about the *eschaton* suggests his concern was other
than with the timing of the *parousia*. The point of his eschatological parables was that God's Kingdom has already dawned in Jesus' person, word, and
work, but it was not yet complete. Geiselmann illustrated this from two
parables. In the parable of the banquet (Mt 22:1–14), Jesus linked his own
destiny with that of the proclamation of God's lordship. The rejection of
the latter is a rejection of Jesus, but its ultimate universal success is also
seen in Jesus' success with Jews and gentiles. In the parable of the tenants
(Mk 12:1–12), Jesus announced his messianic claim in a veiled form and
hinted at the link between his suffering and death and human salvation.
Geiselmann's point was that in his parables Jesus presented himself as the
Christ, even if he did not use that term, and equated his presence with the
onset of the Kingdom of God.[39]

Another issue for modern scholars has been Jesus' authority claims.
Jesus was called Rabbi and Teacher, but his manner of teaching, his audience, and his setting were not those of the pharisaic rabbis. Jesus appealed
to God's authority, not the authority of the law. He illustrated his teaching
from common human experience and used parables to make God's lordship
clear to his audience. It was Jesus' ability to draw on experiences he shared
with his audience that gained him their attention. The uniqueness of Jesus'

parabolic style was that in this way he was able to confront his audience with both his own destiny and that of his message.[40]

Jesus also claimed for himself an authority surpassing that of Moses when he proclaimed, "But I say to you...." Because his contemporaries viewed Moses as their highest authority, Jesus' claim was unique in Judaism.

> Just as Jesus acted and appeared, so could only the Messiah appear. Thus has the messianic nature of the person Jesus, his proclamation, his actions, and the immediacy of his historical appearance come to expression.[41]

Geiselmann illustrated his point with many citations from the gospels where people were amazed at Jesus' claims of authority and began to ask about him instead of his claims.

Geiselmann dealt with many issues concerning the person and work of Jesus Christ, but the heart of his concern lay with the historical character of the gospels and their subject. In the face of attempts to withdraw Jesus Christ from history in order to protect Christian faith from the corrosive effect of modern skepticism, Geiselmann repeatedly asserted the identity of the earthly, historical Jesus with the resurrected, exalted Christ. This identification began with the earliest post-Easter kerygma as recorded in the Acts of the Apostles.

> The foundation of the post-Easter kerygma is the earthly, historical Jesus, the man Jesus, through whom God realized his salvific decision.[42]

> The early Church did not only believe in Christ, but in the historical Jesus as the Christ.[43]

The gospels are historical in content, even if not in intent. But their message is not exhausted by history. People saw Jesus as a prophet yet his message cannot be comprehended solely as prophecy. Jesus did not legitimate himself in the same way the Old Testament prophets had. He also differed from the pharisaic rabbis because of his apocalyptic understanding of the law. Whereas the Pharisees sought to explain the Torah, Jesus was concerned about eschatological revolution. Jesus saw the Kingdom of God as the inbreaking of a new age, of salvation and life with God. His contemporaries saw it as coming in their time and raising them above the other nations. Although Jesus' message contained apocalyptic themes, the apocalyptic was not what made Jesus' message unique. There was something else about Jesus that took him out of the stream of the ordinary and made it impossible to understand him purely in terms of history.

> Before the historical figure of Jesus, the manner of his appearance, his work, and his message, the historian quickly reaches the limit beyond which no further explanation is possible, at which the unsolved mystery can be illuminated no further.[44]

Jesus Christ was an historical person, but he was more than that. Jesus Christ was a human, but he was also more than that. In thus summarizing Geiselmann's main concerns, we notice his was no one-sided approach. As had his predecessors at Tübingen, Geiselmann sought to mediate Christian faith and teaching to his own age. Two opposite and contradictory trends characterized his age. Scholars denied Jesus under his metahistorical and divine aspects in favor of a mere man in history, some going further to deny also the historical and human in favor of an idea or myth. People in the pew, however, neglected the historical and human in favor of the eternal and transcendent.

Geiselmann sought to correct both errors. In attempting to do so, he took advantage of the developing openness in the Roman Catholic Church to the more restrained aspects of biblical criticism. He accepted some of the form-critical conclusions that appeared to help explain aspects of the gospel accounts better than had previous teachings, but he firmly rejected those critical approaches that threatened to overturn the historical value of the gospel witness. At this point Geiselmann drew heavily on the Tübingen understanding of tradition, particularly as developed by Kuhn, to suggest something could be historical and reliable and at the same time theological.

Conclusion

History and theology are not incompatible, said Geiselmann. From this starting point, he proceeded to present a Jesus Christ who was recognizable as the subject of the gospels and yet who could be recognized by Geiselmann's contemporaries. This Jesus was not a man of his age—as Adam tended to portray him—instead, he stood as a challenge and even a threat to the attitudes and values of the age. In trying to defend Jesus

Christ against his modern critics Geiselmann was not afraid to affirm the traditional teachings, but in affirming them he never hesitated to introduce other concerns and to restate tradition in a way his age could understand. This was all part of his concept of living tradition.

Drawing on the contributions of form criticism, Geiselmann explained the four gospels were written as proclamation, not as biography. They did not seek merely to report a person's life but aimed to elicit faith in that person. To say this is not to deny historicity, merely to admit history was not the primary purpose for writing. The gospels are reliable historical records, and they are our only historical records of the life of Jesus.

Geiselmann agreed with the designation of the gospels as salvation history because their content and purpose was kerygmatic. He saw salvation history as adding to the understanding of history instead of subtracting from its content. The story of a person like Jesus Christ can only be understood through the eyes of faith and the possibility of such faith presupposes the validity of salvation history.

Jesus is the God-man, said Geiselmann. Moreover, he knew this during his earthly life and prior to his baptism. Because of this self-awareness, he could speak on his own authority and describe himself in terms that can only be called messianic. His concept of what it meant to be Messiah differed from that of his contemporaries, so he was reserved about the use of the title during his ministry.

Geiselmann's Christology was far from complete because of the apologetic nature of his approach and because his life goal was to revitalize Catholic Tübingen theology, not to write a dogmatic Christology. As with his predecessors, however, when the situation in the Church and outside it required him to involve himself in the contemporary debate about the Jesus of history, he did so using all the resources of his school to argue his position. His work, especially in *Jesus der Christus*, helped Karl Adam in his later christological writing[45] and prepared the way for a theologian of the next generation, Walter Kasper, to make significant contributions to the renewed christological debate.

Geiselmann's work on the history of Jesus displayed an ambivalence toward the use and results of biblical criticism. He admitted the validity of those conclusions he could fit into his basically credal Christology. Other conclusions less compatible with this stance he rejected even though the basis for the latter was little or no different from that for the former. This ambivalence regarding biblical criticism becomes more pronounced in the work of his student Kasper. In admitting to differences in the various gospel accounts, Geiselmann too often contented himself with denying the existence of serious contradictions even though his understanding of biblical inspiration allowed for the existence of contradictions and errors in the text. Geiselmann did not wrestle seriously enough with textual problems even though resolving these problems was a prerequisite for reaching some of the christological conclusions he presented and for responding to the critics with whom he was in conflict.

1. Josef Rupert Geiselmann, *Die katholische Tübinger Schule* (Freiburg: Herder, 1964).

2. Paul Schanz, "Die katholische Tübinger Schule," *Theologische Quartalschrift* 80 (1898):1–49; Philipp Funk, "Die katholische Tübinger Schule," *Der Schwäbische Bund* 1 (1919–1920):293–305. As we saw in chapter 1, Funk's opinion has not disappeared after Geiselmann's research, although the idea of a Catholic Tübingen School has gained widespread acceptance in the theological community.

3. Leo Scheffczyk, "Josef Rupert Geiselmann—Weg und Werk," *Theologische Quartalschrift* 150 (1970):393.

4. Ibid., pp. 392 f.

5. Ibid., p. 395.

6. Josef Rupert Geiselmann, "Der Glaube an Jesus Christus—Mythos oder Geschichte? Zur Auseinandersetzung Joh. Ev. Kuhn mit David Friedrich Strauss," *Theologische Quartalschrift* 129 (1949);435.

7. Josef Rupert Geiselmann, *Jesus der Christus. Erster Teil: Die Frage nach dem historischem Jesus* (second edition; Munich: Kösel, 1965), p. 15.

8. Ibid., p. 201.

9. Ibid., p. 237.

10. Geiselmann, "Der Glaube an Jesus Christus," pp. 434 f.

11. George Tyrrell, *Christianity at the Crossroads* (London: Longmans Green, 1910), p. 44. Tyrrell's precise words were, "The Christ that Harnack sees, looking back through nineteen centuries of Catholic darkness is only the reflection of a liberal Protestant face, seen at the bottom of a deep well."

12. Geiselmann, *Jesus der Christus*, pp. 18 f.

13. Ibid., p. 47.

14. Josef Rupert Geiselmann, *The Meaning of Tradition*, trans. by W. J. O'Hara (London: Burns & Oates, 1966), pp. 11 f.

15. Geiselmann, *Jesus der Christus*, p. 35.

16. Ibid., p. 44.

17. Ibid., pp. 5 ff.

18. Ibid., p. 58.

19. Ibid.

20. Ibid., pp. 104 f.

21. Ibid., p. 119.

22. Ibid., pp. 31 ff.

23. Ibid., p. 34.

24. Ibid., pp. 39 f.

25. Ibid., pp. 40 f.

26. Ibid., pp. 146 f.

27. Ibid., p. 100.

28. See A. W. Mosley, "Historical Reporting in the Ancient World," *New Testament Studies* 12 (1965–66):10–26; and Herbert Butterfield, The Modern Historian and the New Testament," pp. 96–110, on *Herbert Butterfield: Writings on Christianity and History*, ed. by C. T. McIntre (New York: Oxford, 1979).

29. Like Kuhn, Geiselmann never produced a systematic Christology that related all aspects of the doctrine and showed where his primary focus lay. He left this project for one of his students, Walter Kasper, whose work we will examine in the next chapter.

30. Geiselmann, *Jesus der Christus*, pp. 169 ff. Geiselmann's contention that John is the gospel author who presented Jesus' humanity most clearly and played down his deity is not a widely-held view. John's prologue and other portions of the gospel do stress his humanity, and the synoptics do present clearly Jesus' deity in a variety of ways; but most New Testament scholars would say it is the synoptics that are most explicit about Jesus' humanity and John who is most explicit about his deity.

31. Klaus Reinhardt, *Der dogmatische Schriftgebrauch in der katholischen und protestantischen Christologie von der Aufklärung bis zur Gegenwart* (Munich: Ferdinand Schoningh, 1970), p. 369.

32. Geiselmann, *Jesus der Christus*, p. 230.

33. Ibid., p. 224.

34. Ibid., pp. 221 ff.

35. Ibid., p. 227.

36. Ibid., p. 228.

37. Ibid., p. 229.

38. Ibid., p. 217.

39. Ibid., pp. 216 f.

40. Ibid., pp. 213 ff.

41. Ibid., pp. 281 f.

42. Ibid., pp. 235 f.

43. Ibid.

44. Ibid., pp. 210 f.

45. Karl Adam, *The Christ of Faith*, trans. by Joyce Crick, (New York: New American Library, 1962), p. v.

CHAPTER VIII

WALTER KASPER

Since Geiselmann's work, there has been an increasing interest in the Catholic Tübingen School and a greater willingness to be publicly associated with it. Vatican II vindicated the Catholic Tübingen interest in tradition, history, and dialogue with one's contemporaries. The shift in theological perspective that occurred at Vatican II can be attributed in no small measure to the influence of Catholic Tübingers such as Karl Adam. This has changed the status of the School from one of uneasy co-existence vis-à-vis Roman theology and the Church hierarchy to one where today the advice and participation of Tübingers is sought by that hierarchy. This can be seen most clearly with Walter Kasper (b. 1933), recently named bishop of Stuttgart.

No theologian of the Catholic Tübingen School has ever been disciplined for his work, although some ceased publishing for fear of discipline. As late as the 1930's, Karl Adam was forced to rewrite portions of his books in order to obtain Church permission for their publication. Kasper, by contrast, served as theological advisor to the German bishops before himself being named to a bishopric and is widely recognized as a leading spokesman for mainstream German Catholicism.

A second theologian at Tübingen has privately challenged Kasper's claim to be the heir of the Catholic Tübingen tradition, asserting that because the School has been ahead of the Church in theological innovation and risked censure for its theology he is the true heir of the tradition.[1] Hans Küng (b. 1928) is a well-known and influential Catholic theologian. His sharp critique of certain aspects of Catholicism and his responses to contemporary questions have resulted in his censure by Rome. Küng has shown particular concern to respond clearly and intelligently to the questions of his non-Christian and non-religious contemporaries. We have concluded, however, that Kasper best represents the Catholic Tübingen tradition today and believe this chapter will make clear the reasons for our decision. In the next chapter, we will survey Küng's work to show his understanding of tradition and its role in theology differs fundamentally from that of the Tübingers; thus, he does not fit into the Catholic Tübingen tradition. His Christology also differs from theirs in significant ways.

Like most of his predecessors, Kasper is a Swabian and studied at Tübingen. He did his doctoral work under Geiselmann and wrote his *Habilitation* on Schelling's concept of history. Before his call to Tübingen in 1970, Kasper taught at Münster for several years. Kasper is the most prolific member of the Tübingen School, with more than a dozen books and over 50 articles to his credit. As an historical and systematic theologian, Kasper has dealt primarily with theological method, the relation between history and theology, Christology, and ecclesiology. Kasper is familiar with and makes ready use of modern exegetical studies, but relies on others for this exegesis, being content to incorporate their arguments into his work when he finds them helpful. In 1989, Kasper was named Bishop of Rottenberg-Stuttgart.

To English-speaking audiences, Kasper is a relative unknown, but on the Continent he is a major theologian of the center. O'Collins ranks him with Rahner and Pannenberg.[2] Fehr says the 1976 publication in English of Kasper's Christology has brought both Kasper and the Catholic Tübingen School to the attention of English-speaking theologians.[3] He describes Kasper's place among the Tübingers as follows:

> At the Catholic Faculty in Tübingen, however, Drey is well remembered, and the style of theology which he initiated is pursued in conscious continuity by Walter Kasper.[4]

Kasper has described the spirit of the Catholic Tübingen School as meaning that

> one is obligated in many different situations to seek ever new syntheses of scientific study, attachment to the Church, and openness to the times. In doing so, the essence of Catholicism is brought to light in new forms as a witness to life and a service to freedom in the world.[5]

Catholic theology, according to Kasper, is not a principle nor is it an idea; it is a person and a name: Jesus Christ. This is why Christology has returned to the center of theological interest in this last quarter of the twentieth century. The task of theology is to explain how God's once-for-all revelation in Christ is crucial to the needs and aspirations of humanity. Philosophy is a valuable tool at this point because it provides categories and themes by which to organize this explanation. No single philosophical system, however, can ever become normative for theology. Yet because revelation has occurred through a person and in history, some philosophies will prove to be more compatible with revelation than will others. Theology must translate Scripture and dogma into language that is both theoretically comprehensible and capable of reaching people existentially. Kasper attempts to make this contact through a personalist ontology of freedom, relation, and love. He grounds this in the mystery of God as seen in a theology of the Incarnation that places particular emphasis on the Holy Spirit.[6]

Kasper has chosen modern Western civilization as the context for his theology. He does not address other world religions as does Küng, or politics and economics as do the various liberation and political theologians. The setting that interests Kasper is that formed by the Enlightenment and its successors. These have changed the horizon in which we raise the questions of God, humanity, and the world. They have stressed human freedom, but because that freedom is no longer grounded in God, it has become self-destructive. Kasper has been influenced by the later Schelling to make freedom (divine and human) a major theme in his theology, and he cautions that God and Christ should never be seen as antithetical to human freedom. They are the source of that freedom. He offers this to a European readership looking for meaning but finding instead emptiness both within and without. Kasper follows Adam in addressing one particular audience, not attempting to deal with other cultures or all times. This is an aspect of Kasper's Tübingen heritage we must remember as we evaluate his Christology.

Contemporary Catholicism has shown a strong interest in Jesus Christ in recent years. Not all that has been written has met with the same reception, however. Kasper has been well received because his work has been contemporary, responsive to tradition, and attentive to exegetical and historical data. He is sure we can recover authentic Jesus material from the sources, but his historical interest takes second place to the theological consideration that makes this material an intrinsic part of systematic Christology.[7] Kasper is familiar with historical-critical methods, but he rejects their exclusive use because he believes they seek an intellectual mastery over reality in a way that reduces God's freedom and mystery to the limits of human comprehension. As Adam had said, so Kasper repeats: practitioners of the method tend to equate the confidence the method can give with the certainty available only through faith. Historical criticism is popular because our age is experiencing a crisis of faith that has challenged the fundamental assumptions of faith and even the possibility that we can say anything about God. As a result, the dogmatic theology that came out of Vatican II is more dynamic, catholic, and oriented to the world and the future than previous theology, but in many ways it seems also to be less certain than before.[8]

This means to Kasper that we can no longer simply repeat the historic profession of faith but must carry it over into life in a way that can respond to today's questions. Faith deals with truth, and truth can only be one. Human thought should not conflict with Christian faith when each is properly understood.

Before concentrating on Christology, Kasper devoted himself to consideration of theological method for today. We live in a world that has come to understand Christian faith in a variety of ways, not all of which are compatible. Thus, Christian faith risks losing its directness, clarity, and power. Kasper says people have seen this as a crisis of faith because a secular spirit has infected the Church where the barrier between truth and falsity has broken down. Kasper argues it provides opportunity as well as danger. Faith can no longer be unthinking acceptance of what we are told. Today Christians must continually examine their faith intellectually to ensure it is true.

> In our time deluged under words [there is] the need for a reliable word; in a pluralism often become one of limitless choice, by longing for an obligation in the original sense of the word; in a world devoid of history and memory, by the search for the enduring values of tradition... false security is also being sought.[9]

Kasper says the best response to this situation is not to run and hide but to interact with one's surroundings. He draws on the example of the early Church, which took up the best of Greek thought in its effort to penetrate society. Kasper aims to show we can present Christian faith responsibly and compellingly in the face of modern skepticism.

Two major ideologies dominate our age: evolutionism and revolutionary utopianism. Both claim to provide the solution to the future. Evolution depends on the myth of continuing development in every area. Revolution urges us to take control of our destiny. Kasper says neither can provide a general and fully adequate solution. Neither can provide an answer to the question of meaning. Nietzsche's nihilism describes today's reality better than does Marx's utopia, however. Both of today's ideologies presume we can surpass our limits in order to make endless progress. What they offer is the age-old promise to make humans into God.[10]

The content of faith became explicit in the Church only because of the practical need to respond to the pagan society in which the early Church arose. It did not derive from the desire to speculate. As heresies arose within the Church, the content of faith had to be redefined continually in order to exclude these errors.[11] Christian faith has never been merely the sum total of statements about particulars. It has always been a structured whole where the various statements are related organically to each other. In the New Testament we do not find a unity of dogma, but we do find a unity of dogmatic tradition. The various biblical confessions differ depending on the situation to which they were addressed. For Kasper, this shows the limits of a merely verbal orthodoxy. Kerygmatic and dogmatic statements may be made only in light of concrete reality because this is an essential criterion for valid proclamation of the gospel.

The gospel's value for today cannot be found through the simple intellectual process of translation; it exists much more as a mediation through which living Christian and Church practice become visible.[12] Furthermore, the confession that began with the New Testament cannot end there. This "biblicism" would be incompatible with the historical and universal character of the Christian faith.[13]

Kasper cites the Old Testament as an example of faith being reformulated and reinterpreted based on new historical experiences. The old came to be understood differently in light of new experience and the new was interpreted in light of the traditional faith. Faith is not only an intellectual activity. It is the fundamental act of human existence and gives meaning to all reality. Christian truth has to be experienced; we cannot hold to it in a merely intellectual way. We can find the truth of Christian faith only through commitment. Our finitude shows us only God can make an unconditioned reality possible and only this reality and its creator can give us and our world any absolute meaning. In this way, God is no longer a "God of the gaps" but answers our problem of existence and meaning. The truth of God surpasses our ability to speak about it. Therefore, God as the ground of our faith must be clearly distinguished from our statements about that faith. The latter are always historically conditioned and limited. Our statements must make our faith understandable in the current situations in which we and our contemporaries exist. Otherwise they cannot challenge and call people to decision.[14]

The traditional ways of "proving" faith cannot demonstrate the credibility of Christian faith. All they do is show faith to be a possibility that can be both responsible and meaningful. Faith ultimately must be built not on human proofs but on God himself. Thus faith is more than believing what the Church says and doing what it requires.

The path to truth begins with truth. Because tradition is characterized by the search for truth it can put us on the road to truth. No one starts the search for truth from scratch; each of us is working from within a particular horizon. Tradition serves as one such horizon, and as such it raises questions about truth that it cannot fully answer. Too often, says Kasper, tradition gets in the way of answering those questions.[15]

We still need to appreciate Christian tradition and use its diversity as we see it in history. Tradition shows us revelation in a process of "self-interpretation." When we look at the context within which our dogmatic statements were formulated, we can strip from our current understanding many peripheral problems that related only to the original context and no longer apply in our age. These peripherals include historical, philosophical, and conceptual elements. Criticism can help us at this point because faith and criticism do not contradict one another. We cannot preserve faith by maintaining a pre-critical attitude or by chasing each new development uncritically.[16]

In his *Methods of Dogmatic Theology*, Kasper proposes a way of doing theology that combines elements of the modern with the traditional. It is a way which is questioning instead of triumphalistic, and which is particularly concerned to present the faith meaningfully to moderns. It is not yet clear whether this will work out in practice, whether the various elements are mutually compatible, or whether responding to the world's questions might not blunt the challenge of the gospel that raises questions and offers answers people might prefer to ignore.

According to Francis Schüssler Fiorenza, Kasper is trying to locate himself midway between a transcendental philosophical analysis and an historical-critical approach. He has found what he wants in the speculative concept of history that characterized the 19th century Catholic Tübingen School.[17]

Kasper adds that our understanding of dogma and dogmatic theology must be influenced by a realization that the Church is an

> eschatological entity, a reality in the making, a promise as yet unfulfilled, an instrument of service, not an end in itself. Seen in this light, dogma can only be regarded as a relative, historical reality of purely functional significance.[18]

Kasper takes some of the force out of this radical statement by denying dogma is relative in every sense. It shares in the historical form and eschatologically definitive character of divine revelation. Dogma exemplifies the trait of "already, not yet" that characterizes the Church's entire existence in the world. Dogmatic theology thus becomes a process of translation, of setting the word of revelation found in Scripture in the context of present-day realities. Theology moves from exegesis to missionary proclamation.

Kasper says theology today must take the questions and experiences of modern humans and science seriously, but it can provide an answer to today's questions only when it remembers its origin. The origin, and thus the starting point, of theology is the witness of the Scripture embedded in the faith of the Church (tradition). We must read the former in terms of the questions our contemporaries are asking and the latter in the sense of "faith seeking understanding."

Dogmatic history begins with the New Testament because that is where we find the earliest christological formulas. It presents a Christology "from above" as well as a Christology "from below." The latter is salvation-historical and serves to explain what God has accomplished "from above" for our salvation. The path from biblical witness to early dogma was not simple repetition or logical explanation. It consisted of translating the original deposit into new cultural settings with new language and new thought forms. For example, the Bible dealt with history, but the Hellenistic world was more concerned with the continuing substance that underlies history. The great confessions of the Church were formulated in this metaphysical period of the Church's history. The synthesis of the biblical message with Greek thought that occurred at this time is one of the pillars of Western culture.[19] Thus the use of metaphysical terms and categories is valid, and may even be necessary if we are to communicate meaningfully in certain contexts, but we need to be willing to translate these terms into new ones when we move into a new context.

One of the limits to the metaphysical treatment of theology is that theology deals not only with brute facts and propositional statements but also with unique events that Christians claim set forth an eternally valid promise.[20]

Language is an interpretation of reality; ontological questions are thus necessary. When language about God is transformed into meaning and function statements, it loses its cognitive content, becoming code words and impulses toward certain social and ethical actions, a perspective on reality, or the embodiment of a universal idea. Words become allegorical. Used to mean something else, they can in principle then be exchanged for other words.[21] The Christian faith was formed in an age whose language and concepts are no longer understandable. This has led some to see Christianity as an ideology of the past and an impediment to progress. The need for the Church to address the modern world does not mean an uncritical openness to the Enlightenment, but it does require the Enlightenment be taken into account. Kasper suggests new language and thought forms can render the Christian message once more understandable without prejudice to the original message.

The Enlightenment has rendered all standpoints based solely on authority invalid. Today all authority has to prove itself, to show it provides the opportunity for human freedom. A scientific world has arisen in which reason takes precedence over tradition no matter how hallowed that tradition. Humans have become the measure of all things; the world is seen from a human perspective and directed toward a human goal. Yet science does not provide the answer. Science may help us achieve our goals, but it is unable to tell us what those goals should be. Final solutions and answers to theological questions will not come from scientific sources. These sources can provide clarifications of the problems, helping us in our search for theological answers, but they can do no more. The scientific model as generally presented is unsuited to theology because the object of theological inquiry is not repeatable and does not deal with a neatly delimited portion of reality as do the natural sciences.

Theology is grounded in a positive, historical revelation that we can grasp only through the testimony of the early Church. This testimony is contained partly in Scripture and partly in tradition, but we have to deal with each in its own way. Because Scripture is canon, it is both normative and valid as attestation of God's word. So questioning starts from Scripture. We may not go back to Scripture to find proof texts for theses we bring in from outside. At this point, Kasper does not appear to be entirely consistent with his earlier statement that theology today needs to take the questions of the world as its agenda. His actual practice in Christology has been both to respect the authority and power of Scripture and to allow modernity to question Christian faith in its search for meaning and answers.

History is a critical concern of Kasper because through its bond with concrete history Christian faith separates itself from ancient myths and modern ideologies. Unfortunately, says Kasper, Christians are increasingly unwilling to think historically. In the middle of the 19th century, the Church began to view history as a danger and as some thing unable to be assimilated into theology. On the other side of the question, scholars asked if it was still possible to assimilate theology and history because they questioned the relationship between historical truth and universally valid principles. These two groups became increasingly separated because of Lessing's challenge, and theology became increasingly alienated from history.

The problem of historicity in theology is universal. It affects every aspect of modern thought and faith, presenting a radical challenge to Christianity's continuing claims to absoluteness. Because Christianity is an historical faith, its adherents cannot avoid the problems of history in the way some have done. Fideism or withdrawal (*à la* Bultmann) is no answer if history is relevant to faith.[22] This is because we encounter the God of the Bible in history, not in nature or mystical experience. Christianity, says Kasper, is called to proclaim God's mighty works, not some abstract system or general worldview. History is the ultimate framework for all reality.

God's actions in history are different from other actions. There can be no neutral observer to verify that they are from God. Divine actions go *incognito* and can be seen only by faith. Salvation history does have an objective aspect, but it also has a subjective one. History is a series of historical promises and salvific events that make the promises real. Christianity is not a collection of eternal verities and general principles. Neither is the biblical notion of truth solely cognitive; it must be realized in practice, dealing as it does with events that have occurred or not occurred, not with how things are by nature.[23]

Not only is history the environment within which Christian faith exists, it is also the most serious challenge to that faith today. This is because the past two centuries have shown the biblical message is historically conditioned. It depends in some measure upon other religions, literary genres, and the conceptual, imaginative, and linguistic forms of its time. There is a history of the development of Scripture and a consequent tension among various statements.[24]

Historical thinking is essentially critical in nature. It seeks to know "how it really was." Properly understood, historical thinking is set in motion by particular contemporary issues. Historical thinking is limited because it is incapable of selecting one of its many authorities as ultimate. This is a purely theological task because theology alone has the "eyes of faith" needed for such a choice. History has its proper function but it cannot do purely theological tasks. Historical research helps theology only when it is theologically animated. Likewise, theological speculation needs the control provided by historical studies.[25]

Part of the modern attempt to historicize existence is a radical move that would erase all metaphysical norms. Following Schelling, Kasper says no true historical outlook can dispense with metaphysical categories. History is a process of becoming—linking past and future, and creating tensions between them. These tensions issue inevitably in metaphysical questions.

Kasper adds that an authentic historical outlook has no place for skepticism or relativism.[26]

Christ is the key to understanding reality. Because humans are a major element of that reality, they cannot understand themselves apart from Christ.[27] Vatican II said God has revealed in Christ what it means to be human. But, for Kasper, Christology cannot stand in isolation.

> The doctrine of the Trinity is a prerequisite and an original representation of the mystery of Jesus Christ... In the mystery of Christ, the mystery of God, as well as that of mankind is revealed to us in [its] totality.[28]

Kasper says the doctrine of the Trinity is presuppositional to any Christology. Christology without a doctrine of the Trinity must collapse on itself. This is because the Father is purely giver and sender, the unoriginate origin of divine love. The Son receives life, glory, and power from the Father, not in order to keep it for himself, but to empty himself of it (Phil 2:6 ff.) and pass it on. This makes the Son the mediator. Finally, the faithful receive in the Spirit the gift of the Father that has been mediated through the Son.[29] The statement that Jesus is the Son of God already expresses an analogy that represents both unity and distinction within the Godhead. Kasper adds that to prevent this from being understood anthropomorphically, Jesus was also portrayed as the Word of God. This was a decisive step in early Christology's move from image to concept. It drew on both the Old Testament wisdom literature and the Hellenistic Logos concept.[30] Furthermore, the Church is church only as the Church of Jesus Christ. This means Christology is the fundamental doctrine of the Church. It is also why Christology has be come the point of tension today as the Church faces the problems of modernity. Our Christology must color our understanding of what the Church is and does. We cannot answer modernity's problems unreflectively merely by repeating traditional creeds and denying the conditions that lie at the heart of modern problems. But neither can we discard the essence of the faith in an attempt to conform to modernity and its views.

The starting point and the setting for Christology is the Church community's confession that Jesus is the Christ. Hence the title of Kasper's Christology (*Jesus der Christus*). But this one title does not exhaust the content of Christology: no one title does. It is the unity of the earthly Jesus with the risen Christ of faith, and not that of the two natures as presented at Chalcedon, which provides the framework for Christology. Nevertheless, Chalcedon is a valid interpretation of Jesus' history and destiny.[31] Our responsibility today is to speak of Jesus Christ understandably so the identity

of Christian faith remains powerful while its relevance for today becomes clear. This is Kasper's statement of what we earlier called contextualization.
Christians believe the deepest and final mystery of all reality has been revealed in Jesus Christ. This faith requires Christians to be prepared to respond to metaphysical questions. This is not to say Christians are bound to a particular historical expression of metaphysics; pluralism of philosophies and theologies is both legitimate and necessary. Jesus Christ calls all systems of human thought radically into question. Thus, Christian faith may be expressed in terms deriving from philosophy (and other disciplines), but it may never be made captive to any school of thought. In the same way, Christology cannot be derived from human or social needs, but because it makes universal claims it must be open to consideration in terms of these needs.

Although Jesus Christ is the primary criterion of Christology, we can know him only through Scripture and Church tradition. Tradition is alive; this means the process of christological thought continues today. It also means Christology must deal with questions of history, but history alone is not enough. If Christians hope to translate the universal claim contained in the confession "Jesus is the Christ" into the language and thought of today, Christianity must encounter philosophy. This is not, and never has been, a deviation from Christian origins. The encounter with philosophy demonstrates the gospel's power to incarnate itself in new cultural situations.[32]

This does not mean every application of philosophy to Christian theology has been valid and faithful to Christianity, only that the attempt to interact with the philosophy of one's contemporaries has always been legitimate. Because serious discussion of Jesus Christ necessarily leads us to consider ultimate questions regarding reality and human need, an undercurrent of philosophical concerns runs through all Christology. As O'Collins points out, Kasper's Christology frequently shows the influence of German idealism. Both Hegel and Schelling play important parts in it, but neither they nor any other philosopher exercises a controlling influence on Kasper. Kasper says Jesus Christ is the point of reference for all salvation history. Something occurred in Jesus that affects all history. Christ is the definitive beginning, but salvation has not yet reached its conclusion. Thus, the Church sits between the "already" and the "not yet." This definitive beginning, without which Christianity would not be Christianity, is the scandal of the enfleshment of the Logos (John 1:14) and God's reconciliation of the world to himself in Christ (II Cor. 5:19).

This is the message of the kerygma and dogma of the Church. Only through biblical and ecclesiastical confession can we approach Christ scientifically. Kasper says Geiselmann has shown the way along this path to

Christology in his *Jesus der Christus*, and though the details of Geiselmann's program may be dated, his basic thesis is not.[33]

Bernard Ramm has characterized Kasper's Christology as a stout defense of historic Roman Catholic Christology which interacts with the best of German New Testament scholarship. Ramm says Kasper makes considerable and surprising concessions to criticism at points but also offers a sturdy challenge to the mood of current scholarship.[34] Hendrikus Berkhof calls Kasper the most significant Catholic to attempt a Christology "from below" while remaining faithful to Chalcedon. Kasper shows how much biblical-theological and modern insights can enrich classical Christology.[35]

Raymond Brown thinks Kasper's *Jesus the Christ*[36] is less exciting than Küng's *On Being a Christian*,[37] but that Kasper shows a better grasp of the complexities of New Testament studies and handles the post-New Testament developments more adequately. In attempting to demonstrate a continuity between the New Testament and the Church councils, Kasper is more conservative than Küng or Schoonenberg in assessing the Church's doctrinal development. He provides a good analysis of modern biblical studies and a broad, balanced evaluation of critical exegesis. Kasper uses a critical approach to the New Testament but avoids the excesses of Bultmann and Käsemann. Brown concludes that Kasper has written the best Catholic theology of christological origins.[38]

According to John Carmody, Walter Kasper has tried to update christological doctrine and make it credible to his contemporaries. In doing this, his defense of dogma is neither conservative nor uncritical. Kasper is notable for his attempt to do theology within the bounds of tradition.[39]

The article on Christology in the supplement to the *New Catholic Encyclopedia* devoted more space to Kasper than to any other position or author. It says Kasper offers a systematic presentation of classical, conservative Roman Catholic theology. Kasper's method is to examine biblical texts within the developing reflection of the Church and in conversation with contemporary culture and philosophy. Because philosophical questions are unavoidable in Christology, Kasper denies a Christology "from below" can be viable as an exclusive option. Kasper considers the use of Hellenistic language a necessary application of Jesus' meaning to a particular culture. He also rejects the distinction between function and being because function presents what Jesus did as a realization and expression of his being.[40]

These diverse sources—evangelical Protestant, neo-orthodox Protestant, and Roman Catholic—are in remarkable agreement about the nature and tone of Kasper's Christology. Each sees a moderate theologian who is willing to use carefully the best of critical scholarship yet is comfortable with the Church's tradition, who wishes to be faithful to the teaching of his Church yet communicate with his contemporaries. They also show a measure of disagreement about where Kasper stands and what he is saying, but do so within a common appreciation for his work in general. Kasper has been attacked by others on both his theological right and left for being too comfortable with critical scholarship or not being comfortable enough while not being tied enough to traditional Christology, or being tied too much.

Kasper presents three christological tasks for contemporary theologians. They must produce an interpretation of Jesus that corresponds to his life as it has been established by historical research. They must also make Christology relevant to today's questions. Finally, they must produce a Christology that deals with salvation, demonstrating Jesus' liberating and redemptive significance. This is what Kasper is attempting to do. Faithful to the Catholic Tübingen tradition, he begins from the faith of the believing community. Like his Tübingen predecessors, Kasper is not content merely to pass this tradition along, but seeks to translate the once-for-all events that occurred with Christ into something this age can grasp.

Theologians are called upon to explain the confession "Jesus is the Christ" and to show how a unique, historical person can have a universal and thus eschatological and definitive significance. Kasper says theologians have tried to do this in three ways. Some have offered a Logos Christology. Pierre Teilhard de Chardin is a contemporary example of this approach. Others have tried to present Christology in terms of anthropology. Karl Rahner has described the Incarnation as the unique instance of the full realization of human reality, but other anthropological Christologies have been reductionist. The third way has been a universal-historical interpretation. Pannenberg and Moltmann are leading representatives of this approach, which builds on Hegel's philosophy of history. This last way risks submerging Christ's uniqueness in the general flow of history.

Christology must explain how it is possible to understand the dogma "true God and true man": how an individual human can at the same time be God and thus have universal, absolute, and unsurpassable significance. This brings us back to a crucial problem of modernity: how can an eschatological event occur in history?[41]

This is the context in which Kasper attempts a christological reformulation for our time. It is a Christology with little room for a political Jesus. Clarke sees the following as characteristic of Kasper's program: function and ontology are kept together, the existence of an implicit Christology and Jesus' consciousness of his deity during his life are presupposed,

Jesus' freedom and obedience are emphasized, it is pneumatologically oriented, and some critical conclusions are accepted. [42]

Such a Christology, says Kasper, must draw on Jesus' life and work, on his proclamation and behavior. The primary criterion for Christology is the earthly and exalted Jesus Christ. Secondary is the Church's living faith as seen in Scripture, tradition, and worship. The starting point is the phenomenology of the Church's faith in Christ because this is where we meet the living Christ today.[43]

This new approach to Christology also means a Christology centered more in the cross and Resurrection than in the Incarnation, which had been the prevailing view in traditional Catholic theology. This Christology must be soteriological in its intent (although it may never be dissolved into soteriology). It should also lead to a new understanding of God that sees Jesus as the definitive promise of God because he discloses the future as well as presenting a completed achievement. We see here a shift from Kasper's Tübingen predecessors who concentrated their interest on the Incarnation, making this virtually the only event in salvation history. Kasper also departs from Adam's Scotist sympathies. Yet in replacing the Incarnation with the cross and Resurrection as the focus of Christology Kasper has not erred in an equal and opposite way from those he criticizes. These two foci must be recognized as equally important and interdependent for understanding the thrust of Christian faith.

Kasper makes several signal contributions to current christological discussion. He rejects the exclusive emphasis others have placed on Christology from "above" or "below." He also says we cannot separate function and being: Jesus' actions necessarily raise ontological questions. Many modern Christologies view these pairs as polar opposites and require us to choose between them. Kasper says we need to think in terms of both/and, not either/or. He sees ontology and function as complementary, not competing, aspects of Christology. Yet in viewing these two pairs as complementary, Kasper neglects to assign a priority to one element in each pair. For example, does function precede being or vice versa? Our decision on these matters will affect our later choices in Christology.

Recent Catholic theology has demonstrated not only a shift to interest in Christology but also a shift of interest within Christology. Traditional Christology "from above" has been replaced by Christology "from below." Christology "from below," however, means different things to different people. In every case, we see an anthropological orientation, a renewal of biblical theology, and an historical understanding of christological tradition and dogma. Some, however, have reduced Christology to anthropology and replaced Scripture with non-biblical norms.[44]   Kasper is sympathetic to some of these changes but sharply critical of others.

The post-Enlightenment assertion of the autonomy of the human subject has led to the claim that Christology "from above" is incompatible with Christology "from below." Kasper denies this is true. The challenge to Christology "from above" derives from a more basic questioning of God. Jesus, however, reveals to us both God and humanity, answering the modern questions about God and human meaning. It is only in the "above" that the "below" finds its ground and goal. Moreover, we can move from "below" to "above" only if God first has moved from "above" to "below."[45]   Thus, to formulate a one-sided Christology "from below" in opposition to a one-sided Christology "from above" is wrong. Jesus never thought of himself as "from below." He saw himself as the one who sent "from above" as the messenger and witness of the Kingdom of God.

Kasper concludes Christology "from above" is an essential part of any authentic Christology because it reminds us of the necessity of a divine initiative. In traditional Christology, however, this was presented out of context, obscuring Jesus' true humanity and its salvific importance. Any Christology containing a resurrection as an act of God is "from above" because only the creative act of God can call that which is not into being.[46]

Christology "from below" is equally necessary because it reminds us of Jesus' true humanity, which is the "operative and definitive sign of salvation" and the "locus of our encounter with God." Responsible Christology "from below" may not divorce itself from traditional Christology but must provide answers to contemporary experience in order to help moderns better understand traditional Christology. The difficulty for modern people is how to find the "above" in the "below." Christologies "from below" face two serious questions. First, do they accept a real, bodily resurrection, and, if they do, how do they define the relationship between the cross and the Resurrection? Put another way, what is the relationship between the earthly Jesus and the resurrected Christ? Second, do they deal with the human person Jesus who reveals God to us as person, or do they deal with the second person of the Godhead who is revealed in Jesus' humanity? Kasper asks further how in light of the second question the Chalcedonian dogma is to be made understandable today.[47]

We cannot understand Jesus as a case, even the highest case, of a cosmology, anthropology, or philosophy of history. Thus, Kasper rejects the three approaches to Christology he mentioned earlier. He has another approach to Christology which he considers more faithful to the original data and closer to the interpretations of Christ offered by the early Church.

Kasper sees continuity rather than discontinuity as characterizing the relation between Jesus' earthly life and the early Church's appreciation of him as the Christ. Post-Easter Christology is only the ontological unfolding of the reality of Jesus' life. It is wrong to play off the historical Jesus against the Church's christological confessions and dogma.[48] That which was implicit and indirect in Jesus' words and deeds before Easter became explicit and direct after Easter. Even the post-Easter statements are functional, lacking the ontological content we see, for example, in the two-natures doctrine of Chalcedon. As functional, it expresses Jesus' saving significance. Yet because Jesus' person and his message coincide, we must identify Jesus' person with his message, not divide them. It is the historicity of faith in Christ that separates Christianity from modern ideologies. If the christological titles and confessions lack historical content, Christian faith is merely one more ideology.[49]

We may not be able to reconstruct Jesus' life or a significant portion of his words and actions, but this does not justify historical skepticism. The story of Jesus has the quality of an historical occurrence, therefore we cannot include it among the religious myths. In fact, we can understand Jesus' uniqueness only by looking at his concrete history.

Kasper's historical picture of Jesus is consistent with modern critical conclusions. He selects out of the whole of Jesus' life his faith, prayer, obedience, and sacrifice as the key to understanding Jesus. This accords with the personalist ontology that he builds on the concepts of freedom, relation, and love he finds in the later Schelling. Pre-existence is an expression of Jesus' eschatological character, not a retrojection of his historical person into eternity.

Kasper faults modern biblical criticism on philosophical and theological grounds. Philosophically, it operates on the basis of modern human subjectivity. It sees everything solely in terms of continuity, rejecting unique (especially divine) action in history. Kasper considers this particularly devastating to Christian eschatology. Theologically, modern criticism assumes Jesus' earthly reality was the entirety of his reality. Certainly we have access to Jesus through historical research, but the historical Jesus is not the totality of the Christ of Christian faith. Kasper says a two-step Christology derived from Romans 1:3–4 brings together the earthly Jesus and the risen Christ. It was this that developed into the two-natures Christology of Chalcedon.[50]

A central christological problem today is the relationship between dogmatics and exegesis. This relationship remains undefined. Dogmatics sees the original witness of the apostles in terms of the faith of the living

Church; exegesis fixes the original witness in terms of its earliest expression. From this first problem derives the second problem—hermeneutics. This asks how we understand and translate our faith to each new generation. It is not a matter of whether we are going to interpret our faith, but how. We need to distinguish true from false and show the continuity of faith over time. Faith can be relevant only as long as it has something to say to us today, but this something needs to be in continuity with what the Church has said for two millennia. If it is not, it will be of no more than passing value.[51] An historical Christology is a universal Christology because it views all creation as being from Christ. Traditionally this has been expressed in terms of Irenaeus' doctrine of recapitulation. The Church today needs to deprivatize Christianity and reassert its universal significance, but this can be done only appreciating anew the historical significance of Christ.

The present time is a *kairos* in the sense that it provides an opportunity to develop Christology in an historical and personal way. Today's historical way of asking questions is closer to the biblical way of thinking than was Hellenistic thought. The traditional Christology "from above" is able to respond to the historical questions "from below." Furthermore, an historical Christology is a personal Christology. Thus, it is relational. Personhood is established through relations because the essence of personhood is the giving of self to others. In this relational metaphysics which Kasper proposes, love is the meaning of being. Thus, the categories of substance and person, though important, are no longer central to theology. According to Kasper, this new metaphysic has the further advantage of being able to incorporate the modern anthropological turn and yet critically surpass it.[52]

Jesus' value and function for us require we examine and recognize his status at the level of being. Jesus' salvific work tells us something about who he is as well as what he has done. Every soteriological statement has ontological implications.[53] This means the traditional separation of Jesus' person from his work must be overcome so being and function can be considered together.

Kasper has recognized the critical place our understanding of the term "person" has for modern Christology. The context in which person originally was defined theologically for christological and trinitarian doctrine no longer exists. The medieval understanding of person as the actual unique reality of a spiritual being underlies the classical christological confessions. The modern understanding of the term includes concepts, derived especially from modern psychology, that lead people today to understand traditional christological language in ways significantly different from that original intent. Modern subjectivity has detached the concept of person from the context of being. Since the time of Locke, person has been defined in terms of self-consciousness and individual personality. This new concept of person is not fully compatible with the idea of a personal God, and once the new concept became generally accepted, the trinitarian doctrine of three persons in one God became impossible both logically and psychologically.

Kasper agrees the concept of person employed by the early councils is not found in Scripture, but he adds that other important doctrinal concepts are equally absent from Scripture. This does not mean we may not use the concepts in theological discourse; "not biblical" is far different from "unbiblical" or "anti-biblical." The key is not whether a concept occurs in Scripture but whether it represents "an objectively valid interpretation of the biblical testimony."[54]

> Tradition as such is not, of course, a decisive argument. But it becomes one when it gives an objective interpretation and more precise statement of an original statement of revelation itself.[55]

Kasper goes on to say that because a concept is expressed correctly in dogma does not mean there cannot be other words that might express that concept more clearly or precisely. The comparison is not bad to good, but good to better.

The same tradition that used the concept of person in theology also recognized the problematic character of the term. Kasper mentions Augustine, Anselm of Canterbury, and Aquinas as having been aware of the linguistic inadequacy of the term person but unable to find a better one.

> The problem was rendered more acute in the modern age because the concept of person changed in relation to that which was current in the early Church and in the Middle Ages. Ever since Locke, "person" has been looked upon as characterized by self-consciousness.... The ontological definition of person was thus transformed into a psychological definition. Kant added a definition geared to morality.[56]

This shift makes doctrines defined in accordance with the original concept of person at least open to misunderstanding, if not to being totally unintelligible.

In order to make it easier for moderns to understand traditional doctrinal concepts, Kasper suggests we should define a person as a being whose freedom and integrity lie in the self-transcendence of turning to the world, to others, and thus to God. We attain freedom only by experiencing the love and acceptance freely given by others. Thus a person comes to be only through his or her relation to others.[57] The value of this definition today, says Kasper, is that it makes clear that there is no isolated, unipersonal God. Thus, Kasper makes God trinitarian—as opposed to unitarian—by definition.

> We have no choice then, but to say that in the Trinity we are dealing with three subjects who are reciprocally conscious of each other by reason of one and the same consciousness which the three subjects "possess," each in his own proper way.[58]

He further requires that Christ be pre-existent, because if he is not then God cannot be relational.

For Kasper, the ultimate reality is found in relation, not in substance. Thus, while he accepts the continuing validity of the traditional dogmatic statements, he sees a need to reformulate their substance language into the language of relation.

> The definition of God as a person both includes and goes beyond the classical definition of God's essence. It no longer looks at God in terms of substance and therefore does not define him as absolute substance, but thinks of him rather in the horizon of freedom and defines him as perfect freedom.[59]

In asserting the priority of relation over substance, Kasper does not explain how relations can exist before there are entities to relate. This is a variation of the function-versus-being argument in which Kasper denies function provides an adequate foundation for being. Kasper is not saying that a person is a being who has relations but that only through relations can persons exist.

We have looked at Kasper's understanding of person in the context of the Trinity, but we still need to see how this new understanding of person affects his Christology. The use of "person" in Christology is not necessarily the same as it is in the doctrine of the Trinity because the term performs a different function in each of these doctrinal areas. In the former it is the ground of unity, but in the latter it is the basis for distinction.

The question of who Jesus is—a man in whom God has graciously made himself present, or God's unique Son who works through the humanity of Jesus—is a biblical question. It is found as early as Paul's letter to the Philippians (2:5—11), which deals with the identity of a subject who exists in the dimension of God and who in time became flesh and took the form of a servant.[60] Unless we have a clear answer to the question about the person of Jesus, clear-cut Christian faith is impossible. Christianity depends entirely upon faith in Jesus Christ. We need to know who Jesus is before we can believe in him and be his disciples.[61]

Kasper is dissatisfied with how Christologies from "above" and "below" answer the question of who Jesus is. Most Christologies from "above" abridge Jesus' humanity because of their doctrines of an- and enhypostasis. Christologies from "below," however, tend to affirm God has appeared in Jesus but not that he is *the* Son of God. Both perspectives make the unity of deity and humanity in Christ an abstraction, but Scripture grounds the unity of Christ in the concrete, personal relationship between Jesus and his Father. Ontological and functional Christologies cannot be set in opposition to each other. Functional Christology derived from the ontological interpretation of the ontic relation between Jesus and the Father.[62]

The basic christological theme of the New Testament is the unity of the earthly Jesus with the exalted Christ. The fundamental christological motif of tradition is the unity of true God and true human being. Neither factor in each pair may be emphasized to the detriment of the other. Our basic theological task is to explain the unity between the Jesus of history and the Christ of faith, between Jesus' deity and his humanity. It is, says Kasper, a question of human salvation. The seriousness of the matter has led the biblical texts to raise the subjects of pre-existence and incarnation. Had God not incarnated himself in the man Jesus, the salvation of humanity could not occur.[63]

Kasper bases his understanding of the divine-human unity in Jesus on his concepts of person and relation. Persons exist in relations and the meaning of these relations comes from God. Thus, God is part of the definition of the human person. The divine-human union in Christ fulfills the human dynamic and humanity's openness to the infinite. Personal being is essentially mediation because the person is open to everything in an essentially dynamic existence. Yet the human person cannot bridge the distance between God and humanity from the human side. This potential for bridging exists only in a passive sense. Jesus understood his mediatorial role in terms of an existence "from above." He was the savior of humanity because of the specificity and perfection of his mediatorial office. Jesus' origin and mission "from above" show the final meaning of human existence to be external to humanity. Thus, any Christology exclusively "from below" must fail. We can start "from below" only on the basis of God's historical revelation in Jesus Christ.[64]

The personal relationship which Scripture describes between Jesus and his Father was later correctly explained and interpreted ontologically. Unfortunately, the Church allowed the ontological question of the relationship between the natures of Christ to replace the question of personal relationship. Kasper says because the matter of relationship is presented in terms of ancient philosophy, it threatens today to become a cognitive as well as a salvific mystery. But Jesus' Abba experience shows Christology is not abstract speculation but is grounded in humanity and lives out of one's love for God and service to one's fellow human beings. Kasper sees the Abba relationship as containing a complete, albeit indirect, Christology. The relationship shows Jesus' origin and orientation. It presents Jesus as God's self-communication and as the one who from eternity has been for humans. Such a Christology is linked directly to spirituality and Christian practice.[65] Jesus expressed his understanding of his unique relationship to the Father through his prayer life and teaching. The best way to describe this relationship is in terms of sonship, even if Jesus never described himself as the Son of God during his lifetime. This sonship is ontological, but it also has functional significance because it has salvific implications for us.

If we are going to claim an identity or difference between the earthly Jesus and the risen Christ, or between God and the man Jesus, we first must explain what we mean. Schelling's philosophy provides Kasper with a new way of doing this by interpreting the meaning of being and christological identity in terms of love. Yet Kasper has some reservations about Schelling's Christology because he doubts Schelling was correct in charging classical Christology never achieved its aim. With his eschatological vision of divine love, Schelling provided the possibility of a way out of the christological crisis Kasper thinks (1973) confronts the Church.[66]

To say Jesus is one person who is true God and true human being is a valid and permanently binding interpretation of Scripture and is the basis of Christian orthodoxy, but it is not the whole truth about Jesus. This statement deals exclusively with the internal constitution of the divine and human subject. Jesus is the model of true humanity and one to whom divine dignity and worship are due. Furthermore, the interpretation of Chalcedon offered by II Constantinople is legitimate because the Logos must have hegemony as the subject. Because only God is so "surpassingly free" is he able to posit something in itself with an identity which is distinct from God by uniting this something totally with himself.[67]

According to Kasper, John 1:14 contains all that was necessary for later christological development. It asserts divine and human attributes belong to the same subject. Such an assertion is an essential feature of any New Testament Christology. This is not to say John was concerned with one person who possessed two natures; he was interested in the flow of events in sacred history. John's focus was Jesus' unity with the Father, not his unity with the Logos. The christological problem came to the fore when people began to reflect on the ontological implications of the Father-Son unity and of Jesus' earthly life.[68] Scripture teaches divine and human are united in Jesus. It also presents the earthly Jesus as one who characteristically spoke and acted in God's place.

The gospels never discuss Jesus' mental life, so we lack the necessary data from which to write a psychology of Jesus. Because Paul described Jesus' life in terms of obedience we can assume Jesus had reason and free will, but we cannot go further. At this point, Kasper has dissociated himself from Adam's attempt to reconstruct Jesus' self-consciousness. Today, says Kasper, scholars no longer seek Jesus' uniqueness in terms of his self-consciousness, but in terms of the uncommon freedom with which he criticized the law, his love for the downtrodden, and the way in which he spoke and acted as one standing in God's place. We should note, however, that these are the very characteristics of Jesus from which Adam and others have sought to construct a self-consciousness.

Consistent with the emphasis of modern theology, Kasper is interested in Jesus' humanity. Jesus shows us what it means to be human as well as what God is like. We may not judge Jesus' humanity in terms of our own, but must look to Jesus to see what we are intended to be as humans. Jesus' humanity is hypostatically united with the Logos in a way that protects his human freedom and self-consciousness. The relationship between the humanity and deity is dialectical:

> Precisely because Jesus is no other than the Logos, in the Logos and through him, he is also a human person. Conversely, the person of the Logos is the human person.[69]

Kasper attributes this insight to Aquinas, and then cites Scheeben to argue Jesus' humanity shares in the personal being of the Logos because it is in and through the humanity that the Logos forms a human person and thus

subsists in and through this person rather than himself.[70] Christ experienced himself in a human way as an "I" who was actually the Son of God
ontologically. Christ's experience of being one with God was a fundamental
disposition which was realized objectively in special situations where Jesus
became aware concretely of God's will. Furthermore, Jesus' unity with the
Father resulted in a real and essential sinlessness. This involved neither the
elimination nor the suppression of Jesus' human free will, but resulted from
his unconditional decision for God and humanity against the powers of evil.

The New Testament presupposes Jesus' real humanity. Its particular
concern is to show that in and through this man Jesus God has acted definitively to reconcile the world to himself. This means Jesus is the point at
which each person's eschatological salvation is decided.

The modern study of Jesus has treated his humanity according to
specifically modern presuppositions. This new way risks making Jesus into
a mere symbol or cipher, thus raising anew the ancient heresy of Docetism.
Kasper repeats the patristic warning that the reality and corporeality of
human salvation depend upon the reality of the humanity of Jesus.

Jesus shows God is the God of history because he is moved by and
enters into the suffering of his creatures. In terms of his love and life, he
is a God who is becoming. His becoming contains no element of imperfection or lack, but expresses the overflowing of God's being. Because God has
become like us in Christ, there is no situation devoid of him or far from
him.

Contrary to his predecessors at Tübingen but in agreement with
most modern scholars, Kasper approaches the nature of Jesus' sonship from
the perspective of his death and resurrection, not from the Incarnation. We
must begin from the Father's giving of the Son and the Son's self-giving to
the Father and for the many. This approach derives from Philippians
2:6–11. Kasper denies his kenotic understanding includes any transformation of nature or de-divinization of God. "According to this text the kenosis
consists in the taking of the form of a slave and not in the surrender of the
form of God."[71]

Kasper has rethought critically the bifurcations between being and
function and between Christology and soteriology, seeking to relate the elements of each pair and the pairs themselves dialectically. Christ's saving
work points to his being, both in himself and in his relation to the Father.
Any account of Jesus' work that does not consider who he was can only be
considered unsatisfactory. Essence and function are interdependent: what
Jesus did is who he was, and vice versa. Jesus' divine being grounds his
mission and is essential for salvation.[72]

Kasper connects his relating of being and function to the Kingdom of God. Jesus is the physical embodiment and personal form of that Kingdom's coming. Thus his words, deeds, and attitudes contain an implicit Christology which became explicit only after Easter. Jesus' attitude toward sinners was that of one who stands in God's place. In his preaching, Jesus placed his word above the highest authority of Judaism and made no distinction between his word and God's word. Jesus called people to decide finally about the Kingdom and he linked this decision to their decision about him—to decide about Jesus was to decide about God.[73]

Kasper agrees with modern biblical scholars that New Testament statements about the person of Christ are functional in their intent. This is equally true of the early Church's statements. They are soteriological—if Jesus and the Spirit are not true God, we are not truly saved. The early Church's development of christological dogma clearly shows Jesus' salvific significance is grounded in his being. If Jesus is only human he can give us only human nature in its equivocal and conditional nature, but he can do nothing about our deepest need in regard to sin and death. But if Jesus was not equally a true and complete human, God could not reach us in our humanity. Our salvation would be abstract and empty.[74] If Jesus' salvific function is not grounded in his being, then it must be viewed as the mistaken projection of the human desire for salvation. An ontological foundation for functional and relational Christologies also serves to prevent docetic and gnostic understandings of Christ.

Modern critics have pointed out that Jesus was reluctant to use honorific titles for himself and have argued many of the titles found in the gospels were placed on his lips by redactors. Kasper agrees for the most part, but not for the reasons given by biblical scholars. He says Jesus rejected the titles not because they overstated his claims about himself but because they understated them. No christological title can ever encompass the whole of Jesus' claim about his person and mission. Christ was the supreme and central christological title, but in Jesus' day it was susceptible to multiple meanings so Jesus avoided using it lest he be misunderstood. Yet because the title had eschatological significance he could not deny it without surrendering his eschatological claim. This is why he was forced to acknowledge it at his trial. Son of Man was the title Jesus preferred because it was more of a riddle than a clear claim. Son and Son of God show the depth of Jesus' claim about his being. The Church created the latter title to express its understanding of Jesus' person as revealed in the way he spoke.[75] Jesus does not fit into our categories. He transcends every one. Kasper says we can understand Jesus' claims only in terms of the formula "more than..." applied to any title accorded him or person with whom he is compared.

As we have seen, Kasper rejects the Incarnation-centered Christology of his predecessors. If we allow the divine-human person of Jesus to be constituted once for all in the Incarnation, says Kasper, then the remainder of Jesus' history has no constitutive meaning for him. Jesus' death becomes no more than the completion of the Incarnation and his resurrection the confirmation of his divine nature. Kasper has no desire to deny the Incarnation, only to focus his Christology on another point—that of Jesus' death and resurrection.[76] For Kasper, the Incarnation is the dividing line between Christian and anti-Christian. The latter is exemplified historically by Gnosticism, which made everything specifically Christian illusory.

Traditional Christology's emphasis on the Incarnation remains important. With this emphasis, it presupposes the triunity of God and the pre-existence of the Son. It is a Christology "from above," but it has recognized we can reach the "above" only through God's revelation in Jesus—"from below." Thus "above" and "below" cannot be exclusive options. They have become so only because of the anthropological turn in theology and the modern "problem of God."

Kasper sees several limitations in the way the Incarnation has been understood. The Bible never says God became human, but that God became the specific man Jesus. For Kasper this means the limitation of the Incarnation stands in judgment on all those in whom God did not become incarnate.[77] Kasper is also dissatisfied with the traditional understanding of divine immutability because it is inconsistent with the Incarnation. In the Incarnation God has "become" in history. This interpretation does not violate the traditional concern underlying the teaching of divine immutability. God's becoming in history derives not from any lack in God but from his superabundance.[78] Because the doctrine of the Incarnation is a theological formula, it is limited by its context as are all theological formulas.

> The doctrine of the Incarnation of God is, especially in its dogmatic formulation through the Chalcedonian definition, only a theological interpretation of the Christ event— bound by the language and thought-form of a particular time which we today must critically interpret.[79]

The power and effect of sin have made necessary a new beginning in history. The New Testament's proclamation of Jesus as the new Adam

(Rom 5:12–21) heralds this new beginning. The Incarnation is God's breaking in on the disastrous situation in which all humanity lives, and the redetermination of that situation. From this perspective, redemption can be seen as liberation.

Kasper says the Incarnation answers the modern question, "What does it mean to be human?" Because of the way God made us we cannot derive our meaning from ourselves and our environment; only in Christ does an answer become possible. He is for us the unique and highest instance of the fulfillment of what it means to be human. In Christ we can see what God meant us to be, and what we would be apart from sin. But Jesus is far more than the exemplar of perfect humanity.

In the Incarnation the eternal Logos took to himself flesh once-for-all. John's prologue designates flesh as humanity in all its frailty and subjection to death. Thus the Incarnation as presented by John suggests a Christology of cross and *kenosis*. This is what has been lacking in the traditional Logos Christology. Kasper's answer is not to jettison classical Logos Christology but to reintroduce and refine the concept of *kenosis*.[80]

Given his concern for other aspects of Jesus' life than his Incarnation, it is not surprising that Kasper recognizes the importance of Jesus' ministry. With his Tübingen heritage, it is equally unsurprising that the Kingdom of God theme is prominent in his Christology. The gospels provide us with an example of how to proclaim Jesus by the way they tell his story. This historical discourse makes clear who Jesus is and what he is, and it is a more congenial medium to the modern age than is classical metaphysics. They tell us about Jesus in this way because we understand Jesus best by seeing how he acted. We see a Jesus who proclaimed God's love for all because God is the God of all. Jesus offered salvation to all who believed, and this salvation was for the whole person. The Jesus of the gospels was not a social worker or revolutionary; he spent time with the exploiters as well as with the exploited.[81]

The message Jesus proclaimed was about the coming Kingdom of God. This was the center of his preaching. Jesus did not view the Kingdom as a place but as God's exercise of lordship over history. The coming of the Kingdom meant the offer of salvation and the fulfillment of human hopes for a transformed society and a new start. Jesus believed this was being revealed and realized in his ministry. We can understand all aspects of Jesus' ministry more clearly in the light of his concern for the Kingdom of God. The meaning of his addressing God as Father becomes evident only in connection with Jesus' proclamation of the Kingdom. The way Jesus described the Kingdom shows freedom is a key concept for understanding God. The Kingdom is exclusively God's activity. Humans can neither earn nor construct it. The appearing of the Kingdom shows God to be a God of love, and this is most evident in the enfleshment of God's Son in humility and surrender.

Despite all Jesus said about the coming of the Kingdom, he never explained what it consisted of. The Kingdom was an eschatological concept which dealt with forgiveness and reconciliation. Kasper says it was grounded in the eschatological and soteriological character of Jesus himself. Jesus was the one who made possible entry into the Kingdom. Its appearance was bound in some way with Jesus' own coming and his message. Jesus was not the first to proclaim the Kingdom of God; the prophets had done so before him. He differed from the prophets, however, in that he brought the Kingdom as well as proclaiming it.

In proclaiming the Kingdom, Jesus neither proclaimed himself nor taught a specific Christology. In his proclamation Jesus did present an implicit Christology. Because of this the pre-Easter proclaimer became the post-Easter proclaimed. This is because Jesus reveals not only what God is for humanity, but equally what humanity is for God. He shows us human existence consists of receptivity. Because God has accepted us in grace, we can accept ourselves and others. He shows us our ground and meaning come only from God, so we can be free only in God. He also shows freedom comes through obedience, not self-assertion.[82]

Jesus proclaimed the Kingdom in terms of grace, forgiveness, mercy, and love, not divine wrath.[83] He stood with God and humanity against the forces of evil. This was evident in his confrontations with demonic powers hostile to both creation and the new creation. Kasper says these accounts of demonic confrontations cannot be simply erased from the gospels.[84]

Jesus polemicized against Jewish legislation, broke the Sabbath commandment, ignored purification rituals, and addressed God as Father in a way that was for his fellow Jews both inconceivable and amazingly intimate. This, says Kasper, can scarcely be denied historically. His rejection created a situation in which only his death could usher in the Kingdom.[85] In saying this, Kasper appears to admit the possibility Israel might have accepted Jesus and he could have ushered in the Kingdom apart from his death.

Jesus forced people to choose. In Jesus they came face to face with God. Jesus' very life answered their question, "Who is God?" Jesus' life was a mystery to his contemporaries and he did little to shed light on himself.

This is because he cared about God and humanity, not about himself. Thus, it is his mission that shows us most clearly who Jesus was. That is the mission of proclaiming and bringing in the Kingdom.

The miraculous has been a much-argued subject in modern theology. Many have taken a history of religions approach and said Jesus' disciples attributed miracles to him in order to put him on a par with the pagan gods of antiquity. Others have said there was a kernel of powerful actions and great insight that Jesus' contemporaries misunderstood in terms of the miraculous. For Kasper, miracles are signs and anticipations of the coming Kingdom. Miracles are evident in the earliest strata of the New Testament. There is an indisputable core of miracles that Jesus performed,[86] yet we need to examine the miracle claims with care and in the light of modern scientific understanding.

Kasper says some of the miracles are taught more for theological reasons than for historical content. The nature miracles, in particular, appear secondary. These non-historical miracle reports are faith testimonies about Jesus' significance for our salvation. Some miracle accounts must derive from recollections of Jesus' ministry because if this were not so the gospel tradition would be inexplicable.

Miracles are intended to cause us to look toward God. In the miraculous, God never replaces this-worldly causality because that would mean reducing God to the level of this world and becoming an idol. Neither can miracles compel belief if we are to retain human freedom. Science leaves no room for events without a physical cause, so we need to reexamine causality rather than positing a gap in causality. The ultimate question of miracles is theological and philosophical, not scientific. Natural science cannot settle the question of miracles. We need to define correctly the relationship between God and the world, because in the sense of a directly visible action, miracles are nonsense.[87]

Kasper shows a greater openness to the possibility of the miraculous than do many of his theological contemporaries, but he is inconsistent in doing so. He admits historical difficulties regarding miracles, and appears to be influenced by Troeltsch's denial of discontinuity in history, agreeing with him that God does not alter the way the world operates. Both of these limitations appear incompatible with Kasper's understanding of God as free and sovereign. Kasper is inconsistent in rejecting the nature miracles, which are relatively minor, but accepting the more significant and difficult miracles, particularly that of the Resurrection. Kasper's insight that the miracles are not intended to force people to believe but serve as evidence of the coming Kingdom is helpful. He says Jesus' miracles were not part of a systematic attempt to improve the world. This, too, is consistent with his position that Jesus came to proclaim the Kingdom: a new world, not an improvement of the old one.

The greatest miracle, and for Kasper the central theme of Christology, was the Resurrection. The cross and Resurrection must be seen as two parts of one event, not as separate occurrences. They complete Jesus' becoming one with the Father and giving himself for others. They show Jesus' relation to the Father partakes of the Father's eternal essence.

Easter is the ultimate ground of our faith and the ultimate revelation of God. Jesus' resurrection definitively reveals the Kingdom of God. The Resurrection is an object of faith, however; it is not a datum to be presented in support of faith. What we decide about the reality and meaning of Easter is based on our worldview. Are we willing to look at reality from God's perspective alone or not? Are we willing to rely on God or not? The Easter faith of Christians directly challenges the view that the universe is a closed system.

Kasper says we cannot avoid a bodily resurrection without ending in Docetism, but the questions he raises about the meaning of body make his position more complex and problematic than appears at first. If the Resurrection was an historical event—as Kasper thinks—it must have been bodily. The bodily nature of Jesus' resurrection demonstrated God's acceptance of the world. For Kasper, body denotes the entirety of one's person. Kasper also says the resurrection appearances are described in the same way the Old Testament theophanies were. He adds that Jesus' appearances were not objectively tangible. The decisive question is not the nature of the appearances, but whether we are willing to surrender ourselves to Jesus as the first disciples were.[88] Kasper seems to be suggesting commitment need not be linked to an objective reality.

Kasper has made a serious effort to rethink possible meanings of believing in "the resurrection of the body." He begins from the proposition that we are "embodied spirits," not "persons who have bodies." Our bodies make us part of the world and enable us to relate to others. In Scripture Kasper finds both a material body and a more profoundly spiritual body. The former is ever-changing and susceptible to decay, but the latter is the home of all our activities and relationships and continues to exist after the former is gone. As William Thompson notes, Kasper is somewhere between having a crude physical approach to the Resurrection and a spiritual one.[89] Kasper needs to speak more clearly about the differences between Jesus' resurrection body and other bodies at death since it appears each of us has a spiritual body that will survive our death.

The Easter stories do not present a purely historical account of the events surrounding Jesus' resurrection. They were not intended to. The important thing is the proclamation of the Resurrection; the empty tomb is secondary, but this does not mean the empty tomb was not factual. The empty tomb is a positive witness to the reality of the Resurrection. It was the human witnesses, not the tomb, that were central to the proclamation. History can say the tomb was empty, but it cannot tell us how the tomb got that way. All traditions agree Jesus appeared to certain disciples, proved himself alive, and was proclaimed to be such. The existential testimony of these witnesses in their lives and deaths speaks strongly for the Resurrection.

The Resurrection validated Jesus' person and message. In saying this, Kasper identifies the Resurrection and exaltation because the latter expresses Jesus' eschatological significance. God has accepted Jesus' existence in behalf of others and is now reconciled to the world. This has changed the objective situation of all people. All are now free from the power of sin—and thus can decide for God—and from the power of death— it no longer means enslavement and lack of a future.[90] For Jesus, resurrection meant living wholly and forever with God. It is a new way of being, not a new place to be in. Thus Jesus remains with us, but he does so in a way that mediates God's love, justice, and peace to us.

The Resurrection also transported Jesus into God's dimension where he was filled with the Spirit and enabled to share that Spirit with others. Through the Resurrection, Jesus has become the Kingdom he had preached about. Kasper develops this concept in terms of a Spirit Christology which reinterprets the two natures of Chalcedon in terms of the two states of Romans 1:3 f.

The New Testament presents Jesus' death as not only the work of Jews and Romans, but also as God's saving act and as Jesus' self-sacrifice. How Jesus understood his death remains problematic. The gospel reports of his expectation and understanding of it come from the post-Easter community and do not necessarily reflect Jesus' own knowledge. Certainly Jesus would have considered the possibility of a violent death, given the nature of his mission and opposition, but it is unlikely he would have forced a decision à la Schweitzer because this would have contradicted his faith in God. Pollard says Kasper tries to show Jesus understood the salvific nature of his death. Kasper argues we can show Jesus' individual sayings and overall intention (which he calls the *ipsissima intentio*) converge. First, Jesus saw his death in terms of the Kingdom of God, and the Kingdom deals with salvation. Thus, Jesus' death deals with salvation. Second, the essence of Jesus' life was existence for others. He came and lived as a servant among his disciples. Thus, for Kasper, it is legitimate to speak of an implicit soteriology in the same way we speak of an implicit Christology.[91]

Salvation is from sin. Kasper pictures sin in terms of lostness, self-centeredness, self-will, and self-importance. Sin serves to atomize everything, making it impossible to understand reality as a coherent whole. In modern European terms, sin breeds isolation and loneliness, resulting in meaninglessness. The Kingdom of God means the restoration of connection and relationship—with others, but especially with God who gives meaning to all reality.

Sin is the all-encompassing situation into which each of us is born. As humans, we accept the situation ontologically (original sin) and ratify it by our own sinful behavior. Sin characterizes us inwardly at the level of our being. Kasper says biblical teaching bases this condition on a free, historical act in which all later humans were involved and to which they assented. No other perspective would preserve both divine and human freedom. This occurred in history, so only a new beginning in history could overcome it.[92]

Kasper views sin more as sickness and bondage than as rebellion and transgression against God. This would mean it is an ontological more than a moral condition. Salvation thus consists more in healing than in vivifying.[93] In either case, it has serious detrimental effects on all our relationships.

The traditional order of subjects in systematic theology has placed sin before Christology and soteriology because it has been believed we must define a problem before we can solve it. If sin is the problem, salvation is the solution. Normally, theologians have developed soteriologies consistent with their understanding of humanity's need. Kasper's understanding of salvation relates to the modern human condition of existential lostness, estrangement from God, and the need to expiate God's wrath. It has little to say about social, economic, and political evils, or about the concept of corporate sin that plays so prominent a role in liberation theology.

Kasper defines salvation as participation in the life of God, in the Spirit and through the mediation of Christ. It is not something supernatural added to our human nature; it frees us to be ourselves. Thus, argues Kasper, there is no fundamental opposition between the post-Enlightenment idea of emancipation and the Christian message of redemption because freedom means more than doing what we want to do.[94] In our encounter with the free person Jesus we achieve the possibility of becoming free ourselves. Salvation does not consist only of assenting to certain truths; it means equally receiving the power of Jesus in our lives in order to redirect us toward God and our fellow humans.

Christianity teaches the salvation of the world occurred once for all in Jesus Christ. This is the scandal of Christianity. We cannot be vague about this because this truth is the ground for all that is decisively and distinctively Christian.[95]

Until recently, theologians have routinely treated Christology and soteriology as separate subjects. Kasper says we may not sever the two because the ontological statements of the christological councils were soteriologically motivated. Christology deals with soteriology, but it may never be reduced to soteriology. Kasper sees an example of this reduction in Schleiermacher, who began from the experience of redemption and worked back to the redeemer. This path risks making Christology no more than the expression of Christian self-consciousness. Bultmann was equally guilty of making New Testament statements about Jesus' deity refer only to his significance, not to his nature. Meaning must be grounded in being, or religion becomes little more than the projection of human needs and desires.[96]

Christology stands completely under the soteriological statement that Jesus gave his life "for the many." This is the anthropological significance of Christology and it is found particularly in the Adam-Christ typology of Romans and I Corinthians. Jesus' importance for our salvation is expressed by the title *kurios*, which designates him as the risen one who is powerful in heaven. It is a Palestinian, not a Greek title.

Kasper suggests the concept of divinization is a way to express the meaning of salvation. He acknowledges it has a bad press today, but this is because it has been misunderstood as a participation in the divine nature. Kasper understands it to mean that "through the actions of him who is Son of God by nature we become the children of God through grace and divine acceptance."[97] It has nothing to do with any blurring of the distinction between God and humanity.

Kasper contrasts this understanding of salvation with what he calls humanization. He takes this term to mean being a Christian is something people can do for themselves and not something God does for them in Christ. This is the religion one finds in Immanuel Kant. Kasper accuses Küng of teaching salvation in terms of humanization.[98]

Christ's death must be interpreted at least in part as expiatory. Jesus taught it was an expiation, and to deny this aspect would be to approach mythology and ideology. There was also an eschatological interpretation of Jesus' death that equally implied an expiatory soteriology. This is because the liberation Jesus accomplished consists of the remission of guilt toward God. Kasper accepts the satisfaction theory of the atonement proposed by Anselm of Canterbury. He acknowledges Anselm's concept of divine honor reflects Germanic instead of Roman ways of thinking, but says the theory remains relevant for today.

> Kasper [has] argued for the subtlety and splendor of Anselm's theology of satisfaction. This version of the atonement appreciates God's *fidelity* to creation and the moral order in a way that parallels St. Paul's sense of divine righteousness.[99]

Kasper says the idea of representation is alien to modern thought because today we begin from the standpoint of human autonomy. This means we are responsible for our own acts, and no one is able to represent us. Jesus, as our representative before God, establishes a new solidarity with God which leads to a new solidarity among humans. This also results in a restructuring of the universe so the goals society seeks become possible because they are grounded in Jesus Christ, the sustainer of the universe. It is not that Jesus takes our place in the world but that he is the conduit for divine justice, love, and peace to flow into the world.

The Church grasped the meaning of Jesus' work "for us" when it defined him as the man for others. His nature was to exist for others and this was his perfection. He took to himself our sinful history and made a new beginning out of it. Kasper says representation is the essence of the biblical concept of history. Just as Adam represented humanity in its totality and as Israel served as God's priests to the nations, so Jesus is the founder and representative of the new people of God. Representation has been a major theme of the theological tradition, but as our representative Jesus is not our substitute. This would remove our significance. Jesus' salvific work thus consists of restoring meaning to lives that are without meaning because they have lost touch with the ground of their meaning: God. Jesus accomplishes this by canceling our sin against God through his expiatory death. The Resurrection confirms the validity of Christ's work and preaching of reconciliation.

Traditional Christology moves from Jesus' death and resurrection to his return in glory, the *parousia*. Kasper understands the *parousia* in a different way. It is not, he says, Christ's physical return into time and space but his sovereign taking possession of them in a visible and glorious way. That which occurred in a hidden way in Jesus' death and resurrection will occur openly at the *parousia*. This coming of Christ signals the ultimate victory of life and love over death and violence. It also requires judgment so good can be separated from evil.

Christ's final coming in glory is not the end, but the
perfection of the world.... The consolation which lies in
Jesus Christ's final coming in glory is hope in the final
victory of life and love over falsehood and injustice.... [It]
must necessarily include judgment.[100]

Heaven for Kasper signifies the place of the deepest human desire.
It is where God is finally with humans and humans with God. Jesus' ascension means the first human has been finally and entirely taken up by God.
Jesus did not rise to some place or realm; we might say heaven came to be
with his rising. The ascension signifies a new beginning in which Jesus has
been installed as Lord of the world and is its permanent measure and goal.
This event contains both an eschatological fullness and an historical character. This shows the fullness of human hope is God's gift; it is not to be
found "from below."[101]

Kasper's discussion of the *parousia* is not clear. He appears to want
the results of the traditional Second Coming without the event itself.
Kasper is more interested in answering the existential question of human
meaning through Jesus Christ. He is also caught between his desire to affirm traditional Church teaching and to accept critical exegetical conclusions
where possible.

Dogmatic Christology

Catholics, and Catholic theologians in particular, are required to
accept the conclusions of the ecumenical councils as a part of their faith.
For Catholics today, the definition of Chalcedon appears to serve as a touch-
stone of christological belief. We find, however, that Catholics of widely
different and sometimes incompatible viewpoints continue to affirm acceptance of Chalcedon in some way. Not all these ways have been found acceptable by the theologians of Rome's Sacred Congregation.

Kasper states his acceptance of the conclusions of Chalcedon. Doctrine needs to be translated into new cultures and times because it is subject
to the historical limitation of all human language and is true in detail only
in relation to its original context. The current crisis in theology, says
Kasper, has led to the questioning of the basic principles of faith and even
the possibility of speaking about God himself. Thus the questioning of one
or another dogma or reform is only symptomatic of a deeper problem.[102]

Truth cannot normally be expressed in a single statement, so dogma
cannot settle an issue for all time. Even after dogmas have been defined,

they are affected by the history of their reception, interpretation, and integration with other dogmas. Dogmas cannot be studied in isolation; they must be interpreted in the context of Scripture and tradition. Kasper says, "We are not dealing with infallible propositions, but with an infallible 'cause.'" The testimony of Scripture depends historically on witnesses. It is not the propositions contained in the gospels that are infallible, but the living, historical authorities.[103]

A modern concept of orthodoxy based on dialogue does not exclude the setting of clear boundaries. It remains possible to declare formally that certain positions are incompatible with Church teaching. This is especially true with regard to essentials, and it may become more important in the future. Thus it would be naive to think the Church could ever rid itself of dogmas. Vatican II has called for a dogmatic theology more dynamic, more catholic, and more oriented toward this world and the future. The council also presented doctrine as something having much less certainty than had been claimed previously.

Our understanding of dogma must reflect our awareness of the Church as an eschatological reality. It is not yet complete and it is not an end in itself. Thus we must recognize dogma is relative and historical, having only a functional significance. Dogmatics is for us an hermeneutical task of translation. Dogma stands midway between the revelation in Scripture and the modern world in which we must proclaim Christ. Saying this does not mean dogma is in every way relative for Kasper. Dogma shares in the eschatological-definitive character and historical cast of Christian revelation. It is both "already here" and "not yet."[104]

> Dogmatic formulations are never simply the concluding clarification of a dispute but are at the same time always the beginning of new questions and problems. Precisely because dogmas are true they are in constant need of new interpretation.[105]

The mystery of Jesus Christ is always more than can be contained in a dogmatic formulation. Thus a confession is always less than the biblical witness which it interprets. Metaphysical language cannot express fully the personal, historical, and eschatological dimensions of biblical Christology. This means today we are again called upon to make the original witness comprehensible to our age.

Classical Christology was far less naive and uncritical than it appears at first sight. It began with a highly critical view of humanity and saw human holiness only through God's self-communicated love. The divine-human unity in Christ can be grounded only "from above." The early fathers never thought they could usurp God's place through theological speculation; they believed God can be known only through his revelation in creation and history. In classical Christology, says Kasper, approaches "from above" and "from below" co-exist without ultimate conflict. The only route to a Christology "from above" is "from below," but unless Christology ends "above," the "below" is meaningless.[106]

Kasper traces a continuity from the New Testament to the christological councils. The two primary motives of the development were soteriological and rational. A Christology and Christianity which do not confess Jesus' deity would have no salvation to proclaim. Because the Christian is under obligation to account for his or her hope the Christian must be prepared to use philosophical thought to help explain and justify the reality of that hope.[107]

Kasper considers the christological disputes of the second and third centuries the most dangerous to the early Church because they denied Christ's humanity. Taking the early conciliar decisions about Christ's true and full humanity seriously, we cannot have a theology "from above" without a corresponding theology "from below." The world is not the criterion for our faith, but the requirement for a theology "from below" makes the world central for any Christian understanding of salvation.

The Apologists were the first to present the Christian message in philosophical terms. Theirs was a bold and necessary step; it did not result from a feeling of weakness in the Church, but from the vitality that propelled Christianity into new cultural areas. The problems in this early attempt arose from a failure to distinguish the Creator-creation relationship of God and the world from the Father-Son relationship of God and Jesus.

Christology is not merely the interpretation and reinterpretation of kerygmatic and dogmatic confessional formulas. Historically, the "fully developed" dogmatic formulas resulted from patristic debates aimed to achieve "the greatest possible fidelity and exactitude in the interpretation of the biblical datum" [sic]. The conciliar debates were not, contra Gibbon, exercises in useless hair-splitting and quibbling over vowels. Kasper says the patristic endeavors were both difficult and important.

> It was... by no means enough simply to apply concepts from
> Greek philosophy to the traditional confession of faith. All
> such attempts ended in heresy. The need was to reflect on
> the data of scripture and tradition and to break away from

the one-sided existential thinking of Greek philosophy and
into a personalist thinking that did justice to the scriptures,
thus laying the foundation of a new type of thought.[108]

Once the Church took seriously the biblical statements about the
relationship between Jesus and God, patristic Christology was inevitable.
Kasper assesses the early confessions favorably, but he adds that the biblical
data are far broader than the focus of these confessions. This is why they
are both permanently binding and in need of interpretation in terms of the
total biblical witness.

Using new language and thought forms, the Church fathers were
able to counter errors and make the Christian message understandable in
new contexts. This means the distinction between person and nature derives
not from Hellenistic philosophy but from the Christian response to the
Hellenizing tendencies of false teachers. The dogmatic history of the early
Church was a hermeneutical necessity, not an instance of weakness. Using
Hellenistic concepts was not a diminution or weakening of Christianity; it
shows the assertion, not the surrender, of early Christianity. Kasper adds
that it is a model for us today in what appears to be a similar situation.[109]

It is impossible to deny the spaciousness, depth, and
coherence of this classical Word-theology.... Logos
Christology can help us understand that in Jesus Christ
God's innermost being as well as the ultimate ground of all
reality are made known to us. It explains how Jesus Christ
is the head of the whole creation and how in him as the
single Word of the Father all of reality finds expression and
its deepest meaning. Only one who knows Jesus Christ has
an ultimate understanding of man and the world.[110]

Kasper doubts, however, that classical Logos Christology expresses all John
intended by his use of the Logos concept in his prologue.

The Hellenistic world developed the universal significance of Jesus's
history in a new perspective by bringing the metaphysical question of being
to the fore. This metaphysical development in the Church led not to
Hellenization, but to a lack of appreciation for the eschatological content of
the Christian message. Further, the abstract christological formulas are
insufficient to sustain the piety of the Church.

In agreement with many modern scholars, Kasper notes the early
christological confessions were developed according to an "is" formula. We

need to ask what sort of identity was intended by this "is." Kasper says classical Christology was correct in stating the matter in terms of Jesus' identity, but it overlooked the historical background of the titles by which Jesus was designated. Jesus is who he is only in connection with this history. The relationship between the Jesus of history and the Christ of faith is both an historical and an ontological problem. To ignore ontology is as serious an error as to ignore history.

The meaning of the christological "is" continues to be a problem, according to Kasper. This can be seen in the disagreement between Hegel and Schelling. Schelling tried to express the "is" historically with a consequent freedom and lack of necessity that were foreign to Hegel's philosophy of identity. Schelling defined "is" in terms of "*können-sein*" where the power resides within the individual either to be or not to be as one freely chooses. For Schelling, this matter of possibility and reality involves the temporality of being and views the future rather than the past as the essence of time and being.[111]

Nicea, which introduced this use of "is" in the christological discussion, was the *aggiornamento* of the age, an attempt to express the permanently valid Christian message in the language of its day and in response to new questions. Nicea was not a Hellenization but a de-Hellenization of Christianity. Arianism was the illegitimate Hellenization, dissolving Christianity into a cosmology and a morality. The council, on the contrary, sought to hold firmly to that which the New Testament says about the Son and to reaffirm God himself has appeared in Jesus Christ.

In the next generation, Apollinarius posited the mutual exclusivity of God and humanity. This, too, was a Hellenization of Christianity. Kasper says the error of Apollinarius remains the basis of modern criticism of religion.

Chalcedon expressed in the language of its day precisely what the New Testament says we encounter in Jesus Christ, according to Kasper. He adds the doctrine of the hypostatic union affirmed at the council expresses conceptually and ontologically the biblical statement that God manifested himself in Jesus fully and completely in a human way.[112] Kasper criticizes Chalcedon for emphasizing ontology to the detriment of history and eschatology. Chalcedon was formulated according to the intellectual and political assumptions of the time and in rather technical philosophical language. The dogma it formulated dealt with the basic issue of human salvation as well as the speculative concern of mediation between God and humanity. It was the de-Hellenization of Monophysitism. It builds on earlier christological work, but defines this in terms better suited to the changed nature of the problem.

Chalcedon used Greek philosophical language to express something for which linguistic and conceptual resources were not available. Instead of putting forward its own christological theory, the council limited itself to guarding against erroneous presentations of the christological mystery.[113]

Although its formulation remains valid, the definition of Chalcedon needs to be placed within a comprehensive biblical and systematic context. In saying Chalcedon is no longer sufficient, we must go on to say the framework Chalcedon established cannot be ignored because the points it made have not been superseded by any contemporary theology. Chalcedon remains important because it provides a comprehensive framework for understanding the dialogue between God and humanity which reaches its underivable and unsurpassable high point in Jesus Christ.[114]

Thompson suggests Kasper has proposed the most balanced understanding of Chalcedon for today. Kasper for his part suggests a relational model of the person of Christ is implicit in Chalcedon's teaching. This suggestion derives from Kasper's insistence that person is something one becomes through having both vertical and horizontal relationships. For Kasper, Chalcedon says Jesus is a person in that both divine and human resonate through him most completely. The formula implies further that the divine person is the all-encompassing basis of Jesus' being without any detriment to his human will and action.[115]

Spirit Christology

Kasper seeks to contribute to the current christological discussion by restoring the Spirit Christology of the early Church to respectability. He says Jesus' absolute uniqueness as a human can be understood only in terms of the universality of his resurrected and glorified existence. This real existence of Jesus can be accounted for only in terms of his unique relationship to the Spirit of God. In the Old Testament, the Spirit was the life-giving power of God.

Although Pannenberg is a leading opponent of the revitalization of Spirit Christology, Kasper draws on him for his Christology. He even uses Pannenberg to help buttress his arguments for Spirit Christology. According to Pannenberg, the trustworthiness of Jesus' own claim and his vindication by God at the Resurrection is the source of our knowledge of Jesus' deity and thus of his Spirit-filled nature before the Incarnation. Pannenberg denies a Spirit Christology can support this position.[116] Kasper agrees on the significance of the Resurrection, but he understands it as the fulfillment of the Spirit's continuous action in Jesus. This means the Spirit's presence in Jesus can be developed separately without necessarily leading to Adoptionism. A biblically-grounded Spirit Christology, says Kasper, can show Jesus' essential unity with God was an ontological unity before the Resurrection. Thus what was revealed as true at the Resurrection was true of Jesus' entire life. Kasper believes a Spirit Christology that develops out of the Spirit's role in the Resurrection avoids adoptionist overtones while enhancing Jesus' essential unity with God from the beginning of Jesus' human existence and even before that time.[117]

The Spirit's universal mediating function becomes clearest in the person, work, message, and fate of Jesus. In Jesus' resurrection the Spirit inaugurates an entirely new form of human participation in God's trinitarian life. Kasper's stress on ontology and the Trinity points back to the Greek concept of the economic Trinity (God in history) rather than the Latin immanent Trinity (God in himself).[118]

In the Bible, says Kasper, we read that the Spirit of God is equally the Spirit of Christ. Scripture tells us all Jesus' life, from birth to death, took place in the power of the Spirit. Being anointed with the Spirit made Jesus the Christ (the Anointed One). The decisive phases of Jesus' life are linked with the Spirit. The Spirit is the permanent actuality of Christ, yet he is a distinct divine person. The Spirit adapts Jesus' work to each new situation so that it remains liberating, not binding. The Spirit is the moving force of the future, urging us to transcend our limits and drawing us toward the perfection that is beyond our own ability to achieve.

Kasper has opted for a Spirit Christology because he sees serious weaknesses in Christologies coming from explicitly philosophical, anthropological, cosmological, and world historical perspectives. These affirm Jesus' universality at the cost of his uniqueness, but both aspects are important. The biblical framework for Christology was that of the Spirit of Yahweh. This explains both the continuity and discontinuity of the Christ event with the old covenant. In the New Testament, Christology can be seen as an aspect of an overarching pneumatology.[119]

By remaining open to Jesus' pre-existence and to ontological language, Kasper seeks to avoid the danger Adoptionism presents for any Spirit Christology. The gospel writers saw Jesus' uniqueness in terms of his Spirit-filled existence. The Resurrection then transformed Jesus into a "spiritual body." In other words, Jesus can be viewed as the prophetic bearer of the Spirit, the one anointed with the Spirit, yet at the same time the divinely vindicated sender of the Spirit and Lord of creation through the power of the Spirit.

Pneuma-sarx Christology was the Church's earliest attempt to express God's presence in Jesus. It accounted for Jesus' uniqueness in terms of the intensity of his union with the Spirit of God. This Christology contained a tension between Jesus' functional, soteriological role as Lord of the Church and his ontological, substantial role as Son of God. The early fathers drew primarily on Romans 1:3 f. and I Timothy 3:16 as the foundation for this Christology. Early adoptionist tendencies in the Church led to this approach's rejection. The *Pneuma-sarx* Christology was superseded by the now dominant *Logos-sarx* Christology derived from the Johannine prologue. Kasper says an implicit pneumatology was the basis for the early Church's doctrines of God, Christ, Church, sacraments, and liturgy, as well as its moral theology. A pneumatological approach has always characterized orthodox Christianity. The Spirit has always played a prominent role in eschatology, and this eschatological emphasis is another reason Kasper stresses pneumatology.

It was the Spirit who gave the individual person and unique work of Jesus universal significance. Christianity is convinced that only once in history has the Spirit found acceptance in a total and undistorted way. This was in the man Jesus.[120]

Pneumatology has two roles in Christology. It helps express the universality of the salvation that has come in Jesus Christ, but because we must hold strictly to Christ's uniqueness the Spirit is defined as the Spirit of Christ. Kasper links the first role to the universal work of the Spirit throughout history and the self-transcendence of humanity. These two aspects of universality and uniqueness have not been integrated fully in Kasper's Christology.

Jesus differs from other bearers of the Spirit in both degree and kind. He is the culmination of the Spirit's operation and the starting point for the sending of the Spirit. Having attained the goal of the new creation in the Resurrection, the Spirit now must integrate all other reality into this new creation and is sent by Christ to do so. Thus the Spirit is the medium through whom Christ becomes accessible to us today.[121] In the coming of the Spirit at Pentecost, the return of Christ is already happening because the Spirit is the reality of eschatological fulfillment.[122] This exemplifies our earlier concern about the lack of clarity in Kasper's eschatology. Because the truth of Christ continues to be mediated through the Spirit, there is no place for a static understanding of theology; it must be living and prophetic.

Rosato suggests Spirit Christology can make a contribution to interreligious dialogue because the Spirit's filling of Jesus can be understood as creating the goal of all other religions.[123] Kasper agrees, because he sees traces of the Spirit's operation everywhere in the world. He says all religions of the world mediate the Spirit of Christ in part but the fullness occurs only when people explicitly confess Christ as Lord. Where this happens, the Church is. Kasper is offering a form of what has come to be called anonymous Christianity which aims at but does not require an explicit encounter with Christ.[124]

Rosato says Spirit Christology never has and never can be the answer to all questions raised by a genuine Christology. Adoptionism is an ever-present danger as is the loss of Jesus' absolute uniqueness as the God-man. Spirit Christology has been a mixed blessing for the Church. Occasionally it has served to revitalize the inner life and mission of the Church, but it also has been at the heart of every major Church schism. The unresolved problems of the relation of the Spirit to the Word, community, and individual have been the source of both innovation and division within the Church.[125]

Christology is at the heart of the current conflict over the nature of the Church. Different Christologies stand behind the various views about a more open or closed Church. Deeper christological reflection is needed to resolve this and other contemporary Church problems.[126] Furthermore, Jesus Christ is the foundation and meaning of the Church. This means the Church is the objectification of Christianity, not in the sense of subsuming Jesus into the Church but in seeing Jesus as the goal of the Church and the standard against which it must constantly measure itself.

The Church has been a stumbling block for many because of its intolerance and authoritarianism, but as an institution it is necessary for the survival of Christian beliefs. For this reason, the Church must speak unequivocally about at least the fundamentals of the faith. This can be done only by spiritual judgment, not by democracy or authoritarianism in the Church. To show it does not reflect individual whimsy, the judgment must be consistent with the objective testimonies of Scripture and tradition because this word of revelation stands above the Church.[127] Thus the infallibility of the Church is the infallibility of God's faithfulness in Jesus Christ, not the Church's own possession.

It is within the Church that the Spirit who brought to life the New Testament brings to life the hearers and readers of the New Testament. Thus the Church is the proper locus for the tradition about Jesus and for personal encounter with him as the risen Christ.[128] It is where God's saving work in Jesus is made present to humanity by the Spirit. This is why the Church exists at all—it is a sacrament, a visible reality of God's presence in a sign. The Church is not, however, the Kingdom of God. If we take this difference seriously, we can no longer see the Church as the direct representation of God nor as an extension of Christ.[129] The Church of Jesus Christ is all those who are bound to Jesus in love whether they know him or not.[130]

Evaluation of Other Christologists

As a leading Catholic theologian of the center, Kasper has evaluated the work of some of his contemporaries. His primary subjects have been the prominent Catholic christologists of the center and left, Karl Rahner and Hans Küng. Kasper has dealt only briefly with christological interpretations arising from Third World political and liberation theologies.

Kasper is dissatisfied with Rahner's work for several reasons. Rahner's emphasis on the use of philosophy in theology and his heavy dependence on Heidegger are incompatible with Kasper's understanding of the proper role of philosophy in theology in general and in allowing theology to be tied to one philosophy in particular. Kasper also charges that postulating the need for a transcendent ground to make human freedom possible functionalizes God. God becomes a necessary agent in the process of human self-fulfillment, exposing Christianity to Feuerbach's critique. Rahner's transcendental method can show the openness of humanity to the infinite, but it cannot show this infinite to be God.

Rahner's anthropologically-developed Christology impresses Kasper as both significant and fruitful, but Kasper denies theological anthropology can provide a sufficient foundation for Christology.[131] Human nature remains incomprehensible until we consider Jesus Christ. No metaphysic can be accepted as a universal understanding of human existence until it has been tested by the uniqueness of Jesus' life and meaning.[132]

Kasper concludes Rahner's Christology does not lead us to consider the relationship between Father and Son, but to see Christ as the high point in the development of the Creator-creature relationship. Kasper questions whether such a Christology gives sufficient value to the uniqueness and newness of Jesus' history. Does Rahner's Christology result in the concept of the hypostatic union or merely that of an eschatological prophet? In either case, it risks reducing theology to anthropology.[133]

Until 1980, Hans Küng was Kasper's colleague on the Catholic Tübingen faculty. Even before Küng's permission to teach as a Catholic theologian was withdrawn, Kasper and Küng had disagreed publicly over theology. Kasper says the basic difference between the two men is methodological; they disagree over the proper starting point of the christological enterprise. Kasper does not believe it is possible after 2000 years of Church history to put ourselves in the place of the first disciples as Küng attempts to do. Kasper and Küng agree the proper subject of faith is the earthly Jesus who has become the risen Christ and remains present in the Church through the Spirit. Kasper adds the risen Christ meets us only through the witness of the Church as faith community, and this faith rests on the witness of the original apostolic community. Different starting points, says Kasper, lead to different conclusions. This is evident with regard to their different views of pre-existence, the Incarnation, and the Trinity. Kasper questions whether it is possible to say the traditional ontological statements are historically determined and not unconditionally binding conceptual-presuppositional forms belonging to the essence of Christology.[134]

Kasper asks how Küng holds together unity and distinction in the person of Jesus Christ when he talks about the true deity of Jesus at the same time he proposes a functional-hierarchical subordination of Jesus to the Father. Concepts such as unity of revelation and unity of action are not helpful because they are susceptible to a variety of meanings and can be understood in a Sabellian or Nestorian sense.

Küng does not place Christology "from below" in conflict with that "from above," and Chalcedon serves as a guideline for new christological interpretation. Küng's final criterion is the Jesus we meet through historical criticism. Küng's real interest, however, is not in Jesus "as he really was," says Kasper, but in Jesus "as he meets us here and now." Kasper appreciates much of the work Küng has done and says Küng's contribution is evident in his own Christology, but he believes Küng's Christology does not deal adequately with the evidence.[135]

Conclusion

We said earlier that Kasper's Christology shows little appreciation for the social and political aspects of Jesus' life or of salvation. Kasper does not deny Jesus' life, death, and message have implications for the way we live, but he insists that reducing Jesus' significance to the political does not do justice to the phenomenon that was Jesus. Granting Kasper's focus is on the European scene, we must ask if he shows sufficient appreciation for aspects of the salvation Jesus has brought to those who live in situations like those of today's Third World, including the outcasts of the West.

Because of his prominent position in modern Catholic theology, Kasper has been the subject of much evaluation. Most, but not all, of this criticism has been positive, even laudatory. Both Protestants and Catholics have seen value in his work. H. E. W. Turner, writing at the height of the myth of God incarnate debate, called Kasper's work a restatement of orthodox Christology in terms of the contemporary debate. He noted Kasper keeps Christ's person and work together and uses soteriology as the determining factor in Christology.[136] Others see Kasper's appreciation of the need to consider both nature and function in Christology, respect for the miraculous, recognition Jesus' words and deeds contained an implicit Christology and soteriology, and concern to keep Jesus' universal significance and personal uniqueness together as important contributions to the current christological discussion. Kasper also emphasizes the valid role played by the early christological councils with the Greek language and concepts they employed. These are not unique contributions of the Catholic Tübingen School, although it has been active in keeping such concern alive, but they show the contemporary importance of a self-conscious Tübinger for non-Catholic theologians.

Kasper is a complex and subtle theologian. His Christology appears somewhat conservative at first reading, but deeper study shows this to be too simple an evaluation. His theological conclusions do not reflect fully the impact of critical thought on his method. Kasper's attempt to restore Spirit Christology to a major role in contemporary thought has serious implications for Christology which he has not fully worked out. As much as he has sought to avoid completely the expression of Adoptionism in his Christology, it is to soon to know whether Kasper has succeeded. In its current form, his attempt to retain the traditional dogmatic statements and appreciate the results of modern biblical criticism appears ultimately unworkable. At some point, he will be forced to choose between the two. Küng and Leonard Swidler both think Kasper's fundamental direction is more radical than his theology has appeared to date and that Kasper will have to move to the left if he is to be consistent.[137] Gerard Sloyan characterizes Kasper's method as demythologizing the conciliar and credal statements of the early Church in modern existential and phenomenological language without admitting the need to yield anything from the past.[138]

Kasper's concern to ground his Christology in the dogmatic statements of the Church and in Scripture gives stability to his thought. To date, it has counterbalanced the influence of modern criticism. His recognition of the historicity of humanity and of the effect of time and culture on the use of language and concepts offers a realism too often lacking in those who stress tradition. Kasper's difficulty lies in the way he brings the two together. As with many Catholic theologians after Vatican II, Kasper still needs to find a way to use in his theology the tools biblical scholars have made available to the Church during the past four decades without undercutting the dogmas of the faith it has confessed for over 1500 years.

Kasper has sought to present a Christology dealing with Jesus' entire life and message. He has shown a greater appreciation for Jesus' earthly life and his death and resurrection than have his Tübingen predecessors. At the same time, he has not allowed that concern to swallow up Christ's pre- and post-existence. Kasper has recognized the functional nature of much of the biblical and patristic language, but he also has recognized the ontology underlying that function. Küng argues Kasper's shift to ontological language is not supported by the biblical data. For example, Kasper understands the New Testament usage of Son of God to describe Christ ontologically. Küng doubts it is as easy to move from function to essence or from personal to essential relationship as Kasper thinks. He considers Kasper rash at this point. The same is true for the concepts of pre-existence and incarnation: Kasper calls them ontological; Küng says they are functional. Function and ontology cannot be as easily harmonized as Kasper thinks, says Küng.[139]

Several scholars have questioned Kasper's fidelity to the Tübingen School. Gerald McCool says Drey would be dismayed at Kasper's "Heideggerian theology" because Kasper has "abandoned the theological method Drey devised under the inspiration of Schelling's *Discourses on the Method of Academic Study*." He adds that whatever tradition might mean in Catholic theology, it can no longer be defined in terms of faithfulness to an inherited theological method.[140] James Mackey says Kasper takes his stand squarely on the need to use the Church's dogmatic tradition in order to understand Jesus, but when Kasper sets out his picture of Jesus he differs little from Küng on substantial matters.[141]

We believe these conclusions are in the first case irrelevant and in the second erroneous. Even the second generation Tübingers differed from Drey in method, yet the spirit that characterized those early generations has equally characterized these later generations despite differences in method and conclusions. A study of the critiques Kasper and Küng have prepared of each other shows their differences are not "negligible."[142]

Kasper has offered this generation a valuable Christology in the tradition of the Catholic Tübingen School. His work shows the influence and concerns of his late 20th century Western European context and addresses that audience, but that was a characteristic of Karl Adam's work that led Kasper and others to consider him a member of the Tübingen School. Kasper works hard to make Christian tradition relevant to his contemporaries without at the same time making it unrecognizable to its authors. Kasper also provides a clear understanding of how Christology developed from the early Church to our day. That is no small or unimportant accomplishment. It is difficult to chart our path for the future if we do not know where we have come from and where our predecessors have gone wrong or done particularly well.

Kasper has weaknesses in his Christology. Some of these are the reverse side of his strengths. He needs to interact more with those liberation Christologies he has overlooked. When Kasper did his major christological writing ten years ago, however, liberation Christology had only begun to receive the attention it has today. Kasper also needs to deal further with the relation between Church doctrine and biblical criticism. He has yet to show his system does not mask an ultimate methodological incompatibility. Is Küng correct in suggesting Kasper's conclusions are constrained by fear of Rome? Kasper needs to enlarge upon his proposal for a Spirit Christology, both in order to show how it can improve other approaches at specific points and to show his proposal contains no element of Adoptionism. While Kasper continues to work in these areas, his contemporaries can benefit greatly by examining his Christology for ways they might improve their own work either by incorporating aspects of Kasper's into their own or by accepting his challenges in order to improve their own.

1. Discussion with Hans Küng in Tübingen, July 10, 1985. Kasper explicitly claims descent from the Catholic Tübingen School, especially Karl Adam and Josef R. Geiselmann, in his *Jesus the Christ*, trans. by V. Green (New York: Paulist, 1977), p. 9.

2. Gerald O'Collins, *What Are They Saying About Jesus?* (New York: Paulist, 1977), p. 7. O'Collins revised this book significantly in 1983 in the light of major developments in christological research since his first edition. The revision did not affect O'Collins' assessment of Kasper, but it did result in an increase in the space devoted to Küng due to the latter's problems with Rome.

3. Wayne L. Fehr, *The Birth of the Catholic Tübingen School: The Dogmatics of Johann Sebastian Drey*, American Academy of Religion Academy Series Number 37 (Chico, CA: Scholars Press, 1981), p. 7. The Christology in question is Kasper's *Jesus the Christ*.

4. Ibid.

5. Walter Kasper, "Karl Adam," *Theologische Quartalschrift* 156 (1976):258.

6. Daniel Donovan, "Küng and Kasper Compared," *Ecumenist* 15 (1977):22.

7. Brian O. McDermott, "Roman Catholic Christology: Two Recurring Themes," *Theological Studies* 41 (1980):339 f.

8. Walter Kasper, *The Methods of Dogmatic Theology*, trans. by John Drury (New York: Paulist, 1969), pp. 1, 3.

9. Walter Kasper, "The Spirit Acting in the World to Demolish Frontiers and Create the Future," *Lumen Vitae* 34 (1979):93.

10. Ibid., pp. 87 f.

11. Walter Kasper, *An Introduction to Christian Faith*, trans. by V. Green (New York: Paulist, 1980), p. 99. Kasper does not explain the early heresies sometimes were attempts at speculation and the continued redefinitions were consistent with previous statements, sometimes quoting earlier confessions verbatim.

12. Walter Kasper, *Glaube und Geschichte* (Mainz: Matthias-Grünewald, 1970), p. 222.

13. Ibid., pp. 97 f.

14. Ibid., pp. 21 ff.

15. Kasper, *Introduction to Christian Faith*, pp. 89 f.

16. Kasper, *Introduction to Christian Faith*, pp. 89 f. From what Kasper is saying, we can see his understanding of criticism goes beyond the methods of biblical and theological criticism that Adam had characterized as "negative" and "destructive." Kasper holds even these forms of criticism up for criticism. This criticism is a going forward, not a return to the naive acceptance of tradition or Church authority along the lines of what Kasper criticizes as "biblicism."

17. Francis Schüssler Fiorenza, "Christology After Vatican II," *Ecumenist* 18 (1980):82.

18. Kasper, *Methods of Dogmatic Theology*, pp. 24 ff.

19. Walter Kasper, "Neuansätze gegenwartiger Christologie," in *Christologische Schwerpunkte*, pp. 29 f., ed. by Walter Kasper (Düsseldorf: Patmos, 1980).

20. Kasper, *Methods of Dogmatic Theology*, p. 43.

21. Walter Kasper, *The God of Jesus Christ*, trans. by Matthew J. O'Connell (New York: Crossroad, 1984), pp. 92 f.

22. Kasper, *Introduction to Christian Faith*, p. 160.

23. Kasper, *Methods of Dogmatic Theology*, pp. 52 f.

24. Kasper, *Introduction to Christian Faith*, p. 158.

25. Kasper, *Methods in Dogmatic Theology*, pp. 37 ff.

26. Ibid., pp. 56 ff.

27. Walter Kasper, "Christologie und Anthropologie," *Theologische Quartalschrift* 162 (1982):214.

28. Walter Kasper, "The Church's profession of Faith: On drafting a New Catholic catechism for adults," trans. by Sister Josephine Köppel, *Communio* 12 (1985):65.

29. Kasper, *The God of Jesus Christ*, p. 308.

30. Ibid., p. 185.

31. Walter Kasper, "Christologie von unten?" in *Grundfragen der Christologie heute*, p. 166, ed. by Leo Scheffczyk (Freiburg: Herder, 1975).

32. Walter Kasper, "Orientations in Current Christology," *Theology Digest* 31 (1984):109.

33. Walter Kasper, "Einmaligkeit und Univesalität Jesus Christi," *Theologie der Gegenwart* 17 (1974):4.

34. Bernard L. Ramm, *An Evangelical Christology: Ecumenic and Historic* (Nashville: Thomas Nelson, 1985), p. 193.

35. Hendrikus Berkhof, *Introduction to the Study of Dogmatics*, trans. by John Vriend (Grand Rapids: Wm. B. Eerdmans, 1985), p. 106.

36. Walter Kasper, *Jesus the Christ*. Most reviewers of the book have criticized the quality of the translation. Not only is the translation weak, but the indices are far less complete than those in the original.

37. Hans Küng, *On Being a Christian*, trans. by Edward Quinn (Garden City: Doubleday, 1976).

38. Raymond E. Brown, review of *Jesus the Christ*, by Walter Kasper, *Catholic Biblical Quarterly* 39 (1977):584 f.

39. John Carmody, *Theology for the 1980's* (Philadelphia: Westminster, 1980), p. 152.

40. T. M. McFadden, "Christology," in *New Catholic Encyclopedia*, XVII: 115 f., ed. by Thomas E. O'Brien, 17 vols. (New York: McGraw-Hill, 1979). Kasper rated 1½ of six columns in the article.

41. Kasper, "Einmaligkeit," p. 2.

42. Thomas Clarke, "Current Christologies," *Worship* 53 (1979):446 f.

43. McDermott, p. 340. It is difficult to see how Kasper could separate Christ from the Scripture, tradition, and worship of the Church as criteria for Christology because it is through these media that we must approach Christ in the 20th century.

44. Kasper, "Neuansätze gegenwartiger Christologie," pp. 17 f.

45. Kasper, *Christologische Schwerpunkt*, p. 14, and "Christologie von unten?" p. 162.

46. Kasper, "Orientations in Contemporary Christology," p. 107, and "Christologie von unten?" p. 162.

47. Kasper, "Orientations in Contemporary Christology," pp. 107 f., and "Christologie von unten?" p. 150.

48. Kasper, "Einmaligkeit," p. 4.

49. Kasper, *Introduction to Christian Faith*, p. 50.

50. Kasper, *Jesus the Christ*, pp. 34 ff.

51. Kasper, *Christologische Schwerpunkt*, pp. 12 f.

52. Kasper, "Christologie und Anthropologie," p. 220.

53. O'Collins, pp. 35 f.

54. Kasper, *The God of Jesus Christ*, p. 286.

55. Ibid.

56. Ibid., p. 287.

57. Kasper, "Orientations in Current Christology," p. 110.

58. Kasper, *The God of Jesus Christ*, p. 289. If we grant that the traditional understanding of the Trinity is no longer comprehensible, we must ask if Kasper's proposed explanation is any clearer to an audience of non-theologians. In asking this, we assume an audience of theologians will understand the technical language of the traditional explanation and be able to work with it even if they would prefer and are actively seeking more intelligible language.

59. Ibid., p. 154.

60. Kasper, "Christologie von unten," p. 163.

61. Kasper, "Für eine Christologie in geschichtlicher Perspektive: Replik auf die Anmerkungen von Hans Küng," p. 182, in *Grundfragen der Christologie Heute*, ed. by Leo Scheffczyk (Freiburg: Herder, 1975).

62. Kasper, "Christologie von unten?" pp. 166 f. Kasper cites Ernst Käsemann as saying the entire New Testament understands Jesus' role as Son of God in a metaphysical sense. Martin Hengel has also shown the concept of a real, not ideal, pre-existence occurs early in the New Testament and is based on biblical presuppositions. It was presented in order to restrain the threat of mythologizing Jesus. Likewise, the transition from function to ontology in Christology occurred within the New Testament, not between the New Testament and post-biblical writings, "Für eine Christologie in geschichtliche Perspektive," p. 181.

63. Ibid., pp. 164 ff.

64. Kasper, *Jesus the Christ*, pp. 246 f.

65. Kasper, "Neuansätze gegenwartiger Christologie," pp. 28 f.

66. kasper, "Krise und Neuanfang der Christologie im Denken Schellings," *Evangelische Theologie* 33 (1973):384.

67. Kasper, *Jesus the Christ*, pp. 238 f.

68. Ibid., p. 233.

69. Ibid., p. 248.

70. Ibid.

71. Kasper, *The God of Jesus Christ*, p. 189.

72. O'Collins, p. 27 (rev. ed.); Kasper, *Jesus the Christ*, p. 111; Kasper, "Orientations in Current Christology," p. 110.

73. Kasper, *Jesus the Christ*, pp. 101 ff.

74. Kasper, "Christologie und Anthropologie," pp. 203, 205; Walter Kasper, *Faith and the Future*, trans. by Robert Nowell (New York: Crossroad, 1982), p. 71.

75. Kasper, *Jesus the Christ*, pp. 103-109.

76. O'Collins, pp. 3 f.; Kasper, *Jesus the Christ*, p. 37. In attacking the traditional Incarnation-centered Christology, Kasper misses the point of that theological enterprise in the way he criticizes the incarnational position. He seems to be reacting to the one-sided view held by his Tübingen predecessors among others, because viewing the Incarnation as constituting the person of Christ once-for-all need not denigrate the significance of Jesus' life, death, and resurrection. It is a different matter when the Incarnation is seen as realizing human salvation apart from the rest of Jesus' life and then this concern becomes relevant. But if we see the Incarnation as the prerequisite for Jesus' ministry, we can appreciate what occurred in Jesus' life because of the value given it by the Incarnation without denigrating either one. Kasper's contention that Jesus' death and resurrection must play a part in making his person divine is reminiscent of Wolfhart Pannenberg and appears to derive from a particular reading of Romans 1:3 f.

77. Kasper, *Jesus the Christ*, p. 198.

78. Kasper, "Orientations in Current Christology," p. 111.

79. Kasper, *Glaube und Geschichte*, p. 212.

80. Kasper, *The God of Jesus Christ*, p. 189.

81. Kasper, *Jesus the Christ*, pp. 66 f.

82. Kasper, *Introduction to Christian Faith*, pp. 44 ff.; *Jesus the Christ*, pp. 213 f.

83. Kasper's description of the content of Jesus' proclamation of the Kingdom of God indicates a selective reading of the gospels. I am convinced Jesus spoke clearly about impending judgment and divine wrath, and Kasper's use of biblical criticism does not permit him to explain away these statements. Kasper's view of the nature of the Kingdom appears to be a theological interpolation on his part.

84. Kasper, *Jesus the Christ*, p. 86.

85. Ibid., p. 121.

86. Kasper, *The God of Jesus Christ*, p. 168.

87. Kasper, *Jesus the Christ*, pp. 94 f.

88. Ibid., pp. 137 ff.

89. William M. Thompson, *The Jesus Debate: A Survey and Synthesis* (New York: Paulist, 1985), pp. 237 f.

90. Kasper, *Jesus the Christ*, pp. 155 ff.

91. T. E. Pollard, *Fullness of Humanity: Christ's Humanity and Ours* (Sheffield: Almond, 1982), p. 54.

92. Kasper, *Jesus the Christ*, pp. 203 f.

93. Kasper, *Introduction to Christian Faith*, p. 127.

94. Ibid., pp. 126 f.

95. Ibid., p. 190.

96. Kasper, *Jesus the Christ*, p. 63.

97. Kasper, *The God of Jesus Christ*, p. 183.

98. Pollard, pp. 96 f.

99. O'Collins, p. 36 (rev. ed.).

100. Kasper, "Hope in Jesus' Final Coming," *Theology Digest* 33 (1986):153.

101. Walter Kasper, "Christi Himmelfahrt—Geschichte und theologische Bedeutung," *International katholische Zeitschrift* 12 (1983):211 f. In an interview with Kasper in Tübingen in July 1985, I asked Kasper abut his position regarding the return of Christ, saying his writings seemed unclear on this point. Kasper suggested this article as a good statement of his position. I consider the articles in the preceding note to be an equally helpful statement of that position. Kasper appears to hold to a form of realized eschatology in which all that we will see at the *parousia* actually has been achieved in a hidden way in Jesus' resurrection and exaltation. The Spirit has been playing a major role in this eschatological realization since Pentecost. Kasper says there will be an eschatological *parousia*, but the specifics of that event are not set forth clearly in the biblical texts. He does not believe it need be understood simply as Jesus entering into the world in a way all can see.

102. Kasper, *Methods of Dogmatic Theology*, p. 1.

103. Kasper, *Introduction to Christian Faith*, pp. 170 f.

104. Kasper, *Methods in Dogmatic Theology*, pp. 24 f., and *Dogma unter dem Wort Gottes* (Mainz: Matthias-Grünewald, 1965), pp. 126–138.

105. Kasper, *The God of Jesus Christ*, p. 184. In *Glaube und Geschichte*, Kasper says, "Die Vorläufigkeit dogmatischer Aussagen: Das Evangelium ist eine eschatologische Grosse, durch welche die entscheidende und endgültige Wahrheit des Heils ein für allemal in die Welt gekommen ist. Aufgrund der Treue dieser Verheissung wird es immer eine Kirche geben, in der diese Wahrheit im Glauben angenommen ist.... Das Moment der Verläufigkeit

und Offenheit gehirt deshalb ebenso wesentlich zum Glauben der Kirche wie
das der Endgültigkeit. Dogmen können deshalb nur Wegstationen, aber
nicht das Ziel sein; sie müssen ihre Wahrheit daran erweisen, dass sie über
sich hinausweissen und der Kirche den Weg in die Zukunft nicht verschlies-
sen, sondern aufliessen.... Zum Unterwegsein der Kirche gehört es auch,
dass sie nicht nur die heilige Kirche, sondern auch die Kirche der Sünder ist.
An der Sündigkeit der Kirche können auch die Dogmatisierungen partizi-
pieren" (p. 221).

106. Kasper, "Neuansätze gegenwartiger Christologie," p. 25.

107. Ibid., p. 31.

108. Kasper, *The God of Jesus Christ*, p. 260.

109. Kasper, "Neuansätze gegenwartiger Christologie," p. 30.

110. Kasper, *The God of Jesus Christ*, p. 188.

111. Kasper, "Krise und Neuanfang der Christologie," pp. 377 f. Küng also
discusses the use of "is" in early Church confessions in *Glauben an Jesus
Christus* (Zurich: Benziger, 1982), pp. 40 f.

112. Carmody, p. 152; McDermott, p. 342.

113. Kasper, *Jesus the Christ*, p. 238.

114. Walter Kasper, "Einige verwunderte Gegenfragen," *Zeitschrift für
katholische Theologie* 98 (1976):187 f. In *Glaube und Geschichte*, Kasper
writes, "Das Glaubensbekenntnis von der Menschwerdung Gottes ist,
besonders in seiner dogmatischen Formulierung durch das Chalkedonense,
selbst nur eine theologische Interpretation des Christus Ereignisses—
gebunden an die Sprach- und Denkform einer bestimmten Zeit, die wir
heute selbst wieder kritisch interpretieren müssen" (p. 212).

115. Thompson, pp. 329 f.

116. Philip J. Rosato, "Spirit Christology: Ambiguity and Promise,"
Theological Studies 38 (1977):442. On pp. 441 f., Rosato sums up Pannenberg's objections to Spirit Christology.

117. Ibid., pp. 442 f.

118. Ibid., p. 440.

119. Ibid., pp. 423 f.

120. Kasper, *Jesus the Christ*, p. 267. it is statements like this that cause other theologians concern about the adoptionist tendency of Spirit Christology. At another point, Kasper says the creature filled with the Spirit freely becomes an historical figure through which the Son gives himself to the Father (*Jesus the Christ*, p. 252). Taken in isolation from other parts of Kasper's theology, this sounds very much like Adoptionism.
M. M. B. Turner says the biblical evidence makes Jesus' relationship to the Spirit in the New Testament analogous to God's relationship to the Spirit in the Old: "The closest analogy in the Old Testament and Judaism to Jesus' relationship to the Spirit (as specified by Peter at Pentecost), is not that of men anointed with God's Spirit, but the Old Testament picture of God's relationship to the Spirit.... As the Spirit had mediated God's activity, and thus his presence, amongst his people, so, according to the perspective of Acts 2:33, the Spirit has not become the means of Jesus' presence and activity too." M. M. B. Turner, "The Spirit of Christ and Christology," in *Christ the Lord*, p. 183, ed. by Harold H. Rowden (Downers Grove, IL: Intervarsity, 1982).

121. Ibid., p. 256.

122. Kasper, *The God of Jesus Christ*, pp. 208, 211, 305.

123. Rosato, p. 448.

124. Kasper, *Jesus the Christ*, p. 268. In a discussion with the author, Kasper stated that all salvation is in Jesus Christ, but because his Spirit is universally active adherents of non-Christian religions can receive salvation. Kasper said he is not entirely comfortable with Rahner's concept of anonymous Christianity and agreed with Küng's critique of the concept. Kasper agreed that the phrase *extra Christus nulla salus* accurately reflects his soteriology.

125. Rosato, pp. 426, 429.

126. Kasper, "Christologie von unten?" p. 141.

127. Kasper, *Introduction to Christian Faith*, pp. 145 f.

128. Kasper, *Jesus the Christ*, pp. 26 f.

129. Kasper, *Introduction to Christian Faith*, p. 191.

130. Kasper, "Christologie und Anthropologie," p. 218. Kasper cites Thomas, *Summa Theologica* III, 8, 3, as his justification for this view.

131. William P. Loewe, "The New Catholic Tübingen Theology of Walter Kasper: Foundational Issues," *Heythrop Journal* 31 (1980):37.

132. McFadden, p. 116.

133. Kasper, "Christologie von unten?" pp. 158 f.; "Christologie und Anthropologie," p. 209.

134. Kasper, "Für eine Christologie," pp. 179 ff. This response by Kasper as well as the preceding articles by Kasper and Küng in Leo Scheffczyk's *Grundfragen der Christologie heute* show clearly the fundamental differences between the two Tübingen theologians, differences that existed prior to Rome's 1979 action.

135. Kasper, "Christologie von unten?" p. 160.

136. H. E. W. Turner, review of *Jesus the Christ*, by Walter Kasper, *The Churchman* 91 (1977):260 f.

137. In separate discussions with me, both Küng and Swidler expressed the view that the Kasper we see in print is inconsistent with his own presuppositions. Küng said Kasper's presuppositions should lead him to embrace Küng's position. He added that Kasper is in the Tübingen School in the sense Möhler was and, like Möhler, fears the reaction of Rome. This makes Kasper over-cautious and inconsistent. Kasper told me that the question of the relation between biblical criticism and dogma is one of where we find truth. Ultimately we find it in the church, not in the world. This appears to mean that when he cannot reconcile criticism and dogma, Kasper will

support dogma. This interpretation agrees with his practice in *Jesus the Christ*.

138. Gerard S. Sloyan, review of *Jesus the Christ*, by Walter Kasper, *Commonweal* 105 (14 April 1978):252.

139. Hans Küng, "Anmerkungen zu Walter Kasper, 'Christologie von unten?'" in *Grundfragen der Christologie heute*, pp. 175 f., ed. by Leo Scheffczyk (Freiburg: Herder, 1975).

140. Gerald A. McCool, *Catholic Theology in the Nineteenth Century* (New York: Seabury, 1977), p. 265. See note 19 on pages 21 ff. for the understanding of school I have used; I have defined it in a less formal sense than do Küng and McCool.

141. James P. Mackey, "Küng and Kasper Compared," *Living Light* 14 (1977):151.

142. A better alternative, which I was able to take, was to interview Kasper and Küng and ask each about the other's theology. Kasper had a greater appreciation for Küng than did Küng for Kasper, but neither was content with the basic tenor of the other's Christology. Küng said Kasper prefers a Christology "from below," but when that does not work he "flies up in a helicopter" and achieves his desired results from the side of the Trinity. Küng also said Kasper has a view of the union of infinite and finite being that contradicts II Constantinople. This may reflect Kasper's uneasiness with II Constantinople as cited by Sloyan in his *Commonweal* review (see note 138 above).

CHAPTER IX

HANS KÜNG

Hans Küng is probably the best known German-speaking theologian, Catholic or Protestant, outside Germany today. His books are widely translated and read, and in addition to his teaching schedule at Tübingen he lectures and teaches regularly in many parts of the world. Since the Vatican revoked his license to teach Catholic theology in 1979, Küng probably has been more influential outside Germany than he has inside. Despite the Vatican action, however, Küng remains a popular lecturer and best-selling author.

Hans Küng was born in Switzerland in 1928. His earliest desire was to become a parish priest, but his demonstrated brilliance caused him to be sent to Rome for theological study at the Gregorian University and after that at the Sorbonne. At the former Küng gained a solid education in the reigning Neoscholasticism of the pre-Vatican II Catholic Church; at the latter he was introduced to the modern biblical-critical methods that were beginning to gain acceptance within the Catholic Church of the 1950's. It was in Paris that Küng wrote his celebrated study of Karl Barth's doctrine of justification as a doctoral dissertation. After Paris, Küng spent two years as a pastor in Lucerne, Switzerland, and then went to Münster to teach and write his *Habilitation* on the value of Hegel's thought for developing future Christologies. Called to Tübingen to teach in 1960, Küng laid aside his study of Hegel for more than a decade. During Vatican II, Küng served as a theological advisor to the German bishops.

The period immediately prior to the first session of Vatican II marked a major turn in Küng's theological outlook. Trained in Neoscholastic theology and exposed to the new currents in biblical and historical studies, Küng entered into serious discussion with his Protestant colleagues at Tübingen, particularly with Ernst Käsemann. Out of this came Küng's "turn to history." He came to see human experience as a crucial element in theology and, because human experience is historical and limited, concluded that doctrine must be understood relative to its context because it is time-bound in the same way all other human products and experiences are. Since then, Küng has approached theology from the perspective of the human and temporal, no longer from that of the divine and eternal. This in no way means he denies the latter, only that he considers the former a more meaningful way through which to communicate to modern society.

Küng's theological turn has led him to question various traditional Church teachings whose content he considers underivable from Scripture. Küng looked first at the Church, its authority structure, and its tradition, coming to question the teaching of papal infallibility. Later, he wrote about the nature and content of Christian faith, suggesting new interpretations of such fundamental doctrines as the Trinity and Christology. Küng's questions and suggestions have been controversial in the Catholic Church, gaining acceptance from many priests and laity but arousing fierce opposition from others, particularly those in positions of leadership. Opposition has not deterred Küng and he continues to raise questions and offer suggestions about major issues facing not only Catholics but all Christians and even non-Christians.

The secret of Küng's success is twofold. He is interested in speaking to the concerns of his contemporaries in language and thought patterns they can understand. Unlike most theologians, especially German theologians, he expresses himself in language that is easy to read, especially for those not trained in theology. A by-product of this has been increased lay interest in learning about theological subjects. Küng has made clear the apologetic intent of his writings and insists they can be understood properly only in this context.

The same characteristics that have made Küng successful have also created difficulties for him. In identifying with his contemporaries and their concerns, Küng has not always given sufficient weight to the traditions of the Church. Some have suggested Küng has given up too much of that which is peculiarly Catholic in attempting to communicate to those both inside and outside of the Church. In his desire to get back to the Jesus who lived and died in first-century Palestine, Küng may not appreciate sufficiently the Church's response to the historical situations and forces it has faced in the interim. And Küng's clear and crisp German has not always been as clear in what it says as in how he says it. Some have charged that in speaking simply about theological matters Küng has spoken simplistically. Küng's problem with Rome and with the German bishops appears to be as much in what he has not said as in what he has said. Cardinal Höffner suggested to Küng that some of his christological language could be considered equivocal.[1] He was reflecting the view of many conservatives that Küng has offered christological statements which remain open to multiple interpretations and has yet to explain himself to the satisfaction of those who are challenging him.

No study of the Christology of the Catholic Tübingen School can ignore the work of so prolific and eminent a theologian as Hans Küng. This remains the case even if one concludes, as we have done, that Küng does not fit within our definition of that School. Küng's relation to the Catholic Tübingen School is complex, as the course of his theological development has been complex.

Küng's theology, especially his Christology, is far different in 1990 from what it was in the 1950's. His early work might be considered to the right of that of the Catholic Tübingen School. His later theology, however, has gone well beyond the limits envisioned by that School. The catalyst for that change was Tübingen, but it appears to have been Protestant rather than Catholic Tübingen. Soon after his arrival at Tübingen, Küng engaged in serious discussions about the relationship of history to theological study with Ernst Käsemann, the world-famous New Testament scholar. As a result, he increasingly appropriated biblical-critical conclusions into his theological work. All of Küng's work since has reflected this increasing appreciation of the effect of historical thinking on biblical and theological studies.[2]

Küng considers himself to be the heir of the early Catholic Tübingen School because of his appreciation of historicity and concern to communicate the gospel in the language and concepts of his contemporaries. He is correct in recognizing these similarities between his approach and that of the Tübingen School, but there are equally great differences. For example, while it is true that some earlier Tübingers were rebuked by Rome for their theological writings, each chose to submit.[3] Küng has opted for confrontation. Further, the Rome with which Küng is in conflict is a Rome that accepted much of traditional Tübingen's theology at Vatican II. To say Küng is not a part of the Catholic Tübingen School is not to say Küng is in error; it only means his understanding of the Church and of its tradition differs from what we understand that of the Catholic Tübingen School to be. Küng's ecclesiology differs in particular from that of Walter Kasper, whom many consider to be a contemporary representative of the School.

Küng's fundamental difference with the Catholic Tübingen School lies in the area of tradition. We have seen the crucial role tradition plays in Tübingen theology. Küng understands tradition in a very different way from the Tübingers because he considers biblical revelation normative in a way that permits nothing else, even later conciliar decisions, similar normativity. Gerard S. Sloyan notes that it is not differences with Catholic tradi-

tion regarding specific doctrines as much as it is a different understanding
of the role of tradition in establishing doctrines that distinguishes Küng from
most other Catholic theologians today.[4] He says Küng "has left no room for
those Church traditions of which it can be said they are legitimate developments of the gospel tradition."[5]

The heart of Küng's difference with Catholic Tübingen over tradition lies in how each views the development of doctrine. Küng's concept of
paradigm shift is not only different but also incompatible with the organic
understanding pioneered by the Tübingers. Küng's approach relativizes tradition, especially christological tradition, because the theological paradigm
shifts in a discontinuous manner. This requires new statements of doctrine
consistent with the new paradigm because the old statements are irrevocably
tied to the previous paradigm and thus are no longer meaningful to their
hearers. Catherine LaCugna describes Küng's attitude toward the Church's
formulation of faith as follows:

> Not only are all formulations of faith partial and incom-
> plete... they also have a diminished value with respect to
> the present. Past formulations are... worthy of respect, but
> to the degree that they are largely the product of another
> era, an other conceptuality, they are not directly transfer-
> able or applicable to the present.[6]

In this concept of paradigm shift Küng's pastoral and apologetic
concerns come to the fore. Küng desires to present Christianity to his contemporaries not only in Europe and within the Church, but also to those
around the world in other religions or with no religion at all. This concern
is evident in all Küng says and does. We see it in both his language and in
his style. Thomas H. Graves describes Küng's attempt to bridge the gap between traditional Christian faith and the modern lifestyle as dialogical-
interactive. He notes Küng is especially concerned to address those whose
faith is being constructed in a scientific age.[7] One of the more significant
and controversial results of this concern is Küng's shift from the ontological
to the functional and pragmatic idiom that characterizes modernity.

Küng's early Christology is found in *Justification: The Doctrine of
Karl Barth and a Catholic Reflection*.[8] In a concluding excursus, Küng
brought together his early thought in terms of a Christology "from above"
and presented it in traditional language. Much of what he said there stands
in sharp contrast to his later christological writings. Küng said the theologian "cannot confine himself to a simple listing of the biblical findings lest

he renounce theology. He must therefore put questions to the biblical facts."[9] Such theological interpretation is not possible without the use of philosophical categories. Küng added that the use of philosophical and theological categories is firmly based in Scripture.[10]

Küng described Jesus Christ as a divine-human person and spoke of his pre-existence in a divine life. He said, "if Jesus Christ is in God's eternity it is not by virtue of His human nature but by virtue of His divine Person."[11] He also said Paul sometimes referred to Christ as man and sometimes as God.[12]

Küng's Christology at this point reflected his Neoscholastic training; it used all the traditional language and followed the traditional approach. After this study, Küng began to examine Hegel to see whether he might be able to contribute to modern Christology. This study was interrupted by his move to Tübingen. Out of that move came a whole new approach to theology, but particularly to Christology. Küng has described the effect of Tübingen on his theology as follows:

> In my first years it was exclusively a Christology from above that I advocated. My view then was that it was precisely with Hegel's help that this Christology from above... could be renewed for the present day with the help of Hegelian speculation.... The more I occupied myself intensively in Tübingen with exegesis on historical and critical principles... the more difficult it became for me to maintain this speculation in connection with the understanding of God and with Christology. This doesn't mean at all that I had abandoned the positive intentions of a Christology from above. But what increasingly became my goal... was that it was from below that people of today could more convincingly strive to attain and could reach the statement of a "high" Christology.[13]

It appears that part of Hans Küng's controversy with other theologians and with the magisterium derives from this language we find in the earlier Küng. Küng certainly knows the language, concepts, and concerns of traditional Catholic Christology. He may be correct in his program of presenting Christology to the modern world in terms of its concepts and concerns, but some in the Catholic Church expect him to converse in the language he has in common with them when they ask him about what he is saying to those who live outside this theological language. We see here a failure by Küng's ecclesiastical superiors to recognize the task Küng has set for himself. But we also see an unwillingness by Küng to admit the legitimacy of his questioners' approach within the theological community.

The transition in Küng's Christology occurred during his writing of *Menschwerdung Gottes*,[14] the study of Hegel which Küng had begun as his *Habilitation*. Küng had intended to use Hegel in support of the "high" Christology he had presented in *Justification*, but the dialogue with Käsemann altered Küng's outlook in the direction of a Christology "from below." This would begin with the historical Jesus and work toward God's action in him. As LaCugna says, Küng did not intend this new approach to declare his previous approach illegitimate; Küng has since stated that a mythological Jesusology and an unhistorical Christology are equally unacceptable.[15]

Scripture had played an important role in Küng's theology when he came to Tübingen, but it shared its influence with doctrinal formulations and philosophy in a way that has not been evident in Küng's work since the late 1950's. He now describes Scripture as the *norma normans* for theology. But not only is Scripture normative for the content of theology, it appears Küng considers it equally normative for the language of theology.[16]

By placing Scripture at the apex of sources for theology, Küng has lowered all other sources to a secondary role. This is most evident in Küng's approach to the results of Church councils, both ecumenical and local. Scripture alone is "inspired," so we can view councils only as "assisted" by the Spirit. Their conclusions are thoroughly human products and not the word of God; they are only indirect witnesses to that word. These councils stand under Scripture—thus Küng's willingness to critique them in terms of Scripture—and their purpose is to expound, proclaim, and interpret Scripture.[17] The implication of such a position is that the councils are valid only to the extent they do this faithfully.

Küng approaches Scripture from the historical-critical perspective he learned from Käsemann. He is sufficiently sure his conclusions reflect modern biblical scholarship that he can say, "The Jesus of history portrayed in *On Being a Christian* has in its decisive traits the consensus of New Testament exegetes behind it."[18] Küng also believes the historical-critical method provides a fairly reliable picture of the historical Jesus. As Sloyan has noted, it is the New Testament seen through these spectacles that controls Küng's Christology, and Church tradition finds a place only to the extent it agrees with this interpretation of Scripture.

As a consequence of his historical-critical method, Küng brackets the supernatural when he considers history. He admits this is presuppositional, but argues no historically verifiable action can be shown to be a divine action:

> The fact that God is at work in the history of the world and of the individual person is not an observation demonstrated by historical criticism, but... a matter of trusting faith.[19]

Küng contends faith cannot be built on supposed proofs derived from history; he is unwilling to allow faith to be dependent on the contingency of history.

If we cannot verify divine action in history, we are compelled to reconsider the nature of miracles. Traditionally, people have understood miracles in terms of God acting in history contrary to the laws of nature. Küng says God acts in and through humanity and historicity, but never contrary to them. This is what Christians have called providence. Yet Küng notes the biblical miracles are located too deeply in the tradition to be ignored. Some of the accounts are too controversial to be fabrications. As much as he can, Küng explains the nature and healing miracles in terms of natural causes. He does admit some of Jesus' healing miracles remain inexplicable in terms of modern medicine. At points, Küng resorts to explaining particular miracles as embellishments or misunderstandings of actual historical events. He concludes that the burden of proof remains on anyone who wants to accept miracles in the sense of contraventions of the laws of nature. In any case, such an occurrence could never be proven historically.[20]

Küng sees the concept of myth as important for understanding the meaning of the gospels. He says they were written for people who thought mythologically because that was how people explained reality at that time. Mythology was a device used by the ancients to explain out of the ordinary occurrences. Küng says, for example, that

> with reference to beginning and ending, to the birth and death of Jesus Christ, insofar as these things transcend sense experience, the formation of myths is to be expected.[21]

Thus, it is necessary to demythologize. It is equally necessary to recognize the limits of demythologization. He says "myths, legends, images and symbols may not be taken literally," but neither may we ignore them.[22] Myths present truth in a way historical reporting never can. Truth is not the same thing as facticity nor is it equivalent to historical truth. There are different levels of truth just as there are different levels of reality. Sometimes fiction can convey truth better than can history. Küng argues the Bible is more interested in the "truth of salvation" than in historical truth.

> Particularly in the Christmas, miracle, Easter and judgment stories, the main interest is not in what really happened or will happen at that point... but in the practical question of *what it means for us.*[23]

The element of "for me" or "for us" appears repeatedly in Küng's Christology. The subjectivity it appears to express has proven troublesome to many of Küng's conservative critics, and he has attempted to respond to their concern.

Critique of Dogmatic Christology

Küng is troubled about dogmatic statements for several reasons. These can seen most clearly in terms of the source and the content of the statements. Dogmatic statements, says Küng, are unavoidably polemical because they have been constructed in response to heresy and error. But they deal only with that which is untrue in these positions. Because all heresies and errors contain elements of truth—elements not acknowledged in the dogmatic statements—dogmas attack the truth as well as the untruth of heresy. Küng says this makes dogmatic statements half-truths because while they assert that which is correct against that which is incorrect in the heresies, they ignore that which is true in the heresies.[24]

As to their content, all dogmas contain both an implicit and irreformable content and an explicit and reformable form which holds that content. The source of the content is divine, but the source of the form is human. Being human, it is historically conditioned.

Küng's fundamental complaint about the form of dogmatic statements, if not the very idea of dogmatics, deals with the influence of Greek and Roman thought upon the Church. He describes the result of Greek influence as intellectualization, speculation, and sterile mysticism. Roman influence has resulted in an emphasis on form, law, and organization, as well as a taste for tradition, efficiency, and authoritarianism.[25] Küng says the influence of Hellenistic thought on Christology has led to the use of language incomprehensible or misleading in the modern world. He seeks to restate the concepts which that language sought to express and purify them of what he sees as mythological accretions so people today can understand the gospel. He makes no claim to having found the best way accomplish this task, inviting others to suggest better ways of saying what he is trying to say.

Küng says faith in Christ must not be changed, but those terms and ideas which get in the way of belief and practice need to be translated into the modern idiom. This does not mean

> abolishing ancient titles and creeds, does not mean over-looking the long Christological tradition, still less their biblical source. On the contrary, any good translation must be oriented to the original text and learn from the mistakes and strong points of former translations. But any good translation may not merely mechanically repeat, but must creatively sense and seize upon the possibilities of the new language. We need have no more hesitation about new designations of Jesus than about the old.[26]

Küng understands the development of dogma in terms of an un-folding or explanation of that which is already found in either Scripture or another dogma. He does not consider this unfolding to be organic because dogmatic understanding does not necessarily improve over time. Küng sug-gests there can even be false and erroneous developments in doctrine and provides examples. As we have noted, Küng's concept of paradigm shift virtually denies the possibility of continuity in doctrinal development over long periods. Instead, doctrine develops in the same way as does science. The community accepts hypotheses until they are stretched to cover too many inconsistencies. At that point, it constructs new hypotheses to explain those conditions earlier hypotheses were unable to encompass. Küng's favorite example of this process is the replacement of the Ptolemaic concept of the solar system with the Copernican.[27]

When considering Küng's Christology, we need to keep in mind that Küng is asking a different question than are many of his peers. He wants to know what Jesus' life means for existence in the world today. This makes traditional concerns less important because other matters are more critical for Küng. This attitude also governs his method. His Christology "from below" begins from modern humanity's experience, beliefs, and faith. Only then does he examine what the gospels have to say about Jesus' earthly life.[28] Küng calls the historical Jesus a starting point even non-Christians can agree on. This historical Jesus is the norm and standard for all human life. Yet the historical Jesus cannot be separated from the Christ of faith. They may not be simply equated, but there is a continuity between the pre-

Easter Jesus and the post-Easter message. Christology "from below" is not intended to provide a different content from Christology "from above," but to express the same content in a different and more meaningful (for today) way. Whereas some have described the "historical Jesus" as the product of modern criticism and distinguished him from the "Jesus of history," or Jesus as he actually lived, Küng believes the former can be an accurate reflection of the latter.

Beginning with the historical Jesus requires we give greater attention to his message. This was Jesus' proclamation of the Kingdom of God. Jesus' life and ministry focused on this Kingdom. The Kingdom shows God's cause and humanity's cause are ultimately one. Jesus' preaching demanded a response from his hearers and forced them to ask who he was.

Another advantage of Christology "from below" is that it corresponds both to the New Testament evidence and to the modern way of thinking. It means considering Jesus in the same way his first disciples did: by beginning with the historical man Jesus and studying his words, actions, and fate. Having done this, we can ask about the relation between the human Jesus and God. The obvious sources for our answer are the gospels, but these were written after Easter; they are not contemporaneous records of the disciples' experience of Jesus. They were written by men who became witnesses for Jesus. Küng sees a difficulty in this. He says the God who has spoken through Jesus Christ is the only absolutely reliable source for faith.[29] How we get to this source—"God himself as he spoke to believers through Jesus Christ"—Küng does not explain; it certainly is not through some mystical experience. Instead, the New Testament plays a crucial role in this because, Küng tells us, the work of many generations of exegetes and the contribution of the historical-critical method allow us to know the historical Jesus better than perhaps any but the first generation of Christians.

Jesus of Nazareth is the ground of Christianity. Christianity is not a worldview or idealist philosophy. It deals with a man named Jesus, and Küng wants to put us in touch with this man. For Küng, he is "ultimately decisive, definitive, archetypal for man in these various dimensions of his... for man's relations with God, with his fellow man, with society."[30] Jesus is the criterion of what is Christian, but it is the concrete, historical Jesus, and no other, who is this standard. This makes Christianity an historical faith. "It was only as a historical faith that Christianity was able to prevail at the very beginning against all the mythologies, philosophies and mystery cults."[31] The most important thing, says Küng, is not Christology or Christ theory—although these are important—but faith in Christ and following

Christ. Here we see the modern pragmatic and functional interests taking precedence over the more traditional ontological questions.

Küng notes the historical Jesus is also the Christ of faith, and this Jesus is made accessible to us in the Bible. Because the Bible is an historical document it is subject to historical analysis. The Christology resulting from such an historical-critical approach will differ significantly from classical Christology. The fundamental difference will be in the shift from a metaphysical framework which tries to deal with Jesus ontologically toward "more biblical expressions and themes," which Küng believes interpret Jesus functionally.[32] Although Küng's Christology appears to be primarily functional, there are frequent indications of an ontological concern. Gerald O'Collins says an exclusively functional Christology is impossible: we cannot talk about a person's value, significance, and role without making at least implicit claims about that person's nature.[33]

The direction by which we approach Jesus Christ is important for Küng because he believes modern people will accept only a Christology "from below." He says, however, that Christology must combine the best of both approaches: above and below. This is because both God and humanity are involved in Jesus. Küng says, "I have no fundamental objection to starting 'from above'... [but] the method of starting from below strikes me as most suitable."[34] Küng adds the disciples had to ask themselves who Jesus was based on their experience of him and this is the form of the problem for people today.

Küng says the shift from ontological to functional and from "above" to "below" is not "a call to iconoclasm." It is instead a call to translate the ideas of previous generations into the outlook and language of our own.

> Faith in Christ must remain the same, but terms and ideas
> which are unintelligible or even misleading today must not
> make it more difficult or—still less—impossible to accept
> and to live the message of Christ today.[35]

In the same way, Küng is willing to accept the intent of the language of the early christological councils, but he is not willing to be bound by their literal meaning because these are limited by their original context.[36] He recognizes the early Church had no other way to understand the gospel than Greek metaphysical language, but he does not consider Hellenistic concepts a good way to express the contents of the gospel to modern ears. Speculative categories, he says, are always less appropriate than historical ones.[37] Küng

LaCugna notes Küng seems to assume modern historical categories not only make more sense today but also correspond to the New Testament, and thus solve christological problems better than do metaphysical categories. She suggests this approach may serve to bypass Church tradition. Tradition, which had been an indispensable mediator of Scripture until recently, definitely recedes into the background in Küng's theology.[38]

Despite frequent criticism that he disregards tradition, and his own criticism of that tradition, Küng says any theologian who ignores tradition will pay dearly for it in his or her work. Conciliar statements were both brief summaries and defensive demarcations of the faith and must be honored as such. Tradition demonstrates the stability of the Christian faith amid centuries of change. Küng notes the tradition is complex. Its witness to the one Christ is varied, full of contrasts, and not always consistent. He adds that no theologian can deny that every part of the tradition cannot be equally true or even simultaneously true.[39]

A Functional Christology

Küng approaches Christology in terms of the title "Son of God." He understands this as a functional term showing Jesus to be God's spokesman, representative, and deputy. It indicates Jesus stands by the side of God and is no longer within the community. This title came to the fore in the early Church because of its dynamic nature. In the Old Testament, it had been applied to the Israelite kings. After Jesus' death, the Church applied this title to him who by his resurrection and exaltation had been shown to be elected and authorized by God. The disciples' Easter experience had led them to believe Jesus had transcended death and been taken up into God's eternal life. Modern exegetes agree Jesus never called himself the Son of God, but in assuming God's authority he made claims for himself that went far beyond those of the prophets. Thus the title is a appropriate description of Jesus' role. It denotes, says Küng, a juridical and authoritative position, nothing more.[40] "Son of God" expressed more clearly than any other title the early Church's understanding of how much Jesus belongs to God and how much he stands on God's side. Nonetheless, Son of God expresses Jesus' significance, not his nature. This is consistent with Küng's concern: who Jesus was is secondary to what he came to do. The titles tell us what Jesus meant to the early Church, not who he was in himself.

The earliest strata of the New Testament show no interest in questions of essence. Even in John's gospel the unity of God and Jesus is not physical or metaphysical, but a matter of will and knowledge. This is clear from John's stress on Jesus' subordination to the Father. Küng has challenged Walter Kasper in this matter, contending Kasper moves rashly from personal to essential relationship.[41]

Küng says explicit New Testament Christology emerged from the implicit Christology behind Jesus' language, actions, and suffering. Actually, he says, a wide variety of New Testament Christologies emerged, varying in accordance with the individuality of the authors and the different social, political, and intellectual contexts they addressed. This means there is no single normative Christ image.[42] The Hellenistic world was only one of these contexts, and has provided only one of our images of Christ.

That Jesus is the Son of God is the common Christian conviction, but Küng doubts Hellenistic categories and concepts are the only or even the best way of explaining this title. "To put it more clearly," asks Küng, "can the fact that Jesus is the son of God only be explained by the doctrine of the two natures?"[43] He is concerned that the God who stands behind the Christ of the early councils is more the unmoving and passionless god of Plato than the dynamic God of the Bible. We should not belittle the importance of the early councils, but we must recognize they are Greek and Jesus was not born in Greece. The teaching of these early councils "gives expression to the genuine continuity of Christian faith and provides important guidelines for the whole discussion and any future interpretation." Yet we should never give the impression that today Christ's message can or should be stated only with the aid of these Greek categories.[44]

The key question for Küng's Christology is the relationship between Jesus and God. He asks:

> In the language of the New Testament, the question runs this way: How is one to think about and confess the unity of God and Jesus... so that both God's oneness and uniqueness and the identity of person of Jesus Christ are kept intact?[45]

Küng answers his own question through a functional interpretation of the Son of God title. This is probably the most controversial portion of his Christology because some have seen his language here as equivocal.

Küng addresses the question in terms of four fundamental concerns. First, both God and humanity are really involved in the story of Jesus. Jesus reveals to us both who God is and what it means to be human. Second, Jesus of Nazareth is "for faith the real *revelation* of the *one true God*.... God encounters us [and] manifests himself in the work and person of Jesus."[46] Küng says the New Testament expresses this by calling Jesus the image or likeness of God. Word of God and Son of God have the same meaning. Küng explains this relationship by saying, "I know that where Jesus is, there is God."[47] God encounters us in a unique and definitive way in the person of Jesus. By the very nature of this relationship, Jesus confronts us with a decision. We must choose for or against his message, activity, and person, and our decision will affect the course of our life.

According to the New Testament, both Jesus' divine dignity and his relationship with the Father are functional. Küng says Jesus' relationship to the Father is a unity of revelation and a unity of action.[48] Jesus' divinity is not a metaphysical or physical quality, but relates to Jesus' function.[49] There certainly exists a unity between Jesus and the Father, but it is not ontologically unconditional in the sense of the two-natures doctrine of Chalcedon. "God manifested himself really and truly in a unique way in Jesus Christ and *thus* qualified him truly and really as the Son of God."[50] For Küng, form follows function. Finally, this means we can never simply identify Jesus with God. The New Testament reserves the term "God" for the Father, so to call Jesus God would be to confuse the Father and the Son. Jesus is not God the Father, but he is deity. In fact, says Küng, Jesus not only never called himself the Son of God, he directly rejected any simple identification of himself with God.[51]

Since the time of Jesus, it has been difficult to speak of either God or Jesus apart from the other. "This means that our attitude to Jesus determines where we stand with God, how we regard God, what kind of God is ours."[52] Küng says the distinction between Father and Son means we should not speak of a "crucified God." Such language would suggest it was God the Father, not the Son, who had been crucified.[53] At the Stuttgart Colloquium with representatives of the German bishops' conference (1977), Küng pointed out he has never denied the statement, "Jesus is God." He prefers, however, not to express himself in this way because of the prevalence of Monophysitism in Catholic piety. Küng added, "I have always spoken in this sense of the '*Son*' of God because it is important to me, as likewise to the classical doctrine of the Trinity that this '*distinction*' be made clear."[54]

In emphasizing the distinction between God and Jesus, Küng does not ignore what they have in common. He calls Jesus God's will and word in human form. "He, in whom word and deed, teaching and life, being and action, completely coincide, *is* in person, *is* in human form, God's word, will, Son."[55] Küng says that in Jesus God is present to him, is at work, speaks, and acts. Thus, in a unique and definitive way, "Jesus and only Jesus is *for me* the son of God."[56] In response to the criticism that the tone of his affirmation was entirely subjective, Küng clarified his stance in his next major writing by saying

> whether we describe this relationship between God and Jesus in theological terms more functionally or ontologically, whether we start out more from abstract statements about essences or from concrete statements about salvation, is really secondary and need not, anyway, be a contradiction. We may prefer functional statements and yet say that Jesus functions; he not only functions for me as God's Word and Son, he *is* this and he is so not only for me but also in himself.[57]

Küng notes, however, that the principle of unity is not one divine nature common to multiple entities; the principle is the one God. All things come from this God and all things are oriented toward this God. This means the New Testament is not concerned with ontological statements about what God is in himself and his innermost nature. It offers instead soteriological statements about the way God has revealed himself in Christ.[58] Jesus is the word, way, and image of God for Christians.[59]

The interest in ontology and metaphysics that was absent from the New Testament entered Christianity when it spread into the Hellenistic world. The original New Testament concept of Jesus derived from the Old Testament understanding of the term "Son of God" and saw Jesus as appointed to this office, just as the people of Israel and their kings had been chosen by God. There was no divine sonship in a physical sense, merely God's choosing Jesus and granting him full authority. It was the influence of Greek philosophical thinking that led Christians to conceive of Jesus as existing on the same level of being as God the Father.

When Küng considers the person of Christ, he presents Jesus as one who does not fit into our categories. He can not be domesticated or conventionalized. Küng's Jesus challenges our preconceptions, practices, and expectations; it was no different for his contemporaries. That is why he was executed.

Küng believes that who Jesus was is for us secondary to what he came to do. This is the presupposition behind his answer to the christological question. Because he recognizes that what happened requires a who to make it happen and that the Church traditionally has begun with the "who," Küng does not downplay the person of Christ. He says the use of ontological language is neither wrong nor in contradiction to the use of functional language. He prefers functional language because it expresses better for today that which could be expressed only ontologically in the patristic era.

Citing Karl Rahner, Küng says that to say Jesus of Nazareth is God is a Christian, irreversible, and eternally valid truth, but it is a statement open to misunderstanding. "Is" in this case denotes a unity, not an identity, between the man Jesus and God's eternal Logos.[60] This is why Küng prefers the language of divine sonship. Küng believes he can maintain Jesus' uniqueness and unsurpassability with this language as well as others do with the traditional language, and can do so without the problems they face by their use of that language.

> For me, Jesus of Nazareth is the *Son of God*.... The whole significance of what happened in and with him lies in the fact that in Jesus... the God who loves men is *himself present and active*: through him, God himself has spoken, acted, definitively revealed himself.... I want to maintain the uniqueness, underivability, and unsurpassability of his person and the appeal, offer and claim there made articulate.[61]

According to Küng, a critical moment in Christology occurred when the one who called people to believe became himself the content of faith. God has identified himself with the one who identified himself with God. This became clear to the disciples at Jesus' exaltation. At that time, Jesus became the personification of the message of the Kingdom of God which he had been proclaiming. It is only following this exaltation that divine sonship and messiahship were ascribed to Jesus. These titles are not applicable to the earthly Jesus.[62]

The earliest New Testament Christology, says Küng, was an exaltation Christology. It began from "below" and centered on Jesus' death and resurrection. This was an ascending Christology in which Jesus' divine sonship was understood in Old Testament terms of election to and assumption of the status of Son. This approach was increasingly superseded by an incarnational Christology which began from "above" and understood divine sonship in terms of ontological generation. The shift from "below" to "above" was paralleled by a shift in emphasis from function to ontology. The first approach arose from the Jewish tradition of the Old Testament and interpreted Jesus in Hebrew terms. When this biblical language of Spirit conception, pre-existence, and mediation of creation was translated into the environment and language of Hellenism, a very different picture of Jesus resulted. In a Hellenistic context, divine sonship and lordship were understood as divine dignity and nature.[63]

For Küng, statements about Christ's action are also statements about his being. He says functional and ontological statements must not be torn apart.[64] As a result, says Küng, he wants to affirm and make more effective the intention of the two-natures doctrine of Chalcedon. Yet he attacks Chalcedon and Christology of that sort as unintelligible today. Modern Christology cannot begin from dogmatic tradition. Therefore, Küng offers what he calls a paraphrase of Chalcedonian Christology expressed in a way intended to make it both more meaningful for today and truer to the New Testament. The way to do this, says Küng, is to link language about Jesus' deity with the source of his call, offer, and claim, not with his human person.[65] To rephrase the language of Christology is legitimate, but the way it is done may not always be legitimate. Thus it is possible to affirm the traditional creeds at the same time one criticizes their language as inappropriate for modern society. If a problem exists, it is in how this is done, not in the fact of doing it.

The Jesus whom we find in the Bible was "wholly and entirely man." Küng emphasizes this at the same time he says Jesus was the Son of God "without any qualification and with all the consequences." Such a Jesus could suffer, feel loneliness and insecurity, face temptation, doubt, and error in the same way other humans do. But, says Küng, he is no mere man; he is *the* true man precisely as God's Son and Word.[66]

The key event for the Christian message is not Jesus' birth, but his death and new life with God. It was Easter that grounded the disciples' faith. "The disciples did not conclude from Jesus' fate to his resurrection but in fact *experienced* after his death the living person himself."[67] Küng concludes the disciples experienced and truly encountered the risen Jesus in a new way. The Resurrection is not, however, an authenticating miracle but itself the object of faith. Küng says there is no way to eternal life that bypasses faith; we cannot get there by reason alone.

The Resurrection was not an historical event. It occurred in God's dimension, so neither it nor the risen Jesus can be understood or objectified by historical methods. All we can verify historically are Jesus' death and the Easter faith and message of the disciples. God's raising of Jesus is not a miracle in the sense that it violates the laws of nature. It is not a supernatural intervention we can locate and date in space and time. "There was nothing to photograph or record."[68] Similarly, the Resurrection was not merely a way of expressing the significance of Jesus' death. It was a real event even thought it was not an historical event. The Resurrection affected Jesus' person, not only his disciples' attitude.[69]

The Resurrection does not require any continuity of Jesus' body before and after Easter. There was, however, an identity of Jesus' person. Thus Jesus' death was a metamorphosis, not a destruction. In the same way, the corporeality of the Resurrection does not require the tomb to have been empty. Küng considers this a late and secondary tradition in any case. God raised Jesus in a "new, different, unimaginable 'spiritual corporeality,'" not in the body that died.[70] For that body to remain in the grave would not affect Küng's understanding of Jesus' resurrection or exaltation.

Jesus' death and resurrection were primarily God's response to the problem of human suffering. Küng does not appear to see human sin as the most significant issue behind Jesus' death. He says

> Jesus' "sacrifice" must in fact *not* be understood in the Old Testament or pagan sense.... The idea of the death on the cross as an expiatory sacrifice, understandable enough for Jewish Christians at that time, is only one and not the most important model for the interpretation of that death.[71]

For Küng, the Resurrection means the vindication of Jesus' life. As such, it tells us more about what Jesus did than about who he is. This pointing back to Jesus' earthly life instead of forward to universal lordship (as in traditional Christology) may underlie Küng's understanding of Christ's importance "for Christians," and his concomitant acceptance of the normative role of aspects of the other world religions for the salvation of their adherents. Küng recently suggested Jesus is the source of salvation for those who call themselves Christians, but those who hold to the other world religions will be saved in accordance with the precepts of their religions.

The Problems of Pre-existence and Incarnation

Küng believes giving too much prominence to the Incarnation can circumscribe Christology. Associated with the Incarnation in this regard is the concept of pre-existence. When these become the focus of Christology, the rest of Jesus' life becomes secondary.[72] Only in the Johannine prologue do we find the idea of the divine Logos becoming "flesh." The other incarnational language of the New Testament derives from pre-Pauline formulas and understands the Incarnation primarily in terms of emptying and abasement.

Pre-existence is the Church's attempt to say that what happened in and through Jesus cannot be explained solely in terms of human history.[73] It is a way of saying the relationship between God and Jesus had existed from the beginning and was grounded in God himself. Küng contrasts this to a relationship that might have emerged at some later point (perhaps during the life of Jesus?).

Pre-existence need not mean a personal existence prior to the Incarnation. Küng agrees with Wilhelm Thüsing that the mission of the Son did not require he exist prior to his being sent. The "mission of the Son" can include the creation of the man Jesus. Pre-existence can equally be understood in terms of election. In this case, Jesus' pre-existence would be no different from that of all those whom God chose in Christ before the beginning of the world.

This approach to pre-existence, however, does not appear to distinguish adequately between the Logos and the man Jesus. No Christian theologian teaches the preexistence of the man Jesus; the concept deals exclusively with the Logos. Küng's understanding of pre-existence is not derived from Jewish sources. Intertestamental literature posited several hypostatized entities that existed with God, particularly Wisdom.[74] Incarnation and preexistence certainly are not Hellenistic contributions to Christian thought; the incarnation of deity was incompatible with Greek thought of the time and pre-existence would have been meaningless to Hellenistic thinkers.

Küng seeks to make it clear that the Incarnation was not an incarnation of God (whom Küng understands to mean the Father). It is always a matter of the Son or Word of God becoming human. By his language, Küng is trying to avoid any confusion between God the Father and the Son. He notes that, apart from John's gospel, Jesus is designated directly as "God" only in a few, exceptional cases. Thus, to avoid misunderstandings, it is advisable for us to call Jesus "Son of God" and not simply "God" today.[75]

This does not keep Küng from talking about the incarnation of God in Jesus, however. He says,

> The incarnation of God in Jesus means: in all Jesus' speech, in all his proclamation, conduct, and destiny, God's Word and will have received a human form; in all his speech and actions, suffering and death, Jesus proclaimed, manifested, and revealed God's Word and will in his entire

person; he in whom word and deed, teaching and life, being
and acting perfectly coincide is corporeal, is God's Word,
will, and Son in human form.[76]

Küng says the Incarnation should not be identified exclusively with that
point in time when Jesus was conceived or born. It should, instead, be
linked up with Jesus' entire life, death, and new life. What we have in the
Incarnation is a "unity of knowledge, will, action, and revelation between
God and Jesus."[77] Christians have traditionally linked the Incarnation with
the virgin birth. Küng insists, however, that the latter teaching is not central
to the gospel.

Jesus' divine sonship is not dependent on the virgin birth.
He is God's Son, not because God instead of a man
effected his origin, but because he is chosen and destined
as God's Son.[78]

Küng does not consider the virgin birth to be an historical-biological event.
He sees it as symbolizing that God has made a new beginning with humanity
in the person of Jesus Christ. Moreover, the virgin birth is only one of the
ways by which the New Testament symbolizes this new beginning.[79]

If the human Jesus is of particular importance for Christology, his
message may not be ignored. Küng says Jesus did not want to found a new
religion. We can understand his message only in the context of the Old
Testament. The heart of that message was the Kingdom of God. Yet in
speaking of the Kingdom, Jesus never committed himself to formulas or
dogmas. He engaged neither in philosophical speculation nor in learned
casuistry. Jesus lived in an apocalyptic age, and like many of his generation,
he expected the immediate arrival of the Kingdom, and in its train justice,
freedom, joy, and peace. In this, we see both Jesus' culture-conditioned
situation and his liability to error.

Unlike Kasper, Küng attempts to situate his Christology and soteriology in a world context. He sets Jesus in the context of universal human
aspirations, not only in a Church setting. Until recently, Küng contrasted
Jesus with the founders of the other world religions in order to show he
offers a unique and universal salvation. This changed in *Christianity and the
World Religions*, where each religion makes a valid offer of salvation to its
adherents. He rejects the concept of anonymous Christianity as inherently
contradictory because to be Christian means to profess faith in Christ. In
a 1985 lecture at the University of Tübingen,[80] Küng said the other world

religions are conditionally true insofar as they do not contradict the decisive elements in Christianity and can supplement, correct, and enrich Christianity. No religion has the whole truth.

The nature of salvation for Küng is humanization. This means God became human in Jesus so humans might become fully human. Jesus' humanness is thus the paradigm and source of our full humanness. Küng derives this from his reading of the Church fathers, who saw Jesus' full humanness as necessary for the full salvation of humanity.[81] He opposes this to the idea of divinization because to say "man might become God" is not a Christian statement. According to Pollard, the true meaning of what has been called divinization is what Küng calls humanization: in Christ humans become what they were intended to be.

Critiques of Küng

Küng's proposal for a new direction in Christology has caused much discussion. Too often, however, this has generated more heat than light. Many have criticized Küng's Christology, but not all have done so fairly. We will examine only a portion of the criticism and focus our attention on that part which can be considered constructive.

Catherine LaCugna has provided the most complete and objective study of Küng's theology to date. Her study, however, includes Küng's works only through *Does God Exist?* and examines his Christology as but one example of his overall theological method.

LaCugna suggests although Küng has rejected the form of traditional christological statements, he does not deny the intent of those statements. She does believe, however, that the theory of Küng's theological method differs from his practice. In addition, Küng has not always presented his position as clearly as he might have. The other side of this problem of understanding that LaCugna has found is the all too frequent failure of Küng's critics to read him carefully (if at all). Küng's Christology needs to be understood and judged in terms of his methodology, but often this has not been the case.[82]

LaCugna has found what she considers methodological inconsistencies. Regarding Küng's Christology "from below," she writes:

It is noteworthy that Küng's starting point "from below," while not vitiating Christologies formulated "from above," does not contain within itself the means by which one can make an easy transition from "below to "above." That is to

say, once one has determined historically-critically what
Jesus' function is, one cannot pass easily to ontological
statements about his nature or pass from personal communion with the Father to communion of natures, or from the
salvific-soteriological testimony of Scripture to later
dogmatic ontological declarations regarding the
God-man.[83]

She says although Küng experiences difficulty in moving from "below" to
"above" with regard to Christ, he makes the move much more easily with regard to the nature of God. Thus this may be less a methodological problem
than a reservation concerning the dogma. She concludes:

The question may still be raised: what is the justification
for the confidence (of faith?) that the intra-mundane analogy can be applied to divine reality. This seems to be a
problem in systematic theology which Küng is neither prepared nor inclined to answer.[84]

LaCugna affirms the fundamental apologetic concern of Küng's Christology.
But she also appears to think reservations about the content of dogmatic
statements as well as about their form may have influenced the way Küng
presents his understanding of Jesus Christ.

Walter Kasper also looks at theological method when he evaluates
Küng's Christology. Kasper sees this as the fundamental difference between
Küng and himself. Is it possible for us, who have nearly two thousand years
of Church history behind us, asks Kasper, to put ourselves in the place of
the first disciples? Where do we meet the risen Jesus Christ today other
than in the community of faith? Kasper does not agree with Küng that
Christ can serve immediately as the source of faith. Given their different
starting points, Küng and Kasper are certain to reach different conclusions.
Kasper asks: are such teachings as pre-existence, the Incarnation, and the
Trinity only historically-determined forms of presenting a more basic truth,
or are the forms themselves unconditionally binding because they belong to
the very substance of Christology?[85] The difference between Küng and
Kasper centers on the issue of function versus ontology. Küng questions the
validity of Kasper's move to ontology, and Kasper questions the sufficiency
of Küng's remaining with function.

Kasper disagrees with many of Küng's critics because he believes
Chalcedon continues to serve as a guideline for Küng's christological inter-

pretation. It is the Jesus whom we meet through the historical-critical method, however, not the Jesus Christ of dogma, who is the norm for Küng's Christology. Küng's real interest, says Kasper, is not Jesus "as he really was," but Jesus "as he meets us here and now."[86]

Peter Chirico, who expresses sympathy with Küng's aims, says the defects in Küng's Christology result primarily from an inadequate concept of doctrinal development. His point is similar to Sloyan's: Küng works from the implicit premise that all doctrinal development is either the logical conclusion of the initial message of Jesus as heard by the earliest witnesses, or it is the making explicit of that which was implicit in Jesus' earthly actions as seen by those same witnesses.[87] Chirico concludes that if Jesus' earthly life is the supreme norm for christological doctrine, no later development of the doctrines can meet with approval.

> If one holds as Küng does, that all that is normative is con-
> tained in the life of the earthly Christ as grasped by the
> original witnesses, then the emergence of genuine newness
> is ruled out in advance. It is thus quite consistent for Küng
> to take a dim view of the Christological developments of
> the councils and the theologians and even of the NT.[88]

Chirico says Küng errs in distinguishing the earthly Jesus as seen by the original witnesses from all subsequent interpretations of Jesus. He makes the original witnesses normative and requires that all other interpretations to conform to them. Chirico says the original witnesses were interpreters just as much as were those who came after them. None had a complete understanding of Jesus because all viewed him from their own limited perspectives. He says the original witnesses were too close to the events to ask the most searching questions, questions that required reflection before they could be recognized as relevant.[89] Chirico is denying any historical writing can be totally objective and affirming the passage of time enables later authors to provide more complete histories because they can see events in their total context and have access to diverse accounts of what occurred.

Given these criteria, Chirico calls Küng's understanding of development inadequate, both with regard to developments within the New Testament and after. Chirico claims Küng does not believe those who had the gospel accounts available to reflect upon were in as good a position to understand Jesus as were those who wrote the initial accounts. Chirico also argues Küng's view contradicts the dynamic nature of human understanding:

> Genuine human development of understanding is character-
> ized by stages of successively higher viewpoints and per-
> spectives with the emergence of new questions.[90]

Küng claims, however, that the Jesus of history is the ultimate Christian
standard and the best image of him, what he taught and did, is the object of
all attempts to understand him. It is in the search for the clearest image of
the Jesus of history that the earliest scriptural witnesses hold pride of place.
In the light of their witness, later understandings may well discern things
they were unaware of.

We said earlier that the subject of tradition separates Küng from the
Catholic Tübingen School. Some Catholics have suggested Küng's views on
tradition may differ in significant ways from how tradition has functioned in
the Catholic Church. Robert Butterworth, for example, thinks Küng misunderstands the role of tradition in theology and consequently misuses it.
He notes that the Christian interpretation of Jesus did not stop with the
New Testament. As the Church moved through human history, it faced new
problems and the biblical presentation of Jesus took on a new clarity and
depth as the Church applied this to the new problems it faced. Küng
ignores this aspect of christological development, says Butterworth.

> The several questions raised by Küng's book come down in
> the end to a single question about the meaning and use of
> the doctrinal and theological tradition of the Church in the
> presentation of a Christianity which will engage the atten-
> tion of the present day.[91]

Butterworth challenges the validity of Küng's calling all statements
about divine sonship, pre-existence, incarnation, and mediatorship of creation mythological because their reality is functional instead of ontological.
He doubts it is possible to express the Christian belief in Jesus without using
some sort of non-functional language.[92] Gerald O'Collins also denies functional language alone can adequately express the reality of Jesus Christ.[93]

O'Collins sees three weaknesses in Küng's christological method.
Küng appears to presuppose only one picture of Jesus can be true. He also
fails to distinguish clearly between Jesus himself and any picture we might
create of him. Finally, he implies it is possible to achieve objectivity in
studying Jesus. Küng seems to have a confidence in historical study beyond
that which the method warrants. O'Collins says Küng reinterprets certain
biblical accounts (e.g., the virgin birth and the ascension) as *theologumenon*,

and not actual occurrences.[94]   Is there a reason, other than the problem these create for the modern mind, to treat certain events in this way and to consider others as history?

Battista Mondin suggests Küng's Christology is built on three postulates. Epistemologically, only that which is scientifically verifiable is true. He sees this as a combination of the Hegelian identification of the real and the rational with scientific positivism.   Ontologically, Küng eliminates through his approach to nature and history all supernatural events and transcendental reality. Hermeneutically, Küng posits a complete distinction between form and content. The content derives from the writer's intention, but the form comes entirely from the writer's cultural horizon.[95]

In general, Mondin has offered a fair assessment of Küng's Christology. We need to ask, however, whether these three points constitute a methodological bracketing or an expression of Küng's own position. This is an instance of the ambiguity in Küng's theology we mentioned earlier; it may also be an instance of the difference between theory and practice LaCugna found in Küng's work.

The importance of this question is evident in Thomas Clarke's concern for what he calls the limited nature of Küng's christological statements. Küng's description of Jesus' ministry is "eloquent and brilliant," but the hermeneutic behind his major christological statements is unable to yield "more than an impoverished echo of the rich faith of the Church." Clarke doubts Küng's answer to the question, "Who do you say I am?" goes beyond the shallow response of the Enlightenment.[96]   Leo Scheffczyk, who has been sharply critical of Küng, agrees with Clarke that Küng does not succeed in demonstrating theologically the uniqueness of Jesus. "His theology cannot explain why one's trust in God must be expressed precisely through the man Jesus of Nazareth."[97]

We are compelled to agree with Clarke and Scheffczyk. Küng asserts repeatedly the uniqueness of Jesus and of his relationship with the Father, but he does not prove it. Küng's most recent work causes one to ask why Jesus must have such a relationship if his normativity is confined to that portion of humanity which calls itself Christian.

Conclusion

In reading Küng, we find ourselves less inclined to say,-"No! No! That's all wrong!" than to respond, "Yes, but is that all?" It is more what Küng does not say than what he says that leaves us unsatisfied with his Christology. At least two audiences are involved in any theological writing.

There is the author's intended audience and there are his theological peers. Both must be considered, especially when the gap between the two audiences is as large as in Küng's case. Küng writes for a predominantly Catholic and lay audience, so he needs to express himself in language it can understand. But his theological peers read his work and they have questions based on the language he uses for that other audience. It is proper for him to address the first audience in non-technical language, but when his peers ask him to clarify that language he should respond to them in the technical language they have in common. Some accuse Küng of refusing to address his fellow theologians in technical theological language or responding in terms of the questions they put to him. This causes them to ask whether he is able to clarify his popular statements so as to show they are in continuity with the christological councils in both content and intent.

Küng's failure or refusal to use traditional precise christological language raises concern among his more conservative fellow theologians in the area of soteriology. This was the reason, they argue, the councils formulated their statements as they did in the first place. Küng expresses the human problem and thus the nature of salvation in a different way than does the tradition. When some of his peers look at this as a whole, they fear he is altering Christianity in a fundamental way. Were he to express himself more clearly on the traditional concerns of Christology and soteriology, they argue, he might allay the fears of many of his critics.[98]

Küng understands what he is saying and intends his readers should as well. But some of the terms he uses are open to diverse interpretations—which is not a new problem in the history of doctrine. It is at these points of ambiguity that Küng has been challenged. Küng recognizes he needs to say more.[99] *Does God Exist?* answered some of the questions raised by *On Being a Christian*, but Küng still needs to say more. Until he does so, he will continue to be criticized. But depending on what he says, he could face even sharper criticism after he clarifies his stance. In the end, the differences will persist, however, as long as a fundamental difference in mindset, in "paradigm," remains. Küng's mindset is more dynamic, historical, and relational; that of his critics is more committed to a substance philosophy, which tends to be "either/or" and accepting of absolutes in epistemology. Only if a common paradigm is accepted can the sharp differences ever be resolved.

Küng has often said that however important Christology may be, faith in Christ and following Christ are more important. No Christian can argue with this, but to say only this is to avoid the issue the Church has struggled with for nearly two millennia: who is the Jesus Christ we are to believe in and follow? Many Christs have been offered to the Church, but not all merited following and not all could save. Küng agrees with this; he cites Arius and Apollinarius as two who have offered such inadequate Christs. This is why the Church has insisted on using ontological as well as functional language to describe Jesus Christ. Küng acknowledges the validity of the tradition, but his practice tends to ignore it and the substance philosophy in which it tends to be expressed in favor of functionalism.

Hans Küng has caused many to read and think about Jesus Christ and Christianity. In doing this, he has accomplished much of his apologetic goal. He has emphasized elements of christological teaching which have not always received the attention they merit. But in doing so, we think he has not given other aspects of Christology the attention they also deserve. This means the Jesus Christ he presents is less than the Jesus who lived. Küng is not alone in this; all Christologies are guilty of this to some degree. By his method or by his belief—it is unclear which is responsible—Küng presents a Christology that may be more appealing to modern society but which is at the same time less complete and less compelling than the tradition of the Church he seeks to improve upon.

1. Letter of Cardinal Höffner to Professor Küng, April 22, 1977, in *The Küng Dialogue*, p. 123., comp. by the National Conference of Catholic Bishops Committee on Doctrine (Washington: United States Catholic Conference, 1980).

2. See Catherine Mowry LaCugna, *The Theological Methodology of Hans Küng*, American Academy of Religion Academy Series 39 (Chico, CA: Scholars Press, 1982), for an excellent survey of the development of Küng's theology and the influence of various Tübingen scholars on that development.

3. J. B. Hirscher, a moral theologian of the early Tübingen School, had writings placed on the Index at two points in his career. In the 1820's, a piece he wrote on the Mass was condemned. Hirscher later changed his view to conform to that held by the Roman theologians. Two pamphlets dealing with the state of society and the Church that he wrote about 1848 also were condemned. Hirscher also submitted to Rome in this instance.

4. Gerard S. Sloyan, "Jesus of Nazareth: Today's Way to God," in *Consensus in Theology*, p. 50, ed. by Leonard Swidler (Philadelphia: Westminster, 1980).

5. Ibid., p. 55. Robert Butterworth, "Questions to Hans Küng," *Heythrop Journal* 18 (1977):436–446, raises the same issue of Küng's attitude toward Church tradition (see especially pp. 443 ff.).

6. LaCugna, p. 109.

7. Thomas H. Graves, "The Functional Christology of Hans Küng," *Perspectives in Religious Studies* 8 (1981):56 f.

8. Hans Küng, *Justification: The Doctrine of Karl Barth and a Catholic Reflection*, trans. by Thomas Collins, *et al.* (New York: Thomas Nelson, 1964).

9. Ibid., p. 288.

10. Ibid., p. 293. Küng says, "If we hold to the Greek and Scholastic categories (especially those shaped by Plato) at this point, we do so

particularly because even Cullman's book has in no way proved the intrinsic incompatibility of these categories with biblical revelation" (p. 288).

11. Ibid., p. 296. Küng also says, "In Jesus Christ the temporal human nature is integrated with the second divine Person in a substantial unity" (p. 289).

12. Ibid., p. 295.

13. "Interview with Hans Küng," in *Hans Küng: His Work and His Way*, p. 156, ed. by Hermann Häring and Karl-Josef Küschel, trans. by Robert Nowell (Garden City: Doubleday, 1980).

14. Hans Küng, *Menschwerdung Gottes. Eine Einführung in Hegels theologische Denken als Prolegomena zu einer künftigen Christologie* (Freiburg: Herder, 1970). This was translated in 1987 by John Stephenson as *The Incarnation of God: An Introduction to Hegel's Thought as Prolegomena to a Future Christology* (New York: Crossroad).

15. LaCugna, pp. 28 f.

16. Ibid., p. 83.

17. Ibid., pp. 86 f.

18. "Interview," p. 163.

19. Hans Küng, *On Being a Christian*, trans. by Edward Quinn (Garden City: Doubleday, 1976), p. 377. For a different view, see George Elton Ladd, "The Problem of History in Contemporary New Testament Interpretation," in *Studia Evangelica*, vol. 5, pt. 2, ed. by F. L. Cross (Berlin, Akademie, 1968).

20. Kü, *On Being a Christian*, pp. 229 ff., 233.

21. Ibid., p. 419.

22. Ibid., pp. 412 f.

23. Ibid., pp. 415 f. (emphasis original).

24. LaCugna, p. 101.

25. Hans Küng, *et al., Christianity and the World Religions: Paths to Dialogue with Islam, Hinduism, and Buddhism*, trans. by Peter Heinegg (Garden City: Doubleday, 1986), p. 115.

26. Küng, *On Being a Christian*, p. 389.

27. Küng has derived this concept of paradigm shift from Thomas S. Kuhn, *The Structure of Scientific Revolution* (Chicago: University of Chicago, 1962; rev. ed., 1970).

28. Gerald O'Collins, *What Are they Saying About Jesus?* (New York: Paulist, 1977), pp. 13 f. See also Küng, *On Being a Christian*, pp. 25 ff., 119 ff.

29. Küng, *On Being a Christian*, p. 163. "What man can turn to as absolutely reliable for time and eternity are not the texts of the Bible, nor the Fathers of the Church, nor indeed an ecclesiastical magisterium, but it is God himself as he spoke for believers through Jesus Christ. The biblical texts, the statements of the Fathers and ecclesiastical authorities are meant... to be no more and no less than an expression of this faith."

30. Ibid., p. 123.

31. Ibid., p. 146.

32. LaCugna, p. 43. Kung says, "The Jesus of history is not identical with the Christ image of traditional dogmatics... nor... with the speculative idea of Christ fostered by German Idealism... [nor] with the 'liberal' portrayal of Jesus.... If today we are to make statements which are historically certain about Jesus, we cannot start out from a particular image of him.... We shall have to begin modestly with the individual, certainly authentic sayings... and actions of Jesus" (*On Being a Christian*, p. 158).

33. O'Collins, p. 28.

34. "Interview," pp. 164 f.

35. Küng, *On Being a Christian*, p. 389. In *Christianity and the World Religions*, Küng adds, "As a European Gentile Christian, I can thoroughly understand the Hellenistic development of Christology. I can accept the truth of the great Christological councils from Nicea to Chalcedon. The broad outline of their purposes and contents can be roundly affirmed. And so I do not mean to start out from zero all over again, that one should, as it were, become a Jewish Christian" (p. 127).

36. Hans Küng, *Does God Exist? An Answer for Today*, trans. by Edward Quinn (Garden City: Doubleday, 1980), p. 687. Here Küng says, "I am not bound by the [Hellenistic] terminology but by the reality attested in the New Testament: Jesus Christ himself. It is not the literal sense of the term used... that is essential.... With the Fathers of Nicea, we are convinced that our whole salvation depends on the fact that in Jesus we are concerned with the one God, who is truly, really and alone God: in Jesus as his Son made evident.... Jesus of Nazareth in fact has, in the last resort, no decisive meaning for me unless he is proclaimed as the Christ of God. Nor, anyway, does the divine Christ mean much to me unless he is identical with the man Jesus."

37. LaCugna, p. 179.

38. Ibid., pp. 181 f.

39. Küng, *On Being a Christian*, p. 132.

40. Küng, *Does God Exist?*, pp. 682 f.

41. Hans Küng, "Anmerkungen zu Walter Kasper, 'Christologie von unten?'" p. 175, in *Grundfragen der Christologie heute*, ed. by Leo Scheffczyk (Freiburg: Herder, 1975). In *On Being a Christian*, Küng writes: "Originally therefore the title of 'Son of God' had *nothing to do with Jesus' origin but with his legal and authoritative status*. It is a question of function, not of nature. Originally, the title did not mean a corporeal sonship, but a divine election and authorization.... 'Son of God' therefore did not designate Jesus any more than the king of Israel as a superhuman, divine being" (p. 390, emphasis original).

42. Küng, *On Being a Christian*, p. 385.

43. "Interview," p. 165.

44. Küng, *On Being a Christian*, p. 131.

45. Küng, *Christianity and the World Religions*, p. 119.

46. See Küng, *On Being a Christian*, p. 444; *Glauben an Jesus Christus*, Theologische Meditationen 59 (Zurich: Benziger, 1982), pp. 11 f., 40. In *Glauben an Jesus Christus*, Küng says the meaning of this statement is not less than the earlier statement that Jesus is God. "Die Aussage, in Jesu Person offenbare sich in definitiver und unüberbreitbarer Weise Gott selbst, ist nicht weniger als die früher Aussage, Jesus 'sei' Gott" (p. 50).

47. Küng, *Does God Exist?*, p. 686.

48. Küng at the Stuttgart Colloquium, in Leonard Swidler (ed. and trans.), *Küng in Conflict* (Garden City: Doubleday, 1981), p. 237.

49. Küng, *On Being a Christian*, p. 448.

50. Küng, "Anmerkungen," pp. 176 f. (emphasis added).

51. Ibid., p. 316. Küng says that in the New Testament *ho theos* is used only of the Father and never of Jesus. Jesus is designated only by the *theos* without the article, and this only in the Johannine and Pauline schools' writings, both of which were influenced by Hellenism. The New Testament designates Jesus only as "Word," "revelation," and "appearance" of God. Each occurs in the context of a hierarchical-functional subordination of Jesus to the Father ("Anmerkungen," pp. 174 f.).

52. Küng, *Does God Exist?*, p. 681.

53. Ibid., p. 690.

54. Swidler, *Küng in Conflict*, p. 256 (emphasis original).

55. Ibid., p. 685 (emphasis original).

56. "Interview," p. 166 (emphasis added). In his response to Walter Kasper's criticism several years earlier, Küng wrote along the same subjective line that, "In all his speech, deeds, and suffering, Jesus has with his whole person proclaimed, manifested, and revealed the word and will of God. Yes, one can say that in this one in whom word and deed, teaching and life, being and doing completely coincide is personally the word and will of God in human form.... The true man Jesus of Nazareth is a real revelation for belief in the true God" ("Anmerkungen," p. 177).

57. Küng, *Does God Exist?*, p. 687 (emphasis original).

58. Küng, *Christianity and the World Religions*, p. 120..

59. Hans Küng, lecture at the University of Tübingen, June 20, 1985. In this lecture, part of a series given jointly with Wolfhart Pannenberg, Küng has returned to the subjective "for me" language of *On Being a Christian*. The position he presented in the lectures was that for Christians Jesus is *the way*, but he is this only for Christians.

60. Küng, *Glauben an Jesus Christus*, p. 40.

61. Küng, *Does God Exist?*, p. 688 (emphasis original).

62. Küng, *On Being a Christian*, p. 353. Berard L. Marthaler says, however, that the community came to recognize these titles applied to Jesus from the moment of his incarnation. See Marthaler, *The Creed* (Mystic, CT: Twenty-third, 1987), p. 66.

63. Küng, *On Being a Christian*, pp. 437, 440.

64. Küng, *Does God Exist?*, p. 685; Küng at the Stuttgart Colloquium, in Swidler, *Küng in Conflict*, p. 235. In the former, Küng wrote: Functional statements—which are undoubtedly to the fore—and ontological statements must not be torn apart. In this comprehensive—not speculative, but historical—perspective it can be made understandable even today that Jesus before Paul and then also in the Pauline tradition is understood as the revelation of God's power and wisdom, as head and lord of creation, as image, true image of God, as the Yes of God. In this light, it can also be understood and accepted that Jesus is described by John not only as God's Word but also indirectly as equal to God, even as Lord and God. And in

this perspective we can understand such difficult and sublime statements as
that in Christ lives the fullness of divinity, that God's Word became flesh.
This, at any rate, is what we mean when we speak of 'God in Jesus Christ'....
Such statements must be safeguarded against *misunderstandings*" (empahsis
original).

65. Brian O. McDermott, "Roman Catholic Christology: Two Recurring
Themes," *Theological Studies* 41 (1980):352.

66. Küng, *Does God Exist?*, p. 688 (emphasis original).

67. Ibid., p. 373.

68. Ibid., pp. 349 f.

69. Ibid., pp. 351 f. Küng says, "The resurrection message is not the special
experience of a few enthusiasts, the special teaching of some apostles. On
the contrary, it belongs to the oldest strata of the New Testament. It is
common to all New Testament writings without exception. It proves to be
central to the Christian faith and at the same time the basis of all further
statements of faith" (p. 347).

70. Ibid., p. 366.

71. Ibid., pp. 424 f. (emphasis original).

72. Such a devaluation of Jesus' earthly life has accompanied too many
incarnational Christologies in the history of the Church. That this is not a
necessary consequence of giving the Incarnation an important place in one's
Christology has been shown by such modern theologians as Karl Adam.

73. Küng, *Does God Exist?*, p. 683. See also *On Being a Christian*, pp.444–
462. In *Does God Exist?*, Küng wrote, "For someone who commits himself
to Jesus, what happened in and with him is not explained solely from the
course of human history; in its first source, it is explained only in light of the
eternal God. From eternity, there is no other God than the one who
manifested himself in Jesus. Since there is no other God than the one revealed in Jesus, then, in the light of this universal God, Jesus himself has a
universal significance" (p. 683).

74. See, for example, R. H. Fuller, *The Foundations of New Testament Christology* (Glasgow: Collins, 1979), pp. 72 ff., for a discussion of the hypostatization of Old Testament concepts during the intertestamental period and the relationship of this to early christological thought.

75. Küng, *Does God Exist?*, pp. 684 f. Küng lists those exceptional cases where Jesus is designated as God as certainly Heb 1:8, and perhaps II Thes 1:12; Tit 2:13; and II Ptr 1:1. The Johannine designations are Jn 1:1 and 20:28.

76. Küng, *Glauben an Jesus Christus*, p. 20.

77. Küng, *Christianity and the World Religions*, p. 119.

78. Küng, *On Being a Christian*, pp. 456 f.

79. Ibid.

80. See note 59 for details.

81. T. E. Pollard, *Fullness of Humanity: Christ's Humanness and Ours* (Sheffield: Almond, 1982), p. 99.

82. LaCugna, p. 204.

83. Ibid., p. 43.

84. Ibid., p. 184.

85. Walter Kasper, "Für eine Christologie in geschichtlicher Perspektive: Replik auf die Anmerkungen von Hans Küng," in *Grundfragen der Christologie heute*, pp. 179 ff., ed. by Leo Scheffczyk (Freiburg: Herder, 1975).

86. Walter Kasper, "Christologie von unten?" in *Grundfragen der Christologie heute*, p. 160, ed. by Leo Scheffczyk (Freiburg: Herder, 1975).

87. Peter Chirico, "Hans Küng's Christology: An Evaluation of Its Presuppositions," *Theological Studies* 40 (1979):271.

88. Ibid., p. 270.

89. Ibid., pp. 267 f.

90. Ibid., pp. 268 f. Chirico is a Catholic theologian whose criticism of Küng's approach to tradition reflects the common Catholic appreciation of the role of tradition in theology. Protestants would have fewer problems with Küng at this point.

91. Robert Butterworth, "Questions to Hans Küng," *Heythrop Journal* 18 (1977):445 f.

92. Ibid., pp. 438 f.

93. O'Collins, p. 28.

94. Ibid., pp. 22 ff.

95. Battista Mondin, "The Christological Experiment of Hans Küng," trans. by W. Stanley Fleming, *Biblical Theological Bulletin* 7 (1977):86 f.

96. Thomas Clarke, "Current Christologies," *Worship* 53 (1979):444.

97. Leo Scheffczyk, *On Being a Christian: The Hans Küng Debate*, trans. by Peader Mac Seamais (Dublin: Four Courts, 1982), p. 56.

98. See, for example, the comment by Cardinal Höffner cited in Robert Nowell, *A Passion for Truth: Hans Küng and His Theology* (New York: Crossroad, 1981), p. 345.

99. Küng at the Stuttgart Colloquium, in Swidler, p. 257.

CHAPTER X

CONCLUSION

In the preceding chapters we have surveyed the work of those members of the Catholic Tübingen School who have concerned themselves with Christology. We began with Johann Sebastian Drey, the founder of the School, and ended with Walter Kasper, the theologian who represents the School today. We have also looked at the work of one of the most famous teachers at Tübingen, Hans Küng, although we do not consider him to be a member of the School. Now we will assess the strengths and weaknesses of Catholic Tübingen Christology and suggest what it has to contribute to the continuing effort to understand better the person and work of Jesus Christ. Then, drawing on our study of Tübingen, we will suggest some considerations and possible approaches to a Christology for today.

We have surveyed the work of eight Catholic Tübingen theologians over a span of 170 years. These men devoted varying amounts of time to Christology and their conclusions were not always the same. They had different concerns and wrote in different contexts. Yet the spirit of this School has not existed for 170 years in a variety of settings for lack of something worthwhile to say. The approach of the Catholic Tübingen School exhibits both strengths and weaknesses. In examining these, we will concentrate primarily on the 20th century representatives of the School for three reasons. First, Adam and Kasper each wrote more on Christology than did all the other members of the School together. Second, because they are so recent and their writings so easily accessible in a variety of languages, the modern members will have the most influence on other modern Christologies. Finally, because they are closer to us in time, they are addressing problems and attitudes more like those we face than did the 19th century Tübingers.

Catholic Tübingen has significant strengths to offer theology in general and Christology in particular. Individually, these strengths are not unique to Tübingen, but their particular combination and balance does appear distinctive of Tübingen. Sometimes these strengths have become too powerful and become weaknesses. That, however, has been a problem for Christian theology from its earliest days.

Like virtually all theologians today, but in sharp contrast to the Catholic mainstream between Trent and Vatican II, Tübingers have sought to converse with their contemporaries both within Christianity and outside. In chapter one, we described the theological endeavor to speak understandably to one's contemporaries without compromising the deposit of faith as contextualization. This the Catholic Tübingen School has tried to do. It has done so, moreover, by responding to the questions and doubts of its time instead of forcing its agenda upon its intended audience. As Alec Vidler wrote,

> The Tübingen theologians met contemporary thought on its own ground, acknowledging where possible their agreement with it, and criticized it where it seemed to fail to do justice to the rich volume of spiritual truth which was embodied in the Catholic tradition.[1]

In modern Western society, with its questioning of the meaning and worth of existence, Catholic Tübingen's commitment to the intelligibility of history offers reason for hope. The basis for that intelligibility lies in God's revelation in Jesus Christ. Further, this means intelligibility does not arise apart from history. Christian faith, and Christian faith in Jesus Christ, is mediated in history. Christ appeared and lived in history and the Church's understanding of him has developed within the context of his earthly life and the variety of its own earthly experiences. For Tübingers, the faith expressions of this attempt to understand are necessary but never complete. Many understand the claim to the historical setting of the Bible to lead inevitably to the relativity of its truth claims. Tübingers have not surrendered to Lessing on this matter and continue to affirm universal truths can be found in the historical activity of God in the world and particularly in the life of Jesus Christ. Over the years, however, the argument has become increasingly nuanced and sophisticated.

In addressing the issue of history, Tübingers have engaged the intellectual influences of their time. In engaging these trends, they have neither welcomed them unreservedly nor run from them. Not all have done this equally well. The earliest self-conscious christological work came from Kuhn's response to Strauss regarding the historicity of the life of Jesus. Succeeding Tübingers have responded to their contemporaries on the same subject. In each case, they have argued the history of Jesus must be taken seriously. Not only this, but the history of our increasing understanding of Jesus Christ must be taken seriously. Ben F. Meyer has written that

> the heritage of Christian belief affirms as indispensible
> what the heritage of modern culture excludes as impossible,

theological effort... has therefore been concentrated on
mediating between these two sets of claims.[2]

Meyer could have written this about the theological work of the Catholic
Tübingen School.

Related to the Tübingen concern for history is its stress on the concept of the *Kirchlichkeit* of faith and theology. This began with Drey who
presupposed Christian faith is bound to the historical person Jesus Christ.
Such direct binding is possible only because through its liturgy and life the
Church is the objective continuation of Christ. Möhler deepened this identification and other Tübingers have modified it. Today Kasper echoes the
need for this idea of *Kirchlichkeit* in regard to the elements of Christian
theology.[3]

Kirchlichkeit can be seen most clearly in the way Tübingers understand tradition. The Church is the locale in which tradition lives and develops. Thus, tradition is not static but changes over time to meet new situations and reflect increased understanding and better ways of presenting
revealed truth. This connection with the Church also provides stability and
continuity to theological development. Because the Church represents
Christ on earth, it ensures tradition will develop consistently. That which
will develop in the future will be in continuity with that which Christians
have believed in the past. It will not be the same because it will be deeper
and fuller and address different circumstances; but it will not be discontinuous with or contradictory to previous doctrine. Given the turmoil in contemporary christological discussion, this basis for confidence in previous
doctrine and call for continuity is an important consideration for those who
would offer radical rethinking of christological doctrine. The particular
value of *Kirchlichkeit* would also seem to be in expecting that any significant
modification of doctrine needs to receive general acceptance within the
Church before it can claim the status of doctrine.[4]

These various tendencies come together in Tübingen's refusal simply
to repeat past teaching but instead its will to relate theology anew to each
succeeding generation in a way that makes it vital and relevant to its hearers.
It is not the urge to be up to date that drives this desire but instead the
belief revelation needs to be re-presented to each generation, a goal impossible to achieve if revelation is not first made understandable.

Tübingers understand Scripture as an historical document. It is a
relatively reliable rendition of the original revelation, but apart from the
spirit of living tradition it is worthless and dead. To treat the Bible merely
as a subject for grammatical-historical exegesis is to make it use less as the
basis for theology. Yet theology apart from the Bible cannot be Christian

because the Bible is one pole in the dialectic out of which theology grows, our experience being the other. The Tübingers have concentrated on a few major themes from Scripture in their presentation of Christology. Primary among these have been the Kingdom of God, the Adam-Christ parallel, the Son of Man sayings, and eschatology. These themes have become important in much recent Christology, Protestant as well as Catholic.

In their dealing with Scripture, Tübingers have tried to reflect Drey's admonition that our organizing concept for theology must come from Scripture itself. For Drey, this concept was the Kingdom of God. It is not necessary to follow Drey and his successors in choice of theme, but certainly Christians should organize their Christology around biblical themes, not themes derived from philosophy or social thought. These latter sources can provide themes of local and short-term interest but cannot transcend time and place. Theological conclusions should derive from Scripture and be consistent with Scripture. This raises the question of the meaning of Scripture.

Catholic approaches to Scripture have changed significantly over the past four decades as the Church has become increasingly open to the use of modern critical methods in studying Scripture. As a result, the question of hermeneutics has taken on increasing importance for theologians, who have at the same time defined the term far more broadly than earlier generations. This change is evident in the different approaches to Scripture taken by Adam and Kasper among the Tübingers of this century. The definition and limits of hermeneutics remain a subject of debate for theologians today.

Walter Kasper has been particularly vocal in expressing the need for hermeneutical self-consciousness in theology. In saying this, he has advocated using modern hermeneutical approaches insofar as they open Scripture more fully to our understanding. Some have accused Kasper of departing from the Tübingen tradition in his use of modern thought. It would appear, rather, that such use reflects not a departure from Tübingen but the carrying out of the original Tübingen spirit, as epitomized by Drey, of appropriating the valuable elements of contemporary thought. Thus, it is not a matter of using particular methods as much as of using those methods which are most suitable for exploiting the sources to create a modern theology.

In drawing on the Bible, Tübingers have refused to ignore or undervalue tradition in their biblical studies. Instead, they have tried to hold exegesis and tradition in balance. Kasper has been particularly clear in reminding us many early Church conflicts resulted from divergent interpretations of Scripture. At Nicea, says Kasper, the Church rejected Arius' understanding of Christ which he based on a certain philosophical interpretation of the New Testament. A. N. S. Lane warns that some modern theologians have tried to go back to the Bible, ignoring nineteen centuries of tradition, only to repeat some of the christological heresies rejected by their predecessors.[5] For Tübingen, tradition has been a stabilizing influence but also through the Tübingen concept of doctrinal development it has served to push theologians to new understandings of older doctrines.

The essence of Tübingen's concept of doctrinal development is that the content of doctrine remains the same but the expression of its truth differs.[6] Tübingen is not alone in this view, and it faces the universal problem of distinguishing the content of doctrine from its expression. How do the two differ, and at what point does changing the way doctrine is expressed change its content? Tübingers have raised the issue but they may not have provided us with a satisfactory solution.

In their theological enterprise, Tübingers have not hesitated to interact with critical conclusions regarding Scripture. Their responses have not been uniform, however. The Tübingers' response to biblical criticism has been one of the less satisfying aspects of their recent work because of its inconclusive and sometimes contradictory nature. Kasper and Geiselmann have shown critical methods can be synthesized with tradition to develop a Christology that speaks to our time, but they have not always done this well. We believe Kasper will have to decide at some point to move either to his right or left if he wishes to present a consistent Christology (and theology).

Following a period from the late 1960's through the 1970's when theologians wrote intensively about Christology, Catholic theologians have begun to shift their focus to consider the nature of the Church. They have recognized developments in Christology necessarily require concurrent work in ecclesiology. Dietrich notes Tübingen theologians have been particularly aware of this.[7] Traditionally, Christianity has placed a strong emphasis on the supernatural because of its understanding of God and the way God relates to creation. Since the Enlightenment, this understanding has been under attack. In Christology this became particularly clear in the work of D. F. Strauss. Among those who responded to Strauss's mythological interpretation of Christ, Tübingen theologians were in the forefront. This appreciation of the supernatural element has continued among Tübingers. None of the Tübingen theologians we have surveyed would disagree with Pollard when he says

> the intensive concentration on the historical questions
> about Jesus has tended to make us forget that there is a
> supra-historical dimension about the Christ-event without

which Jesus would be no more than another figure in ancient history.[8]

Key aspects of the life of Jesus have been and must continue to be
understood in terms of the supernatural (i.e., relating to the immediate exercise of God's power in the life of Jesus). These include especially his Incarnation and Resurrection. Tübingers have not made this connection explicit,
but the reality of the supernatural finds a parallel in human salvation. Just
as God raised Jesus from death, so God works in others to save them from
sin and its effect. Recent Tübingers have been confronted with the disparity
between critical exegesis and traditional views about the miraculous. They
have experienced difficulty in reconciling this in ways satisfactory to critics
on their right and left.

Modern Christology has gone through a period in which it has been
seen in terms of either/or. This includes the question of whether Christology should be "from above" or "from below," and setting ontology and function in opposition. Kasper has argued these polarities should be understood
in terms of both/and, or we will lose something essential in the way we
understand Jesus Christ. Many christologists today would agree this is the
best approach to biblical and early Church witnesses.

Many have called Kasper a functionalist, but he has shown an
awareness that function needs to be grounded in being. Some have claimed
ontological language is an importation from Greek philosophy, but in both
Old and New Testaments we find that although we know God and Christ
through what they say and do both God and Christ exist apart from and
prior to their actions. Likewise, Kasper has argued Christology must be
from both "above" and "below." We may exclude neither path and we must
end our study "above." In saying this, Kasper affirms the intent of the two-
natures doctrine of Chalcedon that sees Christ as both fully human and fully
divine. Kasper adds, however, that we must not stop with Chalcedon because the Scriptures are far richer in their christological content than
Chalcedon evidences. Doubt about Chalcedon has led to a division over
Jesus: is he God or human? This has been less explicit than the other
polarities because of the continuing authority of the early christological
councils, particularly in Catholic circles. Karl Adam faced this issue and repeatedly reminded his readers only a both/and answer would suffice. Any
other solution must cancel Christianity's claim to be a salvific religion.

Kasper has also brought the subject of eschatology to the fore in
Christology. He has reminded us the early Church looked to the future. In
part, he has drawn on the Tübingen concern for the Kingdom of God to

point out Jesus expected a future establishment of the Kingdom. It did not arrive visibly and powerfully in his ministry, nor did he claim it would. Jesus proclaimed the coming of the Kingdom and described his mission in terms of this Kingdom. In a world looking for hope and meaning, the eschatological vision of the Kingdom of God can provide the ground for such hope. This Kingdom is brought by God; it is not dependent upon human effort and is not to be identified with the Church.

When we look at Tübingen Christology over the past 170 years, we see it has been a balanced Christology. The various members of the School have had their special interests but none has allowed these interests seriously to distort his view of Christ. The School's Christology has not been subject to various theological fads. Instead, it has dealt with the major concerns of the tradition and of the age.

The many strengths of Tübingen Christology are not without off-setting weaknesses. We have seen in several cases the desire to interact with contemporary philosophical, social, and conceptual trends, in our judgment, has resulted in these trends being given too much weight in theology, and in the case of Karl Adam in Christology. Tübingers are far from being the only theologians who have allowed these trends to have more influence than they ought, but because they have so clearly recognized the danger they ought to be less affected than others.

In their conscious attempt to speak directly to the world from their own context, recent Tübingers have created Christologies which may have only limited value for other contemporary contexts and for future generations. While it is important our work address the concerns of our intended audience in language it can understand, the story of Jesus Christ is broader than that. No Christology containing the fullness of the scriptural witness to Christ can omit transcultural elements that address all cultures and generations of humanity. Kasper, for example, needs to respond more to the situation and concerns of those who live outside Western Europe when he discusses who Jesus Christ is and what he has done. This would mean including sociological, political, and economic elements as well as the philosophical and historical ones that already characterize his theology.

Kasper's interest in Spirit Christology reminds the Church of the existence, activity, and importance of the Spirit. The history of Christologies built on the activity of the Spirit has not been good, however. Too often, they have degenerated into viewing Jesus as a man who was uniquely filled with the Spirit, but who otherwise did not differ from other humans. Kasper recognizes the need to avoid this error, but his language is not always as clear on the matter as it might be, given the problematic history of this approach. Further, he has a great deal more work to do if he intends to offer a complete Spirit Christology to the Church for its consideration.

Hans Küng has criticized Kasper and Möhler for drawing back from the logical consequences of their theology (in Kasper's case, his Christology) out of fear Rome might condemn their work. We need to consider this charge for two reasons. One is its ethical implication. If they did modify their conclusions for this reason, these men have been less than honest and less than scholarly. On the other hand, might there not be an unresolved tension in their data or methods? It is different for a person to hold a position from faith which he cannot defend entirely from his evidence than it is for him to hold the position out of fear of retribution if he espouses a contrary position which he may privately accept. From our reading of Kasper and Möhler and our dealing with Kasper, we believe they have held positions they believed in. They may not have been able to defend every element of these positions with the evidence at hand and the methods they chose. In Kasper's case, the problem exists in the way he attempts to reconcile those critical methods and conclusions he accepts with the dogmas of the Church he has committed himself to. There are places where it does not appear possible for his methods to lead to these dogmas unless the dogmas are reinterpreted. For Möhler, the problem was two major shifts in the focus and method of his theology. In each case, he appears to have changed his position as a result of his research.

Kasper's attempt to reconceptualize the meaning of the term "person" in theology also raises problems. It is not the attempt at restatement—theologians are generally agreed the term was used for want of other and better language—but the way in which he attempts a restatement that causes the problem. Kasper's definition of "person" in relational terms becomes problematic when he says a person exists out of his or her relationships. Having previously pointed to the being that underlies function, Kasper appears to substitute relation for function and reverse the statement. Insofar as relations can be understood in functional terms, this is contradictory. Kasper's focus on the personhood and freedom of God and Christ speaks to his Western European audience where personhood has become a devalued concept and freedom turned to license or become a cover word for subjugation. Again, we find both value and danger in the same element of this School's Christology.

We must understand the christological work of the Catholic Tübingen School—of its 20th century representatives in particular—in terms of nuance. Their Christology sounds in great measure like that of the classical statements of the Church, but there is at the same time something different about it. It is not only the attempt to come to grips with the historicity of christological doctrine that makes the difference; there seems to be a different spirit. It may be a matter of accommodating the spirit of the present age. It may be a similar response that leads Küng to question Kasper's intent in his Christology.

AN EVANGELICAL CHRISTOLOGICAL REFLECTION

As we look at the strengths and weaknesses of the Catholic Tübingen School, we find many elements that can help us in constructing a Christology for today. Such a Christology need not be in the spirit of the School. Tübingers have much to offer out of their consideration of the roles of tradition, historicity, philosophy, Scripture, and contextualization in Christology to those who do Christology in other traditions. We will offer some suggestions for such a Christology based on our interaction with Tübingen thought. We may not always agree with the conclusions of its representatives, but we will draw on themes they have emphasized and try to learn from their successes and failures.

The task of creating a Christology for our era is of major importance. Christianity is a salvific religion and as its name indicates this salvation has to do with Jesus Christ. Christ is so important to Christianity that all other areas of Christian belief and practice would be affected by any change in christological teaching.[9]

Despite numerous attempts in history to reconceptualize Christianity as a system of ideas or eternally valid truths, everything comes back to the life, teaching, and death of a Jew who lived in Palestine nearly twenty centuries ago.

> The basic fact which lies behind all the theological terms and titles is the worship of the carpenter. That is a phenomenon sufficiently arresting to require explanation, even if they had never progressed to the stage of openly calling him "God." This worship was no easy option for pious Jews.[10]

In preparing a Christology, we must begin with the Bible. It is here we find almost all the evidence a person named Jesus lived, died, and was honored by his followers as risen from the dead and offering a way to God. Colin Gunton suggests that instead of concentrating on the New Testament as Christians have tended to do, we should make greater use of the Old

Testament. God's activity there provides the backdrop for us to understand Jesus in his Jewish environment.

> Reference to the Old Testament shows a theology not at
> variance with the kind of claim made in orthodox dogma.
> Where the Old Testament is ignored, or ceases to be con-
> stitutive, the danger is that some other framework will be
> provided.[11]

Gunton says that when the salvation-historical framework of the Old Testament is not taken into consideration, the result often is the substitution of a framework in which history is not important. Normally this framework will be an Hegelian system.

Given that we must work with the evidence of the entire Bible, we need to be self-conscious about the way we approach our source. We should be equally conscious of the sources the canonical authors used in writing their documents; not all were canonical. As we have seen from the experience of the Tübingers, modern critics has approached Scripture in a variety of ways, drawing on different presuppositions and methods. Not all are of the same worth. These critical methods have elicited a variety of responses from theologians and people in the pews.

In examining the Bible, we are dealing with a piece of literature. Bernard Ramm reminds us that in proposing theories about how literature is to be understood we are dealing with probabilities. He says, "Statements of New Testament scholars are probability statements and not demonstrated theories."[12]

We need to look not only at what biblical scholars tell us about the text but also at why they say what they do. We have seen that modern theological scholarship is predisposed to reject supernatural explanations. We need to ask whether this is a scholarly conclusion or a bias that is brought to the subject. What are the warrants for believing or disbelieving in the supernatural? Our conclusion here will affect the possibility of doing Christology instead of Jesusology. Here the modern Tübingers have provided us with an affirmation of the reality of the supernatural, but an affirmation that is more cautious than earlier generations have offered. They suggest that we examine claims to supernatural activity with care because natural explanations may explain better the actual occurrence. In saying this, they affirm that in the person of Jesus Christ the supernatural has entered into history, but they want equally to respect the significance of the created order.

History and the Gospel Witness

The gospels do not provide us with biographies of Jesus. That is a commonly agreed conclusion today, but the implications of this continue to be discussed. Different scholars see different informational value in the gospels because for some the value of material from partisan sources remains a problem. Others say we can consider virtually no information objective in any field of study. The absence of modern historiographic standards in the early Church era also poses a problem for many. I. Howard Marshall says, however, that

> although the Gospels were not written by scientific historians, we have found good reason to believe that they incorporate reliable information about Jesus, so that the ordinary reader, who has neither the time nor the scholarly skills to carry out historical research, may rest confident that the portraits of Jesus in the Gospels are based on historical facts.[13]

In viewing the Tübingers' work on Christology we see they have experienced a tension between their dealings with modern biblical criticism and their concern for history. Those who have stressed most heavily the historicity of the biblical evidence have felt the tension most severely. We need to determine whether this tension is inherent in the relationship between history and criticism or whether it results from presuppositions we bring to our study. Our answer will affect our christological method.

Concern for history has characterized Catholic Tübingen from its inception. Today history and historical consciousness have become major themes for both biblical scholars and theologians. Because of the many implications of historical study, this matter of history has been a serious problem for Christology. In one sense, history grounds Christian faith in a particular individual who lived in a specific place at a specific time. In another, however, history raises the issues of limitation and relativity. Lessing's challenge related to the second because he asked how we can derive universal truths from particular events. Gunton contends Lessing erred by setting up false criteria for reliability and credibility of statements because he misunderstood the way in which language relates to reality. Gunton's point is that because our minds and language are finite, we have no assured universal truths of reason. There is no unbridgeable chasm; what we see instead is a continuum.[14] Christianity offers its truths based on divine revelation, not human reason. If God is who Christians have claimed him to be, he is not constrained by our limitations and can thus reveal to us universal truth, even within history.

Troeltsch argued our historical nature limits us and all we do according to our context, subjecting us to the laws of historical development. Because there are many historical contexts and they are always changing, everything in them is limited and relative. This means

> the historical quality of all human achievements... excludes
> all absolutes, that is, all "one and only" or unchangeable
> truth claims.[15]

In taking this position, Troeltsch excluded the supernatural *a priori* and took a particular view of God and God's relation to creation. As he recognized, this position denied the possibility of any value judgments based on more than personal preference. It also excluded the possibility of the Incarnation.

The Christian doctrine of the Incarnation claims God and God's relation to the world differ significantly from Troeltsch's understanding. According to this doctrine, God can and does act within the history of the world, and, *contra* Lessing, God speaks in terms of absolutes into the world of contingency in a way transcending historical and cultural contexts. To say this is not to deny God also speaks in terms of contingency.

The revolution in historiography occurred with the development of modern scientific approaches to research. This brought with it many assumptions, one of which is that anything we cannot explain in terms of the method must be unhistorical. Pannenberg has criticized this position when it is used to deny the historicity of the Resurrection. Gunton criticizes it more fundamentally as attempting to use the wrong tool for the job. He says

> it is not logically necessary that the historical Jesus should
> be discovered by the methods of secular historiography
> alone. All depends upon who the historical Jesus was (or
> *is*), for facts may only be discovered by methods appropri-
> ate to their nature.[16]

Another assumption of the early scientific historians was that we can study and present history in a totally objective manner. This position has been discredited, primarily as a result of recent work in hermeneutics.

Related to the subject of history is the problem of holding together that in Jesus which is new, different, and discontinuous with that which is similar and continuous with the old covenant. If Jesus is totally different from us, we cannot understand him or identify with him; if he is like us, with nothing new, he does not provide the solution to our existential problem. The early creeds affirm both the continuity and discontinuity of Christ with humanity, and we need to explain this in the language of today and demonstrate against Lessing and Troeltsch how this can be.

Hermeneutics

Hermeneutics has become a major concern in modern theology. The Tübingen theologians have approached modern hermeneutic proposals with caution, but have not rejected them. It is important to understand Adam's antagonism toward Bultmann's hermeneutics was based on Bultmann's presuppositions and his conclusions. Adam considered both to be inimical to Christian faith. Kasper has been more sympathetic to the suggestions of Gadamer and others because he believes he can appropriate elements of their work without detriment to Christian faith. Just as Tübingers traditionally have made free use of contemporary philosophies without allowing any one to become master of their theological house, so Kasper wants to make use of contemporary hermeneutics without allowing it mastery over his theology. Following the Tübingers, we can profit from the insights of these hermeneuts, but we need to do so critically and selectively.

Another role of Scripture in Christology is to provide details about Jesus' person, life, and message. The Kingdom of God has been a major Tübingen theme in Christology, but Tübingers have been far from alone in giving this theme an important place in their work. This was a major theme in Jesus' preaching, but is it true Jesus spoke only about the coming Kingdom and never about himself? Such a conclusion appears exegetically unsound if only because it then becomes difficult to explain how Jesus, not the Kingdom, became the focus of all the New Testament books, even those recounting his message of the coming Kingdom.

I. H. Marshall says even Jesus' message about the Kingdom is a message about himself because it contains an implicit Christology. Even Bultmann, he says, admitted Jesus' proclamation of the Kingdom leads inevitably to the question, "Who is this Jesus?" Marshall goes on to say, "Jesus' call to decision must surely have implied a Christology *in his own mind*."[17]

M. M. B. Turner notes Jesus' teaching implied a very high Christology, but it contained no explicit statements that he was ontologically divine;
he adds that the implicit claims are a different matter.[18] Gunton says the
Jesus of the New Testament is a "human and earthly figure whose intrinsic
meaning is to be expressed in expressions employing the word *God.*"[19] Appreciation for Jesus' message of the Kingdom should lead us to recognize
the eschatological thrust of his teaching and to consider what sort of person
he must have been to relate the Kingdom to himself in the way he did.

According to Marshall, the Incarnation is the organizing principle
of New Testament Christology insofar as that Christology concerns itself
with the person of Jesus. It is a Christology "from above" and begins with
the pre-incarnate Son of God who becomes flesh. "It thus deals with the
question of how the Son of God became man rather than how a particular
man, Jesus, could be the Son of God."[20] He adds this is not to exclude any
valid role for a Christology "from below," but it is to say that most of the
New Testament took a different approach. We see here again Kasper's view
that the two approaches used in tandem deal most adequately with the biblical evidence, both approaches existing within the New Testament. Yet, as
the Tübingers have argued, Christology must end "above" or we have lost
Christology in the historical sense of the term.

C. F. D. Moule says the earliest Christology that can be securely
dated is that of Paul's major epistles, and it was as developed and "high"—in
the sense of viewing Jesus as divine, transcendent, and uniquely one with
God—as any that has appeared since.[21] If Moule is correct, the "high"
Christology of historic Christianity is not the product of a long evolutionary
development, but appeared within a generation of Jesus' death. Moule says
further that although not all the christological statements in the New Testament are adequate as modern statements of Christology, they do provide
better insight into who Jesus was than do statements increasingly distant
from Jesus' time.[22] We see here conservative New Testament scholars, but
scholars who make use of the tools of modern criticism, who consider the
New Testament documents reliable sources for modern Christology and
believe the "high" Christology found there to be more complete than
anything that has occurred since, including the statements of the early
christological councils.

Tradition and Christology

We need to recognize explicitly that our Christology is not and
never can be exclusively from the Bible. All of us come out of some tradi-

tion and reflect that tradition in our work. When we recognize our theological roots and see how they influence the way we enter into the theological enterprise, we can compensate for them, if necessary. Tradition plays different roles in our lives and possesses different degrees of authority, depending upon whether we are Protestant, Roman Catholic, or Orthodox. We must ensure our Christology remains biblical despite our traditions, if not always because of them. For some, a biblical Christology may mean pulling back from some aspects of tradition; for others it will mean holding firmly to traditions they might prefer to ignore.

Tübingen has set us an example of concern to deal with tradition not as something constricting, but as a living and active force helping to form the faith of the Christian community. A positive approach to tradition helps us to appreciate the labors of our ancestors. It also reminds us we are not the first generation to wrestle with christological issues. Thus we should avail ourselves of the opportunity to learn from those who have preceded us. It is regarding the place of tradition in theology that Tübingers have been most involved and it is here they have much to offer.

Tübingers have viewed tradition as a living force within the Church, but they have equally recognized it has crystallized into written statements at various times and places. That which has been committed to writing as the result of conciliar decisions must be taken seriously in Christian theology. We cannot ignore these teachings, but we must be ready to interpret the language and concepts of an earlier age for our own. As Gunton writes, christological renewal is to be found in taking tradition further, not in rejecting it.[23] Moreover, we must never cease to measure tradition against the norm of Scripture.

In modern Christology, the statement of the Council of Chalcedon has become a center of controversy. It uses language that is out of favor and out of step with modern thought. It is also an incomplete statement of the biblical message about Jesus Christ. To say this is not to say Chalcedon was wrong in its affirmations and denials. Far from it. Because of its problems, many would prefer to ignore Chalcedon, or, if that is impossible, to reinterpret its difficult parts to mean something other than they have been understood to mean for 1500 years. Most would like to add to it—especially concerning the history and humanity of Jesus—but given the divisions within Christianity a council able to make formal additions is unlikely. Anything less would meet with the same widespread rejection the *filioque* clause added to the Niceo-Constanipolitan creed did.

Chalcedon has two types of weaknesses. Some are in what it does *not* say, and others are in the effects of its teachings on Christian practice.

Some theologians would add that the way in which it expresses itself is a third weakness. The council's definition did not deal directly with the life and historicity of Jesus of Nazareth. The council said, however, that it affirmed and repeated the creed of I Constantinople, which did say some of this. The conflicts to which the councils responded were not cast in terms of history. Those declared to be in error had raised their objections to tradition in terms drawn from Greek philosophy. The conciliar responses thus had to come in the same language, but this did not make them the product of Hellenistic thought.

Ramm says the fathers used Greek language only to the extent it provided them with a way to state more precisely that which they already found in Scripture.[24] Were this not so, were the creeds so formal, so theological and philosophical, so divorced from the gospel text, they never would have received such wide acceptance within the Church.[25] This leads to a problem of the second sort. Chalcedon clearly taught that Christ is fully human and fully divine. The full humanity of Jesus often has been ignored in practice, however, even as its has continued to be affirmed verbally. In the Roman Catholic Church and Eastern Orthodoxy, this has led to the cult of Mary and the saints because some Christians have viewed Jesus as too distant to mediate between God and humanity adequately and sympathetically. Among both Catholics and conservative Protestants there has existed a practical Monophysitism that at times has bordered on Docetism.

In respecting Chalcedon, we are not required to affirm its completeness. It is an incomplete Christology. The proper question concerns its correctness in that which it affirms. It is a commentary on the biblical text, and if it can be shown from Scripture to be incorrect in its comments, it stands in need of correction. It is, however, a statement developed by the Church catholic and accepted for fifteen centuries. Thus we ignore it or treat it disrespectfully at our peril. Our age may possess more information than have previous ones, but that does not guarantee we also have greater wisdom. In saying this, we recognize Chalcedon and the other early creeds do not answer all of our questions and cannot be the final word in Christology. Further work must be done in continuity with and on the foundation of the early creeds, recognizing they set boundaries for future speculation and formulation, without proscribing such activity. The history of the Church shows Christology did not end with Chalcedon, although it has guided itself in terms of Chalcedon.

Because we live in an age different from that of the early creeds, we ourselves must engage in the hard work of defining for today who Jesus Christ is and what he has done. We cannot depend solely on statements over a thousand years old, written for a different age and context, to present the Church's faith in Christ to the modern world.

George Tavard says Chalcedon preserves the realism of the Incarnation. He sees it as a non-philosophical description of a man who is one reality living in two realms at the same time and possessing two consciousnesses and fields of action.[26] Chalcedon, like Nicea, was fundamentally about human salvation; it talks about Jesus Christ because if we are to receive salvation our savior must be able to deal adequately with our need.

The language of the creeds appears strange to some today, but it is the language in which the challenge was presented to the early Church. The New Testament used soteriological, and thus functional, language for the most part to talk about Jesus. The early Church drew ontological conclusions about Jesus because Arius and later critics challenged the Church's understanding in terms of ontology. These ontological conclusions were drawn in order to defend the Church's soteriological affirmations. As we noted earlier, ontology and function are linked. Recognizing their relation is a subject of debate, we would argue being must precede function because only that which already exists can act. If this is the case, the early councils were justified in grounding their soteriological understanding of Jesus Christ in an ontological understanding of his person. In saying this, we recognize the need to define Christ's person and work in concepts that communicate to modern society. These definitions should follow the early Church's example and provide an explanation in continuity with that which has gone before in the same way the fathers provided an explanation in continuity with Scripture.

Tavard writes that classical Christology may have been naïve in its attempt to harmonize the various strands of New Testament evidence but it satisfied the requirements of popular faith and piety. The modern search for the historical Jesus has been faithful to the canons of historical science, but has been so at the expense of popular faith. Hypothetical scholarly reconstructions often contradict the tradition of the Church about the person and work of Jesus.[27] Tavard is raising the issue of the nature of Christian faith here. Is it something we hold intellectually, or is it something we must be able to express in worship (this latter not excluding a rational and intellectual content)? Christians traditionally have argued for the latter, and, excesses notwithstanding, this does appear consistent with the biblical evidence. We would go on to add not only worship but also practice is essential to true and adequate Christology. This is the concern some have raised in recent years under the rubric of orthopraxis, although others have used this term in a way that carries ideological baggage.

As we prepare Christologies for the late 20th century, we can only do so by remembering the contents and lessons of the early christological creeds. We need to be willing to criticize them and go beyond what they have said, but we require a good justification if we intend to go against what they have said. Ramm contends these creeds reflect "in their own way the material found here and there in the New Testament."[28]

If God is as the Bible and Christian theology have portrayed, we are dealing with the infinite when we contemplate God. This means ultimately we are faced with a mystery beyond the power of our finite intellect. Not everything about God and Christ is mystery or we could not speak, but at points we must recognize our faith is dealing with something beyond our ability to comprehend or explain. It is not that this is irrational, but that it transcends reason.

Recent theology, especially that done by Roman Catholics, has appreciated the element of mystery in discussing God, but this appreciation has not been reflected in modern Christology. To recognize our human limitations is not to demean the human intellect, but to be clear about our natural abilities and our relation to reality. This does not mean the creeds and theology are wrong, only that they describe their subject incompletely because Christian faith is commitment to more than we can explain intellectually. Diogenes Allen writes:

> Theological reflection on the way God has related to us thus encounters matters which are beyond our intellect. The notion of mystery is not invoked haphazardly. It is rather the being of God, full and complete in itself, which leads us to invoke mystery at specific junctures in our reflections. It is by means of the intellect that we understand where it is impossible for us to understand.[29]

Whatever its final conclusions, every Christology must consider at some point the elements that have made traditional Christology what it is. These include Christ's pre-existence, the Incarnation, miracles and the supernatural in Jesus' life, Jesus' death and resurrection, and his final return in glory. We have discussed the category of the supernatural earlier. The Incarnation and Resurrection accounts presuppose the supernatural and the various miracle stories make this explicit. If the supernatural element is removed from the gospels we are left with a teacher of ethics and a humanitarian, even if he is a towering one. If we accept the supernatural events of incarnation and resurrection, the other miracles may present difficulties to a natural scientist, but conceptually they ought to be no problem.

Pre-existence and Incarnation

Pre-existence is often either denied or redefined today. For many, the idea of divine being taking human form sounds too much like a fable. Some see it as a story intended to teach some religious truth, but not itself a statement of ontological reality. This is myth in the positive sense. Some theologians have offered a view described as ideal pre-existence. This says Jesus existed in the mind of God as the Christ of the future prior to his incarnation, but that he was not a being who, having the divine nature from eternity, assumed human nature at some point in time. Each of these positions appears to derive from an understanding of the relation between God and humanity that sees the two as incompatible. Thus, for God to become human is beyond possibility. The mythic positions have many difficulties as the book *The Myth of God Incarnate* and the responses it generated showed in the late 1970's. The concept of an ideal pre-existence is weakened severely in that it seems to affirm no more about Jesus than Christians have affirmed historically about God's relation to all humans, namely that God pre-conceives them all.

Pre-existence in the case of the Incarnation says something important about Jesus. The doctrine teaches the relationship Jesus has with the Father is one he has always possessed, and he has possessed it by nature, not as a gift. Pre-existence underlies the Incarnation in an absolute sense and says something about God's attitude toward humanity in bringing about salvation in the way he did.

The meaning of the Incarnation depends upon one's understanding of the pre-existence of the Word. The doctrine of the Incarnation teaches God has entered into creation in a decisive way. It shows an ultimate compatibility between God and humans without erasing a difference in kind between them. If the Son of God who was truly God also became truly human, he provides a link between God and humanity that can overcome the estrangement that has existed in the relationship. The Incarnation shows the extent to which God is willing to go to protect and restore his creation. It also teaches it was God who took the initiative in dealing with his creatures and he is able to accomplish what he planned; in other words, God is both good and powerful. But it only does so if we take seriously the traditional claims about what actually occurred. Kasper has rightly claimed the

Incarnation is the dividing line between that which is Christian and that which is not.

The Incarnation teaches Jesus is fully human, but it does not teach he is human precisely as we are. Were he, he could not later be our savior because we are warped by our sin and unable to save ourselves much less save others, according to Scripture and traditional theology. Jesus' humanity is both continuous with and discontinuous from that of the rest of humanity. He can identify with his fellow humans in their experiences, but he is free of those infirmities that would preclude him from being the savior. Marshall adds the New Testament emphasis is on Christ's full deity, not on his full humanity as we find in much of the modern discussion. The New Testament views Jesus primarily as the Son of God who took the form of a human.[30]

The Resurrection

Jesus' death and resurrection have become the center of much of modern Christology. Few deny Jesus died. If he was a real human, that could only be expected. It is the purpose and effect of his death and what happened after his death that is debated. In terms of history, the Resurrection does not meet the standards of continuity and repeatability of events—it has happened only once according to Scripture. It is also an event that occurred without witnesses. There were witnesses to the effects of the Resurrection, but no one saw the event itself. Lessing's concern about particular events in history having a universal effect has influenced some. Some also have an ethical problem with the death of an innocent individual in behalf of others. This causes them to question the nature of God. A final concern is the nature of the Resurrection, or what kind of a body did the risen Jesus have?

If the Resurrection did not occur, we have several problems. One of these is explaining how the Church came into existence. The Church has taught the Resurrection served as God's vindication of Jesus' message and salvific death. It says Jesus did what he came to do. Another problem is that no one produced a body soon after Jesus' death to put a stop to the resurrection claims. We must remember that while the people of antiquity were not as scientific as we are, they were not more credulous or naive. None of the many theories put forward to explain away the Resurrection has more than a limited following.

The nature of Jesus' resurrection body provides another difficulty. Alan Richardson calls the notion that Christ's resurrection was a purely "spiritual" affair in which the corpse remained in the grave a modern view resting upon disbelief in the possibility of miracles.[31] Various biblical scholars have pointed out the Jews saw no dichotomy between body and soul as the Greeks did. This would mean a resurrection in which the body remained in the ground would be meaningless to Jesus' Jewish contemporaries. It would also serve to deny the importance and value of the material creation, especially the bodies of other humans. Indirect consequences of a "spiritual" resurrection applied logically to other aspects of human existence (e.g., ethics and ecology) would be devastating. Thus a bodily resurrection not only says something about the promise of human salvation, it also speaks to the way in which people should live in this life.

Humanity and Personhood

Kasper notes the importance of our understanding of the concept of person in Christology. He has not been alone in this. From the earliest use of the language, theologians have recognized both the need to deal with the subject and the inadequacy of human linguistic formulations that attempt to do so. The developments of the past two centuries have made the problem even more acute. The term person now has strong psychological overtones that were absent in patristic times when it was primarily ontological.

Lane says the denial of a human person in Jesus Christ was not a psychological statement but a denial of Adoptionism. Use of the term meant the sole subject of the human experiences of Christ was the Logos. Lane says human psychology falls within the realm of nature, not person.[32] If Lane's suggestion that human psychology is proper to one's nature, not to one's person, the statements of the creeds, and even those of anhypostasis and enhypostasis, should become less troublesome for modern people. No longer is there any hint the human Jesus is in some way incomplete. Lane says the difference between Jesus and us that results from this is that while we are merely humans, he is the Logos incarnate, and the Logos was the subject of Jesus' human experiences. "To deny this," says Lane, "is to deny the very doctrine of the incarnation. To call this docetic is simply to state that any doctrine of the incarnation is docetic."[33] We see again the interrelationship between the parts of Christology and how changing one point affects the others. The unexpected results of a change at one point should cause us to be careful in suggesting changes at others.

David Wells says to speak of Jesus' humanity coming to personal completion in the Logos does not in any way diminish the full reality of that humanity. What we see is that the Word of God already possessed everything necessary to be human, so in Jesus Christ we meet God face to face and see human nature in all its perfection. The joining of the two natures in one person, far from diminishing either, only shows deity and humanity are not antithetical.[34]

      We do not offer new language to substitute for the traditional person and nature language. Barth and Rahner both turned their minds to that task in this century, but neither achieved an acceptable substitute. Human language at this point is attempting to express something it cannot explain—the union of the finite and infinite is mystery—so its expression, while necessary, is difficult. The effort to achieve a better language of explanation is valid, but it may not be fruitful. We prefer to look anew at what the original language meant and to clear away the popular misconceptions that have made the classical terminology unacceptable to many. What Lane and Wells have said will not make the earlier formulations more attractive to those who reject the ideal of incarnation, but it does make clear what that doctrine really entails. If one accepts the possibility of the Incarnation having occurred, the credal language properly understood becomes legitimate, even though we might hope to find a better way of expressing it.

Christology and Philosophy

      It was due to a challenge from the side of philosophy that the issue of person entered Christian theology. Some have looked at the problems involved in the relationship of philosophy with theology and suggested theology is better off without any philosophical input. The real issue, however, appears to be whether we are going to have theology with conscious philosophical input or with unconscious input. Because philosophy deals with many of the same issues as does theology, it does not seem possible to exclude philosophy from the theological enterprise. The issue is how best to include it. Our responsibility is to use philosophy as best we can to help us in our task while preventing any particular philosophy from taking over that enterprise.

> Catholic theologians realized that philosophical principles could not be used to derive positive Christianity with its emphasis on the reconciliation of man with God, but that philosophy could help in analyzing the signs of revelation in order to insure that these could support belief.[35]

The use made of philosophy will differ between Catholics and Protestants because they have different opinions about the validity of natural theology and of the role of philosophy. The important thing is that because all theologians are at least informal philosophers, each should be conscious of the philosophy he or she is using.

Equally controversial in modern Christology as the use of person language is the use of ontological language. Modern thinkers prefer function to being not only for Jesus but in all of modern life.[36] People recognize being and function are linked, but they do not agree on the direction of the linkage. We contend function presupposes being; what Jesus did was possible only because of who he was. Wells says Chalcedon separated being from function because the focus of the attack was on Christ's being. Today, people separate Christ's person and work because they pragmatically believe we can understand Jesus only in terms of his actions.[37]

Doing Christology in Context

Not only is it necessary to understand who Jesus was if we wish to understand what he has done, it is equally necessary to understand who Jesus was to understand what the Church should be. O'Collins says, "Questions of ecclesiastical theory and practice will never be satisfactorily resolved unless we go back to our understanding of Jesus himself."[38] He says there exists a mutual relation between ecclesiology and Christology because "the Church is the place where Christians worship, act and suffer. It is Jesus Christ who gives point and purpose to what they do and endure."[39] As we explore questions of Christology, we must recognize their implications for the Church and equally recognize the implications for Christology of the way the Church exists and acts in the world.

We mentioned contextualization at the beginning of this study and have examined various ways Tübingen theologians attempted to place their theology in a contemporary context. We, too, need to contextualize any future Christology. This will mean our Christologies will speak better to some groups than to others, but none will be irrelevant to any context. Contextualized Christology will be a careful and sensitive blend of that which has universal significance with that which is of localized concern.

This was the case with the New Testament writers. No one thinks these authors were miraculously lifted out of their historical and cultural contexts in order to write. Otherwise, how could they have communicated to their contemporaries? But while they were a part of their culture, they transcended that culture as well. This was true for other ancient writers, and it is no less true for the biblical authors. It should be true of us who do theology today as well. But this is not an easy task. Gunton notes every generation of theologians faces the task of communicating to its culture without succumbing to its pressure to "force their content into an alien shape."[40]

The final issue in Christology deals with the purpose of Christology. The creeds speak about Jesus because of what he has done "for us and for our salvation." We may not divorce Christology and soteriology. Jesus was born, lived, and died to accomplish human salvation. That has been the message of Christian faith for nearly 2000 years. The reverse side of that message has been that human salvation is impossible apart from Jesus Christ. If Jesus Christ is he whom the Church has confessed him to be, he is worth study ing in his own right; if he is the sole mediator between God and humanity, the savior of the world, we need to study him in order to learn what this entails.

Christology and World Religions

This requires an examination of the relation of Jesus to the non-Christian world religions. As advances in transportation and communications have made the world smaller, Christians have come into increasingly close contact with adherents of these religions. They have begun to ask about the possibility of salvation for people whose lives appear as ethical as their own but either have not heard of Jesus or have not believed in him. Experience has caused some to reconsider the universal claims of the Christian gospel and the concurrent particularism of salvation in Jesus Christ alone. Some would see Christ as one source of salvation among many, others would see him as savior even of those in non-Christian religions, yet others consider Christ as savior with conscious commitment to him necessary for salvation. This question from modern culture, with the pluralistic attitude it expresses, requires more biblical input than it often has received so that experience is interpreted by Scripture and not *vice versa*.

Conclusion

In looking at some of the issues in Christology and suggesting directions for future christological work, we have sought to learn from the Catholic Tübingen experience. Tübingers were among the first modern theologians to recognize the need to converse with our religious and secular contemporaries so our theology speaks to our generation, not to a previous century, without losing contact with our roots, and then to put their recognition into practice. We appreciate their valuation of tradition in anchoring theology against the latest fad, but we also recognize that tradition at times can obscure truth or be in error. Tradition can never offer a final and complete statement of Christian belief. We need to check it against Scripture. But Scripture was completed nearly 2000 years ago in a foreign language in an alien culture. We have none of the original documents, only copies of copies. Careful use of the modern critical tools can help us to understand better the correct text, the meaning of its language, and the contexts in which it was written.

When this task is done properly, we can know what Scripture says better than many earlier generations did and can apply it to our own age. Tradition can protect us against fanciful exegesis and interpretation. When we turn these tools to understand the society in which we live, we begin to fuse the horizons of the biblical writers and of our own age and can bring Christian theology to bear on the needs of our age. We can query Scripture in terms of those needs. For this age, as for those which have gone before, the heart of this theology is the person of Jesus Christ. In him we come face to face with God. We cannot understand Jesus Christ or what he has done solely in intellectual terms; neither can we understand him or his work in isolation from the other areas of theology. Each area is affected by and affects every other area, and all should lead us to Jesus Christ as the one who gives Christian theology unity and purpose. Apart from Jesus Christ Christianity is inexplicable and without foundation.

1. Alec R. Vidler, *The Modernist Movement in the Roman Church* (Cambridge: The University Press, 1934), p. 35.

2. Ben F. Meyer, *The Aims of Jesus* (London: SCM, 1979), p. 15.

3. Walter Kasper, *Glaube und Geschichte* (Mainz: Matthias-Grünewald, 1970), pp. 21 f. Kasper emphasized the importance of *Kirchlichkeit* not only for the proper appreciation of various doctrines but even more for understanding the spirit of the Catholic Tübingen School in an interview with the author in July 1985.

4. Paul F. Knitter, *No Other Name?* (Maryknoll, NY: Orbis, 1984), p. xiv. Knitter presents an approach to Christology and world religions significantly different from those that many of his fellow Catholic theologians hold to, but he says his proposal, and any other equally radical (in the sense of rethinking a problem from its roots) theological suggestions, must receive general acceptance within the Church before it dare lay claim to doctrinal status.

5. A. N. S. Lane, "Christology Beyond Chalcedon," p. 258, in *Christ the Lord*, ed. by Harold H. Rowden (Downers Grove, IL: Intervarsity, 1982).

6. Donald J. Dietrich, *The Goethezeit and the Metamorphosis of Catholic Theology in the Age of Idealism* (Bern: Peter Lang, 1979), p. 250. Dietrich explicitly mentions Kasper and Geiselmann in this regard.

7. Ibid., p. 81.

8. T. E. Pollard, *Fullness of Humanity: Christ's Humanity and Ours* (Sheffield: Almond, 1982), p. 90.

9. Bernard L. Ramm, *An Evangelical Christology: Ecumenic and Historic* (Nashville: Thomas Nelson, 1985), p. 16.

10. R. T. France, "The Worship of Jesus," p. 25, in *Jesus the Christ*, ed. by Harold H. Rowden (Downers Grove, IL: Intervarsity). See also R. J. Bauckham, "The Worship of Jesus in Apocalyptic Christianity," *New Testament Studies* 27 (1981):322.

11. Colin Gunton, *Yesterday and Today: A Study of Continuities in Christology* (Grand Rapids: Wm. B. Eerdmans, 1983), pp. 79 f.

12. Ramm, p. 130.

13. I. Howard Marshall, *I Believe in the Historical Jesus* (Grand Rapids: Wm. B. Eerdmans, 1977), p. 235. Earlier we cited studies that consider the historiography of the gospels to be adequate for modern scholarly research. See note 28 on p. 199.

14. Gunton, p. 165.

15. Knitter, p. 24. Meyer says: "As in the nineteenth century, the purposes governing the choice of questions in serious historical Jesus research today are explicitly theological or consciously open-ended toward theology. But as long as the integrity of the historian and theologian is felt to be incompatible with the integrity of the Christian heritage, this research is reduced to salvage operations; that is, common cultural assumptions are affirmed and then that much of Christian heritage which is not in clear discord with them is cautiously salvaged—a delicate operation assuredly testing the intellectual integrity of the salvager. Thus, men accepting the dilemma and working within it may define a single dimension of Jesus' history as the visible heritage, and claim that the tension between honesty and Christianity thereby has been resolved. But such salvage solutions leave a residue of nagging dissatisfaction. They neither tackle the root problem of knowledge nor cohere with New Testament faith" (p. 18).

16. Gunton, p. 58 (emphasis original).

17. Marshall, pp. 228 f.

18. M. M. B. Turner, "The Spirit of Christ and Christology," p. 170, in *Christ the Lord*, ed. by Harold H. Rowden (Downers Grove, IL: Intervarsity, 1982).

19. Gunton, p. 83.

20. I. Howard Marshall, "Incarnational Christology in the New Testament," p. 13, in *Christ the Lord*, ed. by Harold H. Rowden (Downers Grove, IL: Intervarsity, 1982).

21. C. F. D. Moule, *The Holy Spirit* (London: Mowbrays, 1978), p. 58.

22. C. F. D. Moule, *The Origin of Christology* (Cambridge: Cambridge University Press, 1977), p. 5.

23. Gunton, p. 201.

24. Ramm, p. 195. A. N. S. Lane says, "It is futile to deny that the Chalcedonian definition is an expression of the doctrine of the incarnation in terms of ancient Greek thought.... But this is not necessarily to criticize Chalcedon.... The impression is soemtimes given that to show that the concepts of patristic Christology arose from the Greek environment is to prove it false. But this is to fall into the genetic fallacy.... While the Fathers used Greek concepts, their resulting Christology was profoundly un-Greek.... The problem with many so-called modern 'translations' of Chalcedon is not that they seek to express it in today's terms, but that the Christology expressed is not that of Chalcedon but one of the heresies there condemned" (pp. 260 f.).

25. Ibid., p. 184.

26. George H. Tavard, *Images of the Christ: An Enquiry into Christology* (Lanham, MD: University Press of America, 1982), p. 44.

27. Ibid., p. 1.

28. Ramm, p. 16.

29. Diogenes Allen, *Philosophy for Understanding Theology* (Atlanta: John Knox, 1985), p. 106.

30. Marshall, "Incarnational Christology," p. 7.

31. Alan Richardson, *An Introduction to the Study of the New Testament* (London: SCM, 1968), p. 196.

32. Lane, p. 273. Bernard Lonergan expressed well the limits of classical terms in both their intent and attainment when he wrote, "The distinction between person and nature is added to state what is one and the same and what are not one and the same. The person is one and the same; the

natures are not one and the same. While later developments put persons and natures in many further contexts, the context of Chalcedon needs no more than heuristic concepts. What is a person or hypostasis? It is in the Trinity what there are three of and in the Incarnation what there is one of. What is a nature? In the Trinity it is what there is one of and in the Incarnation what there are two of." *A Second Collection*, ed. by F. E. Crowe (Philadelphia: Westminster, 1975), p. 259. Eric Mascall adds: "Lonergan's point is plain. It is that, in using the terms 'person' and 'nature,' Chalcedon was not committing the Church to any particular philosophical interpretation of them, but was using them 'heuristically' with just sufficient content to identify the objects to which they are applied." *Theology and the Gospel of Christ* (London: SPCK, 1977), p. 190.

33. Ibid.

34. David F. Wells, *The Person of Christ* (Westchester, IL: Crossway, 1984), p. 178.

35. Dietrich, p. 9.

36. Witness the modern tendency to define individuals primarily in terms of what we do. See my earlier comments on the New Testament basis for ontological language in note 62 on p. 252.

37. Wells, p. 175.

38. Gerald O'Collins, *What Are They Saying About Jesus?* (rev. ed.; New York: Paulist, 1983), p. 3.

39. Ibid.

40. Gunton, p. 206.

SELECT BIBLIOGRAPHY

Primary Sources

Adam, Karl. *Christ and the Western Mind*. Translated by Edward Bullough. New York: Macmillan, 1930.

_____. *The Christ of Faith*. Translated by Joyce Crick. New York: New American Library, 1962.

_____. *Christ Our Brother*. Translated by Dom Justin McCann. New York: Macmillan, 1931.

_____. "Jesus Christ and the Spirit of the Age." In *Germany's New Religion*, pp. 117–168. Wilhelm Hauer, et. al. Translated by T. S. K. Scott-Craig and R. E. Davies. New York: Abingdon, 1937.

_____. *Jesus Christus*. Third edition. Augsburg: Haas und Grabherr, 1934.

_____. "Die katholische Tübinger Schule." *Hochland* 24/2 (1926–27). Reprinted in *Gesammelte Aufsätze*, pp. 389–412. Edited by Fritz Hoffman. Augsburg: Institut. P. Haas, 1936.

_____. "Das Problem der Entmythologizierung und der Auferstehung des Christus." *Theologische Quartalschrift* 132 (1952):385–410.

_____. *The Son of God*. London: Sheed and Ward, 1979 (reprint of the 1934 edition).

_____. *The Spirit of Catholicism*. Revised edition. Translated by Justin McCann. New York: Macmillan, 1946.

Drey, Johann Sebastian von. *Das Apologetik als wissenschaftliche Nachweisung der Gottlichkeit des Christenthums in seiner Erscheinung.*
Zweite Band: Die Religion in ihrer geschichtlichen Entwicklung bis
zu ihrer vollendung durch die Offenbarung in Christus. Three
volumes. Mainz, 1843. Reprinted Frankfurt: Minerva, 1967.

_____. *Kurze Einleitung in das Studium der
Theologie.* Tübingen, 1819. Reprinted Frankfurt: Minerva, 1966.

Geiselmann, Josef Rupert. "Der Einfluss der Christologie des Konzils von
Chalkedon auf die Theologie Joh. Ad. Möhlers." In *Das Konzil von
Chalkedon,* III: 341–420. Edited by Aloys Grillmeier, S.J., and
Heinrich Bacht, S.J. Three volumes. Würzberg: Echter, 1954.

_____. "Der Glaube an Jesus Christus—Mythos
oder Geschichte? Zur Auseinandersetzung Joh. Ev. Kuhn mit
David Friedrich Strauss." *Theologische Quartalschrift* 129 (1949):
258–277, 418–439.

_____. "Die Glaubenswissenschaft der Katholische
Tübinger Schule in ihrer Grundlegung durch Johann Sebastian v.
Drey." *Theologische Quartalschrift* 111 (1930):49–117.

_____. *Jesus der Christus.* Erster Teil: Die Frage nach
dem historischem Jesus (second edition). Munich: Kösel, 1965.

_____. *Die katholische Tübinger Schule.* Freiburg:
Herder, 1964.

_____. *Lebendiger Glaube als geheiligter Überlieferung:
Der Grundgedanke der Theologie Johann Adam Möhlers und der
katholischen Tübinger Schule.* Mainz: Matthias-Grünewald, 1942.

_____. *Die lebendige Überlieferung als Norm des
christlichen Glaubens.* Freiburg: Herder, 1959.

_____. *The Meaning of Tradition.* Translated by W. J.
O'Hara. London: Burns & Oates, 1966.

_____. *Scripture and Tradition in Catholic Theology.*
Theology Digest 6 (1958):73–78.

_____. *Die theologische Anthropologie Johann Adam Möhlers*. Freiburg: Herder, 1955.

Kasper, Walter. *Das Absolute in der Geschichte: Philosophie und Theologie der Geschichte in der Spätphilosophie Schellings*. Mainz: Matthias-Grünewald, 1965.

_____. "Anthropologische Aspekte der Busse." *Theologische Quartalschrift* 163 (1983):96–109.

_____. "Christi Himmelfahrt—Geschichte und theologische Bedeutung." *Internationale katholische Zeitschrift* 12 (1983):205–213.

_____. "Christologie und Anthropologie." *Theologische Quartalschrift* 162 (1982):202–221.

_____. "Christologie von unten?" In *Grundfragen der Christologie heute*, pp. 141–170. Edited by Leo Scheffczyk. Freiburg: Herder, 1975.

_____. "Christsein ohne Tradition?" In *Diskussion über Hans Küngs "Christ sein,"* pp. 19–34. Edited by Hans Ur von Balthazar. Mainz: Matthias-Grünewald, 1976.

_____. "The Church's profession of Faith: On drafting a New Catholic catechism for adults." Translated by Sister Josephine Köppel, O.C.D. *Communio* 12 (1985):49–70.

_____. *Dogma unter dem Wort Gottes*. Mainz: Matthias-Grünewald, 1965.

_____. "Einige Verwunderte Gegenfragen," *Zeitschrift für katholische Theologie* 98 (1976):186–189.

_____. "Einmaligkeit und Universalität Jesu Christi." *Theologie der Gegenwart* 17 (1974):1–11.

_____. *Faith and the Future*. Translated by Robert Nowell. New York: Crossroad, 1982.

_____. "Freiheit des Evangeliums und dogmatische Bindung in der katholischen Theologie. Grundlagenüberlegungen zur Unfehlbarkeitsdebatte." In *Die Theologie und das Lehramt*. Quaestiones Disputatae 91, pp. 210–233. Edited by Walter Kern, S.J. Freiburg: Herder, 1982.

_____. "Für eine Christologie in geschichtlicher Perspektive: Replik auf die Anmerkungen von Hans Küng." In *Grundfragen der Christologie heute*, pp. 179–183. Edited by Leo Scheffczyk. Freiburg: Herder, 1975.

_____. "Geschichtlichkeit der Dogmen?" *Stimmen der Zeit* 179 (1967):401–416.

_____. "Der Glaube an die Auferstehung Jesu vor dem Forum historischer Kritik." *Theologische Quartalschrift* 153 (1973): 229–241.

_____. *Glaube und Geschichte*. Mainz: Matthias-Grünewald, 1970.

_____. *The God of Jesus Christ*. Translated by Matthew J. O'Connell. New York: Crossroad, 1984.

_____. "Hope in Jesus' Final Coming." *Theology Digest* 33 (1986):149–154.

_____. "Hope in the Final Coming of Jesus Christ in Glory." Translated by Sr. Josephine Köppel, O.C.D. *Communio* 12 (1985):368–384.

_____. *An Introduction to Christian Faith*. Translated by V. Green. New York: Paulist Press, 1980.

_____. "Jesus im Streit der Meinungen." *Theologie der Gegenwart* 16 (1973):233–241.

_____. *Jesus the Christ*. Translated by V. Green. New York: Paulist Press, 1977.

_____. "Karl Adam." *Theologische Quartalschrift* 156 (1976): 251–258.

_____. "Krise und Neuanfang der Christologie im Denken Schellings." *Evangelische Theologie* 33 (1973):366–384.

_____. "Liberale Christologie." *Evangelische Kommentare* 9 (1976):357–360.

_____. *The Methods of Dogmatic Theology*. Translated by John Drury. New York: Paulist, 1969.

_____. "Neuansätze gegenwartiger Christologie." In *Christologische Schwerpunkte*, pp. 17–36. Edited by Walter Kasper. Düsseldorf: Patmos, 1980.

_____. "Orientations in Current Christology." *Theology Digest* 31 (1984):107–111.

_____. "Die Sache Jesu. Recht und Grenzen eines Interpretationsversuches." *Herder-Korrespondenz* 26 (1972):185–189.

_____. "The Spirit Acting in the World to Demolish Frontiers and Create the Future." *Lumen Vitae* 34 (1979):86–99.

_____. "Verstandnis der Theologie damals und heute." In *Theologie im Wandel*, pp. 90–115. Edited by the Catholic Theological Faculty of Tübingen University. Munich: Erich Wewel, 1968.

Kasper, Walter (editor). *Christologische Schwerpunkte*. Düsseldorf: Patmos, 1980.

Kasper, Walter and Schilson, Arno. *Christologie im Präsens: Kritische Sichtung neür Entwurfe*. Freiburg: Herder, 1974.

Küng, Hans. "Anmerkungen zu Walter Kasper, 'Christologie von unten?'" In *Grundfragen der Christologie heute*, pp. 170–179. Edited by Leo Scheffczyk. Freiburg: Herder, 1975.

_____. *Does God Exist? An Answer for Today*. Translated by Edward Quinn. Garden City: Doubleday, 1980.

_____. *Glauben an Jesus Christ*. Theologische Meditationen 59. Zurich: Benziger, 1982.

_____. *Justification: The Doctrine of Karl Barth and a Catholic Reflection*. Translated by Thomas Collins, et al. New York: Thomas Nelson, 1964.

_____. *On Being a Christian*. Translated by Edward Quinn. Garden City: Doubleday, 1976.

Küng, Hans, et al. *Christianity and the World Religions: Paths to Dialogue with Islam, Hinduism, and Buddhism*. Translated by Peter Heinegg. Garden City: Doubleday, 1986.

Kuhn, Johannes Evangelist. *Katholisches Dogmatik*, Zweite Band. Die christliche Lehre von der göttlichen Dreieinigkeit. Tübingen, 1857. Reprinted Frankfurt: Minerva, 1968.

_____. *Das Leben Jesu*. Mainz, 1838. Reprinted Frankfurt: Minerva, 1968.

Möhler, Johann Adam. *Die Einheit in der Kirche*. Edited by Josef Rupert Geiselmann. Darmstadt: Wissenschaftliche Buchgesellschaft, 1957.

_____. *Symbolik*. Edited by Josef Rupert Geiselmann. Darmstadt: Wissenschaftliche Buchgesellschaft, 1958.

Schelling, F. W. J. *The Ages of the World*. Translated by Frederick de Wolfe Bolman, Jr. New York: Columbia University, 1942.

_____. *Philosophie der Offenbarung*,1841/42. Edited by Manfred Frank. Frankfurt: Suhrkamp, 1977.

_____. "Vorlesungen über die Methoden des akademischen Studiums." In *Schellings Werke*, III: 229–374. Edited by Manfred Schroter. Six volumes. Munich: C. H. Beck'sche, 1958.

Staudenmaier, Franz Anton. *Encyklopadie der theologischen Wissenschaft* (second edition). Six volumes. Mainz, 1840. Reprinted Frankfurt: Minerva, 1968.

Swidler, Leonard (Editor and Translator). *Küng in Conflict*. Garden City: Doubleday, 1981.

National Conference of Catholic Bishops Committee on Doctrine (Compilers). *The Küng Dialogue*. Washington: United States Catholic Conference, 1980.

Secondary Sources

Aubert, Roger. "Karl Adam." In *Tendenzen der Theologie im 20. Jahrhundert*, pp. 156–162. Edited by Hans Jürgen Schultz. Stuttgart: Kreuz, 1966.

Auricchio, John, S.S.P. *The Future of Theology*. Staten Island: Alba House, 1970.

Berkhof, Hendrikus. *Introduction to the Study of Dogmatics*. Translated by John Vriend. Grand Rapids: Wm. B. Eerdmans, 1985.

Beumer, Johannes. "Theologie und Dogmengeschichte." In *Bilanz der Theologie im 20. Jahrhundert*, III:501–503. Edited by Herbert Vorgrimmler and Robert Vander Gucht. Three volumes. Freiburg: Herder, 1970.

Bouyer, Louis. "Christology from Above and Christology from Below." *Word & Spirit* 5 (1983):20–23.

Brosch, Hermann Josef. *Das Übernaturliche in der katholische Tübinger Schule*. Essen: Ludgerus-Verlag Hubert Wingen, 1962.

Brown, Raymond E. Review of *Jesus the Christ*, by Walter Kasper. *Catholic Biblical Quarterly* 39 (1977):583–585.

Burtchaell, James T. "Drey, Möhler, and the Catholic Tübingen School." In *Nineteenth Century Religious Thought in the West*, II:111–139. Edited by Ninian Smart, et. al. Three volumes. Cambridge: The University Press, 1986.

_____. "The Tübingen School." In *Catholic Theories of Biblical Inspiration Since 1810*, pp. 8–43. By James T. Burtchaell. Cambridge: The University Press, 1969.

Butterworth, Robert. "Questions to Hans Küng." *Heythrop Journal* 18 (1977):436–446.

Buuck, Friedrich. "Zur Geschichte der Theologie des 19. Jahrhunderts." *Scholastik* 18 (1948):54–77.

Carmody, John. *Theology for the 1980's*. Philadelphia: Westminster, 1980.

Chirico, Peter. "Hans Küng's Christology: An Evaluation of Its Presuppositions." *Theological Studies* 40 (1979):256–272.

Clarke, Thomas. "Current Christologies." *Worship* 53 (1979):438–448.

Clayton, John Powell. "Perspectives on Protestant and Catholic Thought in the Nineteenth Century." *European Studies Review* 10 (1980): 247–262.

Dawe, Donald G. "Christology in Contemporary Theology." *Interpretation* 26 (1972):259–277.

Dietrich, Donald J. *The Goethezeit and the Metamorphosis of Catholic Theology in the Age of Idealism*. Bern: Peter Lang, 1979.

Donovan, Daniel. "Küng and Kasper on Christ." *Ecumenist* 15 (1977): 17–23.

Dru, Alexander. *The Contribution of German Catholicism*. New York: Hawthorn, 1963.

Elze, M. "Tübingen I. Universität: Die kath.-theol. Fakultät." In *Die Religion in Geschichte und Gegenwart*, VI:1008–1009. Third edition. Edited by Hans Frhr. von Campenhausen, et. al. Six volumes. Tübingen: J. C. B. Mohr, 1962.

Fehr, Wayne L. *The Birth of the Catholic Tübingen School: The Dogmatics of Johann Sebastian Drey*. American Academy of Religion Series Number 37. Chico, CA: Scholars Press, 1981.

Fiorenza, Francis Schüssler. "Christology After Vatican II." *Ecumenist* 18 (1980):81–89.

Fitzer, Joseph. *Möhler and Baur in Controversy,1832–38: Romantic-Idealist Assessment of the Reformation and Counter-Reformation.* American Academy of Religion Studies in Religion Number 7. Tallahassee: American Academy of Religion, 1974.

Fries, Heinrich. "Paul von Schanz (1841–1905)." In *Katholische Theologen Deutschlands im 19. Jahrhundert*, III:190–214. Edited by Heinrich Fries and Georg Schwaiger. Three volumes. Munich: Kösel, 1975.

_____. "Tübinger Schule. I. Kath. T. S." In *Lexikon für Theologie und Kirche*, X:390–392. Second edition. Edited by Josef Hofer and Karl Rahner. Ten volumes. Freiburg: Herder, 1965.

Fries, Heinrich (editor). *Johannes von Kuhn.* Wegbereiter heutiger Theologie, Volume seven. Edited by Heinrich Fries and Johann Finsterholzl. Graz: Styria, 1973.

Gilmore, George B. "J. A. Möhler on Doctrinal Development." *Heythrop Journal* 19 (1978):383–404.

Graves, Thomas H. "The Functional Christology of Hans Küng." *Perspectives in Religious Studies* 8(1981):55–65.

Häring, Hermann and Kuschel, Karl-Josef (editors). *Hans Küng: His Work and His Way.* Translated by Robert Nowell. Garden City: Doubleday, 1980.

Hegel, G. W. F. *The Christian Religion.* AAR Texts and Translations Number 2. Edited and translated by Peter C. Hodgson. Missoula: Scholars Press, 1979.

_____. *The Phenomenology of Mind.* Translated by J. B. Baillie. New York: Harper and Row, 1981.

Heuser, Adolf. *Die Erlösungslehre in der katholischen deutschen Dogmatik von B. P. Zimmer bis M. Schmaus.* Essen: Ludgerus-Verlag Hubert Wingen, 1963.

Hocedez, Edgar, S.J. *La theologie au XIXe siecle.* Three volumes. Brussels: Descless de Brouwer, 1947–1952, I:231–251; II:297–308.

Hofmann, Fritz. "Theologie auf dem Geist der Tübinger Schule." *Theologische Quartalschrift* 146 (1966):262–284.

Hunermann, Peter. "Franz Anton Staudenmaier (1800–1852)." In *Katholische Theologen Deutschlands im 19. Jahrhundert*, II:99–128. Edited by Heinrich Fries and Georg Schwaiger. Three volumes. Munich: Kösel, 1977.

_____. "Die Hegel-Rezeption Frans Anton Staudenmaier." In *Kirche und Theologie im 19. Jahrhundert*, pp. 147–155. Edited by Georg Schwaiger. Göttingen: Vandenhoeck & Ruprecht, 1975.

_____. "Der Reflex des deutschen Idealismus in der Theologie der katholischen Tübinger Schule." *Philosophisches Jahrbuch der Görres-gesellschaft* 73 (1965–66):48–74.

Hunermann, Peter (editor). *Franz Anton Staudenmaier.* Wegbereiter heutiger Theologie, volume one. Edited by Heinrich Fries and Johann Finsterholzl. Graz: Styria, 1975.

Hunter, Harold. "Spirit Christology: Dilemma and Promise" *Heythrop Journal* 24 (1983):127–140, 266–277.

Kehl, Medard and Löser, Werner. "Situation de la Theologie Systematique en Allemagne." *Revue de Theologie et de Philosophie* 113 (1981):25–38.

Kern, Walter, S.J., "Das Christsein und die Christologie." *Stimmen der Zeit* 193 (1975):516–528.

Klinger, Elmar. "Tübingen School." In *Sacramentum Mundi*, VI:318–320. Edited by Karl Rahner. Six volumes. New York: Herder & Herder, 1970.

Krieg, Robert A. "Is Jesus the Focus of Küng's Christology?" *Heythrop Journal* 22 (1981):243–260.

_____. "Karl Adam's Christology: Toward a Post-Critical Method." *Heythrop Journal* 25 (1984):456–474.

_____. "Zur Aktualität der Christologie Karl Adams." *Theologische Quartalschrift* 166 (1986):92–107.

Lane, A. N. S. "Christology Beyond Chalcedon." In *Christ the Lord*, pp. 257–281. Edited by Harold H. Rowden. Downers Grove: Intervarsity, 1982.

Lachenschmid, Robert. "Christologie und Soteriologie." In *Bilanz der Theologie im 20. Jahrhundert*, III:82–120. Edited by Herbert Vorgrimmler and Robert Vander Gucht. Three volumes. Freiburg: Herder, 1970.

LaCugna, Catherine Mowry. *The Theological Methodology of Hans Küng*. American Academy of Religion Academy Series Number 39. Decatur, GA: Scholars Press, 1982.

Laubach, Jacob. "Karl Adam." in *Theologians of Our Time*, pp. 92–108. Edited by Leonhard Reinisch. Notre Dame: University of Notre Dame, 1964.

Loewe, William P. "The New Catholic Tübingen Theology of Walter Kasper: Foundational Issues." *Heythrop Journal* 31 (1980):30–49.

McBrien, Richard. *Catholicism*. Minneapolis: Winston, 1981.

McCool, Gerald A. *Catholic Theology in the Nineteenth Century*. New York: Seabury, 1977.

McDermott, Brian O. "Roman Catholic Christology: Two Recurring Themes." *Theological Studies* 41 (1980):339–367.

McFadden, T. M. "Christology." In *New Catholic Encyclopedia*, XVII (supp.):113–116. Edited by Thomas E. O'Brien. Seventeen volumes. New York: McGraw-Hill, 1979.

Mackey, James P. "Küng and Kasper Compared." *Living Light* 14 (1977):147–153.

Maurer, Wilhelm. "Der Organismusgedanke bei Schelling und in der Theologie der katholische Tübinger Schule." *Kerygma und Dogma* 8 (1962):202–216.

Meyer, Ben F. *The Aims of Jesus*. London: SCM, 1979.

Modras, Ronald. "Hans Küng—Catholic?" *Currents in Theology and Mission* 7 (1980):215–220.

Mondin, Battista. "The Christological Experiment of Hans Küng." Translated by W. Stanley Fleming. *Biblical Theological Bulletin* 7 (1977):77–88.

Neufeld, Karl H., S.J. "Zu: Walter Kasper, Jesus der Christus." *Zeitschrift für katholische Theologie* 98 (1976):180–185.

O'Collins, Gerald. *What Are They Saying About Jesus?* New York: Paulist, 1977 (second edition, 1983).

_____. *Interpreting Jesus*. Ramsey, NJ: Paulist, 1983.

O'Meara, Thomas F. "Christ in Schelling's Philosophy of Religion." *Heythrop Journal* 27 (1986):275–289.

_____. "F. W. J. Schelling: Bibliographical Essay." *Review of Metaphysics* 31 (1977):283–309.

_____. *Romantic Idealism and Roman Catholicism: Schelling and the Theologians*. Notre Dame: University of Notre Dame, 1982.

Ommen, Thomas B. *The Hermeneutics of Dogma*. AAR Dissertation Series Number 11. Missoula: Scholars Press, 1975.

Pollard, T. E. *Fullness of Humanity: Christ's Humanness and Ours*. Shefffield: Almond, 1982.

Ramm, Bernard L. *An Evangelical Christology: Ecumenic and Historic*. Nashville: Thomas Nelson, 1985.

Reardon, Bernard M. G. *Religion in the Age of Romanticism*. Cambridge: Cambridge University, 1985.

Reinhardt, Klaus. *Der dogmatische Schriftgebrauch in der Katholischen und Protestantischen Christologie von der Aufklärung bis zur Gegenwart.* Munich: Ferdinand Schöningh, 1970.

_____. "Die Einzigartigkeit der Person Jesu Christi." *Internationale katholische Zeitschrift* 2 (1973):206–224.

Reinhardt, Rudolf. "Die katholische-theologische Fakultät Tübingen im 19. Jahrhundert: Faktoren und Phasen ihrer Entwicklung." In *Kirche und Theologie im 19. Jahrhundert*, pp. 55–91. Edited by Georg Schwaiger. Göttingen: Vandenhoeck & Ruprecht, 1975.

Reinhardt, Rudolf (editor). *Tübinger Theologen und ihre Theologie.* Tübingen: J. C. B. Mohr, 1977.

Renz, Horst. *Gesichtsgedanke und Christusfrage.* Göttingen: Vandenhoeck und Ruprecht, 1977.

Riga, Peter. "The Ecclesiology of Johann Adam Möhler." *Theological Studies* 22 (1961):563–587.

Rosato, Philip J. "Between Christocentrism and Pneumatocentrism: An Interpretation of Johann Adam Möhler's Ecclesiology." *Heythrop Journal* 19 (1978):46–70.

_____. "Spirit Christology: Ambiguity and Promise." *Theological Studies* 38 (1977):423–449.

Savon, Herve. *Johann Adam Möhler: The Father of Modern Theology.* New York: Paulist, 1966.

Scheele, Paul-Werner (editor). *Johann Adam Möhler.* Wegbereiter heutiger Theologie, Volume four. Edited by Heinrich Fries and Johann Finsterholzl. Graz: Styria, 1969.

Scheffczyk, Leo. "Josef Rupert Geiselmann—Weg und Werk." *Theologische Quartalschrift* 150 (1970):383–395.

_____. *On Being a Christian: The Hans Küng Debate.* Translated by Peadar Mac Seamais, S.J. Dublin: Four Courts, 1982.

Scheffczyk, Leo (editor). *Theologie in Aufbruch und Widerstreit: Die deutsche katholische Theologie im 19. Jahrhundert.* Bremen: Carl Schunemann, 1965.

Schilson, Arno. "Lessing und die katholische Tübinger Schule." *Theologische Quartalschrift* 160 (1980):256–277.

Schleiermacher, F. D. E. *Brief Outline on the Study of Theology.* Translated by Terrence N. Tice. Atlanta: John Knox, 1977.

_____. *On Religion: Speeches to Its Cultured Despisers.* Translated by John Oman. New York: Harper and Row, 1958.

Schoff, T. M. *A Survey of Catholic Theology, 1800–1970.* Paramus, NJ: Paulist Newman, 1970.

Schupp, Franz, S.J. "Die Gesichtsauffassung am Beginn der Tübinger Schule und in der gegenwartigen Theologie." *Zeitschrift für katholische Theologie* 91 (1969):150–171.

Schweitzer, Albert. *The Quest of the Historical Jesus.* Translated by W. Montgomery. New York: Macmillan, 1968.

Seckler, Max. "Johann Sebastian Drey und die Theologie." *Theologische Quartalschrift* 158 (1978):92–109.

Stockmeier, Peter. "Die Kirchenväter in der Theologie der Tübinger Schule." In *Theologie im Wandel,* pp. 131–154. Edited by the Catholic Theological Faculty of the University of Tübingen. Munich: Erich Wewel, 1968.

Swidler, Leonard. *Aufklärung Catholicism, 1780–1850: Liturgical and Other Reforms in the Catholic Aufklärung.* AAR Studies in Religion Number 17. Missoula: Scholars Press, 1978.

Swidler, Leonard (editor). *Consensus In Theology? A Dialogue With Hans Küng and Edward Schillebeeckx.* Philadelphia: Westminster, 1980.

Tavard, George H. *Images of the Christ: An Enquiry into Christology.* Lanham, MD: University Press of America, 1982.

Thiel, John E. "J. S. Drey on Doctrinal Development: The Context of Theological Encyclopedia." *Heythrop Journal* 27 (1986):290–305.

Thomas, J. Heywood. "J. G. Fichte and F. W. J. Schelling." In *Nineteenth Century Religious Thought in the West*, I:31–79. Edited by Ninian Smart, et. al.   Three volumes. Cambridge: The University Press, 1985.

Thompson, William M. *The Jesus Debate: A Survey and Synthesis*. New York: Paulist, 1985.

Turk, Hans Gunther. "Philosophie-speculative Theologie-unmittelbare Gottesidee: Zum philosophischen und theologischen Denken des 'Tübingers' Johann Evangelist Kuhn." *Zeitschrift für katholische Theologie* 105 (1982):147–171.

Turner, M. M. B. "The Spirit of Christ and Christology." In *Christ the Lord*, pp. 168–190.   Edited by Harold H. Rowden. Downers Grove: Intervarsity, 1982.

Voss, Gustav, S.J. "Johann Adam Möhler and the Development of Dogma." *Theological Studies* 4 (1943):420–444.

Wells, David F. *The Person of Christ*. Westchester, IL: Crossway, 1984.

Welte, Bernhard. "Beobachtungen zum Systemgedanken in der Tübinger katholischen Schule." *Theologische Quartalschrift* 147 (1967):40–59.

_____. "Zum Structurwandel der katholischen Theologie 19. Jahrhundert." In *Auf der Spur des Ewigen*, pp. 380–409. Freiburg: Herder, 1965.

White, Alan. *Schelling: An Introduction to the System of Freedom*. New Haven: Yale University, 1983.

Wolfinger, Franz.   "Johannes Evangelist von Kuhn (1806–1887)." In *Katholische Theologen Deutschlands im 19. Jahrhundert*, II:129–162. Edited by Heinrich Fries and Georg Schwaiger.   Three volumes. Munich: Kösel, 1977.

INDEX

Adam 52, 59, 78, 125, 146, 160, 232, 300;

Adam, Karl 8, 16, 23, 24, 54, 83, **119-178**, 179, 192, 195, 196, 201, 203, 214, 222, 246, 248, 249, 294, 300, 302, 309;
  The Christ of Faith 122, 147-152, 163;
  The Spirit of Catholicism 120, 121, 126, 130;

Adoptionism 6, 11, 240, 241, 242, 245, 247, 257, 317;

Anhypostasis 18, 148, 220, 317;

Anonymous Christianity 242, 257, 280;

Anselm of Canterbury 54, 58, 60, 218, 232-233;

Anthropology 15, 16, 46, 52, 54, 56, 57, 60, 75, 122, 163, 213, 214, 215, 217, 225, 232, 240, 243;

Apocalyptic 186, 194-195, 280;

Apollinarianism 77;

Apollinarius 238, 287;

Apologetics 27, 40, 50, 51, 83, 105, 106, 107, 108, 117, 145, 151, 196, 262, 264, 282, 287;

Aquinas, Thomas 26, 158, 218, 222;

Arianism 95, 238;

Arius 140, 287, 300, 313;

Athanasius 33, 81, 82, 113-114;

Atonement 33, 81, 82, 113-114, 161, 162;

Augustine 95, 120, 121, 125, 126, 127, 160, 218;

Barth, Karl 121, 124, 131, 261, 264, 318;

Baur, J. C. 39, 54, 58, 63;

Bergson, Henri 121;

Bible 2, 11, 13, 16, 17, 45, 47, 48, 51, 57, 81, 112, 113, 121, 122, 123-126, 127, 128, 149, 170, 186, 192, 207, 209, 268, 271, 273, 277, 290, 298, 299-300, 301, 305, 306, 310, 314;

Biblical criticism 7, 11, 48, 51, 79, 86, 87-89, 122, 123, 125, 127, 142, 148, 149, 150, 162, 169, 174, 183-188, 191, 195, 196, 203, 212, 216, 245, 247, 249, 254, 258, 261, 263, 266, 267, 270, 271, 306, 307, 321;

Boethius 148, 151;

Bultmann, Rudolf 87, 139, 148, 149, 162, 184, 186, 188, 190, 209, 212, 232, 309;

Calvin, John 74, 113;

Catholic Tübingen School 1, 6-12, 14, 15, 16, 17, 19, 21-24, 27, 29, 39, 40, 41, 53,

54, 73, 95, 96, 106, 115,
119, 120, 121, 122, 126,
130, 162, 166, 179-180,
196, 198, 201, 202, 206,
246, 248, 258, 288, 322;

Chalcedon 3, 5, 6, 14, 15, 18, 56,
59, 60, 62, 64, 94, 109,
125, 135, 137, 138, 151,
163, 168, 210, 212, 215,
216, 221, 225, 230, 234,
238-239, 244, 246, 263,
274, 277, 282, 284, 291,
297, 298, 299, 302, 303,
304, 305, 307, 311, 312-
313, 319, 320, 324, 325;

Christ (see also Jesus) 1, 5, 16,
18, 19, 29-34, 36, 40, 44,
45, 47, 49-50, 51, 52, 54,
55, 56, 57, 59, 60-61, 62,
63, 66, 74, 75, 76, 77-82,
83, 84, 85, 87-88, 89, 90,
92, 93, 94, 95, 97, 101,
102, 109-111, 114, 115,
133-141, 145-147, 157,
159, 160, 161, 164, 166,
168, 181, 182, 183, 185,
186, 187, 189, 193, 194,
195-196, 198, 202, 203,
210, 211, 213, 214, 216,
219, 221, 223, 226, 232,
234, 235, 236, 237, 238,
239, 242, 243, 244, 246,
251, 255, 257, 265, 267,
269, 270, 272, 273, 274,
277, 281, 282, 283, 287,
289, 290, 294, 298, 299,
300, 301, 302, 303, 305,
311, 314, 315, 317, 319,
320, 321;
Christ of faith 123, 152,

181, 182, 210, 220, 237,
269, 271;
Death of Christ 33, 47,
50, 50, 59, 61, 80, 81, 82,
88, 91, 113, 115, 117, 145-
147, 156, 164, 193, 223,
225, 232, 233, 246, 253,
267, 276, 277-278, 314,
316, 318;
God-man 33, 52, 75, 76,
77, 85, 92, 110, 112, 114,
126, 127, 139, 140, 147,
153, 161, 196, 282;
Person of Christ   120,
122, 123, 125, 126, 133,
140, 141, 148, 153, 156,
157, 160, 165, 188, 193,
194, 216, 220, 224, 239,
240, 245, 253, 265, 273,
275, 278, 280, 306, 313,
319, 321;
Titles 79, 82, 92-94, 134,
144, 188-191, 196, 210,
216, 224, 238, 272, 273,
276;
Work of Christ 1, 6, 47,
49, 52, 57, 59, 61, 76, 78-
82, 83, 91, 93, 120, 122,
126, 133, 146, 153, 157,
161, 182, 188, 193, 194,
214, 217, 232, 233, 240,
245, 273, 313, 319;

Christology 1, 2, 4, 5, 6, 10-12,
14-16, 17, 23, 27, 30, 32,
34, 37, 40, 45, 46, 47, 48,
49, 51, 52, 53, 54, 55, 56,
58-62, 64, 74, 75, 76, 77,
83-85, 89, 91, 92-95, 96,
97, 105, 108, 109, 110,
115, 116, 117, 119, 120,

122, 123, 124, 126, 130-
145, 147, 149, 151, 152-
163, 164, 166, 169, 170,
180, 188-191, 196, 197,
199, 201, 202, 203, 204,
207, 208, 210, 211-214,
215-217, 220, 221, 222,
224-225, 226, 227, 229,
231, 234-247, 248, 251,
253, 259, 261, 262, 263,
264, 265-266, 268-280,
282-283, 285, 286, 287,
291, 294, 295, 297, 298,
300, 301, 303, 305-306,
309-315, 318-321, 322,
324;
"from above" 14-16, 30,
97, 115, 207, 214, 215,
217, 220, 221, 225, 236,
244, 264, 265, 270, 276,
281, 302, 310;
"from below" 14-16, 30,
52, 97, 115, 123, 141, 207,
212, 214, 215, 217, 220,
221, 225, 236, 244, 259,
265, 266, 269, 270, 276,
281, 302, 310;
Pneuma-sarx 241;
Church 1-3, 4, 10, 11, 12, 19, 40,
41, 42, 43, 44, 45, 47, 50,
51, 53-55, 58, 60, 61, 62,
63, 64, 66, 70, 71, 75, 79,
93, 95, 110, 119, 120-121,
122, 123, 124, 126, 128,
129-130, 133, 134, 147,
148-149, 150, 151, 159,
163, 165, 166, 167, 202,
204-205, 206, 210, 212,
214, 216, 233, 241, 242-
243, 245, 249, 251, 258,
272, 287, 296, 298, 299,

300, 301, 302, 304, 311,
312, 313, 316, 319, 320,
322, 325;
Context 3, 16-17, 207, 237, 261,
271, 273, 277, 280, 303,
313, 319-320;
Contextualization 3, 17, 19, 211,
298, 305, 319;
Covenant 50, 61, 81, 161, 240,
309;
Creation 2, 30, 31, 42, 44, 46, 49,
55, 59, 62, 74, 77, 78, 227,
236, 301, 308, 315, 317;
Critical method 270, 283, 303,
306, 321;
Critical scholarship 150, 164,
170, 306, 310;
Cross 3, 30, 49, 50, 52, 61, 64, 97,
110, 113, 114, 117, 146,
164, 214, 215, 226, 229;
Cullmann, Oscar 188;
Culture 3-5, 7, 12, 16, 19, 20,
166, 211, 212, 234, 245,
298, 302, 319-320;
Deification 59, 63, 135, 139, 153,
160, 232, 281;
Deism 54;
Deity 2, 15, 28, 29, 30, 34, 48, 49,
51, 55, 57, 59, 61, 62, 63,
64, 71, 77, 78, 79, 83, 89,
91, 92, 93, 94, 97, 108,
109, 110, 111, 115, 124,
125, 127, 130, 131, 133,
134, 135, 136, 137, 138,
139, 140, 152, 153, 155,
157, 158, 159, 160, 164,
165, 184, 192, 194, 200,
220, 222, 232, 236, 239,
274, 277, 316, 318;
Demythologization 31, 139, 182,
186, 187, 267;

Dilthey, Wilhelm 121;

Docetism 52, 58, 90, 102, 153, 223, 224, 229, 317;

Doctrinal development 40, 41, 42-43, 45, 68, 106, 212, 269, 283, 301;

Doctrine 1, 4, 5, 6, 20, 29, 32, 40, 42, 44, 45, 50, 51, 52, 53, 58, 59, 60, 64, 84, 94, 105, 126, 147, 154, 156, 166, 179, 199, 234, 247, 261, 264, 283, 286, 299, 301, 322;

Dogma 8, 13, 51, 54, 55, 56, 59, 64, 75, 85, 97, 120, 122, 126, 128, 139, 147, 149, 163, 178, 203, 205, 206, 207, 211, 213, 214, 216, 218, 224, 234-235, 238, 258-259, 268, 269, 282, 283, 303, 306;

Drey, Johann Sebastian 9, 10, 11, 13, 14, 16, 27, 29, 34-35, **39-53**, 54, 64, 65-67, 73, 76, 79, 80, 83, 84, 106, 121, 122, 162, 202, 246, 297, 300;

Easter 146, 161, 184, 185, 186, 187, 188, 189, 191, 216, 224, 227, 229-230, 268, 270, 272, 277, 278;

Ecclesiology (see also Church) 8, 40, 55-58, 59, 60, 68, 96, 110, 120, 122, 126, 130, 133, 147, 202, 301, 319;

Education 44, 47, 50;

Enhypostasis 18, 148, 220, 317;

Enlightenment, The 4, 7, 9, 12, 27, 28, 40, 41, 43, 54, 121, 130, 132, 146, 180, 182, 186, 203, 208, 285, 301;

Epistemology 14, 124, 285, 286;

Eschatology 14, 42, 53, 110, 125, 126, 144, 159, 192, 193, 194, 206, 213, 216, 221, 223, 224, 227, 232, 234, 235, 237, 238, 241, 254, 300, 303;

Ethics 46;

Eucharist 60, 133;

Evil 46, 47, 51, 164, 223, 227, 233;

Evolution 105, 204;

Exaltation 33, 82, 190, 230, 255, 276, 278;

Exegesis 31, 80, 84, 101, 106, 180, 202, 203, 216, 299, 300;

Faith 10, 13, 23, 30, 41, 49, 61, 75, 79, 80, 84, 85, 88, 89, 111, 121, 122, 124, 127, 138, 148, 149, 150, 151, 152, 157, 158, 162, 168, 181, 183, 196, 203, 204, 205, 217, 229, 244, 262, 267, 269, 276, 277, 282, 290, 294, 298, 299;

Fall 32, 46, 48, 60, 158, 160;

Freedom 10, 27, 28, 29, 33, 35, 44, 51, 59, 61, 74, 75, 82, 80, 83, 91, 158, 164, 202, 203, 208, 209, 214, 216, 219, 222, 227, 231, 238, 243, 304;

Fries, Heinrich 106, 114, 115, 163;

Function 14, 48, 206, 212, 214, 216, 217, 219, 220, 223, 224, 241, 244, 245, 246, 252, 271, 272-278, 282, 291, 292, 293, 302, 303, 313, 319, 325;

Funk, F. X. 179-180;

Gadamer, Hans-Georg 4, 20, 309;

Geiselmann, Josef Rupert 21, 22, 23, 55, 56, 68, 84, 87, 97, 115, 119, **179-200**, 202, 211, 248;

Gnosticism 2, 58, 122, 153, 154, 186, 224;

God 1-3, 5, 9, 12, 13, 15, 16, 19, 23, 28, 29, 32, 33-34, 41, 42, 43, 44, 45-46, 47, 48, 50, 51, 52, 54, 59, 61, 62, 74, 75, 76, 77, 78, 79, 81, 85, 87, 89, 90, 91- 93, 94, 95, 96, 102, 109, 111, 112, 114, 116, 121, 122, 125, 126, 127, 129, 131, 132, 134, 136, 137, 138, 139, 140, 141, 141, 143, 144, 145, 146, 148, 150, 153, 155, 156, 159, 160, 161, 168, 181, 184, 189, 192, 193, 202, 203, 205, 207, 209, 210, 211, 213, 214, 215, 218, 219, 220, 221, 222, 223, 224, 225, 226-227, 228, 231, 233, 235, 236, 237, 239, 240, 241, 243, 257, 265, 266, 267, 270, 271, 272, 273, 274, 275, 276, 278, 279, 282, 285, 290, 291, 292, 293, 294, 298, 301, 302, 304, 308, 312, 314, 315, 316, 318, 320, 321;

Grace 120, 127, 129-130, 161, 227, 232;

Gunton, Colin 305, 307, 310, 311, 319-320:

Harnack, Adolf von 198;

Hegel, Georg W. F. 6, 7, 8, 10, 12, 27, 28, 29, 35, 54, 55, 58, 62, 63, 64, 74, 84, 141, 211, 213, 238, 261, 265, 266;

Hegelianism 6, 14, 141, 265, 285, 306;

Heidegger, Martin 20, 243;

Heilsgeschichte 184, 189;

Hellenism 14, 19, 154, 174, 189, 207, 212, 217, 236-237, 238, 268, 272, 273, 275, 277, 279, 288, 291, 292, 302, 312, 324;

Hengel, Martin 252;

Hermeneutics 3-7, 17, 20, 169, 181-183, 217, 235, 285, 300, 308, 309-310;

Historicity 13, 16, 17, 42, 50, 63, 74, 75, 85, 88, 90, 91, 96, 127, 141, 145, 157, 162, 180, 196, 208, 216, 245, 263, 267, 298, 305, 312;

Historicism 12;

History 1, 4-6, 8, 9, 10, 11, 12-14, 15, 16, 17, 28, 29, 30, 31, 32, 34, 35, 40, 42, 43, 44, 47, 48, 50, 53, 55, 58, 60, 74, 75, 76, 79, 81, 83, 84, 85, 108, 122-124, 133, 136, 139, 150-152, 153, 161, 163, 168, 179, 181, 182, 184, 185, 186, 187-188, 194-195, 199, 202, 203, 206, 209, 211, 213, 215, 216, 222, 223, 225, 226, 230, 231, 234, 235, 236, 238, 261, 263 266, 267, 268, 272, 278, 279, 285, 289, 294, 298, 299, 306, 307-309, 311, 313, 316;

Hofmann, Fritz   120-121, 163, 165;

Humanity 1, 2, 15, 19, 31-34, 40, 41, 42, 44, 45, 47, 48, 49-50, 52, 54, 55, 56, 58, 59, 61, 62, 63, 71, 76, 77, 78, 79, 89, 91, 97, 110, 111-112, 115, 117, 120, 122, 124, 125, 126, 127, 128, 129, 131, 132, 133, 134, 135-136, 137, 138, 139, 140, 143, 146, 151, 153, 154, 156, 157, 158, 159, 160, 163, 164, 165, 169, 182, 192-195, 200, 202, 203, 215, 220, 222, 223, 227-228, 233, 235, 236, 238, 239, 269, 270, 271, 273, 281, 303, 311, 315, 316, 317-318;

Humanization 232, 281;

Hypostatic union   18, 56, 109, 110, 140, 156, 157, 158, 160, 165, 192, 222, 238, 325;

Idealism 9, 10, 13, 14, 30, 40, 41, 42, 46, 51, 54, 58, 59, 61, 62, 64, 74, 75, 76, 81, 132, 164, 211, 270, 290;

Incarnation 3, 30, 32-34, 44, 47, 48, 50, 55, 56, 57, 60, 61, 62, 63, 64, 66, 70, 74, 77, 78, 90, 91, 96, 97, 102, 108, 109, 110, 125, 127, 135, 136, 137, 138, 139, 146, 151, 156, 157, 158, 159, 160, 161, 164, 170, 192, 203, 214, 220, 223, 225, 226, 239, 244, 246, 253, 276, 278-281, 282, 284, 293, 294, 302, 308,

310, 314, 315-316, 317, 318, 324, 325;

Irenaeus 52, 54;

Jeremias, Joachim 185;

Jesus (see also Christ) 1-3, 5, 12, 13, 15, 16, 18, 19, 27, 30-34, 43, 45, 47, 48, 50, 52, 55, 56, 62, 63, 75, 76, 77, 78, 79, 85, 86, 87-88, 89, 90-91, 93, 96, 107, 108, 109, 111, 117, 120, 121, 122, 123-125, 128, 129, 131, 132, 133, 135, 136, 137, 138, 140-147, 148, 150, 154-156, 157, 158, 160, 161, 162, 163, 165, 166, 168, 171, 174, 181, 182, 183, 185, 186, 187, 188-189, 190, 192-195, 196, 200, 202, 203, 210, 211, 213, 214, 215, 216, 220, 221, 222, 223, 225, 227, 228-229, 232, 233, 234, 235, 236, 237, 238, 239-240, 241, 242, 243, 244, 246, 252, 255, 257, 262, 265, 266, 267, 269, 271, 272, 273, 274, 275, 276, 277, 278, 279, 282, 283, 285, 287, 289, 290, 291, 292, 293, 294, 297, 299, 301, 302, 303, 305, 307, 309, 310, 311, 312, 315, 316, 317, 319, 320, 321, 323;

Historical Jesus 13, 123, 141, 152, 181, 182, 196, 220, 238, 266, 269, 270, 271, 284, 290, 323;

Jesus of Nazareth 132, 141, 185, 270, 273, 276,

285, 291, 293, 312;

John, Gospel of 34, 47, 48, 77, 88, 89, 107, 109, 111, 124, 142, 148, 155, 157, 168, 169, 189, 190, 200, 211, 222, 226, 241, 272, 278, 279, 292, 295;

Judaism 31, 76, 90, 92, 130, 192, 224;

Justification 261, 264;

Kant, Immanuel 6, 7, 41, 54, 232;

Käsemann, Ernst 212, 252, 261, 263, 266;

Kasper, Walter 9, 10-11, 13, 14, 15, 16-17, 23, 26, 27, 34, 37, 84, 119, 123, 139, 164, 165, 166, 196, 199, **201-259**, 263, 273, 280, 282, 293, 297, 297, 299, 300, 301, 303, 305, 309, 310, 315, 317, 322;

Kenosis 30, 31, 34, 37, 125, 156, 157, 170, 223, 226;

Kenoticism 6;

Kerygma 85, 86-87, 88, 90, 92, 181, 183, 185, 186, 187, 194, 196, 211, 236;

Kingdom of God 23, 27, 35, 40, 41, 42, 43, 44, 45-46, 48, 49, 50, 51, 52, 53, 71, 79-80, 81, 125, 126, 129, 130, 143-144, 156, 159, 182, 184, 189, 191, 193, 194, 215, 224, 226-229, 230, 231, 243, 254, 270, 276, 280, 300, 301, 302-303, 309, 310;

Kirchlichkeit 299, 322;

Knitter, Paul 12, 322;

Kuhn, Johann Evangelist 14, 35,

73, **83-97**, 100-102, 106, 111, 115, 119, 121, 122, 161, 162, 181, 183, 188, 190, 195, 199, 298;

Küng, Hans 6, 24, 53, 65-66, 201, 203, 212, 243, 244, 245, 246, 247, 248, 257, 258, **261-296**, 297, 303, 309;
Does God Exist? 281, 286, 291, 293-294;
On Being a Christian 266, 286, 290, 291, 294;

Lamentabili 122, 168-169;

Leontius of Byzantium 18, 148, 151;

Lessing, G. E. 13, 208, 298, 307, 309, 316;

Liberalism 6, 30, 122, 123, 127, 133, 151, 163, 170, 182, 198;

Locke, John 218;

Logos 18-19, 60, 77, 85, 89, 90, 93, 108, 151, 157, 158, 160, 165, 189, 192, 210, 211, 221, 226, 237, 241, 276, 278, 279, 317;

Luke, Gospel of 77, 89, 107, 108, 112, 115, 143, 144, 155, 187, 188, 189, 190, 193;

Luther, Martin 134;

Mariology 20, 127;

Mark, Gospel of 34, 89, 107, 109, 115, 146, 189, 192, 193;

Marshall, I. H. 307, 309, 310, 316;

Mary 127, 171, 312;

Matthew, Gospel of 48, 77, 88, 89, 107, 125, 144, 148, 155, 188-189, 190, 193;

Mediator 31, 49, 60, 79, 81, 89, 125, 127, 133, 140, 160,

165, 210, 276, 312, 320;

Messiah 50, 82, 85, 86, 88, 89, 90,
    91, 92, 93, 109, 111, 113,
    115, 144, 148, 153, 154,
    165, 168, 183, 188, 189,
    190, 194, 196;

Metaphysics 14, 15, 28, 41, 75,
    153, 155, 156, 158, 207,
    209, 211, 217, 226, 235,
    243, 252, 271, 272, 274,
    275;

Miracles 50, 51, 62, 78-79, 80, 84,
    86, 87, 89, 109, 111, 114,
    124, 132, 137, 141, 146,
    150, 151, 189, 228, 267,
    277, 314, 317;

Modernism 122, 162, 170;

Möhler, Johann Adam 10, 11, 14,
    22, 35, 39-40, **53-64**, 66,
    68-71, 73, 83, 96, 106,
    110, 120, 121, 122, 126,
    127, 162, 179, 258, 299,
    303;
    Die Einheit in der Kirche
    39, 54, 56, 57, 60;
    Symbolik 39, 54, 57, 59,
    60, 63;

Monophysitism 5, 18, 19, 52, 62,
    94, 115, 125, 134-135,
    138, 139, 140, 151, 158,
    163, 182, 192, 238, 274,
    312;

Moltmann, Jürgen 213;

Moule, C. F. D. 310;

Myth 29, 48, 58, 63, 75, 81, 85,
    87, 90, 95, 96, 101, 128,
    133, 182, 184, 186, 187,
    188, 195, 208, 216, 232,
    252, 268, 284, 301, 315;

Nature (human or divine) 2, 3, 5,
    18, 19, 32, 46, 47, 49, 52,

60, 74, 78, 80, 82, 89, 93,
    102, 107, 109, 112, 125,
    126, 138, 139, 147, 151,
    156, 158, 160, 190, 192,
    210, 222, 224, 225, 232,
    245, 265, 271, 273, 274,
    277, 282, 289, 291, 302,
    315, 317, 324-325;

Neo-Romanticism 121, 134, 139,
    142, 162, 164;

Neoscholasticism 35, 83, 105,
    119, 123, 138, 170, 261,
    265;

Nestorianism 18, 33, 34, 85, 193,
    244;

New Testament 2, 15, 31, 49, 72,
    76, 80, 87, 90, 93, 94, 107,
    109, 110, 125, 127, 142,
    148, 152-162, 164, 181,
    184, 186, 190, 191, 205,
    212, 222, 223, 224, 225,
    228, 230, 232, 236, 238,
    240, 242, 246, 252, 257,
    266, 270, 272, 273, 274,
    275, 276, 278, 280, 283,
    284, 291, 292, 294, 300,
    305, 309, 310, 311, 313,
    314, 316, 319, 323, 325;

Nicea, Council of 3, 37, 62, 94,
    135, 151, 168, 238, 291,
    300, 313;

Nietzsche, Friedrich 204;

O'Collins, Gerald 202, 211, 271,
    284, 319;

Old Testament 31, 48, 50, 76, 78,
    79, 80, 81, 88, 91, 92, 102,
    107, 113, 115, 125, 137,
    148, 153, 161, 162, 174,
    188, 194, 205, 210, 229,
    239, 257, 272, 275, 276,
    278, 280, 295, 305-306;

Ontology 14-15, 48, 54, 77, 93,
    190, 203, 207, 212, 214,
    216, 217, 218, 219, 220,
    221, 222, 223, 224, 231,
    232, 238, 240, 241, 244,
    246, 252, 264, 271, 274,
    275, 276, 277, 282, 285,
    287, 293, 302, 310, 313,
    315, 317, 320, 325;
Original sin 133, 160, 231;
Pannenberg, Wolfhart 202, 213,
    239, 253, 256, 293, 308;
Parousia 159, 193, 233, 234, 255;
Particularism 12, 320;
Pascendi 152;
Patristics 1, 8, 11, 52, 57, 58, 60,
    62, 64, 84, 107, 148, 157,
    158, 169, 191, 223, 236,
    237, 246, 276, 290, 317,
    324;
Person 1, 3, 5, 6, 18, 31, 32, 33,
    47, 49, 50, 55, 57, 59, 60,
    61, 62, 75, 76, 77-78, 83,
    91, 92, 93, 94-95, 109-111,
    125, 132, 135, 140, 148,
    151, 157, 158, 215, 217-
    218, 220, 222, 223, 239,
    240, 271, 299, 304, 317-
    318, 324-325;
Phenomenology 121, 124, 169,
    245;
Philosophy 3, 4, 6-8, 9, 10, 14,
    18, 19, 27, 31, 40, 41, 45,
    52, 58, 62-63, 75, 96, 121,
    131, 138, 148, 150, 202-
    203, 211, 212, 213, 215,
    216, 221, 236-237, 238-
    239, 240, 243, 265, 270,
    275, 287, 300, 305, 309,
    312, 318-319, 325;
Pluralism 14, 320;

Pre-existence 30, 47, 48, 77, 90,
    93, 101, 109, 142, 155,
    156, 157, 216, 219, 220,
    225, 240, 244, 246, 252,
    265, 276, 278-281, 282,
    284, 314, 315-316;
Prophecy 31, 50, 51, 78, 87, 92,
    111, 113, 115;
Propitiation 50, 52;
Protestantism 6-8, 10, 27, 40, 51,
    110, 123, 133, 135, 137,
    138, 149, 151, 186, 198,
    261, 263, 295, 311, 312,
    318;
Psychology 121, 145, 152, 217,
    218, 222, 317;
Rahner, Karl 6, 14, 110, 139, 193,
    202, 213, 243, 257, 276,
    318;
Ramm, Bernard L. 212, 306, 312,
    314;
Reconciliation 79, 211, 318;
Redemption 49, 60, 61, 75, 76,
    81, 110, 112, 113, 125,
    133, 136, 154, 160, 161,
    226, 231, 232;
Religion 6, 12, 29, 43, 44, 46, 54,
    58, 74, 76, 84, 97, 123,
    134, 149, 241-242;
Renan, Joseph Ernest 145;
Resurrection 1, 18, 34, 47, 59, 78,
    82, 86, 88, 89, 91, 114,
    117, 137, 145-147, 148,
    153, 156, 161-162, 164,
    168, 185, 214, 215, 223,
    225, 228, 229-230, 233,
    239-240, 241, 246, 253,
    255, 276, 277, 278, 302,
    314, 316-317;
Revelation 2, 16, 28, 29, 31, 34,
    40, 41, 42, 43, 44, 45, 46,

48, 50, 52, 54, 58, 75, 76,
85, 88, 89, 93, 120, 121,
129, 180, 202-203, 207,
242, 244, 263, 274, 276,
292, 293, 298, 299, 308,
318;
Ricoeur, Paul 20;
Roman Catholicism 14, 22, 28,
34, 40, 42, 43, 51, 54, 55,
91, 105, 110, 119, 129,
130, 136, 137, 138, 149,
163, 180, 201, 202, 203,
212, 262, 273, 298, 311,
312, 314, 318;
Romanticism 9, 10, 13, 27, 28,
42, 51, 55, 74, 121, 133,
142, 180;
Sacraments 105, 127, 139, 165,
241;
Salvation 2, 5, 6, 15, 16, 33, 47,
49, 50, 52, 54, 55, 59, 75,
79, 80, 82, 85, 89, 92, 110,
113-114, 127, 128, 129-
130, 133, 136, 139, 140,
144, 146, 147, 153, 154,
155, 158, 159, 161, 171,
184, 189, 193, 194, 207,
209, 211, 213, 214, 215,
217, 220, 221, 223, 226,
228, 230, 231, 233, 236,
238, 241, 244, 253, 257,
275, 278, 281, 282, 286,
291, 302, 305, 313, 317,
320;
Salvation history 29, 88, 148, 162,
180, 181, 196, 207, 209,
211, 306;
Schanz, Paul 23, 105-118, 179;
Scheeben, M. J. 222;
Scheffczyk, Leo 115, 180, 285;
Scheler, Max 124;

Schelling, Friedrich Wilhelm
Joseph 6, 7, 8, 9-10, **27-
38**, 40, 41, 42, 44, 45, 52,
54, 55, 58, 62, 74, 84, 87,
202, 203, 211, 216, 221,
238, 246;
Schillebeeckx, Edward 6;
Schleiermacher, Friedrich David
Ernst 6, 7, 10, 39, 41,
52, 54, 55, 56, 58, 59, 62,
63, 64, 74, 87, 232;
Scholasticism 58, 121, 288;
Schoonenberg, Piet 6, 212;
Schweitzer, Albert 186, 230;
Science 6, 29, 45, 117, 208, 228,
269;
Scripture 13, 16, 17, 19, 23, 45,
61, 75, 77, 80, 85-86, 92,
96, 107, 121, 124, 126,
128, 137, 139, 148, 149,
152, 154, 158, 163, 166,
181, 183-184, 203, 207,
208, 209, 211, 214, 215,
218, 220, 221, 222, 229,
235, 236-237, 240, 242,
262, 265, 266, 272, 282,
299, 300, 301, 309, 311,
312, 313, 316, 320, 321;
Seckler, Max 11;
Second Adam 52, 59, 82, 125,
139, 140;
Secularism 204;
Sin 46-47, 49, 52, 54, 59, 74, 78,
81, 82, 110, 111, 113, 145,
158, 160, 161, 174, 224,
225-226, 230, 231, 233,
278, 302, 316;
Sinlessness 49, 63, 78, 93, 113,
158, 223;
Sloyan, Gerard S. 245, 263-264,
266, 283;

Sobrino, Jon 6;
Son of God 30, 32, 48, 71, 78, 89,
        92, 111, 112, 113, 125,
        139, 140, 141, 142, 148,
        152, 153, 156, 158, 165,
        168, 186, 189, 191, 210,
        220, 221, 223, 224, 232,
        241, 245, 246, 252, 272,
        274, 275, 276, 277, 279,
        291, 310, 315, 316;
Son of Man 82, 125, 141, 144,
        148, 155, 165, 174, 190,
        224, 300;
Soteriology 45, 106, 122, 156,
        158, 214, 217, 224, 227,
        231, 232, 241, 245, 257,
        275, 280, 282, 313, 320;
Spirit, Holy 10, 11, 13, 30, 43, 44,
        45, 49, 54, 55, 56, 58, 59,
        61, 62, 75, 91, 92, 94, 128,
        147, 152, 162, 167, 183,
        189, 203, 210, 224, 239,
        240, 241-242, 244, 255,
        257, 266, 276, 286, 302;
Spirit Christology 11, 239-243,
        245, 247, 256, 257, 302;
Staudenmaier, Franz Anton 10,
        24, 35, 44, **73-83**, 97, 98-
        99, 119;
Strauss, David Friedrich 28, 48,
        63, 64, 75, 77, 84, 85-86,
        87, 88, 90, 92, 95, 96,
        108, 133, 141, 150, 183,
        184, 188, 298, 301;
Swidler, Leonard 245, 258;
Syllabus of Errors 115;
Synoptic gospels 88, 107, 108,
        110, 111, 125, 142, 145,
        148, 157, 168, 182, 187,
        189, 191, 200;
Synoptic problem 107;

Tavard, George 313;
Teilhard de Chardin, Pierre 213;
Thomism 14, 26;
Thüsing, Wilhelm 279;
Tradition 1, 2, 8, 10, 11, 13, 14,
        16, 22, 23, 43, 44, 48, 54,
        57, 58, 63, 64, 83, 84, 95,
        97, 122, 128, 148, 149,
        150, 163, 170, 179, 180,
        181, 183-184, 195, 204,
        206, 235, 236, 242, 246,
        249, 251, 262, 263-264,
        272, 284, 287, 295, 298,
        299, 300, 305, 310-315,
        320-321;
Trent, Council of 84, 297;
Trinity 15, 30, 44, 46, 59, 62, 85,
        94, 95, 111, 122, 125, 135,
        141, 148, 157, 159, 210,
        218, 219, 225, 240, 244,
        252, 259, 262, 274, 282,
        325;
Troeltsch, Ernst 12, 151, 228,
        308, 309;
Tyrrell, George 182, 198;
Vatican II (council) 6, 40, 47,
        119, 130, 138, 149, 166,
        170, 201, 203, 210, 235,
        245, 261, 263, 297;
Vidler, Alec 298;
Virgin birth 3, 77, 280, 284;
Word of God 15, 44, 45, 49, 74,
        94, 135, 210, 274, 275,
        277, 279, 292, 293-294;
World religions 30, 32, 47, 51,
        77, 93, 96, 203, 278, 280,
        320, 322;